India and Central Asia
Exploring New Horizons for Cooperation

India and Central Asia

Exploring New Horizons for Cooperation

Editors

Rajiv K Bhatia
Meruyert Abusseitova
Laura Yerekesheva
Athar Zafar

ICWA

Institute of Oriental Studies
Almaty

SHIPRA

Rs. 1400; US$ 70

ISBN: 978-81-7541-786-1

First Published in India in 2014

India and Central Asia: Exploring New Horizons for Cooperation

Published by:
SHIPRA PUBLICATIONS
LG 18-19, Pankaj Central Market,
Patparganj, I.P. Ext.,
Delhi-110092
Tel: 91-11-22235152, 22236152
E-mail: info@shiprapublication.com
www.shiprapublication.com

Foreword

Geographical contiguity between the Indian subcontinent and Central Asia and the intermingling of cultures and ideas has resulted in a centuries-long shared history in this critical region. India considers Central Asia as its 'extended neighbourhood', important for its economic and security interest. The five Central Asian republics of Kazakhstan, Kyrgyz Republic, Tajikistan, Turkmenistan and Uzbekistan became independent nation states in early 1990s. Since then, they have made substantial political, economic, social and cultural progress. After the initial phase of stabilization from the unexpected disintegration of the Union of Soviet Socialist Republics, these countries are now politically and economically stable and socially outward-looking. Obviously, the Central Asian countries and India are keen to strengthen their relationship and explore complementarities.

India, which was among the first countries to establish diplomatic relations with each of these republics, considers Central Asia as a vital hub for resources and its economic diversification. Greater economic, political, intellectual and cultural exchanges are required for mutual economic development. Though the two sides enjoy a close and cordial relationship, bilateral trade has not yet progressed on the expected trajectory. The two sides have huge economic potential to explore in the future. Their development objectives as well as challenges faced are similar.

A robust India-Central Asia relationship necessitates optimal intellectual engagement, which constantly ensures inputs and critiques on the progress made by the two sides. It is incumbent upon the academia, diplomats, strategists, media and, more importantly, the entrepreneurs from the two sides to suggest ways and means for enhanced economic engagement and growth. In this context, the annual India-Central Asia Dialogue, held under the aegis of India's 'Connect Central Asia' policy, plays a crucial role in bringing together the people having deep interest in promoting ties between the two sides.

This volume on the Second India-Central Asia Dialogue, held in Almaty in June 2013, brings out the contours of relations clearly and makes the reader further aware of regional and global interplay in the region.

Meruyert Abusseitova
Almaty

Rajiv K. Bhatia
New Delhi

List of Contributors

Part I

Prof. Hari Vasudevan: Professor, Department of History, Calcutta University, and Director, Centre for the Study of China and Neighbourhood

Dr. Sultan Magrupovich Akimbekov: Director, Institute of World Economics and Politics at the Foundation of the First President of the Republic of Kazakhstan

Dr. Ibragim Radjabovich Mavlanov: Head of Practical Diplomacy Chair at the University of World Economy and Diplomacy of the Ministry of Foreign Affairs of the Republic of Uzbekistan.

Ambassador Paramjit Singh Sahai: Hony. Principal Advisor, Centre for Research in Rural and Industrial Development (CRRID), Chandigarh, India

Dr. Aksanat Zhakitzhanovna Panzabekova: Deputy Director of International Cooperation, Institute of Economics, Ministry of Education and Science, Republic of Kazakhstan

Mr. Abdurahmonov Marufjon Kholmuminovich: Attaché, Ministry of Foreign Affairs of the Republic of Tajikistan

Dr. Leila Muzaparova: First Deputy Director, Kazakhstan Institute for Strategic Studies under the President of the Republic of Kazakhstan

PART II

Prof. Nirmala Joshi: Research Advisor, United Service Institution, New Delhi, and Director, India-Central Asia Foundation, New Delhi.

Prof. Kuldip Singh: Professor and Head, Department of Political Science, Guru Nanak Dev University, Amritsar, Punjab, India

Prof. Ajay Kumar Patnaik: Professor, Centre for Russian & Central Asian Studies, School of International Studies, Jawaharlal Nehru University (JNU), New Delhi

Prof. Pradeep Agrawal: Professor and Head, RBI Chair Unit, Institute of Economic Growth, Delhi

Dr. Seema Sangita: Assistant Professor, Institute of Economic Growth, Delhi

Prof. R.S. Yadav: Chairman, Department of Political Science & Defence & Strategic Studies, Kurukshetra University, Kurukshetra, India

Dr. Gulnara Muratovna Bekmagambetova: Head of the Department for Complex Transport Problems, Research Institute for Transport and Communications, Kazakhstan

Mr. Sarsembekov Tulegen Tadjibaevich, Deputy Chief of Technical Assistance at the Analytical Department of Eurasian Development Bank (EDB), Almaty, Kazakhstan

Dr. Yelena I. Rudenko: Research Fellow, Department of Central and South Asia, R.B. Suleimenov Institute of Oriental Studies, Almaty, Kazakhstan

PART III

Dr. Vijay Laxmi: Research Assistant (Central Asia) at the Centre for Research in Rural and Industrial Development (CRRID), Chandigarh, India.

Dr. Gurinder Kaur: Research Assistant (Central Asia) at the Centre for Research in Rural and Industrial Development (CRRID), Chandigarh, India.

Prof. Farhad Musayevich Dnishev: Professor, Head of the Department of Innovative and Technological Development at the Institute of Economics at the Ministry of Education and Science, Republic of Kazakhstan

Mr. Dudar Zhakenov: Deputy Head of the Representative Office in Almaty, Ministry of Foreign Affairs of the Republic of Kazakhstan

Dr. Punit Gaur: Assistant Professor (Central Asia) at the Centre for Research in Rural and Industrial Development (CRRID), Chandigarh, India

Dr. Rafik Tairov: Director, Department of Military and Defence Researches, Centre for Military-Strategic Researches, Kazakhstan

Prof. Habibullo Rajabov: Professor and Head, Indian Department, Oriental Institute of the Academy of Science of the Republic of Tajikistan

Prof. Kuralay Baizakova: Doctor of History, Director of the Institute of Security Problems and Cooperation at Al-Farabi National University, Kazakhstan

Professor Cholpon Turdalieva: Doctor of Historical Sciences, Anthropology Program, American University of Central Asia, Bishkek, Kyrgyz Republic

Ms. Aizhamal Marat: MA student, Istanbul University, Turkey

PART IV

Султан Акимбеков: к.и.н., Директор Института мировой экономики и политики при Фонде Первого Президента РК

Ибрагим Мавланов: д.э.н., профессор, зав. кафедрой практической дипломатии Университета мировой экономики и дипломатии, Узбекистан

Маруфджон Абдурахмонов: Атташе, Министерство иностранных дел Республики Таджикистан

Гульнара Бекмагамбетова: д.э.н., зав. отделом комплексных транспортных проблем, Институт транспорта и коммуникаций, Казахстан

Рафик Таиров: Директор департамента военных и оборонных исследований АО «Центр военно-стратегических исследований», кандидат юридических наук

Владимир Додонов: д.э.н., г.н.с., КИСИ при Президенте РК

Алишер Расулев: д.э.н., профессор, Директор Института экономических исследований, Узбекистан

Олег Егоров: д.э.н., профессор, г.н.с., Институт экономики МОН РК

Куралай Байзакова: д.и.н., профессор, директор Института проблем безопасности и сотрудничества при КазНУ им. аль-Фараби

Галымжан Дуйсен: д.э.н., доцент, зам. Директора, Институт востоковедения им. Р.Б. Сулейменова, Казахстан

Фархад Днишев: д.э.н., профессор, Институт экономики КН МОН РК, г.Алматы

Дудар Жакенов, заместитель Главы Представительства МИД РК в г.Алматы

Message

INAUGURAL ADDRESS

Mr. E. Ahamed
Minister of State for External Affairs
Government of India
17 June, 2013

Prof Derbisali, Director, Institute of Oriental Studies;
Madame Abusseitova, Head of Department of Oriental Source Studies;
Excellency Mr. Kuanyshev, Ambassador of Kazakhstan to India;
Distinguished scholars and academics;
Excellencies, Ladies & Gentlemen,

I feel pleased and privileged to inaugurate the Second India-Central Asia Dialogue in this beautiful city of Almaty. I am no stranger to this city or to the region and therefore, I am happy to be on familiar territory again amongst all of you.

I recall with pleasure, the inauguration of the first India-Central Asia Dialogue last June in another picturesque capital Bishkek, Kyrgyz Republic. During that inaugural event, we took a decision to have this Dialogue annually on a rotational basis. So now here we are, a year later, inaugurating the Second Dialogue. I think this is a reiteration of India's deep and sustained commitment to enhance links with Central Asian countries and the warm response from all of you to this common objective.

For over two decades of the independence of our neighbours in Central Asia, India has been focusing on this region and evolving ways and means of reinforcing the centuries of bonds. As part of this exercise, during the inaugural of the first Dialogue, I had spelt out our "Connect Central Asia" policy. The policy marks a more pro-active approach to engaging our friends in Central Asia. It is in fact an attempt to re-connect in newer ways with a region with which we have been closely connected in our hearts and minds for centuries. We now need to update the means to connect our physical spaces and connect our common economic goals.

The elements of India's Connect Central Asia Policy are in various stages of formulation and implementation. High level political exchanges are taking place. Recently, in April and May, India's Vice President paid very productive visits to Tajikistan and Uzbekistan. Our External Affair Minister was in Almaty two months ago when he met the President of Kazakhstan. We have had other high level engagements with all Central Asian countries. We have also worked on our common quest to build strong connections between our peoples.

We are continuously engaged in efforts to further our level of trade and economic cooperation, currently well below potential. To improve commercial relations, a major goal is enhancement of surface connectivity and access-route options. We are seeking to re-energise the North-South Transport Corridor and bridge the gaps in rail-road connections. We are looking at alternate routes through the Chabahar Port in Iran, and other Trans-Afghan links. I see that this Dialogue is devoting a full session to discuss connectivity-related issues. I have no doubt this will throw up some fresh ideas which can create breakthroughs in this vital area.

Another priority area is energy cooperation. Central Asian countries possess energy resources in abundance and India has a big energy appetite. We have to find viable solutions whereby Central Asia could be a reliable and sustained source and India could be a reliable market for Central Asian hydrocarbons and other resources.

Partnership for development is an important aspect of India-Central Asia relations. India believes in sharing its developmental experience in nation building with our friends. We are happy to provide economic and technical assistance for viable projects in the region. We have completed some modest projects like fruit & potato processing plants; machine and tool rooms; upgradation of a mini hydel plant and computerization of post offices. We are looking at connecting the region through an e-network to deliver tele-medicine and tele-education projects. We are also pursuing proposals for setting up collaborative India-Central Asia Universities and are discussing business models to set up hospitals and clinics with Indian expertise.

India has the privilege of contributing to capacity building and human resource development in the region and here I am happy to note that annually about 485 slots under our Indian Technical and Economic Cooperation Programme, are utilized in Central Asian Countries. Some students from the region are also pursuing studies in India under other scholarship schemes. We are delighted to share our experience in this important area.

We are also working with our partner Governments to resolve problems like non-tariff barriers and stiff visa regimes so that business flows improve and we stimulate bilateral trade relations. India sees great potential for tourism and towards this end since last July has announced 14 weekly flights for each Central Asian country from India. Uzbekistan, Kazakhstan and Turkmenistan are well connected by air with India. Now, we need similar sustained air connectivity with Tajikistan and Kyrgyzstan.

Both India and Central Asia are multicultural and pluralistic. We share civilizational bonds and ancient commercial links through the Silk Route. Our friendship is a fact of history and we must tap more effectively this natural reservoir of goodwill. It is our firm belief that enhanced interaction and collaboration between India and Central Asia will contribute to stability and development in the entire Central and South Asian region. We also believe that Afghanistan is an important factor for peace and stability in the region. At the "Heart of Asia" Istambul Process conference held at this very venue barely two months ago, all of us agreed that a cooperative approach towards Afghanistan would benefit the entire region's stability. India chairs the CBM on Trade, Commerce and Investments in the Istambul Process and our cooperation in Afghanistan can become a possible driver of its economic development.

Beyond Afghanistan, I am glad to see that the Dialogue has devoted a session to Security and Strategic Cooperation. We in the region face common threats of terrorism and extremism and we need to counter these tendencies in a coordinated manner- through expanding political and security dialogue and evolving common positions on terrorism and security and cooperating in economic growth. India is ready to offer cooperation in military training and joint research in defence.

The ambitious TAPI pipeline project which envisages transit of gas via Afghanistan and Pakistan to India is a welcome development. It could be the realization of a vision to connect

Central and South Asia through an economic corridor. The success of joint regional initiatives will open new vistas of economic cooperation between India and Central Asia.

Here, I would also like to underscore India's commitment to develop a multi-lateral relationship with the region through close and consistent cooperation in various multilateral fora. We support the CICA process, contribute as Observer in the Shanghai Cooperation Organisation (SCO), and have proposed a Comprehensive Economic Cooperation Agreement (CECA) with the Customs Union. We note with satisfaction the evolving economic inter-dependency and integration in the Eurasian space. We recognise this strong and positive contribution of Kazakhstan to these trends and commend its constructive role in the region.

Today, in Almaty, I am happy to particularly note India's growing bilateral relations with Kazakhstan, the largest country in Central Asia with a truly impressive and vibrant economy. Between 2000 and 2007, Kazakhstan has doubled the size of its economy and is targeted to triple the size by 2015. Our bilateral relations also have received a boost in 2012 with bilateral trade at US$525 mn. By 2050 we expect Kazakhstan to be among 30 most developed countries of the world. We rejoice in the success of President Nazarbayev's vision of Kazakhstan and are willing to be close partners in its resolute march to greater prosperity.

I congratulate the Indian Council for World Affairs, New Delhi and Institute of Oriental Studies, Almaty and special sponsor CRRID, Chandigarh for putting together this Dialogue. A special thanks to Kazakhstan, our hosts for their graciousness and enthusiasm and to all participants, whose deliberations would provide valuable inputs to research scholars, academicians, experts and policy makers.

I am confident that the India-Central Asia Dialogue, which was initiated on the 20th Anniversary of India's diplomatic relations with Central Asian countries in 2012, will be sustained. It will no doubt impart further momentum to academic exchanges and people-to-people contacts. It will help connect us in the most important way, it will connect our hearts.

Thank you

Reflections

H. E. Ashok Sharma
Ambassador of India to Kazakhstan

Hon'ble Minister of State for External Affairs, H.E. Mr. E. Ahamed

Hon'ble Director of the Institute of Oriental Studies, Almaty, H.E. Mr. Absattar Derbisali

Hon'ble Representative of the Ministry of Foreign Affairs of the Republic of Kazakhstan, H.E. Aidarbek Tumatov,

Hon'ble Dy. Director, Institute of Oriental Studies, Almaty, Ms. Meruyert Abusseitova

Hon'ble Heads of Delegations of ICWA and CRRID, Ambassador Mr. Chandrashekhar Dasgupta and Mr. P.S. Sahai,

Hon'ble Ambassador of Kazakhstan to India, H.E. Mr. Doulat Kuanyshev

Hon'ble Director of Kazakhstan Institute of Strategic Studies, Mr. Bulat Sultanov, Academicians and Scholars from India and Central Asia,

Dear Guests and Friends,

It is a matter of honour for me to welcome you to the Second India-Central Asia Dialogue in Almaty, which is known for its beauty and hospitality.

I would like to thank the Indian Council of World Affairs (ICWA) for selecting Kazakhstan for holding this conference. I also thank the Centre for Research in Rural and Industrial Development (CRRID) for being a partner to this dialogue.

My special thanks to the Institute of Oriental Studies, Almaty, and its Director for agreeing to become the host of this Seminar in

Almaty. I would especially like to mention the role of Dr. Laura Yerekesheva of the Institute of Oriental Studies for making all necessary arrangements. Her continuous and untiring efforts and hard work have made this event a success. I also compliment my counterpart in India, Mr. Doulat Kuanyshev, for his presence here, which is an example of his commitment and support to this conference.

Excellencies and friends,

Globalisation is not a recent phenomenon: Globalisation is a process which has been affecting human civilization since the beginning of documented history. This is also true of the continuous interaction between Central Asia and South Asia. This process continues due to advances in technology over the last 150 years. The future model for the human civilization is likely to be based on the oceans, and whose success will depend on a common borrowings and synergies. For this purpose, all geo-cultural domains (both material and non-material) must succeed.

We have witnessed during the course of history that India and Central Asia are a fine example of trans-cultural and trans-national integration of human and non-human activities. The discussion during this conference will provide an opportunity for understanding the historical and evolutionary process of integration between the two regions. The scholars are also likely to discuss the future course of this interaction and its implication, not only in the development of our two regions, but even beyond. The challenges before us, and subsequent responses, will have long-term impact on the future of this relationship and will certainly promote development, welfare of our societies, global security and stability.

Thank you

Perspective

H.E Chandrashekhar Dasgupta
Council Member
Indian Council of World Affairs
New Delhi

OPENING REMARKS

Your Excellency Shri E. Ahamed, Hon'ble Minister of State for External Affairs, Government of India,

Excellencies, Ladies and Gentlemen,

I am privileged to participate in the Second India-Central Asia Dialogue. Thank you for a very warm welcome to this beautiful city, Almaty.

The India-Central Asia Dialogue is a Track II initiative launched last year by the Hon'ble Minister of State for External affairs, Shri E Ahamed, under the 'Connect Central Asia' policy. The dialogue provides a forum for scholars, policymakers and entrepreneurs to engage in candid discussions of important policy issues and initiatives. The Indian Council of World Affairs is proud to be a partner in the India-Central Asia Dialogue since its inception. The Council is inspired by the vitally important objective of connecting the peoples of India and Central Asia more closely.

The cultural and economic ties between India and the countries of Central Asia go back to ancient times. These deep historical ties explain our mutual appreciation of one another's cultural heritage. These ties also create a solid foundation of goodwill for consolidating and strengthening our future cooperation.

India and Central Asian countries have registered impressive growth rates in recent years. Indeed, Kazakhstan has witnessed truly remarkable economic and social development. Economic growth in our respective countries has opened up new vistas for trade and investment flows between India and Central Asia. India is actively engaged in the region to meet its growing energy requirements. We are also ready to share our skills in Information Technology and other sectors of a knowledge-based economy. We should mutually explore and benefit from the synergies in our development patterns.

International terrorism and drug trafficking pose grave threats to regional and global security. India and the countries of Central Asia are actively engaged in countering these threats. We have a common interest in strengthening our cooperation in this vitally important area.

In this context, we also share a common interest in maintaining peace and stability in Afghanistan after the withdrawal of ISAF. International terrorists and drug traffickers thrive in conditions of conflict and instability. Three Central Asian countries share a common boundary with Afghanistan, and all are vulnerable to the fallout of instability in that country. India shares these concerns of its Central Asian friends. I am sure that the Almaty session of the India-Central Asia Dialogue will discuss the issue in some detail.

The challenge posed by geography to India and Central Asia can be overcome only through greater connectivity. During his recent visit to Tajikistan and Uzbekistan, Shri Mohammad Hamid Ansari, Hon'ble Vice President of India and President of the Indian Council of World Affairs, underscored the need for establishing road and rail connectivity between India and Central Asia. This would increase not only our economic engagement but also people-to-people contacts.

South Asia and Central Asia have a great deal to offer each other. I am confident that our two-day deliberations will come up with valuable proposals to further strengthen our ties. I am particularly delighted that Uzbekistan has joined this dialogue; its participation will enhance the value of our dialogue.

In conclusion, I wish all success to the Second India-Central Asia Dialogue at Almaty.

Thank you.

Ambassador's Note

H. E. Doulat Kuanyshev
Ambassador of Kazakhstan to India

Жоғары мәртебелі Үндістанның сыртқы істері мемлекеттік министрі Е.Ахамед мырза!
Құрметті Үндістанның Қазақстандағы Елшісі А.Шарма мырза!
Құрметті Шығыстану институты директоры Ә.Дербісәлі мырза!
Құрметті Үндістанның халықаралық істер кеңесінің мүшесі Ч.Дасгупта мырза!
Орталық Азия мен Үндістаннан арнайы келген мәртебелі мамандар мен зерттеушілер!
Мәртебелі ханымдар мен мырзалар!

Бүгін алыстан ат арытып жеткен мәртебелі қауымды осындай маңызы зор халықаралық басқосуға келгенімен құттықтай отыра сұхбат шеңберінде Орталық Азия мен Үндістан арасындағы ықпалдастықты дамыту бойынша келелі ойлар мен ұсыныстар айтылып, өзекті мәселелерді шешудің әрқилы тиімді жолдары қарастырылады деген ойдамыз. Әсіресе, өңіраралық ынтымақтастыққа серпін берер сауда-экономикалық, энергетика мен көлік байланыстары салаларының дамуы және дүниежүзілік жаһандану үдерістерінің салдарынан орын алған экономикалық дағдарыстан шығу мәселелері қатысушылардың қызығушылығын тудырары хақ.

Сондықтан, 2012 жылы маусым айында Бішкек қаласында сәтті өткен бірінші сұхбаттағы пікір алмасулар мен оның кейбір шешімдері өзара өңіраралық байланыстарды нығайтып, оларды жоғары деңгейге шығуына үлес қосқандығын ескере отыра бүгінгі отырыс жұмысына үлкен табыс тілеуге рұқсат етіңіздер.

Excellencies, Ladies and Gentlemen,

It is a privilege for me to speak to such a distinguished audience here in Almaty. Taking this opportunity, I congratulate Kazakh Institute of Oriental Studies and the Indian Council of World Affairs for establishing a permanent dialogue platform by facilitating the exchange of views of experts and think tanks, academics and business leaders of both sides to develop measures to deepen our cooperation.

Kazakhstan lays great importance on its relations with India. And it was proved recently here in Almaty by the meeting of President of Kazakhstan, Nursultan Nazarbayev, and Minister of External Affairs of India, Salman Khurshid, when the Ministerial Meeting of the Istanbul Process took place.

Kazakhstan respects and recognizes India's global and regional standing. India is one of the key players in political, economic, global and regional affairs. We acknowledge the growth of India and fully appreciate the opportunities this growth presents to the world and to our part of the world.

Kazakhstan's relations with India have always been warm and friendly. Bilateral relations between Astana and Delhi are based on equal partnership, mutual respect and understanding. The maturing ties between the two countries every year show great potential to once again bring Kazakhstan-India relations to a new level of cooperation. Establishing new contacts and the signing of large-scale projects demonstrates the progressive development of bilateral mutually beneficial cooperation.

Over the past two decades Kazakhstan's foreign policy has focused on developing and strengthening our relations with our key partners, and establishing a safe and friendly environment around us. We want to use our geography to our advantage; as a country at the heart of Eurasia, we can benefit from the trade flows between the European and Asian markets.

The key to making the most of Kazakhstan's strategic location is to promote integration between West and East, and to keep the wider Central Asian region in the focus of the international community.

The implementation of this policy starts at the regional level through active cooperation and coordination with our Central Asian neighbors, both in bilateral relations and through regional forums, including the Shanghai Cooperation Organization and the Conference on Interaction and Confidence-Building Measures in Asia, amongst others.

Today, Kazakhstan accounts for more than half of India's trade with the Central Asian countries. The total trade between Kazakhstan and India in 2012 reached USD 525 million; it increased by more than hundred per cent as compared to the corresponding period of 2011. However, both sides agree it is still a modest figure, and lack of direct land connectivity between the countries hampers greater economic engagement.

Construction of new routes within the international North-South transport corridor will play an important role in trade development and economic cooperation between Kazakhstan and India. This will reduce by half -and even more -the trucking distance and reduce transportation costs.

Kazakhstan has already completed the construction of its part of the Kazakhstan-Turkmenistan-Iran railway route. In May, President Nursultan Nazarbayev of Kazakhstan and President Gurbanguly Berdimuhamedov of Turkmenistan opened the Bolashak (Kazakhstan) – Serkhetyaka (Turkmenistan) railroad crossing, which is set to become one of the key links in the growing network of railway and road connections restoring the ancient Silk Road in the modern world. We hope that our Iranian friends will complete their part of the route, and soon we will be celebrating the completion of the whole railroad to the Persian Gulf.

The Government of Kazakhstan developed and approved the state strategy for the development of transport sector by 2015. Our transport sector will be organically integrated into the global transport system.

Currently, a lot of attention in the world is focused on the proposal of the ONGC to buy a stake of 'Conoco Phillips' in Kashagan consortium, and this issue is being considered by Kazakhstan within the context of national economic interests. Let me stress that Kashagan is not the end of life. We have a very successful example of cooperation in the same Caspian Sea region but on a bilateral basis with India on the Satpayev block, which is a promising block. We will keep our vision on energy, oil and gas cooperation broad and not narrow, and will continue to seek more opportunities for bilateral cooperation in offshore and onshore fields in Kazakhstan.

We recognize today that the 21st century presents enormous opportunities. But it is also full of various challenges. Only by joining hands we will be able to efficiently address those challenges and utilize multiple opportunities.

The prospects of cooperation between Kazakhstan and India are bright. We have agreed to work very closely and pragmatically to develop connectivity between South Asia and Central Asia. This is the key answer to many opportunities which lie before us. We hope that with the strength and potential of India, we will absolutely be able to develop these connectivities in multiple ways.

In our opinion, as a follow-up, we should continue the practice of holding regular events of bilateral cooperation, including the exchange of visits at various levels, regular meetings of the Intergovernmental commission and joint working groups, the exchange of information and experience, scientific and expert cooperation, and the strengthening of the legal framework.

We intend to support the creation and development of various forms of bilateral cooperation, including business councils and friendship associations, etc.

I look forward to further deliberations with all of you. I am also hopeful that we will be filled with an even greater sense of achievement when we meet at the next India-Central Asia Dialogue.

Thank you for attention.

Remarks

H. E Paramjit Sahai
Hony Principal Advisor, CRRID
Chandigarh

I was honoured to associate myself with the Second India-Central Asia Dialogue held at Almaty, Kazakhstan, on June 17-18, 2013. For me personally, my participation had greater significance, as I was directly involved with the establishment of India's diplomatic relations with the newly independent countries of the region in 1991. I worked on the visit of President Nazarbayev to India in December, 1991, when a number of agreements, including the 'Framework of Bilateral Cooperation', were signed. It was a good opportunity to get a first hand feel of the direction in which the relationship had moved over the years, and where it was headed for.

India has always viewed Central Asia as central to its ties with the region, given the old historical links going back to the Silk Road. Over the years, India's relationship has grown and it now enjoys a strategic partnership with many countries in Central Asia. I was happy to get a reaffirmation that Central Asian countries also viewed their relationship with India in a positive spirit, as they continued to perceive India as a benign power.

India and Central Asian countries are highly connected at the political level, but this has to percolate to other levels. We need to give greater economic content to the relationship and promote greater connectivity at the people-to-people level. The Indian diaspora is growing and it could be actively involved. Post-2014 Afghanistan developments would have a great impact in the region and there is need for India and Central Asia to work together.

India-Central Asian Dialogue is an important activity, under the flagship programme called 'Connect Central Asia' policy of the Ministry of External Affairs, Government of India, which was launched in Bishkek in June 2012, during the First India-Central Asia Dialogue. It takes New Delhi to the doorsteps of the capitals in Central Asian countries, as India connects with officials, the academia and business leaders in these countries.

Our Centre for Research in Rural and Industrial Development (CRRID), Chandigarh, India, was, therefore, happy to join hands with ICWA in connecting with the Ministry of External Affairs, as it connects to Central Asia through this programme. We brought to the table our experiences in bringing about India's connectivity with South Asia, under our rubric programme of 'Peace, Security and Development'. Some of the approaches could be successfully replicated after adapting the same to country-specific situations.

At the personal level, I was happy to associate myself with Ajay Bisaria, Joint Secretary, MEA, with whom I worked in Moscow during 1991-92; Ambassador Rajiv Bhatia, Sarvajit Chakravarti, Athar Zafar from ICWA, and Ambassador Ashok Sharma, India's Ambassador to Kazakhstan, who worked tirelessly for the success of the Conference. Our thanks to the host institute at Almaty, the R B Suleimenov Institute of Oriental Studies and its Director Absattar Derbisali, and former Director Prof. Meruyert Abusseitova, and Dr. Laura Yerekesheva, for extending full support and assistance to all the participants at the Dialogue.

I hope that India-Central Asia Dialogue results in promoting connectivity in three C's – Communication, Culture and Commerce – which could add vitality to the existing relationship, and CRRID would be happy to be a part of this exercise and gladly play its part.

A View from the Desk

Ajay Bisaria
Joint Secretary, Eurasia Division
Ministry of External Affairs
Government of India

Central Asia constitutes an important priority for India's foreign policy; India is treading on a path of closer cooperation with this region through its 'Connect Central Asia' policy, announced during the First India-Central Asia Dialogue in Bishkek, Kyrgyz Republic, in June, 2012. The 'Connect Central Asia' policy addresses India's relationship at both the regional and bilateral level. For tackling issues of regional political and security stability, such as the situation in Afghanistan; for meeting energy requirements such as through energy pipelines; for connectivity between South Asian and Central Asian regions, such as the North South Transport Corridor; and for mutual economic benefit, such as the Eurasian Customs Union, the policy has a collective vision of Central Asia. On the other hand, the policy recognised the unique personality of each Central Asian country and the need to address them bilaterally.

Though Central Asia is close to India politically and culturally, economic links are nowhere near potential. We are hopeful that these links will intensify in the near future. We see an evolving economic interdependence in the Eurasian region, and India is ready to contribute as a partner in the region's growth. The roles played in this direction by Track II deliberations are very significant. The instrument of the India-Central Asia Dialogue is emerging as a critical platform, enabling government authorities, academia, diplomats as well as business leaders from India and Central Asia to candidly exchange views on a wide range of issues.

I feel privileged to be a part of the India-Central Asia Dialogue, the second edition of which is being held in Almaty. I am confident that the participants of the Dialogue would contribute to further deepening the India-Central Asia relationship with their assessments and inputs.

I would like to thank the Indian Council of World Affairs, New Delhi; the R.B. Suleimenov Institute of Oriental Studies, Almaty; the Centre for Research in Rural and Industrial Development, Chandigarh; the Embassy of Kazakhstan to India; the Embassy of India to Kazakhstan, and all the participants for their efforts towards making the Second India-Central Asia Dialogue a successful intellectual exercise.

Thank you

Contents

PART II

INDIA-CENTRAL ASIA: ENHANCING COOPERATION

PART III

INDIA-CENTRAL ASIA: BILATERAL RELATIONS

PART IV

Papers in Russian Language

Introduction

The emergence of Central Asia as a separate geographical and political space in India's neighbourhood in the early 1990s has been a significant development in the last century. Since ancient times, the region maintained close cultural, political and economic relations with Indian subcontinent, affected briefly during the colonial era. Central Asia – comprising of 65 million people and about four million square kilometres of area – has always been an area of interest and priority for Indian policymakers, strategic community, academicians as well as for common people. With their independence, the regional countries of the erstwhile Union of Soviet Socialist Republic (USSR) were once again able to connect with their historical, civilizational and cultural siblings in Asia, especially its Silk Route partners, including India. Wide interest in both India and Central Asian countries in each other, ranging from the strategic and economic to the cultural, shape the new agenda of cooperation.

As it was in the past, the geographical construct of Central Asia makes the region a land bridge between Asia and Europe. The ancient Silk Route served as a trading route and also as a passageway for the convergence of many cultures, religions and philosophies. Besides their strategic location -enabling them to become a corridor- the countries of the region are endowed with hydrocarbon, hydropower and rich mineral resources, and are capable of becoming an important economic pole in the world. Since 2009, Kazakhstan has become the largest producer of uranium in the world; Turkmenistan has the fourth largest natural gas deposits in the world as well as huge oil reserves; Uzbekistan and Kyrgyzstan are among the largest gold producers in the region; Tajikistan's hydroelectric potential is estimated sufficiently to meet the needs not only of the country but also of the whole region.

The geographical proximity of both Central and South Asian regions to each other and the intermingling of cultures and ideas resulted in centuries-long shared history. After the initial phase of stabilization, in implementation of their structural reforms the Central Asian countries are reaching out to the world, and especially to nations in their neighbourhood, including India. This interest is driven by a number of factors. The countries of the region consider India as an important actor on the international arena, a strategic partner, a rising economic power, a potential investor and a technological leader.

India, on the other hand, considers these countries its neighbours and is more than willing to share its experience of 65 years of economic, political, social and technological development. Both India and Central Asian countries face similar global and regional challenges, such as sustainable development, need for knowledge-based economies, resource exploitation, capacity-building, regional integration, connectivity issues and security concerns, etc. The similar nature of these challenges requires a cooperative approach and a shared response.

To address the common challenges and further deepen its engagement with the region, New Delhi launched the 'Connect Central Asia' policy in June 2012 during the first "India-Central Asia Dialogue" at Bishkek, Kyrgyzstan. The objective of the Dialogue process is to build a robust and sustained relationship between the two regions, and suggest ways to further deepen the cooperation. Consequently, it was agreed to hold an annual "Connect Central Asia-India Dialogue" on Track II to facilitate discussions amongst scholars, experts, business leaders and decision-makers from India and Central Asian countries. The Dialogue is planned in each Central Asian country one by one. The Ministry of External Affairs, Government of India, has entrusted Indian Council of World Affairs (ICWA) as the nodal think tank to conduct the dialogue in collaboration with a suitable institution of the host country.

Pursuing these objectives -and encouraged with the success of the first Dialogue- the ICWA successfully hosted the Second "Connect Central Asia-India Dialogue" at Almaty, Kazakhstan, on 17-18 June 2013, in collaboration with the R B Suleimenov Institute of Oriental Studies (IOS), Almaty, Kazakhstan, and the Embassy of India, Astana, Kazakhstan. The Dialogue was supported by the

Ministry of External Affairs, Government of India, and the Centre for Research in Rural and Industrial Development (CRRID), Chandigarh, India, an autonomous research institute, was the special sponsor of the Second Dialogue.

Besides India, participants from Kazakhstan, Kyrgyzstan, Tajikistan and Uzbekistan participated in the Second Central Asia-India Dialogue. There were more than 30 paper presentations in Russian and English languages during the six sessions spread over two days. The delegates discussed in detail progress made in key thematic areas during the past 20 years of India's engagement with the region, as well as with individual countries. The present volume comprises edited papers presented during the course of this Dialogue. The sessions covered international political and economic scenarios, regional developments and the status of bilateral relations with regional countries, as well as ways to further strengthen the ties.

In a global world, the India-Central Asia relationship cannot be advanced and studied in isolation. The Central Asian countries are pursuing the 'multi-vector' foreign policy which has helped to engage – and interact with – both regional and extra-regional players at multiple levels. Their relations with the EU, China, Iran, Japan, Pakistan, Russia, Turkey and the US will continue to impact on the geopolitical, geo-economic and social dynamics of the region and its neighbourhood. India's 'Connect Central Asia' policy is a response to the regional developments and the 'multi-vector' policy pursued by the regional countries. It is pertinent to analyze the Central Asian republics' political and economic engagements during the last two decades with their immediate and near neighbours, as well as the world, to have a holistic understanding of the region and to advance cooperation in different areas.

To increase cooperation in the security, economic, social and political issues, the Central Asian states have become members of many regional political, security and economic organizations such as the Shanghai Cooperation Organization (SCO), Collective Security Treaty Organization (CSTO), Conference on Interaction and Confidence-Building Measures in Asia (CICA) and Eurasian Economic Community/Customs Union, etc. There has been an evolving economic interdependency in Eurasia, and the formation of a Eurasian Economic Union in the region is bound to boost inter-region trade. It is important to understand the current and future dynamics of these institutions and their role in shaping the regional milieu, and analyze India's potential in expanding the horizon of relationship with organizations active in the region. New prospects are emerging due to regional countries adapting international trade regimes, such as Tajikistan becoming the second country in the region (after Kyrgyzstan) to join the World Trade Organization (WTO). However, the integration process has not been pretty efficient, and greater harmonization is needed in different areas, such as the tax regimes. Regional integration takes longer and may also be uneven, and many countries of the region differ over the use of water resources and sharing Caspian Sea resources, which sometimes poses a threat to the regional security environment.

Traditional and non-traditional security threats are crucial to understand the regional security environment. Afghanistan has been disturbed for many years and is currently in the middle of multiple transition, including political and security. The post-2014 scenario in Afghanistan is of concern for Central Asian countries, especially those sharing borders – Tajikistan, Uzbekistan and Turkmenistan – as well as for India, while the non-traditional threats are common to the two regions. After presidential elections in Afghanistan, the reconciliation process is one of the urgent tasks on the agenda in the country. A stable Central Asia is in the interests of all regional states – and of India's. Response to terrorism is important, as it was acquiring new dimensions due to availability of modern technology, international financing and pan-region ideology. Short-term and long-term security concerns (including drugs and human trafficking) and the scope for security cooperation needs to be identified. Cyber-security has been emerging as a new challenge, and strong cooperation between India and regional countries would be beneficial for both sides.

Sustainable economic cooperation is the key to India-Central Asia relationship. The countries of the region are opening and diversifying their economies. Interests between India and Central Asia converge, as India needs energy for rapid economic development while the Central Asian states want to diversify their energy markets to include South Asia. India has expertise in software, services, technology and education and is willing to share it with the countries of the region. Investment, technology development and building human resources in the region would be beneficial for both sides. Potentials in agriculture, mineral resources, tourism – including medical and religious tourism – and the banking sector needs to be explored. Indian and Central Asian countries' cooperation with local, regional and multilateral organizations – for example, the Eurasian Union and financial institutions such as Asian Development Bank and World Bank – will be beneficial for the two sides in economic, security and political terms. Besides, discovering the Greenfield value-added manufacturing and processing activities, idle/dormant industrial units in the region can be identified for modernization. The Governments of India and Kazakhstan, for example, can also explore the possibility of a direct energy pipeline between the two countries.

Being an energy rich region, Central Asia attracts interest and investment from across the globe. There is ample scope for cooperation between the two sides in the areas of both traditional and new forms of energy: hydrocarbon, hydroelectricity, Caspian Sea resources, nuclear energy and renewable energy technologies. Central Asia-South Asia Energy Transmission Project (CASA-1000) and the proposed Turkmenistan-Afghanistan-Pakistan-India (TAPI) pipeline bring the two regions economically closer. The present Strategic Partnership between India and three Central Asian countries – Kazakhstan, Tajikistan and Uzbekistan – has not yet translated into economic advantages. There is a need to adopt a multipronged approach and including human resource development by employing the young generation from both the sides. Economics needs to be the thrust area of India's relationship with the region. Kazakhstan, because of its size and location, is central to all routes passing to or from Central Asia. Given the difficulties in connectivity, land routes via Afghanistan-Pakistan and China can be other alternatives.

Economic cooperation is closely linked to transportation and connectivity between the concerned sides. Central Asia needs to explore and upgrade the existing transport infrastructure as well as develop new ones. Development and modernization of infrastructure: automobile and railroads, roadside services, container transportation, air, rail and access points to the sea, etc. is needed. Iran, the Caspian Sea and INSTC are gateways for Central Asia to India, and vice versa. For seamless movement of people and goods, e-connectivity infrastructure needs to be created.

To have robust relationships between India and Central Asian

Republics, it is important to understand the dynamics of bilateral relations amongst the countries of the region. India and all Central Asian countries enjoy mutually close and cordial relationships. In particular, Kazakhstan and India are important strategic partners that can significantly boost India-Central Asian cooperation, particularly through initiatives such as Conference on International and Confidence-building Measures in Asia (CICA), Eurasian Union, Congress of Leaders of World and Traditional Religions, to name a few. Bilateral cooperation can be enhanced in power, nuclear, space, medical and IT fields. Peaceful use of nuclear technology, the situation in Afghanistan as well as multilateral organizations such as the UN Security Council are important areas of bilateral cooperation. The two countries can also invite another regional partner – China – in a trilateral format to explore economic and political opportunities. These countries are already engaged through the SCO, and they can collaborate on Afghanistan.

In the bilateral economic context, areas of mutual importance are energy, agriculture, pharmaceuticals, micro, small and medium enterprises, information technology and tourism. There is a need to study successful business models that can be used in the region with suitable modification. India can assist in value addition to Kazakhstan uranium output, and a 'scientific dialogue' between India and Kazakhstan can be useful. Humanitarian field is another much-needed dimension, allowing advancing cross-cultural and people-to-people contacts going far beyond geo-economics and geo-politics, and thus promoting better understanding of each other. Education, science and culture are instrumental in furthering people-to-people contacts between India and the countries of the region. Many Indian students are studying in different education institutions in the region, and there is a need to sensitize students in India of the opportunities available in their neighbourhood. With other regional partners like Tajikistan, India can explore available hydrocarbon resources.

Absence of direct connectivity between India and Central Asia has been a major hindrance in deepening commercial relationship between the two sides, and is a special issue of concern. With an eye on this, after the conclusion of the Second Dialogue, a special session was devoted to issues of connectivity. Representatives from Kazakhstan and Indian business and transport sectors, including from Kazakhstan railways, Kazakh Temir Zholy and KazTransOil, shared their views with academics on ways to address the challenges and issues related to transfer of consignments from India to Central Asian countries and vice versa (particularly shipment delays up to several months via China). It is expected that interregional trade would get a boost with the North-South Corridor via Iran becoming fully operational. However, to overcome the issue of geographical connectivity, both India and Central Asian countries could focus on other areas of cooperation; for example, India can step up its presence in the services sector, which is India's niche area and is not dependent on geographical connectivity.

It can be summed up that complimentary economies and a convergence of interests on various political and international issues have been instrumental in advancing mutual engagement of Central Asian countries and India. There exist enormous prospects for economic cooperation in various fields. Shared history, cultural and people-to-people links are also crucial to Central Asian and India's relations. Yet, in view of rapidly occurring changes in regional and world affairs, and developments in national milieus, there is a much -needed urgency to fill in the existing lacunas and make further efforts at deeper, extensive and comprehensive cooperation.

New Delhi
Almaty
July 2014

Athar Zafar
Laura Yerekesheva

PART I

India-Central Asia and the Regional and International Developments

1

India-Central Asia and International Milieu: Prospects for Economic Engagement

Hari Vasudevan

Introduction

Since 1992, India's relations with Central Asia have developed with each state on a bilateral basis. Many connections derive from a network of links that evolved during the existence of the USSR and were based on either the technology or the production and distribution units that existed there. But these, together with important cultural and political factors and common geopolitical concerns, have ensured a special interaction with the region as a whole, based on issues that distinguishes each such interaction from that exists with other CIS states. Bilateral relationships between India and the states of the region overlap in various ways in such a setting.

This chapter gives a balance sheet of how relations between India and Central Asia have evolved over the post-1992 period. It deals with the specifics of trade and cooperation on energy and the role these have come to play in the overall connection between India and the region. The chapter stresses that although the volume of what is involved has not been large, a steady pattern has evolved and shown significant staying power.

The chapter also deals with challenges to the character of relationships and important opportunities that have been under-explored institutionally. Crucial amongst the challenges is the emergence of the Eurasian Community on a firmer and more stable footing than ever previously – a development that has not, significantly, undermined the India-Central Asia relationship hitherto.

Opportunities that have been under-explored include a dynamic approach to participation in multilateral ventures that involve an Indian component and that feature an India component.

The chapter suggests the formation of a time bound Research Agenda, located in the ICWA, and drawing from support bodies to examine how challenges and opportunities may be approached.

I. India-Central Asia Relationship: Broad Parameters

(i) Pre-1992

Before the emergence on the international scene of the five states of Central Asia as sovereign political entities in 1992, recognition clearly existed of their long-term historical connection with India. Cultural and educational initiatives had led to exchange of personnel between institutions under the Indo-Soviet cooperation programmes, and especially amongst medieval historians and archaeologists, close cooperation was well known. Teaching of Hindi in Central Asia was common at the school level. Study of the other country was well established in all major institutions devoted to Oriental Studies in Central Asia and the Aligarh Muslim University and Jamia Millia Islamia in India, as well as in Area Studies Centres in Kashmir, Jawaharlal Nehru University and Mumbai University. These links drew from a closeness that was truly historical in every sense of the word. The proximity in territory had led to trade and cultural connections and networks between the major cities of the area – Samarkand and Bukhara and regions such as Ferghana – drawing, as has been often repeated, from the commercial networks of the Silk Route era.

If the presence of an Indian Consulate in Tashkent symbolized the special link between India and the region before 1992, its very existence was an acknowledgement of connections that went much deeper.

(ii) Post-1992

Following 1992, various Silk Road initiatives have projected the Central Asian states as subjects of history. While doing so, they have also projected the links between South Asia and Central Asia generally, while giving attention to Russia and China in the course of the work.

An example of this projection is in the UNESCO History of the Civilizations of Central Asia, where South Asia features as a distinctive part. Significantly, South Asians have contributed significantly to the volumes concerned.

Elsewhere, at the official level, the Government of India has established connections with the Central Asian states on a bilateral level by opening Embassies. In addition, the Indian Council for Cultural Relations (ICCR) has been involved in the creation and development of lively India Chairs in the countries concerned, as well as opening of cultural centres, which have inspired close interaction and people-to-people contact. An active student exchange programme has brought a number of Central Asian students to Indian universities. These points may be said to hold true for all the states of Central Asia.

At the research level, the Government of India gave special encouragement to the University Grants Commission (UGC) to begin Area Studies programmes in various universities to deal with Central Asia. The Maulana Abul Kalam Azad Institute of Asian Studies (MAKAIAS) under the Ministry of Culture focused cardinally on Central Asia from the time of its formation in 1992. Most of those who pursued higher studies from Russian language departments focused on Central Asia if they stayed on in India.

The past two decades have witnessed, therefore, a firm reinforcement of India's political and cultural presence in the region, as well as to develop serious expertise in the area. In turn, in Indian universities and in India generally, a Central Asian presence has been registered as never before, with many students from Central Asian states enrolling under different programmes.

There is no doubt that such initiatives have taken place within the framework of a multidimensional development of Central Asian states on the international arena. South Asia's legacy of links with the region is shared between India and Pakistan, and Pakistan has projected and developed its own projection of South Asian relationships with the region, independent of India, based on Islam. Such a position drew its strength from networks that existed between the Pamir region, Afghanistan and Pakistan. It also coincided with (and competed with) the projection of the Islamic character of Central Asian identities, as contextualised by Saudi Arabia, Turkey and Iran. A less Islamic projection of the identity of the region has figured in perceptions of the People's Republic of China (PRC) about the region.

The Government of India has been more "secular" in its approach. It has not denied the importance of religious affinities that have linked India with the region, but it has pointed to their historical complexity, drawing attention to Buddhist and Islamic legacies. It has projected these as part of a cultural fabric that has many aspects and which needs to be viewed along with experiences of imperialism and engagements with nationalism. This has not been unlike the approach of the USA or Europe and Russia. However, the engagement by these countries/communities has been more substantially linked to specific economic and strategic initiatives, especially after complex operations that followed 9/11 in the region. To deny that India has been concerned with strategic and geopolitical issues would be inaccurate. However, the Government of India's projection of these interests has been as a concerned party that can provide assistance to sovereign Governments, rather than as a force that can play a role in directing the course of events.

In Central Asia, in response to changing circumstances, Governments and communities have oriented themselves around notions of "nationalism" and nation building, with Islam and notions of Eurasianism being a subtext in the story. Here, globalization and memories of the Soviet experience have been factors that have shaped the quality of nation building. Hence, whilst all countries accept their "Islamicate" character, their Governments are equally concerned not to stress the centrality of Islam in politics and statecraft. Again, most states are multi-ethnic in character and, hence, a straightforward construct of nationalism on the basis of ethnicity is not feasible. This reflects the unusual way in which states were established in the Soviet era and the problems associated with boundaries. "Eurasian" identities, on the other hand, while in accord with migration patterns and the Soviet legacy, do not allow for neat nation building.

II. Economic Relationship

(i) Background: General Features

In this context, the economic relationship between India and the region has been marked by the following factors:

In the period during economic reforms in India and the inclusion of India in the World Trade Organization (WTO), two aspects of India's economic relations with the countries of the CIS have been clear.

(a) First, in the realm of India's trade relations, the standard advantages of proximity (as in the case of South East Asia, West Asia) do not apply – neither do the advantages of technological superiority (manifest in trade with a number of African states). In the case of Asiatic Russia and Central Asia, enterprises of the PRC have distinct advantages in these fields, except in the case of goods of small volume and substantial value (as in the case of pharmaceutical products or gems and jewellery). The exception is European Russia, where the Indian trader and producers faces the same advantages that he has in the European Union (EU), and may compete effectively with enterprises of the PRC and elsewhere. These advantages apply to the Western-most areas of Central Asia, where imports into European Russia are easily traded and have logistical advantages over goods of the PRC. Territorial proximity, it must be stressed and is well known, is important not as an absolute. Geographically, access to Central Asia via Iran or Pakistan is much easier than access to the United States – a major trading partner of India. But in the case of Central Asian states, the character of land and sea connectivity has never reached the sophistication as was in the case with the United States and Europe. This is why improvements in ports and matters relating to "trade corridors" are ever the focus of conversations between diplomats and businessmen in the Central Asian case. Clearly, a reason for the slow development of connectivity is the size of the market here – roughly forty million – and access to that market, which is hemmed by various protective barriers and limited institutionalization.

(b) In the case of *economic cooperation*, there is considerable potential in the states of Central Asia, where cultural advantages also weigh in. India, furthermore, has the advantage of having professionals with Soviet-era experience, who are able to work with the basic infrastructure in these states. India also has long-term affinities that have seldom been called into play but which are stressed in the local histories of these states. Major competitors are Pakistan and Iran. However, their advantages of proximity and religious affinity are outweighed by the complexity of such affinity and the cultural capital India possesses as a secular state. Close integration of Indian enterprise with Euro-US enterprises and easy fluency in English are also advantages. However, the advantages that an Indian occupies has to give way to the local entrepreneur, as well as those from Turkey, West Asia and (most importantly) Russia.

(c) The relationship between India and these states has been supported in a supplementary manner by international enterprises that have an Indian component and which are involved in activities of specific importance to the Indian economy.

Against such a background, it has been possible for Indian and Central Asian actors to take advantage of favourable factors as stated above with some degree of vigour only in the period following the economic "recovery" of the region in the 2000s, which also witnessed important Indian initiatives in Kazakhstan and Uzbekistan. Such initiatives have faced and survived the impact of the "meltdown" in the area after September 2008. The relationship has to now adapt to the increasing presence of the Eurasian Economic Community in the area.

(ii) Background: Central Asian Economies before 2000

More specifically, in the course of the period since 1992, growth in the Central Asian states has depended on factors such as:

(a) The persistence of production systems that were still tied trade and distribution systems that were centred on Russian units and companies. These included systems for distribution of oil and natural gas through the Russian pipeline system to European markets, as well as production systems, especially in the case of cotton production in Uzbekistan, but also in the case of iron and steel production and coal mining.

(b) Dislocation that was the consequence of disintegration of the USSR and the subsequent Russian reforms, which threw almost all established systems mentioned in point (a), into recession.

(c) The creation of distinct economic spaces by the Central Asian states, either individually or as a whole – whether in the creation of distinct monetary arrangements, customs codes and barriers, migration bars or de-linking from the old USSR-era arrangements (as in the case of separation of CIS region from the electricity grid that connected them to Russia through Northern Kazakhstan).

(d) Individual state responses to the dislocation and recession that took place, like when the Kazakh Government tried to develop policies based on privatization while the Uzbek, Kyrgyz and Tajik economies were more oriented towards regulation and the Turkmen economy resisted limited deregulation that was followed elsewhere.

(e) International initiatives to improve the state of the economies (through ventures such as the TRACECA or the Baku-Ceyhan pipeline).

(f) The development of bilateral or multilateral trade relations with countries in the neighbourhood (Russia, China, Afghanistan, Pakistan and India, the Caucasus states and Turkey). The relationship extended to patterns of migration in this greater neighbourhood – patterns which had a global dimension that stretched into the USA, EU and West Asia.

This post-Soviet development was marked by restricted resources available for services and training – the most sophisticated of which were connected to bodies in the Russian Federation (RF) or in the Ukraine, Belarus and the Baltic states before 1992. In these states, many training institutes themselves went through a crisis period in the course of the decade – leading to even more limited availability for Central Asian states as a whole.

Adapting to circumstances in different ways, each of the Central Asian states developed a definite economic profile by 2000, when a degree of prosperity came to the region for the first time, "fuelled" substantially by the global rise in oil and natural gas prices; this affected Turkmen and Kazakh economies, which then were able to play host or provide investments to neighbouring countries based on close economic, legal and linguistic customs and traditions.

(iii) Background: India's Economic Relationship With Central Asian States Before 2000

This period of dislocation and depression in the Central Asian region was marked in India by structural adjustment and adaptation to the requirements of the WTO. Major trade partnerships were developed primarily with the EU and the USA.

Establishing relations with Central Asian states took time, since the logistics of travel within the area had normally been handled by Soviet state enterprises and which was decreasing with every passing year. The monopoly of the Soviet-owned airline, Aeroflot, which normally handled local travel, had quickly faded by the mid-1990s before a slew of newer national airlines.

The Indian public sector had no specific connection with Central Asia in the past, and no major Soviet Foreign Trade Organizations based in this region had fronted for economic relations with India. In fact, no organization existed that had experience in dealing with the public sector of these newly independent states and the Indian public sector. In the case of the private sector, all major business with the former Soviet Union had been handled through the medium of FTOs based in Moscow – and through local branches in Moscow of Indian concerns (opened in the course of the 1980s). There were no local networks into which businesses could tap into, and the monitoring that the Indian consulate in Tashkent had been able to achieve over Hindi-trained Soviets was not practical anymore after *perestroika*.

Post-1991, consequently, the course of establishing links with these economies was largely along the following lines:

(i) The Government of India (GoI) set up diplomatic missions and provided information to new entrants in the region;

(ii) Companies based in Moscow scouted for opportunities in the region (primarily in Kazakhstan, where close interaction with the Russian Federation was possible). Thermax of Pune is a major example;

(iii) Companies in India which had Moscow bases organized a distinct and separate initiative to deal with Central Asian states. By the end of the 1990s, in the case of Indian pharmaceutical exports, Cadilla had two distinct sides to its operations, as did Ranbaxy.

(iv) International traders of Indian origin, with solid Indian connections, began operations in the region. A major instance was Pramod Agarwal, who began business in Bombay in 1975 in a family firm which dealt with textile exports to the USSR, handled company business in Hong Kong and founded Texuna International Limited to trade commodities-cement, cotton, grain, etc .–throughout Asia. He entered the Soviet market during *perestroika*. Post disintegration, he opened his first CIS branch in Tashkent in 1992, and following his setting up of a Moscow office in 1993, developed branches in Almaty, Ashgabat, Baku and Odessa, with a turnover reputedly reaching US$ 200 million by 1995.

It is worth remembering that there were few opportunities for developing a proper consumer market in Central Asia at this time. Transport was difficult and expensive – mainly limited to small volume goods that could be transported by air. There were no financial institutions that could undertake transfer of funds into the region. Inflation was high and currency values fluctuated – which made repatriation of funds, which was anyway seldom permitted, highly

Table 1.1: India's Trade with the Central Asia (US$ millions)

Central Asian States	*1992-93***	*1993-94*	*1994-95*	*1995-96*	*1996-97*	*1997-98*	*1998-99*	*1999-2000*	*2000-01*	*2001-02*
Uzbekistan		5	22	25	29	65	54	43	43	31
Tajikistan		3	Under1	16	2	4	2	10	16	5
Turkmenistan		5	2	4	5	6	8	24	12	21
Kazakhstan		8	26	29	16	56	160	117	229	218
Kyrgyzstan		*	*	*	*	*	*	59	80	52

Source: Statistics of the Foreign Trade of India, by Countries and Commodities. Vol. 1 (Exports), Vol. 2 (Imports). (Director General of Commercial Intelligence and Statistics, Ministry of Commerce, Government of India). Annual Figures as published in March.

** Gross CIS statistics only available.

* No figure given.

problematic. And, most importantly, consumption was low, being highly unstructured and based on a population whose per-capita income was very low. By and large, the market favoured Russian goods – when they were available – or Chinese products that came from the bottom-end of the PRC's production line (i.e., they were of low quality and cheap, but had no reuse value).

(iv) The "Recovery" of 2000-08 in Central Asia

The economic recovery that was seen in the Central Asian states during the 2000s was the result of:

(i) Greater sobriety in public spending and import of goods following the crisis of 1998, which affected all the economies to greater or lesser degree.

(ii) The general prosperity of neighbouring countries (especially Russia and China) during this period, and the ability of state and private enterprises to react to such a situation.

(iii) The increase of capital availability in two major states of the region – Kazakhstan and Russia – which made investments available to other states in the area and whose increased internal prosperity led to a demand for labour, in turn contributing to the income of donor countries such as Kyrgyzstan and Uzbekistan.

It should be mentioned that the large increases in GDP of Kazakhstan and Russia, based on the increases in oil and natural gas prices globally and, consequently, revenues at home, led to willingness to invest in the construction industry in the region as a whole, and also acted as a draw for labour from donor states. Hence, the prosperity of these major centres was responsible for a broader upturn in the local economies of the region, and promoted a series of local enterprises.

(v) Indian Approaches to the Economies of the Central Asian States During the Period of Recovery

Although there has been mention of improvements in bilateral trade during the period after 2002, it is clear that the scale was small (all trade coming to under US$ 500 million at best).

Table 1.2: Central Asia and Russia volume indices of GDP (constant prices, 2000 = 100)

	2001	*2002*	*2003*	*2004*	*2005*
Kazakhstan	113.5	124.5	136.2	149.3	163
Kyrgyzstan	105.3	106.3	112.7	120.7	120
Tajikistan	109.6	121.4	134.8	149.1	159
Uzbekistan	104.2	108.4	112.9	121.6	
Russia	105.1	110.0	118.1	126.6	135

Source: *Statistical Abstract, Commonwealth of Independent States in 2005* (Interstate Statistical Committee of the Commonwealth of Independent States, Moscow, 2006), p. 26.

Note: Figures for Turkmenistan not available.

Table 1.3: Exports from India to the Central Asian states 2002-08 (US$ million)

	2002-3	*2003-4*	*2004-5*	*2005-6*	*2006-7*	*2007-8*
Kazakhstan	46.88	74.84	81.42	90.86	83.27	111.91
Uzbekistan	5.08	15.14	21.35	24.44	29.66	40.32
Kyrgyzstan	14.62	38.20	49.57	38.20	37.21	31.58
Tajikistan	8.65	4.47	6.59	6.24	7.45	12.42
Turkmenistan	10.29	19.21	15.26	18.83	33.81	36.08

Table 1.4: Imports into India from Central Asian states 2002-08

	2002-03	*2003-04*	*2004-05*	*2005-06*	*2006-07*	*2007-08*
Kazakhstan	12.73	9.26	15.39	26.3	88.13	76.83
Uzbekistan	20.54	27.70	34.46	26.13	33.85	16.08
Kyrgyzstan	0.47	0.54	0.63	1.47	0.77	0.91
Tajikistan	0.08	3.95	4.09	5.89	8.05	9.69
Turkmenistan	5.40	9.34	10.87	12.35	12.05	8.58

Source: Table 3 and 4: *Statistics of the Foreign Trade of India, by Countries and Commodities. Vol. 1 (Exports), Vol. 2 (Imports).* (Director General of Commercial Intelligence and Statistics, Ministry of Commerce, Government of India). Statistical Database as available on website.

However, economic collaboration did make significant breakthroughs.

(i) In the case of Kazakhstan, the GoI regarded investments in the Kazakh oil sector possible on the same lines that investments were made in the Sakhalin fields in the Russian Federation. But in crucial cases, ONGC Videsh (OVL), the Indian public sector company that represented Indian interests, was unable to match the competition from China. A standard round of international companies, together with Russian and Chinese players, dominated the output of the Kazakh oil and natural gas sector under the watchful eye of privatized state corporations. However, the formation of ONGC Mittal Energy Ltd. in 2005 led to a strong showing in the region indirectly, despite the poor competitive showing of ONGC Videsh itself.

(ii) In Uzbekistan, though, major changes in linkages between the two countries came to be established. The automotive parts' company, Minda, made a fundamental investment in a company in Uzbekistan (US$ 25 million) to maintain the production line, which was in dire straits following the collapse of Daewoo's Uzbek operations, and to distribute from the country. A large investment was also made by Spandex Textiles – one of India's largest yarn exporters to Europe – in an Uzbek production unit. Significantly, these were not the only enterprises that were thinking of beginning production from the country in the future; others, especially the pharmaceutical industry, the Adani Group (which was interested in food processing) and Bharat Heavy Engineering Limited (BHEL), began work on projects that were of importance to the power sector.[1]

(vi) Impact of the Meltdown of 2007-08

The economies of the Central Asian states were affected by the "meltdown" in two phases. First, there was a clear problem of foreign investment in Kazakhstan (the second leading investment and employment source in the region after Russia) from mid 2007 – with implications for investment by the Kazakh banking sector in the Kyrgyz and Uzbek economies. The trend may have been linked to increasing problems faced by investment agencies in Europe and the US at this time. But the overall impact was partly offset by the continued sturdy performance by Russia – and reasonable support from Russia to a whole gamut of Central Asian economies as well as continuity in employment opportunities all around. Undoubtedly, the worsening of the global investment environment during 2008 led to deterioration of this state of affairs since it affected foreign investment in Russia and Kazakhstan further, as well as limited FDI in other states of the region.

The impact of the "meltdown" following the fall in oil prices from mid 2008 was more acute, leading to a fall in investment and employment opportunities in almost all countries of the region as the meltdown affected both Kazakhstan and Russia especially. Although official controls in force in Uzbekistan prevented the carryover of these problems to the Uzbek economy (and even had some positive effect since energy costs decreased), there was nevertheless increased pressure and fall in orders for textile products, which created major problems, as did the decline in remittances. Kyrgyzstan was affected more hard since there was a sudden depression in the construction industry and in employment outside the country. The same was true of Tajikistan, while Turkmenistan being marginally affected in view of the less catastrophic fall in natural gas prices (gas being the primary revenue earner of this country).

As the crisis bit deep, Uzbekistan evolved a variety of policies 2008 onwards – measures that were applauded by the World Bank.

(vii) India-Central Asia Trade Relations after the Meltdown

The consequences of the meltdown for India-Central Asia trade relations are shown in the following tables. As is clear, while in two cases, there was a brief dip in trade during the period that followed 2008, in all cases there was a steady rise in exports from India. Imports from the region into India suffered briefly, with an overall trend towards improvement. The message is clear. India plays a competitive role in the industry of the region – possibly owing to the sound relationship it has developed with each country, but also because of the larger steadfastness of its trading community and the commerce that is involved. It has been able to hold its own in adverse conditions. Equally, with the exception of Tajikistan and Kyrgyzstan, trade and commerce between India and Central Asia seems to have acquired a robust quality.

Table 1.5: Exports to Central Asia states from India (US$ millions)

	2008-09	2009-10	2010-11	2011-12
Kazakhstan	131.68	136.54	172.16	244.39
Uzbekistan	45.53	54.03	60.42	89.39
Tajikistan	16.71	15.71	18.31	21.28
Turkmenistan	41.40	36.15	26.16	43.95
Kyrgyzstan	22.92	26.84	25.79	30.55

Table 1.6: Imports into India from the Central Asia states (US$ millions)

	2008-09	2009-10	2010-11	2011-12
Kazakhstan	159.03	154.91	138.42	166.35
Uzbekistan	70.74	29.97	20.63	61.58
Tajikistan	17.47	16.85	23.02	7.09
Turkmenistan	12.10	10.00	9.73	16.89
Kyrgyzstan	1.03	0.64	1.03	0.64

Source: Table 5 and 6: *Statistics of the Foreign Trade of India, by Countries and Commodities. Vol. 1 (Exports), Vol. 2 (Imports)*. (Director General of Commercial Intelligence and Statistics, Ministry of Commerce, Government of India). Statistical Database as available on website.

(viii) The "Eurasia" Factor

Significantly, this consistent improvement in trade has taken shape despite a new dimension to the Central Asian scenario. The notion of a "Eurasian Economic Community" (*Evraziiskoe Ekonomicheskoe Soobshchetvo*) leading to a "Eurasian Economic Space" (*Evraziiskoe Ekonomicheskoe Prostranstvo*) – which was mooted in the mid-1990s but which showed little signs of life at the time – has now passed through two major stages in the 2000s.[2] It is now possible to speak of a formal "Eurasian Customs Union" in the area, and it is significant that despite its existence, improvements in trade with India has carried on regardless.

(ix) Prospects for Development of Indian Trade and Collaborations

Under the circumstances, though it is unlikely that trade with the Central Asian states will improve at a rate higher than what already has been achieved, given the variations in incomes and consumption levels in these countries, steady growth as well as possibilities for innovative economic collaboration are undoubtedly considerable. This is evident in almost all countries. For example, in the case of Uzbekistan, this has been seen in the case of the Spandex operation, where the Government has shown itself to be able to intervene forcefully to promote cooperation. Both transport logistics (low airfares) as well as access to a large market in Uzbekistan encourages the prospect for Indian investment in the region as a hedge to operations in South Asia itself.

In fact, in the case of economic cooperation, Central Asia seems to have found a niche in trans-global Indian operations that are run by non-resident Indians, who have major Indian investments in Central Asia, although they are focused in multiple global locales. This is clearly the case in the Indorama operation in Kokand – undertaken by a group that was established in South East Asia (Indonesia), and run by the Kolkata-born tycoon SP Lohia. The group has bases in Mumbai, Nagpur and Himachal Pradesh as well as interests in Indonesia and Nigeria. It drew Uzbekistan into its network in 2011.[3]

Elsewhere, similar opportunities are seen in the case of the offer of Mittal Investment Sarl, the investment agency linked to LN Mittal's ArcelorMittal. Schemes included the initiative to sell off Mittal's interests in Caspian Investment Resources in Kazakhstan to ONGC Videsh. Fifty percent of the company's investment – originally obtained from the Russian company, Lukoil – was on offer, and the sale was approved by Kazmunaigaz, a Kazakh national oil company that has pre-emption rights. It is clear in this case that the possessor company, faced with problems in the international investment environment, wanted to divest itself of some of its acquisitions – and this allowed the GoI to pursue its own interests in energy security. The overlap between national interests, global Indian capital and the faceoff between the interests involved soon became evident in this case, where Mittal ultimately focused on Sinopec, the Chinese oil and natural gas giant.

Such strategies have been possible owing to a straightforward partnership that has existed between ONGC Videsh and the Mittal group in the form of the ONGC-Mittal Energy Company, which has existed since 2005. It may further be noted that the very existence of such an operation and its recent interest in the Satpayev field in Kazakhstan is an example of how operations by overseas Indians' need to be seen independently and deserving to be considered in a bracket by themselves.[4]

III. Looking Ahead

A. The three major issues discussed in the greater part of this paper, I suggest, must be central to any scheme for looking ahead in developing economic policy for Central Asia.

(i) A close eye needs to be kept on the pattern of trade with individual states and how far they rely on different parameters. This is clearly true in the case of Kazakhastan and Uzbekistan, where the trade pattern with India differs, with trade with Kazakhistan based on a greater variety of products/services. Inputs from Import-Export committees and the Ministry of Commerce of the Government of India are essential for establishing these patterns.

(ii) The precise implications of the Eurasian community's commercial arrangements also require attention in such a context – and a projection of opportunities if there are any.

(iii) A firm examination of possibilities of exploring multilateral ventures that involve an Indian component requires more attention than has been the case in the past. A position that non-resident Indian ventures have marginal significance for foreign economic policy is an unwise perspective to follow in the case of Central Asian states.

Such points may be integrated into a Research Agenda to be sponsored by the ICWA and other supporting bodies to provide a firm set of guidelines that can act as a reference point for policymakers in the short-term. The implication of the work of the Eurasian Community requires to be provided to those in the field by the Ministry of Commerce, as part of its Focus Central Asia initiatives.

B. The initial section of this paper looked to cultural connections and geopolitical issues. The latter, which touched on problems associated with the changing situation in Afghanistan, are not the central concern of this Balance Sheet.

Cultural policy has received more attention and the following may be noted as suggestions for the future, which also has an economic angle:

(i) India's cultural policy in the region, while successful, has been restricted to a projection of straightforward aspects of culture – dance, music and film. India Chairs support such ventures, as do placements in Indian educational institutions of students from Central Asian states. Visiting lectures in Central Asia further add to this. Given financial demands on the state that such policy involves, further extension beyond a point is not possible. This has been clear to those involved with Area Studies Programmes.

(ii) A broader venture of educational institutions into the region – and a link with Central Asian units through Skype – and sharing of educational agenda is called for and may not involve substantial outlays. Common points interest – from planning school and university agenda to straightforward teaching of English – are many and require attention.

(iii) A wholesale failure to project Central Asia in India is clear and unfortunate. Despite the closeness of these countries with India historically, seldom do exhibitions of Central Asian subjects ever take place in India, or active discussions in the media. These shortcomings clearly require attention.

These issues may be taken up by the ICWA and support institutions as part of strengthening India's cultural policy in Central Asia.

Endnotes

1. See www.indianindustry.com for the information.
2. The basic history of the community is sketched out on its website, http://www.evrazes.com/
3. http://www.indorama.com/for the operations of this concern, including basic information concerning the Uzbek operation.
4. Indian Express "ONGC Mittal join hands for energy products", 23 July 2005.

2
Transport Corridors from South Asia to Central Asia: Post-2014 Scenario

Sultan Akimbekov

The situation in post-2014 Afghanistan has an important dimension associated with the revival of the earlier transit potential of the country. This aspect is relevant not only for the development of trade relations between India and Central Asia, but also for the peaceful settlement of a number of long-standing conflicts.

The first point is the future Afghanistan could benefit from the transit of goods from Central Asia to South Asia-Pakistan and India – and vice versa. This will partly allow for reducing the current financial burden on international bodies for financing Government institutions in Afghanistan. The second point is development of transit routes through Afghanistan could be important for ensuring stability of the country. The local population and the elite will benefit from the transit revenues and help support the initiative. The third point is the revival of transit potential in Afghanistan will allow for the establishment of an overland trade between the two rapidly developing regions – Central Asia and South Asia. In Central Asia, this can help decrease internal tensions existing amongst regional countries, such as the regular closure of borders between Uzbekistan and Tajikistan. The level of bilateral trade amongst the Central Asian republics is extremely low- especially between Turkmenistan and Uzbekistan- as well as between these two countries' and the rest of the region. In South Asia, the development of trade relations with Central Asia will automatically position Pakistan as an important transit country, which will potentially reduce tensions in Pakistan-India relations.

In general, boosting the transit potential of Afghanistan looks like a feasible way to resolve not only the long-standing conflict in

Afghanistan but also contribute to the settlement of a number of inter-state conflicts in the region.

It should be noted that the termination of trade and economic relations between Central Asia and South Asia was not the result of conflict in Afghanistan (which began with the April 1978 revolution and the consequent Soviet invasion). Historically, trade between these regions reduced sharply as a result of differences between British and Russian empires in the 19th century. The creation of the Soviet Union led to its land mass dividing Soviet Central Asia and South Asia. It should also be emphasized that overland trade in Asia declined sharply in volume approximately around the 16th century, when overland trade between Asia and Europe was replaced by maritime trade. Accordingly, the Great Silk Route, which passed through Central Asia, lost its earlier economic and political significance. A branch of this route, which led from Central Asia to India, was also affected by these developments.

The conflict in Afghanistan further led to the isolation of Central Asia and South Asia. Consequently, current plans for reviving trade and economic relations between these two regions represent a very ambitious task. They have huge potential to radically change the economic and geopolitical landscape of these regions respectively; however, implementation of this plan seems very difficult because of the ongoing geopolitical conflict in and around Afghanistan, as well as the unsettled political situation in the region generally.

Current Set of Contradictions

Currently, there are fundamental contradictions associated with the Central Asian region. In particular, the US supports opening the region from the South. Related to this is the idea put forward by Washington of developing a New Great Silk Road through Afghanistan. However, Russia and China believe that behind the US plan lies a desire to establish its influence in the Central Asian region, which is strategically important for both countries. Moscow and Beijing are, in principle, opposed to the interference of third parties in the region. Their concerns relate to the fact that these countries will be able to exert pressure on vulnerable regions of both China and Russia. In China, this is Xinjiang while for Russia, it is the vulnerable seven thousand kilometre long border with Kazakhstan. At the same time, Russia has traditionally played a greater role in Central Asia than

China. Therefore, Russia has a more proactive approach in the region, as it does towards Afghanistan as well. The US supports the opening up of the Central Asian region and developing trade and economic relations between the Central Asian region and the South Asian countries. However, Russia's main focus is on security issues. From the Russian point of view, in the post-2014 Afghanistan, security issues will only aggravate, in particular, the potential threat of the "Taliban" coming to power. Accordingly, this needs to be closely monitored and ensured that the interests of both the national minorities in Afghanistan on one hand and of the Central Asia states on the other are protected against the Afghan threat.

There are two possible scenarios. One involves going back to the situation in Afghanistan as it existed before 2001– that is, restoration of the former anti-Taliban Northern Alliance, which is a coalition of national minorities . The second scenario stems from the idea that the states of Central Asia will come together on a common platform against the security threats faced by the region as a whole. It is obvious that these two scenarios theoretically hinder the idea of restoring trade and economic relations between Central Asia and South Asia. Thus, the existing geopolitical contradictions between the Great Powers striving both for influence inside Central Asia and for physical access to this strategically important region directly affects any future course of events. In the end, it all depends on how events will unfold in Afghanistan after 2014.

Interests in Central Asia

For the newly independent states of Central Asia, the issue of Afghanistan and any future plans around it are primarily linked to their security. The priorities of economic development give way to potential security risks associated with the Afghan conflict. Also, the geopolitical game being played by the Great Powers forces Central Asian countries to exercise caution in their foreign policy orientation. At the same time, opening trade and transport corridors to the South is also a policy priority of countries bordering Afghanistan, which include Turkmenistan, Uzbekistan and Tajikistan.

Turkmenistan, since the mid-1990s, has been in favour of constructing a gas pipeline to Pakistan. It is seeking to acquire new markets for Turkmen gas to reduce its dependence on Russia. Today, the situation in Turkmenistan is more favourable than the earlier decades of 1990s and early 2000s. Since 2009, some gas is being exported by Turkmenistan to China via the new gas pipeline through Uzbekistan and Kazakhstan.

Uzbekistan needs to open trade routes to the South because its industrial policy needs to reduce costs of production, especially since transporting cargo through Kazakhstan and Russia is very costly.

Tajikistan, which has extremely difficult political relations with Uzbekistan, became economically more isolated because transport through Uzbekistan faced difficulty. Therefore, in addition to local trade, development of relations with north Afghanistan has been important for the Tajik leadership. They would also like to explore new markets in Afghanistan, particularly for electricity generated by the Tajik hydro-power plants.

All three of the above-mentioned countries belong to the "front-line" – they have a common border with Afghanistan. It is obvious that any global processes which influence regional development will also affect them all to some degree or the other.

At the same time, Kazakhstan is far from Afghanistan and is not directly involved with events occurring in the country. Kazakhstan's economic situation gives it more confidence. Further, it has more options in trade and transport. For example, besides the option of the route across Russia, there is also the option of transporting cargo through China and the Caspian Sea to the Caucasus. In geopolitical terms, Kazakhstan has been able to maintain stable relations with all major powers. Ideologically, the country has a multi-vector approach. For Kazakhstan, it is important to monitor any geopolitical scenario that unfolds in the region, and keep a close eye on trade and economic trends as they prevail in the region. For, on one hand, the potential opening of transit trade with Pakistan – and further to India through Afghanistan – is quite acceptable. Kazakhstan, for sure, will benefit from it, taking into account its level of economic development in terms of infrastructure and financial institutions. On the other hand, Kazakhstan will also not lose if there are no major developments, and the emphasis continues to be on security issues.

In general, all Central Asia states are landlocked countries. Theoretically, the rehabilitation of overland trade through the centre of the continent – across Eurasia – is in the interest of all countries of the region and their immediate neighbours. The issue, by and large, lies in the outcome of geopolitical rivalry amongst the Great Powers in the region.

India and Pakistan

It is obvious that the old rivals – India and Pakistan – have different interests in the way the situation evolves in and around Afghanistan. For Pakistan, there are two problems: first, the need to open transport corridors to the North – to the Central Asian region – while the second is the probable political configuration of various stakeholders in Afghanistan after 2014, and who will come to power in Kabul. The latter is of importance from the point of view of demarcation of the Durand Line. The Durand Line is de facto the border between Pakistan and Afghanistan. Any independent Afghan Government dominated by Pashtuns will no doubt raise the issue of legality of the Durand Line, something that the Pashtuns have traditionally questioned. The only acceptable solution for Pakistan is being fully in control of any Government in Kabul. Such a Government – until 2001 – was the Taliban. At the moment, there is no reason to believe that the rivalry between the Great Powers for influence in the region will lead to the repeat of the situation as it existed before 2001. At the same time, issues of economic development still have priority for any Government in Pakistan. We can, therefore, expect that opening transport and trade corridors through Afghanistan to Central Asia will be in the interests of Pakistan.

It should be noted that the interests of India are more in line with the question of geopolitics and security than with opening of transport corridors through Afghanistan to the North. In economic terms, India, unlike Pakistan, can afford to simply maintain status quo.

This position of India is, to some extent, close to the position taken by Kazakhstan. Both these countries are willing to accept the fact that revival of overland trade through Afghanistan, and consequently, Central Asia's value as transit a route, is an interesting project in itself. Similarly, both countries are also willing to accept the current status quo in the region.

3

India's Geopolitical Interests in Central Asia and Economic Diplomacy

Mavlanov Ibragim

Introduction

A unique feature of the Indian economy has been achieving a high growth trajectory with stability, and it has proved its strength and resilience. India's economic diplomacy with Central and South Asian nations shows a continuing positive trend. High-level visits are exchanged on a regular basis. The chapter attempts to analyse that today, India is not only a reliable business partner bilaterally but is one of the best experienced countries in the Asian region to actively promote economic development between Central and South Asian regions. It reflects a process of shift of geopolitical interests of Central Asia (CA) to economic diplomacy initiatives taken by India. Further, the author analyzes the conceptual approach of India and Uzbekistan to the challenge of global economic crisis. The author examines how the Global Financial and Economic Crisis (GFEC) of 2008-2009 has affected the Indian economy, and suggests a comparative analysis of approaches taken by India and Uzbekistan to the challenge of GFEC. It is demonstrated that India succeeded in achieving high economic growth largely due to the rise in its foreign trade. Indeed, it was seen that implementation of foreign trade initiatives as part of India's economic diplomacy played a crucial role in framing the Export and Import policy of the country. The chapter emphasizes that India's political and economic diplomacy approach vis-a-vis Central and South Asian nations is strategically important from the perspective of inter-regional cooperation.

I. India's Economic Development after the 2008 Global Financial and Economic Crisis (GFEC)

The Indian economy is one of the fastest growing economies in the post-crisis period. Analysis of the reform process shows that India's foreign policy and its bilateral and multilateral economic diplomacy enabled the country to achieve considerable success in creating a favourable investment climate and economic liberalization of exports and imports.

As per the latest information released by the Central Statistics Office, the growth of Gross Domestic Product (GDP) at factor cost was estimated at 6.9 per cent in 2011-2012, with agriculture and allied activities growing at 2.5 per cent, industry at 3.9 per cent and services at 9.4 per cent. The corresponding growth in GDP in 2010-2011 was 8.4 per cent, with agriculture and allied sector, industry and services growing at 7.0, 7.2 and 9.3 per cent, respectively.[1]

Despite the world financial crisis in 2008 that greatly influenced global FDI flows, the analysis demonstrated increase in FDI flows in 2011, when the role of the developing countries increased, including India. Thus, it was felt that these changes were caused by some 2,377 amendments made to foreign investment legislation for the period 1992 to 2008; 2,650 changes were made at improving the investment climate.[2] Thus, only from 2007 to 2009-10, FDI inflow into India increased from US$ 8.5 billion to $ 19,791 billion.[3]

Today, India is fourth amongst developing countries in East, South, and Southeast Asia in terms of investments made abroad. According to UN data, India was second in the list of most attractive countries for FDI, following China and remained ahead of the US, Russia and Brazil.[4] Indian trade deficit was higher at US$ 85.7 billion (9.4 per cent of GDP) during 1st quarter of 2011-2012 vis-a-vis US$ 68.9 billion (8.9 per cent of GDP) in first quarter of 2010-2011.[5]

Studying the Indian economy, we tried to analyze how the GFEC of 2008-2009 affected the economy, and it was suggested that a comparative analysis of approaches taken by India and Uzbekistan to the GFEC must be carried out. The analysis showed that GFEC had minimal impact on India due to the fact that Indian banks were not directly exposed to the external financial crisis since growth in India was largely driven by domestic consumption and domestic investment, while demand for exported goods was less than 15 per cent of GDP. However, the Government of India implemented three anti-GFEC crisis packages worth of 75 billion dollars (7 per cent of GDP).

Conceptual approaches of Uzbekistan to the GFEC challenge, as formulated by President of Uzbekistan Islam Karimov, were praised by foreign scholars and political analysts in international conferences. However, a comparative analysis of the Governments' response in Uzbekistan and India to the GFEC suggests that the approach of both countries was very similar. This is particularly evident in areas like structural economic reforms, diversification of production, active pro-investment policy to help implement strategically important projects, development of social infrastructure in rural areas, etc. These steps were the main factors that influenced strategic bilateral mutual guarantees and inter-regional and international economic cooperation between India and Uzbekistan.

An analysis of the financial crisis showed its underlying cause could be attributed to economic systems in general and unique features of the model of economic framework followed by each country. Therefore, a study of models of economic systems should be one of the first tasks of economic diplomacy to identify possible sources of any future crisis. An analysis of scientific methods and indicators for assessing the economic crisis allowed the author to identify shortcomings in existing models and early warning indicators. Therefore, this study continued to undertake further systems research and development of new models of sustainability indicators of economic systems in general. One of the most important tasks of economic diplomacy is the need to redirect investment flows into Uzbekistan and effective use of "mirror" effect on the dynamics of global FDI flows. This requires a radical improvement and development of new diplomatic tools and approaches to investment, and the need to work on complex projects in the constructof inter-regional trade and economic zones. Accordingly, economic diplomacy has to accomplish the following objectives: to develop new filters, identifying and mitigating internal and external threats to economic security in the early stages, better monitoring and analysis of fundamental causes of financial crisis, improvement and development of new methods for understanding the current financial crisis, and improving system analysis and monitoring of economic security.

II. India's Geopolitical Interests in Central Asia

First of all, India has strong historical relations with the Central Asian region (Kazakhstan, Kyrgyzstan, Tajikistan, Turkmenistan and Uzbekistan). Both India and Central Asia were two powerful Centres of ancient oriental civilisations with a high degree of interaction. The historical past of both Centres has a strong foundation in exchanges in cultural, political and economic sphere. The ancient "*Silk Route*" was a strong link between India and the Central Asian region, whether it was trade or people-to-people contacts.

Secondly, in the past, many Indian and Western scientists have been trying to analyze the role of India in Central Asia. BB Kumar has written: "India and Central Asia have a long tradition of socio-cultural, political and economic contact since the remote past. The two regions have common and contiguous borders, climatic continuity, similar geographical features and geo-cultural affinity".[6] In the book "India and Central Asia: Cultural, Economic and Political Links"[7], many scientists underscored the fact that India's relationship with the Central Asian countries was excellent, underpinned by deep historic and cultural bonds, especially since the independence of these countries. Analyzing the presence of Indians in Central Asia in 16th and 17th centuries and Indian traders in Uzbekistan, Surendra Gopal said: "Indians were able to gain access to important trade centres in Central Asia…".[8] Researching economic relations between India and Central Asia, Devendra Kaushik remarks: "…economic relations between India and Central Asia continued to exist, notwithstanding the numerous obstacles…".[9]

In the book "India and Central Asia",[10] edited by Indranil Banerjie, many scientists were of the view that high-level visits between India and Central Asian nations were a regular feature. These were complemented by industrial and consumer goods exhibitions, besides visits of trade delegations. Indranil Banerjie specifically said: "…India's contacts with CARs (Central Asian Republics) have developed at various levels".[11] He also noted: "Some of the largest oil exploration, drilling, and pipeline projects of recent times have been signed in this region… If these contracts prove lucrative, India could bid for bigger energy projects".[12]

Studying Indian strategy in Central Asia, Dr. Stephen Blank underlined: "India's growing interest in Central Asia is not confined merely to the linked threats of terrorism, separatism, drug trading and incitement to civil violence. It also has deep and long-standing strategic and economic roots".[13] He also added: "Central Asia's large gas and oil reserves and India's rising demand for energy sources also suggested a naturally complementary relationship".[14]

An analysis of Indian energy strategies in Central Asian by Maj. Gen (Retd.) SCN Jatar emphasized: "The Central Asian region, with its modest reservoir of hydrocarbons compared to West Asia, is important to India due to geo-strategic and geopolitical reasons".[15] He also said: "the emergence of Central Asia as a region with hydrocarbon potential offers India the opportunity to beef up its energy security in the short term up to 2025".[16]

Researching prospects for India's trade and investment in Central Asia, TK Bhaumik says: "Indian industry can develop long-term partnership with the region and help the CARs achieve their goal of growth of exports. Indian companies can play a major role by investing in sectors that have export potential. Some prominent export sectors of the region are aluminium, textiles, general purpose machinery chemicals, agricultural products, oil and gas, and other energy products. Incidentally, these are also potential sectors for foreign investment in this region… While such a strategy would contribute significantly to the CARs' economic growth, it would also enable Indian companies to explore new global markets… Strategic investment in this region may, thus, offer access to larger markets in the future".[17]

Third, in the present times, India is seeking to evolve a common and strong relationship with each of the Central Asian countries. There is a lot of common ground for building on this relationship. Secularism and democracy are two features that are shared by Central Asia and India. Moreover, Central Asia has a positive and extremely friendly disposition towards India. India's recent diplomatic thrust into Central Asia is in keeping with its view on future energy requirements and strategic positioning through bilateral visits and trade.[18] Clearly, oil and gas continue to be primary economic factors motivating India to play a role in Central Asia.

Another article says: "With the global race for scarce energy resources intensifying, India is increasingly looking to Central Asia, both as a reliable source of oil and natural gas and a focus of its strategic interests in Asia. Besides oil, Central Asian Republics including Turkmenistan, Kazakhstan, Uzbekistan, Kyrgyzstan and Tajikistan are important for India from the viewpoint of national security, especially in combating terrorism fuelled by radical Islam. The potential for cooperation between India and Central Asia is huge and can encompass areas such as IT, biotechnology, telecom, service sector and education. Tourism to picturesque towns of Central Asia is yet another area that may lead to not only more business but also more people-to-people contacts with India. If India is to play its role as a major Asian power, it will have to deepen its engagement and raise its profile in the region"[19]. Another scientist say: "India suffered a tremendous decline in its trade with Central Asia during 1991-94 that highlighted its faltering competitiveness with an already reformed China".[20]

Prof. Martin C Spechler in his book[21] is trying to analyze the situation in Central Asia after the dramatic terror attacks of 11 September 2001, which drew the attention of the US and the West in general to Afghanistan and Central Asia, and created expectations in some – and fear in others- that the security and economic situation there could change.

Prof. Nirmala Joshi, studying India's current relations with Central Asia, said: "Today, Indian interests are substantial and are in the sphere of strategic, security, political and economic security. Any competition amongst major powers for control and influence in India's extended neighbourhood would have a bearing on its policy and diplomacy in the region. If the competitive element in Central Asia becomes a dominant tendency, India would have to take hard decisions".[22]

Prof. SD Muni, marking "Central Asia's geo-strategic location and its rich mineral and hydro-carbon resources", noted: "India focused on three major areas of mutual interests namely: economic cooperation, terrorism and the challenge of political stability and issues of regional security and strategic order".[23] He also emphasized: "The newly-emerged Central Asia provides immense strategic and economic opportunities for India, and Indian policymakers are trying to harness these opportunities… It is true that India suffers from the connectivity hurdle in harnessing the full potential of Indo-Central Asian co-operation, but there is also much scope for India to improve economic aspects of its diplomacy".[24]

Fourth, during the 3rd India-Central Asia Regional Conference, jointly organized by the Institute for Defence Studies and Analyses (IDSA), New Delhi, and the Institute for Strategic and Regional

Studies (ISRS) at Tashkent, former Uzbekistan Foreign Minister Dr. Sadik Safoev, underlined "the need of broader cooperation between India and Uzbekistan in economic and technological arenas" and "...to coordinate their efforts in the fight against terrorism, religious extremism, drug trafficking and organized crime in the Central Asian region." Former Indian Minister of External Affairs, Mr. Yashwant Sinha, in his keynote address, focused on these areas: historical linkages between India and Central Asia, economic and energy potential of Central Asia, bilateral initiatives between India and Central Asian states in the international security situation.[25]

Former Foreign Secretary and National Security Adviser, Government of India, Mr. J N Dixit, speaking at the same conference shared "some general assessments and recommendations about structuring India's relations with Central Asian countries", and said: "India must be more active in associating with new economic cooperation and regional security arrangements, which are being initiated by Central Asian Republics".[26]

Dr. Ravshan Alimov, considering "India's important role in ensuring the regional security in Central Asia", noted: "India's interest in the implementation of major transportation-communication and hydropower projects in the region, in order to ensure stable suppliers of energy raw material, can also facilitate increase in the potential of these projects at the international level". He also underscored: "Moreover, the growth of the Indian economy can enable India to increase its trade, financial and economic cooperation with the countries of the region, taking into account, in particular, the present need of the Central Asian Republics for foreign investment".[27]

Fifth, considering the potential that the Central Asian region offers and India's insignificant presence in that market, Focus CIS Programme[28] was launched by Commerce & Industry Minister, Government of India, in 2003 at the time of announcement of the EXIM Policy on 31st March, 2003. Under this Programme, the Government of India extended assistance to exporters, business chambers, etc. to visit these countries, organise trade fairs, invite Central Asian trade delegations to visit India and undertake various other market promotional activities. The initiatives taken up by this programme received encouraging response from the Indian trading community, and are likely to further boost bilateral trade in the coming years.

In the recent past, economic liberalization undertaken by countries of the Central Asian Region and India, establishment of institutional mechanisms for mutual interaction and development of fast/direct links to Central Asia have all contributed to increased economic interaction between countries of the Central Asian region and India. However, the full potential is yet to be realized. Recognizing the need for enhancing trade and stimulate interest amongst businessmen on both sides, a number of high level visits and a range of initiatives have been undertaken.

Finally, the Central Asian countries have considerable economic potential to cooperate with India. The potential for expansion of trade and investment is great, since this region is extremely rich in mineral resources that need to be tapped, exploited and converted into value-added products.

III. Transformation of India's Geopolitical Interests in Central Asia Into Economic Diplomacy

The analysis of official documents in India as well as those of international organizations and other researches by politicians and diplomats prove the presence of India's geopolitical, strategic and economic interests in Central Asia. These interests have found practical reflection in the foreign policy of India, and are being implemented through the instrument of economic diplomacy that is not limited to negotiations by Presidents, Prime Ministers, Ministers and Government institutions, but are also shaped by private sector participation.

By analyzing mechanisms of implementation of economic diplomacy, it becomes clear that it has had a positive influence on trade with Central Asian countries (Table 3.1).

The actual model of Indian multilateral economic diplomacy with Central Asia and its trend show how theoretical concepts and practical possibilities of India's multilateral economic diplomacy are effectively implemented in Central Asia, as demonstrated during the Conference on Interaction and Confidence-building Measures in Asia (CICA), and the Shanghai Cooperation Organization (SCO).

The study found out that India's diplomacy with countries of CICA is aimed at developing cooperation mechanisms in economic, environmental and humanitarian fields, as well as cooperation on energy security and the development of transport corridors.

Table 3.1: India's trade turnover with Central Asian countries and members of SCO for 2001-2010 (million dollars)*

The countries	*Fiscal year*					
	2001-02	*2003-04*	*2006-07*	*2007-08*	*2008-09*	*2009-10*
Kyrgyzstan	11,53	38,74	37,84	32,43	23,95	27,48
Tajikistan	2,56	8,42	15,41	22,21	34,18	32,56
Turkmenistan	6,30	28,55	45,94	44,64	53,50	46,15
Uzbekistan	23,80	42,84	63,60	56,52	116,27	84,00
Kazakhstan	53,09	84,07	171,48	188,77	290,71	291,45
In total with the Central Asian countries	97,28	202,62	334,27	344,57	518,61	481,64
China	2988,34	7008,33	25796,89	38017,75	41850,52	42441,90
Russia	1333,69	1673,39	3312,74	3418,77	5424,62	4547,48
In total with member of Shanghai Organization	4413,01	8855,79	29397,96	41736,45	47740,25	47424,87
The general trade turnover of India	95240,02	141991,66	312149,29	414786,19	488991,67	467124,31

* It is made by the author on the basis of data of Department of commerce of the Ministry of commerce and the industry of India. http://commerce.nic.in/eidb/iecnt.asp

An analysis of official documents and statistics on India makes it clear that Indian diplomacy towards CA is mainly focused on trade and investment due to the following reasons: rich natural resources of CA; the increasing involvement of the region in global and regional geopolitics; and CA countries as major regional trade and investment as well as political and security partners (with Uzbekistan being the priority).

Studies have also identified strategic Indian economic interests in the SCO region, which is determined by the following: (1) SCO countries have enormous economic and natural potential, (2) Two members of the SCO are UN Security Council permanent members and play an important role in world politics, (3) The SCO appears to India as a large economic market with strategic potential, and (4) A developed system of transport and communications in the SCO region that could provide India with access to adjacent regions and efficient trade-economic and investment cooperation. In 2001-2010, Indian trade with the countries of the SCO increased by more than 10 times.

An analysis shows that India is a strategically important country for the SCO and Central Asia, which is defined as follows: (1) India is actively involved in discussion of issues of global political and economic world order, (2) India's participation in regional economic and security issues has increased, (3) The growing economic, scientific and technological potential (especially in information technology, pharmaceuticals, biotechnology, etc.)es: makes India a country with strategic importance, and (4) India is a promising market for exports and investment.

Thus, the author states that mutual strategic interests define the new trend in institutionalization of regional economic diplomacy of India with Central Asia. According to research, one possible trend in the expansion of India's economic cooperation with Central Asian countries to strengthen bilateral and multilateral interaction could perhaps be the creation of a full-scaled institutional model "India+Central Asia" (Figure 3.1). Further development of this model could possibly be a "Bipolar model of inter-regional economic cooperation Central and South Asia" (Figure 3.2).

These projections may be implemented in the near future, since the formation of new trade and economic institutions in Central and South Asia is an objective reality in international relations, especially amongst developing countries.

Conclusion

India's economic diplomacy in Central Asia is based on a promising economic, investment and trading market, which has strategic potential for joint ventures in small and medium-sized businesses that can give India an advantage in the long run. The region of Central Asia is of important focus for India for implementation of transport and communication projects that Central Asian countries contribute to the rapid integration of Central Asian countries with world markets. Central Asian countries have considerable energy resources (oil, gas, nuclear raw material, etc.) while the possibility of development of gas pipelines and exploration of huge reserves of mineral resources opens up prospects for collaboration in their exploration, production, processing and transport to markets. Technically advanced countries of Central Asia will allow India to quickly develop cooperation mechanisms in all spheres.

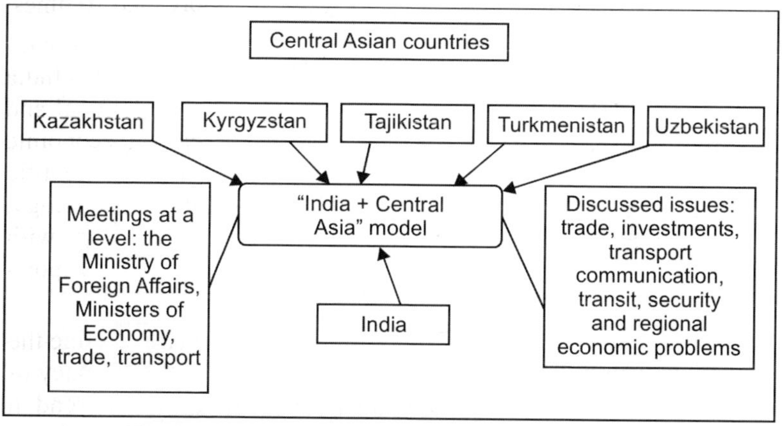

Fig. 3.1: Institutional model "India + Central Asia".*

1. India will fully exploit its multilateral diplomacy with the region of Central Asia and SCO, using existing and new models of inter-regional economic cooperation in Central and South Asia. From the perspective of India's new role in global politics and economy, its presence in Central Asia is strategically important and necessary, not only from the standpoint of India's traditional sphere of influence in

* It is developed and offered by the author.

South Asia, but also from the perspective of the country claiming its rightful role as an emerging political and economic power in this century.

2. The development of a model of economic cooperation on the format of "India+Central Asia", and – in the future – the "Bipolar model of interregional economic cooperation Central and South Asia" – would serve the interests of Uzbekistan and also serve as a basis for active cooperation with the Southeast Asia region .

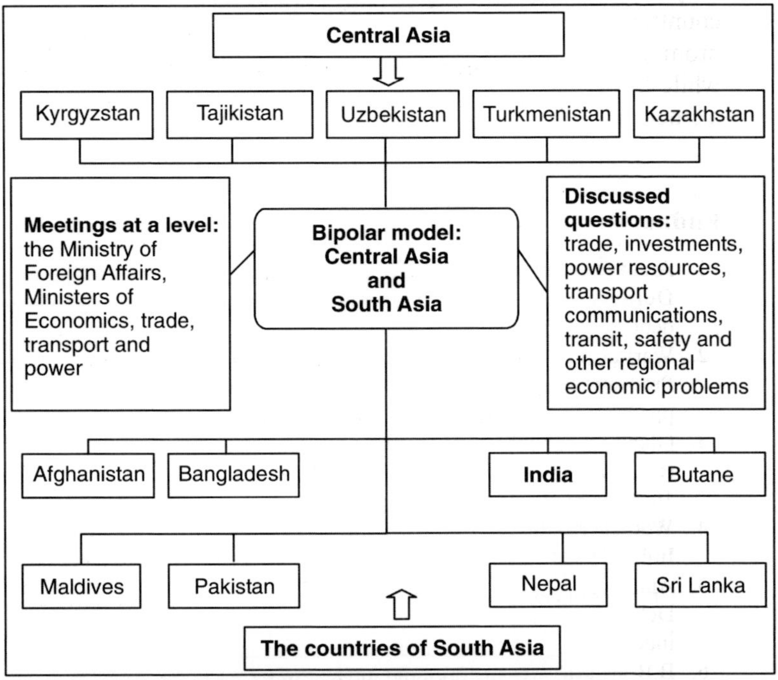

Fig. 3.2: Bipolar model of inter-regional economic cooperation of Central Asia with South Asia.*

3. Given that the Global Financial Crisis was largely due to the framework of country-specific economic systems, attention is drawn to addressing the following scientific and practical problems: (a) In-depth study of Indian economic system model as a possible source of dealing with not only current but also future crises, (b) An analysis

* It is developed and offered by the author.

of economic diplomacy and its resistance to the Global Financial Crisis and the possible introduction of sustainability indicators, (c) The timely diagnosis of Global Financial Crisis, and (d) Improvement and development of new diplomatic tools and approaches to attract investments during crisis.

4. On a daily basis, as Indian analysts recognize, India's economic power is perhaps significant in creating in Central Asia a region of economic security. India's economic growth shows that India is not only a reliable business partner, but one of the most experienced countries in the Asian region that can use its economic potential to promote the active economic development of the Central Asian region while ensuring economic security and stability. Thus, these factors play a crucial role in shaping India's economic policy towards Central Asia.

Endnotes

1. Annual Report 2011-2012. Ministry of Finance, Government of India, New Delhi, 2012, pp. 1-3. http://www.finmin.nic.in/the_ministry/dept_eco_affairs/index.html
2. World Investment Report 2009: Transnational Corporations, Agricultural Production and Development, New York and Geneva: United Nations, 2009, pp. XXII, 16, 31
3. Global Economic Crisis and its Impact on India, New Delhi: Research Unit (LARRDIS), Rajya Sabha Secretariat, 2009. – p. 28; Annual Report 2009-10. New-Delhi: Ministry of Finance, Government of India, 2010, p. 33.
4. World Investment Report 2008: Transnational Corporations and the Infrastructure Challenge, p. 33.
5. Annual Report 2011-2012. Ministry of Finance, Government of India, New Delhi, 2012, p. 3. http://www.finmin.nic.in/the_ministry/dept_eco_affairs/index.html
6. B.B. Kumar. Central Asia: Indian Literary Perception, *Dialogue*, January-March, 2004, Volume 5 No. 3. http://www.asthabharati.org/Dia_Jan.04/central%20asia%20kumar.htm
7. *India and Central Asia: Cultural, Economic and Political Links*, Edited by Surendra Gopal, Shipra Publications, New Delhi, 2001, pp. 200.
8. *Ibid.*, p. 25.
9. *Ibid.*, p. 71.
10. *India and Central Asia*, Edited by Indranil Banerjie, Brunel Academic Publishers Ltd., UK, 2004, p, 357.
11. *Ibid.*, p. xiv.
12. *Ibid.*, p. xv.

13. *Ibid.*, p. 262.
14. *Ibid.*, p. 264.
15. *Ibid.*, p. 304.
16. *Ibid.*, p. 325.
17. *Ibid.*, pp. 339-340.
18. India and Central Asia, Rahul Bedi, *Frontline*, Volume 19, Issue 19, September 14-27, 2002 http://www.flonnet.com/fl1919/19190600.htm
19. Central Asia, new focus of India's oil diplomacy, Manish Chand (IANS), New Delhi, April 6, 2005. http://www.hindustantimes.com/news/181_1308782,0002.htm
20. Richard Pomfret. The Economies of Central Asia. Princeton, NJ: Princeton University Press, 1995, p. 155.
21. Martin C. Spechler. Economy and Security in Central Asia since 9/11: A Skeptical Look, http://www.ca-c.org/journal/eng-01-2003/05.speprimen.shtml
22. *Central Asia: The Great Game Replayed: An Indian Perspective*, Edited by Prof. Nirmala Joshi, New Centure Publications, New Delhi, 2003, p. 8.
23. *Ibid.*, pp. 97-110.
24. *Ibid.*, pp. 126-128.
25. Ramakant Dwivedi, 3rd India-Central Asia Regional Conference, Tashkent, November 6-8 2003. *Strategic Analysis. Quarterly Journal of the IDSA*, Oct-Dec 2003, Vol. 27. No. 4. p. 621.
26. *India and Central Asia: Advancing the Common Interest*, K. Santhanam, Ramakant Dwivedi, Anama Publishers, New Delhi, 2004, p. 20.
27. *Ibid.*, pp. 91-94.
28. FOCUS CIS – Programme 2004-2005, A Programme for Developing and Enhancing India's Trade with CIS. Government of India, Ministry of Commerce and Industry, Department of Commerce, New Delhi, 2004.

4
India's New Policy Thrust in Central Asia

Paramjit S Sahai

Introduction

To start certain basic questions, assumptions and terminologies need to be raised in the context of this paper. 'Connectivity' is the buzz word, whether it is amongst peoples, faiths, businesses or nations. Later, it will be explored how it operates in the context of India's relationship with Central Asia. Seen from another perspective, connectivity can take place only through communication. This raises the question: communication amongst whom – Leaders? Or peoples? Or both? How do you promote this dialogue? The quintessence of dialogue has to be that it leads to peace and development. There is a primary aspect to communication, which is the presence of adequate physical infrastructure. Does this exist and how does this facilitate? A good physical infrastructure can at best be a facilitator, but real communication is amongst peoples. How do people enhance such connectivity amongst different groups, in particular students, academia and the business community? The triumvirate of connectivity would include the 3 Cs – Communication, Culture and Commerce – even though not necessarily in the same order. Having accepted the inevitability of connectivity, people have to see how they realize this and give it a push? Will it come from their idea on their interests? How are people placed with one another? How would these be channelized? Are existing institutional frameworks adequate or additional structures need to be created? An attempt will be made to answer all these, and other, related questions as we look at the ground reality and explore ways to enhance connectivity between India and Central Asia.

Scenario in Central Asia

The first step, therefore, is to understand the present day scenario in Central Asia. There are no two opinions that Central Asia has re-emerged as a strategic space. The opinion, however, is divided, as to whether it has emerged as a geopolitical space or it merely remains a geographical entity. Its emergence as a geopolitical space is delayed, as no common view has developed amongst the five countries since they still have to discover compatibility with one another. For the world, however, Central Asia remains a strategic space. It further assumes greater importance in the context of the post-2014 Afghanistan scenario. This has resulted in a new Great Game, as the Great Powers move to gain or strengthen their foothold.

China has definitely emerged as the dominant power in Central Asia as it entrenches itself, in particular, in the energy sector. This has, however, not been endearing at the people-to-people level, where mistrust of China remains despite the stellar role played by its Confucius Centres. Russia is regaining its lost pre-eminence as it gains acceptance in its natural backyard. America is now sitting on the fence as it quietly watches the unfolding of developments. India still remains a distant partner, although its benign presence is welcome.

Central Asia aspires to be a link between Asia and Europe as it gets commercially intertwined, in particular, in the energy sector. There is, however, no coherence of policies at the regional level, as each country pursues its own national interests. This results in variations in the level of their linkages, with Kazakhstan emerging as the dominant link with Europe and sending negative vibes to Uzbekistan, which is demographically dominant in the region. At the people level, the Russian diaspora still has a sizeable presence, as does the growth of Central Asian diaspora in Russia. Similarly, there is uneven integration of individual countries in regional groupings that are emerging, be it Shanghai Cooperation Organization (SCO), Eurasian Community or the Collective Security Treaty Organization (CSTO). The incentive for such cooperation still remains pursuance of respective interests by each individual country of Central Asia. New socio-economic structures are still evolving, while the old ones have not been dismantled yet. Democratic forces are being set in motion, and these are slowly making their way into the polity of these nations.

India and Central Asia

The next step would be to see how India fits into the present-day scenario prevailing in Central Asia. What are the pluses and minuses of its connectivity? Central Asia stands high at the perception level, being viewed as India's extended neighbourhood and 'central' to its relationship with countries in Central Asia. India harks upon its 'deep historical bonds',[1] which are often recalled by Indian dignitaries. Indian cultural connectivity has not led to any commercial advantage, given the problem of 'access', since access via the land route stands denied by Pakistan. The total trade turnover is meagre - less than US $ 500 million. What is missed at the level of land connectivity is compensated at the level of political connectivity.

India, perhaps, has the highest number of exchange visits at the level of Heads of State/Government, with some leaders having visited India five times. The present level of this relationship has been summed up by Vice President Hamid Ansari as 'extremely cordial, politically very good relations, commercially modest'.[2] The trickledown effect of high level visits is missing at the people-to-people level, given existing constraints of physical infrastructure linking India with Central Asia. It is a kind of being 'too near, yet too far'.

Where else, then, is the strength of India's relationship with Central Asia? India and Central Asian countries are multi-cultural societies. They also hold more or less similar views on global issues. They would like to play their respective roles in post-2014 Afghanistan, in any process that is Afghanistan-led. They are supportive of India's aspirations to be a member of the UN Security Council. India is perceived to be a 'benign power', which is not involved in the 'New Power Game'. India also perceives Central Asian countries as 'Partners in Development'. They would, therefore, like to see greater involvement of India in strengthening bilateral ties and focusing on economic and commercial areas, including energy.

India was one of the first countries to accord diplomatic recognition to the newly independent states in Central Asia after the collapse of the Soviet Union. India also became the first destination for foreign visits by leaders from Central Asia. They felt a sense of greater identity with Asian countries, as against Russia, which started looking up to the West notwithstanding that it donned the Euro-Asian hat. The author was personally involved in organising these visits during 1991-92. These visits resulted in laying the foundation for cooperation, as a number of framework agreements were signed during these visits. This was followed by the establishment of resident diplomatic missions by India and Central Asian countries in India. All this had resulted in creating a good infrastructure and framework for cooperation. India was an 'early bird' in Central Asia. Did its presence translate into any meaningful cooperation? If not, what were the constraints? Has India arrived in Central Asia?

India and Central Asia: Level of Bilateral Relations and Emerging Trends

As stated earlier, the strength of India's relationship is connectivity at the top political leadership level. This relationship stands upgraded to the next level of strategic partnership with Kazakhstan, Uzbekistan and Tajikistan. Here again, the regional component is missing, despite India's participation in some of the regional groupings. The relationship, therefore, is at the bilateral level, as it responds to interests of each country. There is asymmetry in the nature and level of bilateral relationship. The thrust, therefore, varies; economic and strategic partnership with Kazakhstan; economic and cultural connectivity with Uzbekistan; education and security links with Tajikistan; regional economic links (TAPI) with Turkmenistan and establishment of democratic institutions with Kyrgyzstan. India and Central Asian countries share common concerns on terrorism and narco-trafficking, resulting in the establishment of Joint Working Group Mechanisms on Counter-Terrorism with Kazakhstan, Tajikistan and Uzbekistan.

The trickledown effect of this high-level political relationship is missing in other spheres, given the constraint of a viable surface route. The North-South Corridor is still not fully operational. A consignment of dry fruits from Afghanistan managed to make its way through this route in September 2013. Our trade level, however, is still under US$ 500 million, as both sides are punching well below the potential. Some beginnings have been made in the energy sector, with India acquiring a stake in the Satpaev Exploration Block in Kazakhstan. There are prospects for uranium import from that country. Turkmenistan–Afghanistan–Pakistan–India (TAPI) Pipeline project, which has been through 'on now, off now' stages at different periods, is again back on the radar. If implemented, this would have the potential of emerging as a friendship pipeline, as economic benefits would coalesce with political and security interests.

Where else, then, is the strength of India-Central Asian relationship? It is in the area of 'Capacity Building' and 'Human Resource Development'. India provides around 450 training slots annually under its Indian Technical and Economic Cooperation (ITEC) Programme. Besides these, India offers scholarships to students under Indian Council for Cultural Relations (ICCR's) scholarship scheme. ICCR also provides facilities for research scholars. On the other hand, Indian students avail facilities for study in medicine in some universities in Central Asia.

India also actively connects with Central Asia through its 'Development Partnership Programme'. It is in the area of Information Technology that such cooperation has borne fruit. At present, Information Technology Centres of Excellence are functional in Ashgabat, Bishkek, Dushanbe and Tashkent. Another centre is planned for Astana, thereby covering all the five countries. Another partnership project of significance has been India's assistance to the Varzob-I mini-hydel plant in Tajikistan. India has also helped in setting up industrial units, such as a Fruit Processing Plant in Dushanbe and a Potato Processing Plant in Talas, Kyrgyzstan. Other projects include Machine and Tool Room in Dushanbe and Entrepreneurship Development Centre in Tashkent.

India's New Policy Thrust in Central Asia

India took a new initiative with the launch of its 'Connect Central Asia' policy in 2012. This was spelt out by Minister of State for External Affairs, E Ahamed, at the First India-Central Asia Dialogue at Bishkek in Kyrgyzstan. This provides for a framework for 'proactive political, economic and people-to-people engagement with Central Asian countries, both individually and collectively'.[3] The India-Central Asian Dialogue has emerged as an important forum to promote such connectivity. The first Dialogue was held at Bishkek and the second at Almaty in June 2013. Three more Dialogues are planned in the remaining countries.

What are the key elements of this 'Connect Central Asia' policy? These were highlighted by the Minister of State, Ahamed, at Bishkek[4] and are as under:

1. To build strong political relations through the exchange of high level visits

2. To strengthen strategic and security cooperation – military training, joint research, counter-terrorism coordination
3. To promote close consultation on Afghanistan
4. To set up engagements through existing multilateral fora-SCO, Eurasian Economic Community (EEC) and the Customs Union — To enter into a Comprehensive Economic Cooperation Agreement (CECA)
5. To promote long-term partnership in energy and natural resources
6. To promote cooperation in the agricultural sector, generating value addition through cultivation of profitable crops
7. To consider setting up of civil hospitals/clinics in Central Asia, to meet growing requirements of health
8. To set up a Central Asian University in Bishkek, as a centre of excellence to impart world class education in IT, Management, Philosophy and Languages
9. To set up a Central Asian e-network, with a hub in India, to provide tele-medicine and tele-education
10. To help in setting up several medium size steel rolling mills for specific products
11. To provide a viable banking infrastructure
12. To promote Central Asian countries as holiday destinations and exotic foreign locales for the film industry (Bollywood)
13. To promote exchange between youth and the future leaders, building upon a robust exchange of students
14. To encourage regular exchanges of scholars, academics, civil society and youth delegations, to gain deeper insight

India's New Thrust on Development Partnership

India's 'Connect Central Asia' policy has to be linked to its Programme on Development Cooperation, given the thrust on development cooperation with these countries. To ensure better coordination and implementation of its programmes under different umbrellas, a new Department called the Development Partnership Administration (DPA) was set up under the Ministry of External Affairs in January, 2012. It is headed by a senior official at the level of Special Secretary.

It is expected to bring about greater transparency, speed and efficiency, as it streamlines technical assistance programmes and project assistance, from conceptualisation to implementation

The heart of this Programme lies in:

1. According priority to the needs of the countries.
2. Creating a single window for successful implementation.
3. Creating in-house specialized technical, legal and financial skills.
4. Merging of all aid and technical assistance programmes under one Entity.

Conclusion

In recent years India has reinvigorated its policy on Central Asia; however, much needs to be done at a faster pace. In this regard, India could consider creating a Central Asia Fund, which could take into account its experiences with the Africa Fund, even though it covers a large number of countries. This would be in keeping with thc country's stated objective of becoming a Development Partner of Central Asia. This would also result in getting the much needed visibility in those countries. An important sector would be development of infrastructure, both physical and social. Health and Education would be the ideal sector for development partnership.

Allied to this would be to give enhanced focus to human resource development. This is an area where Central Asian countries have shown keen interest, given our willingness to share knowledge and technical knowhow. This is reflected in the increased intake of ITEC slots, totalling over 450 during 2012-13. The country-wise breakup of intake of ITEC slots is indicated in brackets: Kazakhstan (55); Kyrgyzstan (95); Tajikistan (100); Turkmenistan (35) and Uzbekistan (150). There is a need to conduct a social audit of this programme, as evaluation is considered useful. Our aim should be to make it more demand driven and even consider creating training modules/courses, which are of particular relevance to Central Asian countries.

This takes us to the next step. How do they provide greater content to our economic and commercial linkages? As trade is hostage to a viable surface route, they could cross this bridge by moving in the direction of investments. In the early stages, Indian entrepreneurs had not adopted this route; it is high time they do so. At the level of Government, it could only give a push and enter into framework agreements, which exist. There is now also increasing interest in Central Asian countries, in particular Uzbekistan, followed by Kazakhstan to take the investment route. To suggest, we should focus on investments at the Third Central Asia Dialogue and, through that, enthuse Indian entrepreneurs.

While India's focus would primarily remain bilateral, New Delhi must be alive to developments taking place in the regional context. In this regard, it would be in our interest to push for full membership at the SCO and look for openings jointly in other economic regions, such as the Eurasian Countries Union.

Steps also need to be taken to bring about greater awareness about one another, as this could give a push to cooperation. There is a need to involve the media and also promote increased cultural activities and students exchanges. The presence of the Indian diaspora is increasing. Steps need to be taken to involve them increasingly, since both the diaspora in conjunction with other initiatives help build India-Central Asian connectivity. Apart from that, there is a need to focus on greater academic exchanges, in particular in identified areas for joint research, as this would not only help in bridging the information gap, but also provide each other the knowhow to achieve objectives.

Endnotes

1. Media Statement by Hon'ble Vice President, Shri Hamid Ansari at the Joint Press Event with the President of Tajikistan, Dushanbe, 15 April, 2013.
2. On board Media Interaction with Hon'ble Vice President En Route to Dushanbe, 14 April, 2013.
3. Keynote Address of EAM E. Ahamed, Bishkek, June 12, 2012.
4. *Ibid.*

5
Globalization: Central Asia and Economic Security

Aksana Panzabekova

Contradictory Process of Globalization

Due to their integration with the modern global economic system, coupled with growing economic reforms, many countries are increasingly experiencing the adverse impact of the global economic crisis and the new challenges and threats that accompany it, with one challenge being the globalization of each country's economy itself.

Currently, specialists who are studying the challenges of globalization have not agreed on a single accepted understanding of this process and scope, as well as its implications on development. There is an extremely broad range of interpretation. Some experts see globalization as the main driving force for progress, while others consider it to be a threat to vital interests, national identity and global development.

Certainly, globalization has many positive aspects, since it opens up new opportunities for development. It contributes to the spread of information, knowledge and new technology, more than ever allowing countries to take advantage of various benefits. These include, but are not limited to, an international division of labour, industrial cooperation and more efficient use of resources. On the other hand, however, globalization also sharpens the contradictions that exist in the world, giving rise to new challenges and new threats.

In recent decades, the process of globalization has become more intrinsic to international relations. Taking this into account, it would be impossible to analyze or predict the trajectory of development of a state, or to design political and economic measures that help maintain or strengthen a country's standing in the world community.

Three contradictory processes of globalization directly affect the national security of states: democratization, economization and informatization[1] (Figure 5.1).

The democratization of the modern world is irreversibly changing the hierarchy of national security objectives. At the top of this hierarchy is identity, followed by society, with the state in third place. Under this hierarchy, the state thus becomes primarily an instrument to protect the interests of the individual and the society.

Therefore, any country that claims to play a significant role in world affairs today must strictly abide by this hierarchy. As democratization increasingly becomes the norm – though being inconsistent and contradictory in practice – it means that democratic norms and human rights cannot be ignored. No modern state can afford policies that are fundamentally different from these norms.

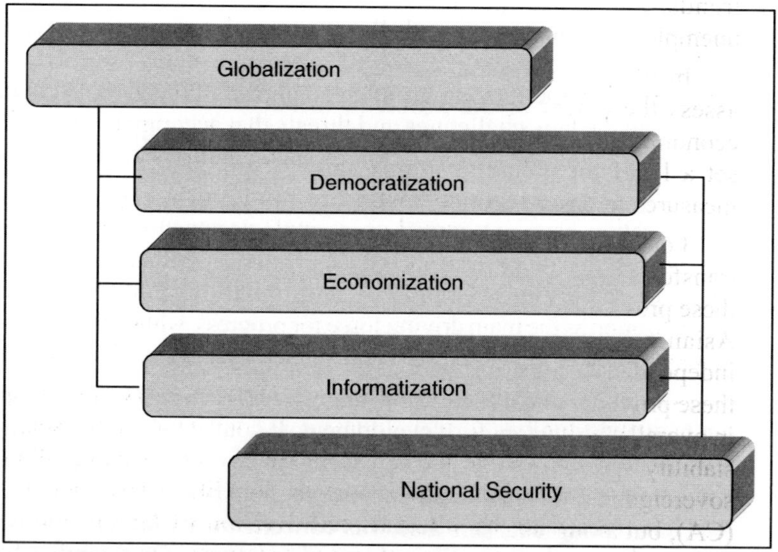

Fig. 5.1: Contradictions in Globalization and National Security

Economization is steadily leading to the formation of a single global economic space. A model of national security that takes this into account is the only way of defending national interests. Limiting integration is, in essence, refusing to develop to potential, though it can be also seen as a key element of a country's national security strategy. No society can be competitive without becoming part of the global economic space.

Computerization has led to the formation of a single global information space, leading to a global information network and an increasingly globalised society, accessible to people of all countries. It provides access to material goods and helps multiply intellectual and other human resources. It promotes sustainable development and well-being of individuals and society at-large. On the other hand, information technology is not an absolute 'good' or product: it creates new possibilities for the control and manipulation of public consciousness in internal politics, and works as an effective tool for interstate conflict or confrontation. Consequently, it is a new threat to national security. In recent years, information technology has been associated with the globalization of negative phenomena, such as the vulnerability of national economies to unfavourable international trends, and a decline in living standards as a result of rising unemployment and worsening social indicators.

In many countries, intensive research has been carried out to assess the extent of the problem, to analyze risks and threats to economic security, to identify indicators of economic security and set a level for their thresholds and to formulate and implement measures to ensure economic security.

For Central Asian countries which are undergoing socio-economic transformation while trying to also preserve their regional interests, these provisions are particularly important and relevant. The Central Asian region is currently experiencing development as newly-independent countries in global geopolitics. Through trial and error, these provisions will form their internal architecture and find a place in overall architectonics. It should be noted, however, that the current stability and security in the region is far from ideal. A "parade of sovereignties" brought independence to the countries of Central Asia (CA), but along with this also was concern for their viability.[2]

Recently, the process of establishing a new security framework amongst the independent states of Central Asia has taken on a new meaning. Potential sources of conflict can be found not only within the region, but also emanate from beyond its borders. A primary task, thus, is to identify the risks and craft urgently-needed solutions. According to Kazakh political scientists " major security threats in Central Asia are equitable use of water resources, environmental degradation, ethnic conflicts, drug trafficking, organized crime, international terrorism, religious extremism and population growth. However, today there are more acute internal problems in the region that could lead to conflict between the Central Asian states in the future ...".[3]

The states of Central Asia have different levels of socio-economic development. According to the 2013 Human Development Report by UNDP (United Nations Development Programme), which provides data about living standards, social protection, health indicators, education and cultural development, crime, environmental issues and popular participation in the decision-making processes, the only country in the region with a high level of human development is Kazakhstan, while Kyrgyzstan and Tajikistan ranked relatively low in the UN's definition of human development (Table 5.1).

Table 5.1: Ranking of Central Asia Human Development Index in 2012

Country	*Ranking*	*The level of human development*
Kazakhstan	69	High
Turkmenistan	102	Average
Uzbekistan	114	Average
Kyrgyzstan	125	Average
Tajikistan	126	Average

Source: http://hdr.undp.org.

Security issues in the Central Asian region have a complex and unique character. This is primarily due to difficulties faced by countries of Central Asia since independence, including economic decline and instability in society and political weakness. The Central Asian region is strategically important from a geopolitical point of view. Being at the crossroads of several civilizations, the region is influenced by many countries: Russia, the United States of America, China, Iran and Turkey, as well as by the European Union. The emerging system of regional security, lack of a unified approach to some regional issues and varied national interests in economic and political development – all of these could form the basis for differences between the countries of Central Asia[4].

Key Economic Threats to Central Asian States

Without claiming to be exhaustive, this chapter focuses on key economic threats to Central Asian countries, both external and internal.

External threats in the context of globalization are of particular importance. This is due to the fact that development in the modern day is fundamentally different from that of previous decades. Faced with external threats, misguided responses to these threats have serious implications for national security. On this basis, in our opinion, the following are the main external threats currently to the economies of Central Asian countries:

1. Natural resources-oriented economies (for Kazakhstan, Turkmenistan and Uzbekistan)
2. Growing technological dependence on industrialized countries
3. Rising foreign debt
4. Brain drain and
5. Capital flight

Internal threats include an inability to ensure self-preservation and self-development, difficulty in taking advantage of innovations, and inefficient state economic regulations. These are compounded by the more general inability of nations to strike a reasonable balance of interests to overcome the contradictions and social conflict that impede the development of society. In our opinion, the greatest internal threats to Central Asian countries include:

1. Growth of structural deformities in the countries' economies
2. Increasing dependence on imported food and consumer goods
3. Destruction of scientific and technical potential
4. Criminal activity in the economy and society
5. Widening economic stratification
6. Environmental degradation

Currently, there has been a pronounced rise in external threats. An acute problem are the raw materials-oriented economies. Large reserves of natural resources of global significance, primarily hydrocarbons, are concentrated in Central Asia, which has attracted the attention of developed countries to the region. Central Asian countries, thus, pursue geopolitical policies designed to maximize, as much as possible, their control and influence over the export of their hydrocarbon resources to world markets.

Kazakhstan, for example, ranks sixth amongst the most resource-rich countries in the world, and seeks to become a leader in export of natural resources. It is endowed with 99 of the 110 elements of the Mendeleyev Periodic Table, of which 70 have been explored and 60 extracted.

Currently, more than 80 per cent of strategic enterprises in Kazakhstan are under the control of foreign investors. The critical threshold of control of strategic enterprises by foreign investors which could constitute a threat to economic sovereignty is in the range of 30-50 per cent. The actual ownership of land and natural resources as compared to actual right to exploitation of recoverable reserves of natural resources in the country can be clearly seen from the distribution of assets in the hydrocarbon industry (Table 5.2). The state owns only 18 per cent of the hydrocarbons while the remainder belongs to multinational companies and investors.

Threats in Central Asia are also a result of internal factors, such as the index of development of a region. This can also include, primarily, socio-economic backwardness and the continuation of detrimental policies in economic development. The result could lead to significant socio-economic stratification and a rise in unemployment and poverty. The surplus labour force in the countryside has to move to urban areas for employment and wages, but in many cases, the migrants cannot find stable employment. This problem is especially acute for rural youth, who lack the necessary knowledge and skills to be employed gainfully in cities, and are thus often doomed to very low standards of living.

Increasing levels of poverty have forced a significant section of the population of the region to seek work in other countries. It is estimated that about two million low-skilled workers and small traders from Kyrgyzstan, Tajikistan and Uzbekistan have left to earn a living in Russia or Kazakhstan. Remittances from migrant workers and traders form an important segment in the informal economies of Central Asia.

In turn, migration, especially illegal migration, can be cause of internal threat in both destination and source countries. Source

Table 5.2: Information on Kazakhstan's Major Oil Fields of Kazakhstan (in billions)

Name of field	*Recoverable reserves*	*Owners of shares*
Tengiz	6-9 billion	Tengizchevroil (TCO) Chevron (UWB) 50%, ExxonMobil (U.S.) 25%, KazMunaiGas 20%, Bow Arco (Russia) 5%
Karachaganak	2.5 billion	Karachaganak Intertrade Organization (KIO): Agip (Italy) 32.5%%; British Thermal Power Plant (UK) 32.5%, Chevron (USA) 20%, Lukoil (Russia) 15%
Kashagan	13 billion	Agip Kazakhstan North Caspian's Operating Company (former OKIOK): Eni, Total, ExxonMobil, Shell and KazMunaiGas (by 16.5%), Conoco Phillips (9.26%), Inpex (8.33%)
Kurmangazi	6-7 billion	KazMunaiGas (50%), Rosneft, Zarubezhneft (50%). "Total" as a shareholder is under the share of KMG
Darkhan	9.5 billion	KazMunaiGas. Other potential owners are a consortium of Chinese companies, including the SPRS and Rexona
Janajol	3 billion	SPRS - AktobeMunaiGas (88%). Remainder under other investors including IG International and Werth
Zhetibay	2.1 billion	MangistauMunaiGaz
Nursultan	4.5 billion	Potential owners include Conoco Phillips, Shell and KazMunaiGas

Source: http://inosvkz.com.

countries lose tax revenue and also face demographic changes in the social, educational and ethnic areas.

The countries of Central Asia face severe environmental problems. The most visible of these is the rise of sea levels in the Caspian Sea, which threatens to flood vast areas, and the drying of the Aral Sea, which has significantly impacted environmental, social-economic and health of people in the region. Then there is the issue of is dangerous radioactive waste lying in in Kyrgyzstan. According to experts, this waste is a threat not only to the country's own population, but, due to the cross-border nature of the problem (for example, flooding), it acquires a regional dimension. Remedies for these complex environmental threats would require huge financial resources that most countries in the region, unfortunately, do not have.

The threat to economic security of Central Asian countries is, thus, obvious. Each of the factors described above, as of today, can cause or contribute to negative developments in the region. New challenges brought on by rapidly globalising economies have led to new issues that threaten national interests. All Central Asian states must develop effective and practical solutions to the problem of economic insecurity in the region. In the face of global instability and fierce competition, states must seek a stable economic environment to provide for the welfare of the peoples and future economic growth. To achieve this goal, the state must lay the foundations of competitiveness and seek out all possible benefits and advantages. Economic security in Central Asia requires strong international cooperation in areas such as banking regulations and the fight against corruption, money laundering and transnational crime. Much will depend primarily on the joint efforts of these states themselves. In particular, interaction amongst the Foreign and Economic Ministries of the region's countries, as well as amongst their security forces, will play a major role in economic stabilisation as they pursue their individual goals at the local, national, regional and international levels. Understanding these strategies is exactly what allows one to understand the level of coordination amongst the various branches of power and their commitment to the implementation of international treaties, projects and programmes. Crucial factors here include trust amongst member countries and continuity in policies and decision making.

The most important factor in ensuring the security of the states of Central Asia, as seen by the international community, is deepening the process of integration within the region.

The President of the Republic of Kazakhstan, N A Nazarbayev, in his speech at the International Meeting of Culture and Science, which brought together Kazakhstan, Kyrgyzstan, Tajikistan and Uzbekistan said: "If we do not have the political will to create a system of national interests, conflicts will arise between the national interests of our states. We cannot allow this to happen. The leaders of the countries of Central Asia already have the will to harmonize their mutual interests".[5]

Therefore, only by uniting the efforts of everyone, respecting international law, freedom and democracy, preserving human values, traditions and the identity of nations, interacting effectively on the basis of cooperation, harmony and justice, can a joint market and a new security architecture be created.

Endnotes

1. Kortunov S.V. *Kontseptualnye osnovy natsionalnoi i mezhdunarodnoi bezopasnosti* [The conceptual foundations of national and international security] (Moscow, State University - Higher School of Economics, 2007), p. 308.
2. Eshamanova E.Zh. *Realii i perspektivy integratsii stran Tsentralnoi Azii* [Realities and prospects for integration of the countries of Central Asia], (Chimkent: M.Auezov South Kazakhstan State University, 2007). http://www.postsoviet.ru/publications
3. Saidaliev W., A. Khokhlov. Problemy obespecheniya regionalnoi bezopasnosti v Tsentralnoi Azii v XXI veke [Problems of regional security in Central Asia in the XXI century]. In *Security, Diplomacy and International Law: Proceedings of the International Regional Conference* (Astana, January 18-19, 2001).
4. V. Niyatbekov. *Rol Kazakhstana v obespechenii regionalnoi bezopasnosti* [Kazakhstan's role in regional security]. http://www.easttime.ru/analitic (Accessed July 8, 2011).
5. Nazarbayev N.A. *Strategiya transformatsii obshchestva i vozrozhdeniya evraziiskoi tsivilizatsii* [The strategy of social transformation and rebirth of the Eurasian civilization] (Moscow: Economics, 2000), p. 423.

6

India and SCO: Current State of Cooperation and Development Prospects

Marufjon Abdurahmonov

Fundamental changes in the international situation after the Cold War could not but impact change in India's foreign policy. The collapse of the Soviet Union and the subsequent almost-total reorientation of Russia to the West demanded that India look for fresh approaches in its security calculations. India did not take any drastic moves in its foreign policy. In keeping with its traditional way of calmly and in depth study of foreign policy strategy and tactics, it decided to flexibly adapt to the new world order while pursuing the protection of national interests and security. For India, this task was made easier by the fact that it did not choose a path that abandoned past policies. At the same time, it was not easy under the changed circumstances to recalibrate its rightful place in the world.

In the current context of increasing globalization, high growth rates and economic development and expansion of political influence the world over, India could not remain aloof from the play of international processes in the region of the former Soviet Union, where other powers were also pursuing their own national interests. By becoming an Observer in the Shanghai Cooperation Organization (SCO) in July 2005, India once again not only confirmed its historical ties with SCO member states – based as they are on deep roots laid down since the Great Silk Road – but also emphasized its strategic interests in the region.

At the meeting of the SCO Heads of Governments in 2005, Minister of External Affairs of India, K Natwar Singh, said that India's goal is "to play an active role in the SCO… to increase inter-regional trade and economic cooperation… especially in the energy sector…

the development of transport corridors that will provide a shorter and more efficient trade route to Russia and the countries of Central Asia". In 2006, at the meeting of the Heads of Governments of SCO, the representative from India, noting that "the SCO has evolved into an important organization that ensures security, stability and economic cooperation in the region", pointed out enormous opportunity for India to "participate in energy, transport, information, communication and agriculture projects". At the meeting of Heads of SCO Member States in 2007, India maintained that the country's interests in the activities of the SCO focus on the energy sector, economic development, fight against terrorism and drug trafficking. Hence, it is evident that with the geostrategic vision of its regional role in South Asia, India certainly has geopolitical interests in the SCO region.

Most Indian scholars also point out that India's relations with Central Asia is excellent, strengthened by deep historical and cultural ties. Both regions share a common and adjacent border, integrity of climate, similar geographical features and geo-cultural affinity.

In 2008, the SCO had six member countries. Amongst Observers were India, Pakistan, Iran and Mongolia. Besides, Pakistan and Iran showed the greatest interest in becoming full members of the SCO.

In June 2009 in Yekaterinburg, along with the BRICS summit, a regular meeting of the leaders of member states of the SCO was also held. It was attended by the heads of the six countries – Russia, China, Kazakhstan, Uzbekistan, Tajikistan and Kyrgyzstan – as well as by the leaders of four Observer countries – India, Pakistan, Mongolia, Iran and Afghanistan. It was decided therein to expand trade and investment ties between SCO member states and the Observer states. Particular attention was paid to projects on transport, communications, trade, tourism, innovation, energy saving and renewable energy technologies. The SCO leaders have stated their goal is to turn Central Asia into a transcontinental bridge between Europe and Asia. This would require new transport corridors and modernization of existing railroads and highways.

During 2010-2012, the SCO adopted a series of documents aimed at strengthening the fight against terrorism and extremism. Special attention was also paid to security. A document on political and diplomatic mechanisms for responding to situations that threaten peace, security and stability in the region was adopted.

The situation in Afghanistan was also discussed in SCO meetings. The SCO expressed deep concerns over the deteriorating situation in the country, and decided to strengthen cooperation with SCO Observer and other states (and organizations) to strengthen the fight against terrorism and drug trafficking. The Russian view is that the Afghan problem cannot be resolved without normalization of the situation in some provinces of Pakistan, and without the elimination of terrorists who have taken refuge there.

In turn, India has not been a bystander to what is happening in Afghanistan after the beginning of military operations by the coalition forces, led by the United States. It did not take part in the military operations but carried out extensive work on restoration of civilian facilities in Afghanistan, to which it has contributed more than $1.2 billion in 2009. For this purpose, there were about 4,000 Indian workers in Afghanistan.

India's diplomatic ties with the SCO and its member states are developing on both bilateral and multilateral levels. Bilateral diplomacy between India and the countries of the SCO is driven by the diplomatic missions in each country. Their activities in the SCO states before India was admitted as an Observer were aimed at promoting the image of India in these countries and reinforcing India's contribution to the SCO as an Observer state. The bilateral diplomatic contacts and visits at various government levels have intensified and active cooperation between India and the SCO member countries during the last decade was manifested in the form of mutual (reciprocal) visits of Presidents, Prime Ministers, Foreign Ministers and Parliamentary delegations to each others' countries. The fillip to India's relations with countries of the SCO is important not only from the point of view of effective cooperation to combat threats of terrorism for stability and security in Asia, but also in terms of addressing key issues in international politics. Indian diplomacy is not limited to above mentioned issues; it is active in all fields, particularly economic, trade and investment. In the framework of India's economic diplomacy, multiple meetings have been held through economic and trade commissions, business councils, trade fairs and exhibitions. Different trade and industrial delegations have signed numerous contracts. This active economic diplomacy by India in recent years has allowed it to significantly increase trade turnover with the countries of the SCO, which has even greater potential for further development.

Strategic economic interests of India in the SCO region are defined by the following factors:

1. The SCO includes countries with considerable economic potential and natural resources. The SCO members encompass vast territory and huge demographic resources.
2. The SCO includes two states which play an important role in world politics and are Permanent members of the UN Security Council.
3. The SCO region, including countries of Central Asia, has become increasingly active in geopolitics, which is very important for promoting their economic interests and security.
4. India views SCO member countries as natural partners in political, trade and economic cooperation, as well as ensuring mutual security

Accordingly, the geo-economic space of the SCO appears to India as a huge new economic market, which has enormous strategic potential, including the following:

- With extensive land mass, the SCO region provides India a geo-strategic passage to Europe in the West and the Asia-Pacific region in the East. The developed system of transport communications in the SCO give India access to the neighbouring regions and the possibility of effective trade, economic and investment cooperation;
- Huge investments and markets of SCO member states, where establishing joint ventures in small and medium-sized businesses is key, offers Indian industry and the economy long term benefits The SCO can be a powerful tool for India to implement new transport and communication projects that may help it to access Central Asian countries and connect them to world markets further a field;
- Some SCO member states have substantial deposits of energy resources (oil, gas, raw materials for nuclear power plants), as well as pipeline networks;
- Development, exploration, production, processing and

transportation of huge reserves of mineral resources opens up broad prospects for Indian and SCO-based industries;

- A developed and technically sound SCO region will enable India to rapidly develop cooperation in all spheres of the economy on mutually agreed terms;
- SCO countries have been undertaking economic reforms in all areas that contribute to the increasing inflow of capital from other developed countries;
- The people of SCO member countries and India are well aware of each other's culture and produce, which also creates a huge and effective stimulus for the development of mutual cooperation.

Analyzing the overall prospects of India's participation as an observer in the SCO and its cooperation with member countries, it is necessary to take into account the strategic importance of India to the SCO region, which is:

1. India is actively involved in addressing issues of global political and economic world order
2. Over the years, India has been enhancing its role and importance in addressing regional security issues and combating terrorism
3. The growing economic and scientific-technological potential of India (especially in the field of information technology, pharmaceuticals, biotechnology, etc.) brings this country to a level of strategic importance
4. India is a prospective market for the export of products from SCO countries

Economically stable and progressive development of India during the last decade strengthened its position in world politics and trade. With an enviable international profile, India today is able to positively impact and contribute to the development of other parts of the world, including the SCO region. A country with a population of more than a billion people and tremendous economic, scientific and technological potential, India is already a great power and shows responsibility towards the fate of the people across the globe by actively participating in international and regional organizations. All this indicates that India, which has become an important entity in international relations between nations, is poised to play a very positive role in the SCO, especially in the domain of economic integration, Asian regionalization and security. It should be noted that the SCO region, over the years, will get increasingly stronger, creating a solid foundation for economic stability and security in Asia and exerting significant influence on the shape and nature of geopolitical situation in Asia, and India's role in these processes will steadily increase.

7
Energy Security in the Caspian Central Asian Region

Leila Muzaparova

Recent developments in North Africa and the Middle East once again bring out issues of international and regional security. Therefore, the issue of energy security is increasingly important for international security given that conflicts have occurred or are likely to occur in countries and regions that are either rich in strategic reserves of hydrocarbons or have important transport routes through their territory.

Thus, the possibility of military conflict in close proximity to the Caspian and Central Asian region triggered by one of the Central Asian states can also be a result of the competition for access to natural resources of the region and control over its transit facilities.

Given the above mentioned factors, and considering the global focus on the region, Indian experts shared the energy policy and security for the Caspian and Central Asian region, and the focus will hence be on this topic.

There are currently a number of interrelated issues in the region and the approaches of Central Asian states to their national security - including energy security – reflect this complexity. In their relationship with each other and with the external actors interested in the Caspian and Central Asian energy resources, the countries of the region need to take into account the following challenges and threats to regional stability:

I. Disputed Oil and Gas Fields in the Caspian Sea

In the absence of a consensus or documentation that defines the legal status of the Caspian Sea, there is still a certain probability that the countries of the Central Asian region may opt to resolve the matter of individual control over Caspian Sea resources by force. Iran has already displayed its intent to use force when its navy forced Azeri vessels to stop fieldwork on the offshore oil field in the "Araz-Alov-Sharq" in 2001, claiming them to be in Iranian territorial waters. This scenario is plausible for those littoral states that have not settled their borders with their neighbours over disputed oil fields.

The Southern part of the Caspian Sea seems to be more conflict-prone, primarily because delineation has not happened so far in the Azerbaijani-Iranian and Azerbaijani-Turkmen sectors of the Caspian Sea.

As there is no legal agreement on the status of the Caspian Sea, Iran, Azerbaijan and Turkmenistan continue to defend their positions aggressively on purported offshore boundaries and, most importantly, build up their naval forces. Although the three countries claim that negotiation and dialogue to resolve disputes are their priority, stability and security in the Southern Caspian remains fragile and vulnerable in the long-term.

II. Expanding Activities of Extremist and Terrorist Groups

Terrorism today could be the new tool in the Caspian and Central Asian geopolitics to settle scores. The pipelines crossing the territories in the region as well as offshore oil and gas platforms in the Caspian Sea may be potential targets for terrorist attacks.

The explosion on the "Baku-Tbilisi-Ceyhan" oil pipeline in August 2008 is an example of vulnerability of the energy infrastructure. According to Turkish media, the responsibility was taken by a Kurdish terrorist organization. As a result, the supply of hydrocarbons to European consumers was suspended for a few days.

A slightest disruption in supply of Caspian oil and gas to the world markets, especially given the shift in export routes from Iran due to the on-going sanctions, would cause an immediate ripple in the local and international oil and gas markets and can also have other negative effects, such as political destabilization in the Caspian states or a sharp decline in investments in the region, leading to considerable loss for companies supplying hydrocarbon resources.

These threats need to be prevented by enhancingmeasures to strengthen defense of these assets by individual countries. Conducting joint military exercises in the Caspian Sea to enhance defenses against possible attacks – is the need of the hour and, therefore, worth serious consideration.

III. Involvement of Extra-regional Powers in the Formation of Regional Security Systems

Western powers, the USA in particular, are trying to 'park' their military presence and political visibility in the region to defend their investments in the oil and gas industry of the Caspian states, and also secure the various pipelines. In order to eliminate any potential threat of sabotage and terrorist attack on the Caspian energy infrastructure, the United States has focused on providing military-technical and material assistance to Azerbaijan and Kazakhstan.

IV. Accelerating Militarization

Until 2002, the countries of the region had not taken any steps to augment their military capabilities in the Caspian Sea, but the situation changed dramatically after the first Caspian Summit in Ashgabat ended in failure. Since then, the coastal countries have seen their navies as an additional element of security to defend their national interests in the Caspian region. Quite alarmingly, the Caspian states are building up their naval power. Military alliances are regarded as a deterrent against possible threats and risk, particularly those posed against the oil and gas fields. The militarization of the Caspian Sea continues despite official statements about the formation of a regional security system. While agreeing on cooperation amongst the various national border and law enforcement agencies, the coastal states are yet to address the question of qualitative and quantitative composition of their navies deployed in the Caspian Sea.

V. Disagreement Over Building Transport Infrastructure and its Use

The location of the Caspian Sea determines its significance in the global transportation system. However, projects aimed at increasing traffic volumes, especially that of hydrocarbons, face complexities of a geopolitical nature. Since the legal status of the Caspian Sea has not been settled, the prospects of trans-Caspian oil and gas projects is pretty vague. However, Ashgabat does not consider the fact that the legal status of the Caspian Sea is an obstacle to developing the trans-Caspian route. At the third Caspian Summit in Baku in November 2010, Turkmen President, Berdymukhamedov, claimed that underwater pipelines in the Caspian Sea could be built only with the consent of those parties whose territories are criss-crossed by such a pipeline. The consent of the others was not needed, he said.

The revitalization of the Trans-Caspian project to transport Turkmen gas crucial for the "Nabucco" pipeline and is consistent with the interests of the EU to ensure its energy security. The European Council authorized the European Commission to negotiate with Azerbaijan and Turkmenistan on the legal basis of the Trans-Caspian gas pipeline. It should be noted that the 2020 EU Energy Strategy sees the Trans-Caspian gas pipeline as a key element for its realization.

At the same time, the fact that the negative stance of Russia and Iran on the Trans-Caspian gas pipeline project was ignored brings additional complexity into relations amongst the coastal states. The transportation of gas from the Eastern to the Western coast of the Caspian Sea via an underwater pipeline is directly related to the unresolved issue of delimitation of the Caspian Sea. The contradictions can be resolved only by ensuring an internationally recognised legal status to Caspian Sea resources and which clearly defines the boundaries of each nation therein, thereby regulating all mining. In the meantime, as long as there is no legal binding treaty or agreement, the situation remains deadlocked.

VI. Unresolved Environmental Issues

The adverse impact of intensive industrial development, especially in mining, has significantly aggravated the environment in and around the Caspian Sea, thus jeopardizing its environment and biodiversity. Considerable measures are needed to restore this balance and the Caspian states have introduced a number of environmental regulations designed to minimize adverse impact of industrialisation on the ecosystem of the Caspian region. However, in practice, their implementation is subordinate to the political and economic interests of the geopolitical players in the Caspian region.

The Caspian Sea is also prone to man-made disasters, especially when the largest offshore project of "Kashagan" is launched. Therefore, closer coordination amongst all Caspian states is needed to maintain ecological security of the Caspian Sea region.

In other words, the Caspian region faces a number of region-wide challenges, while their solution requires convergence of interests of all Caspian countries, like:

1. Unresolved legal status of Caspian Sea hampers the prospects for an agreement on distribution of Caspian shelf offshore oil production;
2. Unique bio-resources of the Caspian Sea need to be preserved;
3. There is a need for raw materials-oriented economies of all countries in the region to modernize their national fuel and energy complexes and, more importantly, develop a new economic model of growth and development;
4. There are environmental and technological risks associated with the rise in production of hydrocarbons, especially given that it will only increase once exploitation of offshore fields starts;
5. The transportation of hydrocarbons is related to existing options in connectivity of oil and gas supply routes to the world markets; in other words, there exists a problem of diversification of export routes;
6. There are various external actors shaping the economic debate in the region;
7. There is no shared Caspian region development strategy that defines an integrated socio-economic system, and, consequently, stipulates priorities of regional economic cooperation for the Caspian states;
8. Each country of the region attaches great importance to Caspian energy resources; For Kazakhstan, Azerbaijan and Turkmenistan, the Caspian Sea is the only sea route they have access to, though it is not linked with any other water bodies in the region. In fact, unlike Iran and Russia, these countries have no any other alternative but to develop the marine and energy resources of the Caspian Sea.

All of these problems require solutions via regional energy cooperation that should be based on the following four principles:

1. The Caspian region should be regarded as a single and unique

socio-economic system, and its destruction would be equivalent to an ecological and economic catastrophe on a global scale;
2. The socio-economic interests of the states in the region should prevail over the interests of external actors;
3. Priority should be given to foreign economic cooperation that would facilitate regional interface;
4. A convention on the legal status of the Caspian Sea should be key to maintaining stability in the region.

There are a number of internal and external factors that are influencing economic cooperation amongst the Caspian countries and the economic development of the region as a whole. The external factors are currently predominant; these include global appetite for energy and the geopolitical interests of non-regional global market players in Caspian resources. External factors have both positive and negative impact on the Caspian socio-economic system. On the one hand, they stimulate growth of the economies of the Caspian countries – in particular, their energy and commodities sectors – and, on the other, they can even threaten economic stability in the region and destroy its unique biodiversity.

The internal factors include the following:

1. Limited resource base of the Caspian shelf;
2. Fragility of bio-resources of the Caspian Sea; and
3. Complicated nature of intra-regional relations.

All these factors (both external and internal) contribute to the following trends in regional cooperation:

1. Increased influence of extra-regional factors and players in the economies of both the region as a whole as well as individual Caspian states
2. Intensified competition amongst various pipeline projects
3. Transit and transportation of energy resources used as a major incentive for cooperation amongst Caspian states

These trends aggravate regional tensions, hamper stability of the regional economic system and slow down economic convergence of the Caspian countries.

The lack of a joint strategy for regional economic cooperation, which should be developed by all concerned states, also prevents the convergence of economic interests of the countries of the Caspian region. Such a strategy should be aimed at achieving a common goal, that is, to maintain stability of the unique socio-economic system of the region. It can also serve to maintain an appropriate balance of global, regional and national interests, to identify priorities for economic development within the region, and offer solutions to resolve issues that can possibly escalate inter-regional tensions .

Prospects of economic cooperation in the region are likely to improve if the following conditions are met:

1. Optimization of regional ties in the energy market, so that it could contribute to common regional security and economic sustainability of the region
2. Modernization of the fuel and energy sectors of the countries of the region
3. Establishment of an International Union of Caspian states
4. Diversification of trade and economic relations amongst the countries of the region through transition from bilateral (trilateral) to multilateral format of regional cooperation in all sectors of economy. The current bilateral agreements on a number of "non-energy" issues are consistent with such a multilateral format, like cooperation in the banking sector, food (grain) market, fishing industry, transport and port infrastructure maintenance, etc.

The two primary goals of energy cooperation in the region are:

1. Modernization of the energy exploration, manufacturing and transport system of the Caspian region; and
2. Diversification of export routes for supply to world markets.

Thus, there is an obvious need to intensify regional integration and formulate key areas of cooperation in the energy sector; this is how the global economic stature of the region can be enhanced.

PART II

India-Central Asia: Enhancing Cooperation

8

Indian and Central Asian Perspectives on Regional Security

Nirmala Joshi

The security scenario in the Central Asian region is in a state of flux. For India, the Central Asian region holds immense geopolitical and strategic significance. In Indian strategic thinking, all the five states of Central Asia are part of its extended neighbourhood. At stake are India's security and economic interests. The Central Asian countries are comparatively young states and in various stages of their systemic transformation. For the Central Asian Republics (CARs) therefore, stability and security of the region is crucial. Similarly, for India also, the stability of the region is important. It would not like the region to be destabilized by forces of religious extremism and terrorism. This shared perception has become a crucial input into building ties with CARs. India and CARs perceive that non-traditional threats such as religious extremism, international terrorism, drug trafficking, smuggling in small weapons and organized crime are the principal challenges to the security of the region. They believe that these challenges emanate from the various militant groups and organizations located in the Afghan-Pakistan borderlands. These negative impulses are strong and have the capacity to destabilize the region. The negative impulse of religious extremism and terrorism receive support from certain quarters across the border. In turn, it has provided impetus to drug trafficking, which is a source of sustenance for the extremists. Nevertheless, it is a matter of deep concern to the CARs for the social disharmony it causes within the countries. Hence, both India and CARs share a wide area of security and strategic interests. Their aim is to see that the common neighbourhood remains peaceful and stable.

Since the last two decades, Afghanistan has emerged as the fulcrum of regional security mainly because the extremists and terrorists are well entrenched in the borderlands and operate from this safe haven. Despite the continuing 'war on terror', these forces have not been completely destroyed. A great deal will depend on how the situation in Afghanistan evolves. Between now and the end of 2014, two crucial developments are the Presidential election in Afghanistan, and the withdrawal of US-led coalition forces from the country. Linked with these crucial developments is the status of the reconciliation process on which President Hamid Karzai has staked a lot. However, this process was a non-starter and has led to nowhere. Although the war on terror has dented and weakened the Taliban, they remain a resilient force. Probably that is the reason why they are not keen on the reconciliation process. The question is -would the Taliban and likeminded groups join the future political set up and accept the sanctity of the Afghan Constitution? An equally important issue is the capability of the Afghan National Security Forces (ANSF) and the Afghan National Police (ANP) to safeguard its sovereignty and territorial integrity, and protect its citizens and enforce the rule of law. These are, no doubt, difficult imponderables, nevertheless regional security will be shaped by these developments.

At this juncture, it is difficult, however, to predict how the future scenario will evolve. The situation could get more complex with large scale violence breaking out, or some semblance of peace and stability could emerge. The predictions are that the security scenario would be a mixed one of certainties and uncertainties. Due to the compatibility of their geopolitical and strategic interests and shared perceptions on regional security, India and the CARs will have to work closely to ensure that non-traditional threats are contained. They will have to energise existing mechanisms and work on new ones, if necessary, so that they are able to meet the challenges in a coordinated and sustained manner

Issues in Regional Security

The main concern is, as mentioned, the challenge of non-traditional threats. From their safe sanctuaries in the borderlands, extremists and terrorists have been carrying out strikes in neighbouring countries with the goal of promoting *jihad*. India has faced cross border terrorism in the state of Jammu and Kashmir, where it has been battling insurgency and separatism for more than two decades. The Fergana Valley of Central Asia has also witnessed an upsurge in extremism and aggressive nationalism. Several groups and organizations such as Islamic Movement of Uzbekistan (IMU), Hizb-ut Tahrir (HuT), Islamic Renaissance Party of Tajikistan (IRPT), and others continue to exist, although underground. They challenge the ruling regimes by violent means, like for instance, in the 1999 attempt on the life of President Islam Karimov, the blasts in Osh Valley, kidnapping of Japanese tourists, etc. which are proof of their intent. A few years ago, some terrorists moved to the Rasht Valley along with their supporters. The possibility of terrorist infrastructure relocating to the Tajik province of Gorno Badakhshan is real. It could destabilize Tajikistan and thereby increase vulnerabilities in the Fergana Valley – and subsequently the whole of Central Asia.

In reality, it is an ideological struggle. It is between a religious order versus democratic and secular values. The outcome of this struggle will impact on regional security. India and CARs are committed to building a democratic, secular and modern polity. These cardinal principles are enshrined in their respective Constitutions. Religious extremism aims to strike at these core values of democracy and secularism. What is even more pernicious is the mindset against which India and CARs will have to fight. In addition, CARs will have to address the grievances of the people, particularly the youth, whose main driving force often has been economic gain.

A crucial dimension of religious extremism is the impetus it has provided to drug trafficking. Under Taliban rule, Afghanistan emerged as the highest producer of heroin. Ninety per cent of world's heroin is grown in Afghanistan. It is well known that drug profits sustain extremism and terrorism. Reportedly 30 per cent of the contraband cargo passes through Central Asia. While some unemployed youth in Central Asia may have been lured into this nefarious activity, its impact on society is substantial in terms of addiction, corruption and escalation of social violence. For instance, President Nursultan Nazarbayev, in his book "The Critical Decade" mentions that in Kazakhstan, there are 45,505 people – including 1927 adolescents and 4420 women – who have been registered for drug abuse. In its dual approach to the reconstruction and stabilization of Afghanistan by coalition forces on the one hand and military operations on the other, the process however did not include eradication of poppy cultivation. Today, Afghanistan has emerged as the highest producer of heroin. Central Asia is one of the routes through which heroin is transported. However, it has caused a lot of tension within each country in terms of addiction, violence and corruption. Reportedly, drug cartels have come up along borders that ensure that this contraband is transported safely. However, non-governmental organizations working in Afghanistan are focusing on agriculture and teaching the locals the benefits of growing wheat rather than poppy. A related issue is the region is flush with small arms, which has kept up the level of violence and increased insecurity in the region.

Another factor is Pakistan's ability to rein in the dangerous groups that are residing in its Federally Administered Tribal Areas (FATA), such as the Haqqani network, Jamaat-ud Dawa, Lashkar-e-Toiba, Hazb-i-Islami, etc. – appears limited. Either Pakistan is unable to do so – or is unwilling to do so – as it considers such elements as "strategic assets". There is no doubt that developments in Pakistan – especially the activities of the Pakistani Taliban – will have a strong bearing on regional security. Indeed, cooperation between Afghanistan and Pakistan is essential, but for that Pakistan will have to give up its long-cherished goal of "strategic depth"; in other words, a weak Afghan state and a pliable leadership under its influence. The notion of strategic depth, initiated by the then President of Pakistan, Zia-ul-Haq, aimed at creating a vast strategic integrated region that included Afghanistan and Central Asia, based on religious order. India and CARs, by adhering to democratic and secular principles, have countered this notion. As mentioned, it is an ideological competition for influence.

Linked with the growth of religious extremism in Pakistan is the danger of nuclear weapons, technology and resources falling in the hands of such forces. The notion of a 'dirty bomb' is a horrendous prospect. In this regard, CARs feel a greater sense of vulnerability. They have propounded the idea which needs wider acceptability by the international community.

The ethnic factor resulting in aggressive nationalism is present in the Central Asian region. Ethnic discord between Uzbeks and Tajiks and Uzbek and Kyrgyz is an important issue in the region. However, the most potent ethnic issue is the one between Afghanistan and Pakistan; the Pashtun issue that has bedevilled Afghan-Pakistan relations since 1947. The Pashtuns reside on both sides of the Durand

Line and have been working for unification. How this factor will shape up post-2014 remains an uncertainty, but its outcome will have implications for the region. The ethnic factor between Afghanistan on the one hand and Tajikistan, Uzbekistan and Turkmenistan on the other, is not a divisive issue.

A geopolitical change will occur in the region post 2014, even if a contingent of US troops remains. While active combat activity will cease, the focus will now shift to training, guidance and capacity building by the International Security Assistance Force (ISAF). In the economic sphere, the emphasis will be on economic development and reconstruction. But a larger shift in focus has already occurred. It is a shift from fighting extremism and terrorism to controlling the natural resources of Afghanistan. It has already sparked off a fierce competition amongst major powers for this purpose. Afghanistan is rich in energy resources and vital minerals. It is estimated that this wealth is valued at USD 1 trillion. What has further added to the geopolitical significance of Afghanistan is its geographical proximity to Central Asia, which is equally endowed with abundant natural resources including energy, hydel power, uranium, etc. As a consequence, the region has assumed tremendous geopolitical significance. In fact, Afghanistan and Central Asia are part of the same geopolitical space, and both are landlocked. All external and regional powers are involved in the region. This competition post 2014 would increase. Whether the alignment of interests remains benign or conflictual only time will tell.

What will have a beneficial impact on regional security is for India to connect with CARs through Afghanistan. It will provide this landlocked region an opening in the South. The ancient trade route went via Afghanistan and was the hub of trade and transit routes; routes from China, the Indian Subcontinent, Persia, Central Asia and the Caspian Sea region criss-crossed its territory, bringing prosperity to it. In view of sea commerce getting risky and congested, a revival of the overland route would not only be beneficial, but also necessary as well. The huge transit revenues that will accrue to the countries needs to be considered dispassionately. The Istanbul Conference on Afghanistan – "Security and Cooperation in the Heart of Asia" held in November 2011 – highlighted the importance of Afghanistan as a land bridge to Eurasia. Meanwhile, plans for the Pan-Asian Highway and the Trans-Asian railway need to be operationalised at the earliest, and this will only enhance economic prosperity of the region. If the countries of the region accord higher priority to economic considerations, it will facilitate regional cooperation amongst these countries and have a positive impact on security. It will dispel the notion of Afghanistan as a "buffer state", and instead promote the concept of the latter as the pivot of trade and transport route.

Besides, India has developed immense economic interest in CARs. Apart from procuring Central Asian energy resources, India is interested in Central Asia's economic growth. In the long run, it is development that will ensure stability of CARs. Moreover, Indian involvement in Afghanistan has gone up tremendously. If Indian efforts in Afghanistan are to succeed, stability and development of Central Asia is equally important. This whole geopolitical space should remain stable and secure, if Indian interests are to be ensured. At the political level, the commitment to build open and democratic polity and a free market economy in CARs needs to be supported and strengthened. Perceived as a friendly country with no hidden agenda, India is well placed to deepen its ties with CARs.

Indian and Central Asian Perspectives

For India, the breakup of the Soviet Union in 1991 and the rise of religious extremism and terrorism in Afghanistan had a drastic impact on its perception of regional security. Another historic development that occurred simultaneously was the emergence of CARs as independent sovereign states. The CARs had embarked on the road to a systemic transformation. They had no experience or expertise to build a new system. What was required was a peaceful external environment.

When Operation Enduring Freedom (OEF) was launched in October 2001, India and the CARs backed the Western initiative. OEF aimed at defeating the Taliban by military action and, within no time, they were routed. India was able to restore its traditional ties of friendship with Afghanistan, which had been under severe strain during the Taliban rule. Since then, India has been deeply and extensively involved in reconstruction activity in Afghanistan. It is the fourth largest aid giver of USD 2 billion, and probably the biggest investor in its mining sector and other areas. Besides, Indian efforts are aimed at capacity building in security, military and economic spheres. Like many other countries, India also believes that economic growth and development are the best way to not only prosperity, but also to keep the youth and the unemployed away from negative activity. It must be mentioned that poverty is not the only reason that drives some people towards religious extremism. It is deep ideological commitment nurtured in the *Madrassas* that creates a mindset which is difficult to counter. However, by and large, people take up such activities for monetary gains.

The CARs have shared India's concern at the growing forces of extremism and terrorism in the common neighbourhood. The beginning of the Tajik civil war, the wholehearted support the Tajik Opposition received from their brethrens in Afghanistan and the talk of "greater Afghanistan" were perceived as grave threats to their newly-emergent independence. They turned to Russia for security and the peacekeepers began to guard the Tajik-Afghan border. This way, they were able to keep hordes of extremists at bay. Meanwhile, India and some CARs supported the Northern Alliance that was fighting the Taliban. Apart from the threat posed by religious extremism, terrorism and its offshoot – the danger of drug trafficking – is the main concern of CARs in the prevailing ethnic discord within the region, which could be exploited by extremists to further their religious agenda.

When the war on terror was launched by the US and the North Atlantic Treaty Organisation (NATO), the CARs supported and extended cooperation to the coalition forces. Kyrgyzstan, Tajikistan and Uzbekistan offered military base facilities to the Western forces, while Kazakhstan and Turkmenistan offered rights to overfly their territory. Since then, the CARs have been cooperating with the coalition forces.

The CARs cooperation with coalition forces scaled new heights in 2008, when Pakistan blocked the transportation of vital materials through the Khyber Pass. The CARs offered passage through their territory. Today, the Northern Distribution Network (NDN) is a vital link for the coalition forces in terms of transporting personnel, equipment and non-military cargo. It passes through Russia, Kazakhstan, Uzbekistan, Kyrgyzstan and Tajikistan. In the NDN, Uzbekistan plays a crucial role and a new 75-km long railway line connects Uzbekistan with Afghanistan, thus enabling faster and voluminous transport of goods. As a consequence, the Taliban have mounted insurgency operations in the North, aimed at this crucial railway link. Similarly, the International city of Navoi in Uzbekistan is a crucial link for air lifting supplies to Afghanistan. The Manas Transit Centre in Kyrgyzstan has played a vital role. The Manas Centre facilitated the flow of US troops and supplies from Afghanistan. Kazakhstan not only supports the NDN, but plays an important role in the field of education as well. India has set up Joint Working Groups (JWG) on terrorism with Kazakhstan, Uzbekistan and Tajikistan. India has raised the level of its relationship with Kazakhstan, Uzbekistan and Tajikistan by signing the Strategic Partnership Agreements. A security dialogue and the 'Connect Central Asia Policy' are attempts by the Indian Government to energise its engagement with CARs.

At the broader level, India and CARs have cooperated in all the initiatives for the stabilization of the region. They have extended support to the key pillars of stabilization initiated at the London Conference in January 2010. These key pillars were "reintegration" and "reconciliation". While the concept of reintegration aimed at bringing back the disillusioned into the mainstream and was supported by all, the idea of reconciliation, however, implied that there were good or moderate Taliban who could be encouraged to become part of a coalition Government and isolate the hard-core elements, was viewed with a high degree of scepticism. The Kabul Conference of July 2010 carried this process further. Both India and the CARs do not subscribe to the view of moderate and hard core Taliban.

The Istanbul Conference in October 2011, the Bonn Conference in 2011 and the Tokyo Conference in July 2012 are grappling with the issue of stabilization, economic development and capacity building measures. While these are steps in the right direction, cooperation amongst all stakeholders in peace and stability in the region is absolutely essential. So far, regional cooperation has proved to be a distant goal. Nevertheless, India and the CARs share similar perspectives on issues of regional security. It is imperative that they work closely for expanding the contours of peace and stability.

9

India's Economic Interests in Central Asia and Kazakhstan

Kuldip Singh

Writings that visualize the centrality of Central Asia in terms of its richness in hydrocarbons are in abundance. This was particularly so in the initial years of post-Soviet Central Asia. However, of late, studies have appeared arguing that the real significance of the area does not lie in its richness in hydrocarbons, but rather in its geo-strategic location, which has led to renewed interest in the geo-politics of the region. Nevertheless, there are scholars like Andre Gunder Frank who go beyond the familiar narrative to stress the perceived centrality of Central Asia. Frank has written recently that Central Asia and its history is the most important part – and the most neglected – in the world. Amongst reasons for such neglect are victors mostly write history for their own purpose and for legitimizing their victory, while Central Asia, for a very long period, has been home to many victors. As the area lost out to others, it could not find place it deserved in world history. Secondly, scholars writing history have been infected by the virus of Euro-centrism, which blinded people to Central Asia, especially to anything important or good about it. Moreover, political circumstances in the Soviet and Chinese Central Asia virtually closed much of the area to foreign researchers for nearly two generations. Therefore, he concluded that Central Asia was waiting to be discovered by the outside world. As a prelude to the discovery of Central Asia and bestowing on it its due status, Frank argued that it was time to abandon the historical and the (still) popular image of Central Asia as home to nomads and barbarians because empirical evidence suggests that Central Asia was also home to many highly civilized and urbanized people. Coming to the present epoch, he writes that Central Asia, which remained at the economic cross-roads of the region until at least 1800, was the region where the 'Great Game' was earlier played for its domination by others in the nineteenth century, and which be again – in the twenty first century – be the region for yet another 'Great Game' of geo-political domination, and where the rewards will be huge reserves of petroleum for Russia, China, US, India, Pakistan and Western Europe (Frank, 2007).

Geo-strategic and Economic Dimensions

The estimates of hydrocarbon resources of Central Asia, which are mostly concentrated in the Caspian Sea region, vary. The US Deputy Secretary of State, Strobe Talbott, gave a figure of up to 200 billion barrels of oil, while others put it as low as 30 to 40 billion barrels. Geoffrey Kemp puts the oil and gas reserves of the Caspian Sea as high as 200 billion barrel of oil and 279 trillion cubic feet of gas, which puts the region in third place after the Middle East and Russia. If the latter is true, Central Asia assumes key place in supply of energy resources not only for the region but also at global level, because oil consumption in world is likely to increase from 78 million barrels per day in 2002 to 103 million barrels per day in 2015 and 119 million barrels per day in 2025. These projections suggest that an increment of 42 million barrels per day is needed by 2025 for meeting enhanced demand. At such a juncture, the Central Asian region, Azerbaijan included, is likely to contribute about six per cent of the global output by 2025. The discovery of large gas deposits in the Shah Deniz offshore field and Absheron oil field in Azerbaijan and the Kashagan oil field on the coast of Kazakhstan have further raised the hope of increased deposits of oil and gas in the region (Singh & Laxmi, 2006).

However, a lack of consensus on oil deposits estimates has led scholars to argue that the US State Department invoked rich potential of energy resources of the Caspian region only to justify its geopolitical strategy. Such an argument was warranted by estimates of Energy Information Administration (IEA), Paris, putting oil deposits in the range of 17 to 35 billion barrels and around 6.5 trillion cubic meters of natural gas, with Turkmenistan holding the largest deposits outside Russia. Those who argue on these lines subscribe to the view that hydrocarbon resources are just a sugar coating for the entry of the US in the region (Chenoy, 2005).

In such a context, it has been argued that the 19th century 'Great Game' was enacted because of the strategic significance of Central Asia owing to its geopolitical location as the gateway to the Indian sub-continent and the Persian Gulf. While analyzing the geo-strategic significance of Central Asia, it has been argued that US interests in the Caspian region are not motivated just by the need to protect the country from oil blackmail or develop the area as an alternative source of energy, rather these are driven by the 'Cold War syndrome', wherein Washington continues to pursue rather vigorously the objective of marginalizing Russia for further consolidating its victory in the Cold War, a victory that was achieved with the ultimate collapse of the Soviet Union (DK). The argument has been extended to conclude that oil for indigenous use may not be the consideration; rather, behind its interest in controlling Caspian oil may be the US desire to deny oil supplies to China and India, for isolating and marginalizing the influence of Iran and Russia and using Turkey as a proxy to expand its political, economic and military interests in Central Asia and Caucasus. In its efforts at controlling oil transit routes towards Turkey lies its desire to weaken Russia economically by ending its monopoly over the transport of oil to the West through its territory (Kaushik, 2005).

In such a scenario, the former Soviet Republics in Central Asia and Trans-Caucasus are to be seen as potential footholds for the US, along with its traditional area of influence in Turkey and Israel. Colour revolutions in Ukraine and Georgia were viewed as a web of geo-political moves for creating a much wider region of US influence to be used for containing rivals. Such a design has been sought to be implemented through the West-sponsored NATO's Partnership for Peace Programme and US desire to work closely with Ukraine and Georgia as part of naval exercises in the Black Sea. The network of political maneuvering being created, the pipeline politics resorted to and the policy initiatives taken by the US for cultivating the countries of this region are all seen as the manifestations of the new 'Great Game', in tune with the realities of the 21st century (Mahapatra, 2005).

The geo-strategic paradigm does not take away the economic significance of the Central Asian region. Moreover, to think of this region primarily in terms of oil and gas resources, ignoring key natural resources available in the region, amounts to be blind to its real economic worth. For instance, Kazakhstan is endowed with abundance of ferrous and non-ferrous metals. The country is an important producer of steel, and is blessed with abundant iron ore, chrome, manganese, and alloy minerals deposits. It has approximately 19 per cent of the world's lead, 13 per cent zinc, 10 per cent copper, 25 per cent manganese and 30 per cent chrome. During the Soviet era, Kazakhstan produced uranium from a number of deposits, and had substantial resources of this metal. Likewise, Turkmenistan – best known for its gas reserves – has deposits of Sulphur, Iodine, Celestine, Potassium Salt, Magnesium Salt, Sodium Chloride, Bentonite Clays, Limestone, Gypsum, Brown Coal, Basalt and Dolomite. Similarly, Uzbekistan – widely known for its cotton products – is amongst the largest producers of Gold, Copper, Uranium, Silver, Zinc and Tungsten. It ranks tenth in the world for its Copper reserves, seventh or eighth in Uranium reserves and fourth in its extraction (Sachdeva, 2007). Thus, to underscore the geo-strategic importance of the Central Asian region and emerging geopolitics while ignoring vital economic facts of the region is not correct. The centrality of Central Asia, as invoked by Andre Gunder Frank, is not merely rhetoric; rather, it can be sustained in view of contemporary reality. The diverse richness of the area and its geo-strategic significance culminating in neo-geopolitics should be seen as reinforcing each other for determining the centrality of Central Asia in the present global scenario.

India-Kazakhstan Relations

Relations between India and Kazakhstan are rooted in history. During the Soviet era, India's first Prime Minister, Jawaharlal Nehru – along with Indira Gandhi – visited Almaty in 1955. In the post Soviet era, after the emergence of Kazakhstan as a sovereign country on the world map, diplomatic relations were established in February 1992. India was the first country outside the Commonwealth of Independent States (CIS) region to be visited by President Nazarbayev after the independence of Kazakhstan. This visit in 1992 was followed by the visit of Prime Minister of India, Narasimha Rao, in 1993, which gave impetus to India-Kazakhstan relations. President Nazarbayev also visited India in December 1996, February 2002 and January 2009. A fresh impetus to bilateral trade and commercial relations was given as a result of the visit of President Nazarbayev to India in January 2009. During the visit, a Joint Declaration on Strategic Partnership was adopted, which foresaw comprehensive cooperation in all spheres.

An agreement between ONGC Videsh Ltd. and KazMunaiGaz on Satpayev oil block and a Memorandum of Understanding between NPCIL and Kazatomprom, envisaging cooperation – including supply of uranium to India, among others – was signed during the visit. A memorandum of Understanding for cooperation in the field of space; an extradition treaty between both countries and protocol on the accession of Kazakhstan to WTO was also signed during the visit (Ministry of External Affairs, 2009). Prime Minister Manmohan Singh visited Astana on 15-16 April 2011. During the visit, several Agreements were signed. Important amongst them included: (a) Agreement between ONGC Videsh Limited and Kazmunaigas on Satpayev Exploration Block, (b) Agreement for Cooperation in the Peaceful Uses of Atomic Energy, and (c) Joint Action Plan for furthering Strategic Partnership between India and Kazakhstan (Ministry of External Affairs, 2011).

On 16th April 2011, an Agreement was signed between ONGC Videsh Limited and Kazmunaigaz on the purchase of 25 per cent stake in the Satpayev Oil Block in the Caspian Sea. Another agreement envisages a legal framework for mutual cooperation between the two sides on peaceful uses of nuclear energy, including fuel supply, nuclear medicine, use of radiation technologies for healthcare including isotopes, reactor safety mechanisms, exchange of scientific & research information, exploration and joint mining of uranium, design, construction and operation of nuclear power plants. The roadmap outlines the joint action plan for implementation of projects to be undertaken by both sides during the period 2011-2014 and for the implementation of Inter-Governmental Agreements (Ministry of External Affairs, 2011).

Economic Relations: Trade and Investment

Kazakhstan is the largest economy in Central Asia and the second largest, after the Russian Federation, in the CIS. During 2000-2007, it registered an impressive annual average growth rate of about 11.6 per cent. In the aftermath of the global financial crisis, this growth rate fell to 3.3 per cent in 2008 and further to 1.2 per cent in 2009. However, the Kazakh economy has shown strong recovery since 2011 (CUTS, 2012). Over the years, the Kazakh economy has structurally shifted from agro-based to manufacturing and services, accounting for 42.8 per cent and 51.8 per cent of its GDP, respectively. The country is endowed with enormous fossil fuel reserves and abundant supplies of other minerals and metals such as Uranium, Copper, Iron and Zinc. More than 1,200 types of minerals are reportedly available in the region (CUTS, 2012). The country is an important producer of steel and is gifted with Iron ore, Chrome and Manganese as well as alloy minerals deposits. The Canadian company, Cameco, is developing sites for producing Uranium for use as fuel for nuclear power plants. A French company has shown interest in investing US$100 million for the development of the Moinkum Uranium deposits in Southern Kazakhstan. Gold has received a lot of attention from foreign investors in recent years, as the country contains several thousand known gold occurrences and possesses enormous exploration potential. Much of Kazakhstan's gold, at present, is produced as bi-produce metal at the Copper and Lead/Zinc smelters. However, a number of primary gold mines are in the process of being developed for production. In addition, Kazakhstan-based ABS Group of Companies is developing a series of deposits and has facilities for ore flotation and conventional and heal leaching of gold ores. Kazakhstan refines around 16.2 tonnes of gold and 900 tonnes of Silver. It has the world's biggest reserves of Tungsten and Barite, the second largest reserves of Phosphate and Chromium ores and Uranium (accounting for 25 per cent - 30 per cent of world reserves). Amongst CIS states, its reserves of Chromic ores and Lead are 97 per cent and 38 per cent, respectively, of all CIS reserves; it is second in oil, Silver, Copper, Manganese, Zinc, Nickel and raw Phosphor; and third in gas, coal, and Tin, fifth in Molybdenum and sixth largest in gold reserves (Singh & Laxmi, 2006).

In spite of the abundance of resources, the single most important challenge before Kazakhstan is to overcome its predominant reliance on natural resources so as to diversify into sectors such as telecommunications, financial services, transport, construction, pharmaceuticals and food processing. With the possibility of developing many key industrial sectors and modernisation of the services sectors, Kazakhstan offers enormous opportunities for trade and investment.

India is not a significant player in terms of trade in Central Asia. India's total trade with Central Asian countries is less than one per cent (0.91 per cent) of its total volume of trade (Figure 9.1). In 2012, India's bilateral trade with Central Asia was US$ 728.7 million (Kazakhstan US$ 426.9 million, Uzbekistan US$ 143.7 million,

Turkmenistan US$ 78.7 million, Tajikistan US$ 44.9 million and Kyrgyzstan US$ 34.2 million). As these indicators show, Kazakhstan is India's largest trade partner in Central Asia. India-Kazakhstan bilateral trade has grown from US$ 113.14 million in 2005, US$ 280.59 million in 2009. During this period, India's imports from Kazakhstan have grown much faster than exports (Figure 9.2). In 2012, India-Kazakhstan trade reached US$ 426.9 million, and has been constantly rising since 2005 (UN Comtrade).

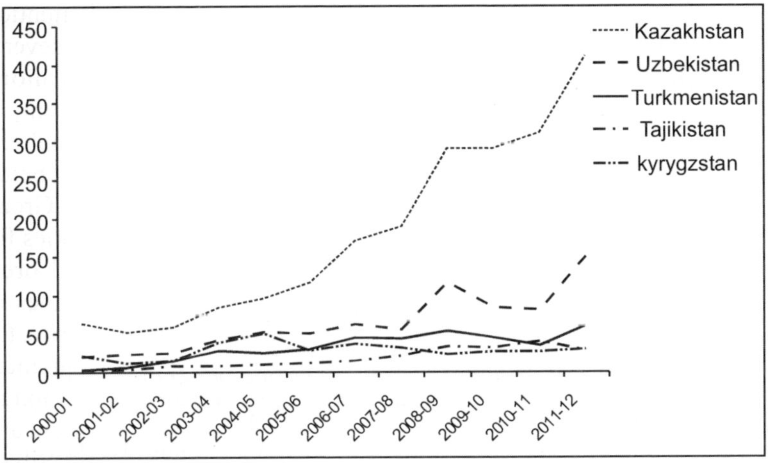

Source: Directorate General of Foreign Trade, Government of India.

Fig. 9.1: Trade between India and Central Asian Republics (US Million $)

Since Kazakhstan is fast becoming a major source for metals and minerals, iron and steel accounted for about 50 per cent of India's imports from it. Furthermore, Zinc and its compounds constituted another 27.7 per cent of imports and about 16 per cent was accounted for by salt, Sulphur, Lime and other minerals. Thus, more than 90 per cent of India's imports are on account of these commodities. Significantly, oil and natural gas do not feature in this list of major import items. On the other hand, pharmaceuticals, coffee, tea, spices, textiles and apparel are the main categories of exports from India. However, except for pharmaceutical products, among the top 15 merchandise imports to Kazakhstan Indian exports are less than one per cent. Even in case of Indian pharmaceutical exports to Kazakhstan, the percentage share (as a percentage of total Indian exports of

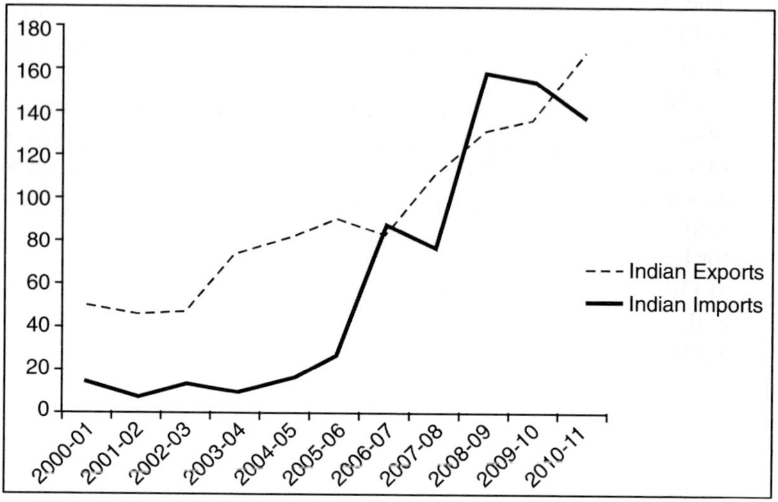

Source: Directorate General of Foreign Trade, Government of India.

Fig. 9.2: Trade between India and Kazakhstan: 2000-01 to 2010-11 (US Million $)

pharmaceutical products) is less than one per cent. Finally, India's export of services to Kazakhstan is negligible (CUTS, 2012).

It is important to note that India's share in major Kazakh imports from other Asian countries is less than 10 per cent in all categories of products, except iron or steel products. It would be interesting to look at India's revealed comparative advantage in those product categories, and compare it with that of its Asian competitors to understand future potential of Indian exports to Kazakhstan. However, over the years, the composition of bilateral trade (exports as well as imports) has remained more or less unchanged. There is hardly any sign of product diversification in the overall growth in trade volume. Trade deepening through exploring prospects in other commodities and reaping full potential of bilateral trade is yet to materialised (CUTS, 2012).

Kazakhstan's FDI flow to India has been minimal till date. Kazakhstan's outward FDI initiatives are driven by the need for economic diversification beyond mining and improvement in competitiveness through overseas experiences, adoption of internationally accepted standards of corporate governance, etc. Therefore, its FDI destinations have been to developed countries like

The Netherlands, Italy and The UK. Likewise, India's contribution in FDI stock of Kazakhstan is also low. Despite having an investment treaty (bilateral investment promotion agreement) between India and Kazakhstan, which came into force in July 2001, cross-border investments are weak (CUTS, 2012). But, since 2009, a number of investment avenues opened up in Kazakhstan, mostly in sectors such as oil and natural gas, pharmaceuticals, banking and information technology. It is clear that energy security is the primary motivation for India's investment interests in Kazakhstan. The long-standing bid of Oil & Natural Gas Commission of India for joint oil exploration with KazMunaiGaz (both are state-owned oil and gas companies) in the Satpayev Block has been a highlight of this motivation, and with the signing of the deal, the ONGC is expected to invest a considerable sum in Kazakhstan (Ministry of External Affairs 2009).

Future Prospects of India-Kazakhstan Cooperation

Apart from cultural goodwill, Central Asia was an attractive option for India for a variety of reasons. Even though Pakistani diplomacy and security-related issues throughout the 1990s tended to impede India's reach in Central Asia, India did try to explore opportunities in the region's oil and gas deposits. Kazakhstan's failure to fulfil its past commitment for giving a slot to India in its oil fields was certainly a discouraging move. Nevertheless, India failed to get a share of the Kazakh energy pie due to a variety of reasons, but fresh vistas are now opening up for bilateral cooperation with Kazakhstan in the post-nuclear India scenario. From all accounts, indicators are that Kazakhstan is keen to cooperate with India in nuclear commerce and would be ready to supply uranium for India's existing and future civil nuclear power plants. Kazakhstan was, in fact, one of the first countries to support India at the NSG. What is clearly emerging is a positive environment of cooperation between the biggest Central Asian country, Kazakhstan, and the biggest South Asian country, India (Stobdon, 2009).

India attaches immense importance to Kazakhstan in the field of energy security. After Russia, Kazakhstan is the only country which has endowed to help meet India's energy security. This includes nuclear fuel and hydrocarbons. Kazakhstan has huge reserves of Uranium as well as oil and gas. The nuclear agreement signed with Kazakhstan makes it the fourth country besides the US, France and

Russia who would supply Uranium to India for civil energy purposes. Under the proposed agreement, the Nuclear Power Corporation of India (NPCIL) will begin to import at least 120 tonnes of uranium annually from Kazakhstan. Energy cooperation between India and Kazakhstan is not limited only to nuclear fuel. As mentioned earlier, Kazakhstan has huge hydrocarbon reserves which offer a strong prospect for cooperation (Hussain, 2009).

While petrochemicals and uranium are of key strategic interest to India, building momentum in other sectors is hindered mainly by lack of adequate and authentic information in both countries about the business potential and prospects. An important study on India's future trade prospects in the light of financial crisis, identified Kazakhstan as one of India's trading partners with a high unexplored trade potential. The gap between actual and potential bilateral trade was estimated at 86.19 per cent of potential trade volume. In fact, the corresponding figures are very high for other prominent CIS countries – Uzbekistan (81.95 per cent), Tajikistan (94.39 per cent), Armenia (82.47 per cent) and Kyrgyzstan (93.34 per cent). This, coupled with the fact that Kazakhstan fares far better in the Central Asian region in terms of economic stability and governance indicators, shows the huge potential it has in improving (net of trade creation by taking into account trade diversion factors as well) trade relations in future (CUTS, 2012).

Considering the potential, the current scale of economic interaction – including trade and investment between the two countries – is not very big. However, there exists vast scope to expand and increase both the volume of trade as well as quantum of investment, a view shared by both India and Kazakhstan. The volume of bilateral trade between India and Kazakhstan is – insignificant. It is characterized by two factors: first, Kazakhstan is the largest trading partner of India amongst all Central Asian countries, approximately accounting near 60 per cent of the total trade between India and the Central Asian Republics (Figure 1). Second, trade has recently registered faster growth than earlier (UN Comtrade, 2012). In the field of investment, Kazakhstan offers huge scope. Currently, there are 280 companies, including those in the oil and gas sector, which are doing business in India and Kazakhstan. Furthermore, Information Technology (IT) and pharmaceuticals provides rich ground for Indian companies in Kazakhstan. The pharmaceuticals industry in Kazakhstan provides a market of US$ 500 million (Hussain, 2009).

As an emerging power, India ought to be taking note of Kazakhstan's potential more seriously. This would pave the way for India keeping pace with the new geopolitical reality evolving in Eurasian region. Kazakhstan has been supportive of India in all multilateral fora like the United Nations and others. Kazakhstan backs India's candidacy for permanent membership of the UN Security Council. Astana has also facilitated India's entry into the Shanghai Corporation Organization (SCO) as an Observer. For India, Kazakhstan offers the best possible opportunity as a gateway to the Central Asian region. Economic diplomacy with Kazakhstan must take into account the larger goal of increasing better trade and investment ties with the CIS region. Increased bilateral ties would help to leverage the larger market potential of Belarus-Russia-Kazakhstan Customs Union as well as the combined market potential of CIS countries.

Notes

1. Andre Gunder Frank, "Central Asia's Continuing Role in the World Economy to 1800" and "The Centrality of Central Asia", www.rrojasdatabank.org/agfrank/research.html (October 17, 2007).
2. Anuradha M. Chenoy, "Oil Politics of Central Asia and Caspian Sea Basin: The US Game Plan" *Contemporary Central Asia,* Vol. IX, No. 1, 2005, pp. 27-45.
3. Chintamani Mahapatra, "US Policy Toward Caspian Region" *Contemporary Central Asia,* Vol. IX, No. 1, 2005, pp. 1-26.
4. CUTS, *A Note on India Kazakhstan Trade and Investment Relations,* http:/ /www.cuts-citeeorg/pdf/briefing_paper-india-kazakhstan_trade_and_ investment_relations.pdf as Accessed on 03-05-2013.
5. Directorate General of Foreign Trade http://dgft.delhi.nic.in/ as accessed on 03-05-2013.
6. Gulshan Sachdeva, (2007), *"India" The New Silk Roads: Transport and Trade in Greater Central Asia*, a monograph produced by the Central Asia, Caucasus Institute & Silk Road Studies Programme.
7. Hussain Zakir (2009), *India and Kazakhstan: New ahead,* Wayshttp://www idsain/idsastrategiccomments/IndiaandKazakhstan ZHussain_180209 as accessed on 05-03-2013.
8. Kaushik, Devendra (2005), "The Caspian Cauldron: New Geopolitical Game," *Contemporary Central Asia*, Vol. IX, Number 2 and 3, pp. 1-12.
9. Kuldip Singh and Vijay Laxmi (2006), "Economic Profile of Central Asia and Emerging Politics," Project Report, Centre for South-Central Asian Studies, Guru Nanak Dev University, Amritsar.

10. Ministry of External Affairs, Government of India (2009), *Joint Declaration on Strategic partnership between India and Kazakhstan* http://mea.gov.in/bilateraldocuments. htm?dtl/4776/Joint+Declaration+on+Strategic+Partnership+between+India+and+Kazakhstan as Accessed on 05-03-2013.
11. Ministry of External Affairs Government of India (2011), Bilateral Agreements concluded during PM's Visit to Kazakhstan.
12. P. Stobdan (2009), *India and Kazakhstan should Share Complementary Objectives,* http://dx.doi.org/10.1080/09700160802579553 as accessed on 03-05-2913.
13. UN Comtrade, (2013) http://comtrade.un.org/db/ as accessed on 06-03-2013.

10
India-Central Asia Energy Partnership: Trends and Future Outlook

Ajay Patnaik

Introduction

The past ten years or so have witnessed increasing Indian engagement in Central Asia. It was in 2003 that the Indian Prime Minister, Foreign Minister and the Defence Minister visited the region. Since then, Indian policy makers and scholars have used the expression "Extended Neighbourhood" to define the closeness between India and Central Asia. Today, the relationship is being elevated to a higher level through what is called the "Connect Central Asia" Policy. This author himself uses the expression 'India's Look North' policy, which can also be a part of India's "New Silk Road Vision" in which India-Central Asia connectivity is pivotal. Energy remains a major variable in the "Connect Central Asia" policy. It can economically and geographically link India and Central Asia through investments, pipelines and energy trade. Central Asia is rich with different sources of energy in abundance – it has oil, gas, coal, Uranium and hydro-energy resources in large quantities, though different countries have different resource potentiality.

The year 2003 was also the year when the Iraq war made India aware of the risk associated with excessive dependency on West Asia for its energy supplies. The visit by the highest Indian dignitaries to Central Asia that year may not have been a coincidence. In any case, India's Central Asia policy took a decisive turn from then onwards.

Since the Iraq war, India has realised that the West Asian region is going to be a less stable source of supply. Iran is a latest example of this. The sanctions regime is already affecting Indian imports from Iran. India has been moving into the energy sector in Africa and Latin America. However, the nearest source for energy is Central Asia, which, since the disintegration of the Soviet Union, has opened up to the wider world.

While Kazakhstan is the eighth largest producer of oil in the world, it, along with Turkmenistan and Uzbekistan, also possesses substantial reserves of gas. Turkmenistan currently ranks in the top six countries for natural gas reserves and the top 20 in terms of gas production. Turkmenistan has some of the largest natural gas reserves in the world. Kyrgyzstan and Tajikistan have huge potentialities for producing hydro-electricity. With about 17 per cent of world reserves and 15 per cent of total global Uranium production, Kazakhstan is emerging as a major partner to meet the needs of India's expanding nuclear energy sector.[1]

Current Energy Cooperation

As far as India is concerned, more vigour has been shown in the last few years to pursue its energy interests in Central Asia. In August 2005, the Indian state-owned company, ONGC, collaborated with Mittal Industrial Group to form OMEL, and made a serious effort to acquire energy assets in Kazakhstan. The creation of ONGC Mittal Energy Limited (OMEL) was meant to give more teeth to India's global energy search. Mittal had earlier acquired Russian company Lukoil's assets in Kazakhstan, and thus was expected be a powerful factor in India's efforts for overseas energy deals.

The OMEL put a very high bid of US$ 3.9 billion to acquire the Canadian-owned Petrokazakhstan Company, which has its operations in Kazakhstan. Though it did not succeed, the bid established the fact that India is serious about its energy diplomacy in Central Asia. India's engagement in the energy sector of Central Asia has only grown since then.

During Indian Prime Minister Manmohan Singh's visit to Astana in April 2011, India and Kazakhstan signed an agreement for ONGC's acquisition of 25 per cent stakes in Satpayev exploration bloc in the Caspian Sea. Three energy agreements, according to reports, between India's ONGC Videsh and Kazakh state company, Kazmunaigaz, were worth US$ 400 million.[2] Earlier, ONGC Videsh had acquired stakes in two oil fields in Kazakhstan.

The invitation to President Nazarbayev as the Chief Guest at the 60th Republic Day celebrations on 26 January, 2009, in Delhi is a strong testimony to the importance India places in its relationship with Kazakhstan. This visit was preceded by a breakthrough agreement on supply of Uranium to India and comprehensive cooperation in the civil nuclear energy programme. Kazakhstan is emerging as a major partner to meet India's energy security needs. Its state sector company, Kazatomprom, has already signed an MoU with Nuclear Power Corporation of India Limited (NPCIL) to supply Uranium following the Inter-Governmental Agreement on Cooperation for the peaceful uses of nuclear energy.

Not only has Kazakhstan assured India of supplying 2,100 tons of Uranium, its Foreign Minister also hoped that this cooperation would lead to "cxchange of technology and creation of joint ventures" in the nuclear field. The two sides have already agreed to set up a Centre of Excellence in Information and Communication technology at the Eurasian National University in Astana.[3] Currently, Kazakhstan has no nuclear power stations and does not use any Uranium by-products, but has recently embarked on a programme to provide materials for the entire nuclear cycle – from raw uranium to nuclear fuel and reactors. India's technology and expertise can be of use to build nuclear power plants in Kazakhstan.

Uzbekistan has emerged as another strong partner of India in Central Asia. During Prime Minister Manmohan Singh's 2006 visit to Tashkent, Uzbekistan offered exploration facilities to Indian companies in the hydrocarbon sector, with a proposal for an equal share for both countries in the extracts.[4] Singh stated that India saw Uzbekistan "as an important element in any effort to optimally utilize the energy resources of Central Asia", and Karimov added that "Uzbekistan, based on its cooperation with a number of countries, ...is ready to allocate geological territory to Indian companies to explore the resources of gas, oil, and other hydrocarbons".[5]

During President Karimov's visit to India in May (17th-18th) 2011, India and Uzbekistan signed a total of 34 agreements, which included a Memorandum of Understanding between ONGC Videsh Limited and Uzbekneftgaz on Cooperation in hydrocarbon sector, and another Memorandum of Understanding for cooperation in Oil and Gas sector between Uzbekneftgaz and India's private sector ESSAR group.[6] The Uzbek Government declared that ONGC would undertake exploration work in the Central part of Uzbekistan.[7]

Turkmenistan has also drawn attention as an important source for India's energy search. Indian companies have acquired stakes in exploration blocks in offshore Turkmenistan in the Caspian Sea. OMEL holds 30 per cent stake in Exploration Block 11-12 in offshore Turkmenistan in the Caspian Sea. Covering an area of 5,663 sq km, the block is located close to discovered and producing fields. The other partners in the project are Wintershall, a German company and Maersk Oil, a Danish company.[8]

Though Tajikistan has hardly much oil and gas resources of its own, it has abundant hydro-electric potentiality. India is beginning to back its strategic engagement in Tajikistan by greater economic activism. Energy again is a driving force in this respect. Tajikistan's importance as a source of hydro-electric energy has attracted India's attention. Tajikistan is the third largest producer of hydro-electric power after the US and Russia. On its part, Tajikistan has shown interest in India's involvement in its energy sector. At the 2005 summit of SCO in Astana, President Rahmon told Indian Foreign Minister that he welcomed India's investment in Tajikistan's power sector.[9]

In response, following Tajik President's visit to New Delhi in August 2006, Indian companies invested US$ 17 million in the reconstruction of the Varzob-1 hydroelectric power station, which supplies part of Dushanbe with electricity.[10]

Indian President Pratibha Patil's visit to Tajikistan during 6-9 September, 2009, further boosted Indo-Tajik energy ties. During the visit, it was announced that Indian companies plan to invest US$12 million in the development of gas fields in the country's south. New Delhi is interested in gaining access to Tajikistan's Uranium reserves which, according to the Tajik President, account for 14 per cent of the world reserves.[11]

Pipeline Projects

Some potential routes for Caspian region states to supply Asian demand would be to pipe oil and natural gas through Iran to the Persian Gulf, or Southwest to Afghanistan, apart from pipelines to China. Turkmenistan has been promoting the Afghanistan option, which would entail building pipelines across Afghan territory to reach markets in Pakistan and India. The Turkmenistan-Afghanistan-Pakistan-India (TAPI) pipeline would span over 1,000 miles from a point in Turkmenistan to Fazilka (India) on the Pakistan-India border, and have a proposed annual capacity of over 1,200 Bcf. Major issues holding up construction, according to the US Energy Information Administration, are security concerns, uncertainty of pricing and fees, and lack of financial commitment.[12]

While the project was not moving ahead for quite some time, the visit of Turkmenistan's President, Gurbanguly Berdymuhamedov, to New Delhi in May 2010 gave momentum to energy cooperation between the two countries. Following Turkmen President's visit, India signed two important agreements on 20 September 2010 for the TAPI gas pipeline project – one initialising the gas pipeline framework agreement (GPFA), the other being the proposed Gas Sales Purchase Agreement (GSPA) – along with three other partner countries.

There was more activity the following year. The four nations involved in the TAPI pipeline project began discussing gas sales and other details of the US$ 7.6 billion project in New Delhi in April (25th-28th) 2011. India hosted the official-level dialogue which, among other things, deliberated on a Gas Sale and Purchase Agreement (GSPA) and project structure. Turkmenistan and Pakistan signed a Heads of Agreement in November 2011, regarding import prices.

Quite recently, there has been a proposal for a pipeline from Chimkent in South Kazakhstan to India. During visiting Kazakh Foreign Minister's meeting with India's External Affairs Minister, Salman Khurshid, on 5 March, 2013, in Delhi, the idea of a 1,500 km pipeline that would pass through Uzbekistan, Afghanistan and Pakistan before reaching Delhi was discussed. The proposal was expected to be revived when the two were to meet again in Almaty for the Istanbul Process on Afghanistan, and again when they were to have a bilateral meeting in Astana. This would open up a new route on the North-South axis for Central Asia energy.[13]

According to some, this pipeline would have the potential to be extended to Russia, thus solving the problem of getting Russian energy to India. The proposal would undergo a 240-day vetting process by Kazakhstan, and Kashagan oil resources could be the source of supply to this pipeline. It has been reported in the Indian press that India is interested in acquiring stakes of an American company (Conocophillips) in a very big block in the Kashagan fields. The proposed Indian interest in the US$50 billion Kashagan project will cost about US$5-US$6 billion, which would make it the biggest ONGC investment overseas.[14]

Since extensive energy linkages already exist between Central Asia and Russia, the proposed route can further extend North to open Russian hydrocarbon exports to South Asia, according to Gulshan Sachdeva. The issue was also discussed during the Indian External Affairs Minister's visit to Moscow in late April 2013. From the Gazprom's Central Asia-Centre pipeline, built during the 1960s, linkages have previously existed to Mazar-e-Sharif in Afghanistan, and these could be revived again. The distance to the Indian border from Mazar-e-Sharif is about 1,200 kilometres. This proposed pipeline would help in establishing an energy corridor of gas and oil pipelines linking South Asia into Eurasia. If needed, parallel road corridors could also be constructed, adds Sachdeva.[15]

Convergence of India-Central Asia Energy Interests

I. Supply and Demand Compatibility

The Central Asian countries not only have high levels of proven reserves of oil and gas, but also have the huge potentialities for expansion. All the countries are trying to expand their present production and export capacities.

Kazakhstan's oil production has seen an impressive expansion since 1995, and surpassed the 1.0 million bbl/d production level in 2003 and has steadily grown to be the second-largest oil producer in the former Soviet Union, second only to Russia. Kazakhstan's exports are going to expand in the coming years, as new fields, particularly Kashagan, come on line. However, the rapid growth of oil production and exports will require an expansion of export capacity.[16]

Uzbekistan exported approximately 24 per cent of its gas production in 2010, and exports have generally increased since 2002. Uzbekistan plans to triple its gas exports by 2020 and diversify gas markets.[17] In the case of Turkmenistan, recent major discoveries at South Yolotan in the Eastern part of the country are likely to add to the current proven reserve amounts.[18] Tajikistan has the potential to produce more than 300 billion kilowatt hours of electricity per year, but currently produces only 16.5 billion kilowatt hours.[19] Similarly, Kyrgyzstan, despite being an upstream county with huge water resources, produces only 11.19 billion kilowatt hours of electricity. It is planning big investments in its hydro-electric projects.[20]

Table 10.1: Central Asia's oil and gas reserves, 2011

Country	Proven reserves of crude oil (million bl.)	Current production (thousand barrels per day)	Proven gas reserves (trln.cu.ft)	Current production (bln.cu.ft per year)
Kazakhstan	1552.94	30.0	85	401
Uzbekistan	594	60	65	222,6
Turkmenistan	600[a]	202	265[b]	1,600[a]

a. Data for 2010
b. Data for 2012
Source: US Energy Information Administration, EIA, 2013
For Kazakhstan : http://www.eia.gov/countries/country-data.cfm?fips=KZ
For Uzbekistan : http://www.eia.gov/countries/country-data.cfm?fips=UZ
For Turkmenistan : http://www.eia.gov/countries/country-data.cfm?fips=TX

Uzbekistan plans to triple its gas exports by 2020 and diversify gas markets.[21] In the case of Turkmenistan, recent major discoveries at South Yolotan in the prolific Eastern part of the country are expected to offset most declines in other large, mature gas fields, and will likely add to the current proven reserve amounts.[22, 23]

India could provide not just a close and big market for Central Asian energy. Its economic growth has enabled its public and private sector companies to invest large amounts of capital outside the country. India's foreign policy in 21st century is driven mainly by economic growth and energy security. In the first decade of this century, India grew dynamically by 7 per cent to 9 per cent per annum, which created growth in energy demand. Even the future growth is projected to be on the same scale, though the current global crisis has pulled down the growth rate. According to the estimates by the US Energy Information Administration (EIA) about 45 per cent growth in world oil demand would be from India by the year 2030. Nearly 75 per cent of India's oil requirement/consumption is imported.[24]

As per British Petroleum (BP) information, India's net natural gas imports reached 10.8 billion cubic meters in the year 2008 from 2.7 billion cubic meters in the year 2004. Imports increased by four times in four years. There was a sharp increase in consumption of natural gas during 2005-2010. IEA projects that India would import one-half of its natural gas demand by 2030. Natural gas is expected to be an increasingly important component of energy consumption, as the country pursues energy resources diversification and overall energy security.[25]

Nuclear energy could be one of the long-term solutions to India's energy security. The country has announced ambitious plans to expand its nuclear energy programme by nearly 15 fold in the next 20 years. However, the shortfall in the supply of domestic Uranium has affected the operation of nuclear plants in India. None of them have been working at full capacity. There are 20 operational nuclear plants across the country, with a total installed capacity of 4,780 MWs. India's need for Uranium would increase ten-fold by 2020 as it boosts nuclear power generation.[26]

The supply and demand scenario calls for greater energy collaboration between Central Asia and India, be it oil, gas or the nuclear sector.

II. Diversification

'India Hydrocarbon Vision-2025' (Planning Commission, 2000) has the key objective of achieving energy security through self-reliance by increased indigenous production and investment in oil equity abroad. The main objective of India's energy policy is to diversify its energy supply sources and not depend only on OPEC countries. For this, India has been working hard for pipeline projects, and has invested in joint investment projects. It is making efforts to diversify towards Russia and the energy producing nations in Central Asia.[27]

Central Asian states are also diversifying their energy markets, which are reflected in their multi-vector policies. Kazakhstan and Turkmenistan have built pipelines to China in recent years. Turkmenistan also has a pipeline to Iran, and it is willing to supply energy to the proposed TAPI pipeline. Kazakhstan has receptive to the idea of a pipeline from Southern Kazakhstan to India through Uzbekistan, Afghanistan and Pakistan.

Uzbekistan has sought foreign investment in its energy sector through PSAs (Production Sharing Agreements) or JVs (Joint Ventures), primarily with different international oil companies, primarily with Gazprom, Lukoil, CNPC, Petronas, and KNOC of Korea. Uzbekistan also signed several energy cooperation agreements with other companies such as India's GAIL and ONGC, PetroVietnam, and ExxonMobil to attract their technical expertise and support in the country's hydrocarbon production. Uzbekistan recently began easing legislation to attract foreign capital. In 2004, Uzbekistan passed PSA legislation to attract more foreign investment. Also, in 2007, the country lowered taxes on subsoil hydrocarbon extraction to give producers more incentives to reverse oil production declines.[28]

Similarly, Turkmenistan is eager to diversify export routes for its oil and gas resources, but must obtain capital, technical assistance and political support for alternative pipelines, according to Energy Information Administration (EIA) of the United States. The Turkmen Government began reforming the country's energy sector and regulatory environment to attract more foreign investment and diversify export routes. For example, in March 2007, the Government established a hydrocarbon regulatory authority, State Agency on Management and Use of Hydrocarbon Resources, to issue licenses and contracts for oil and gas field development, and provide greater revenue transparency. In 2008, Turkmenistan also passed a Hydrocarbon Law to provide greater legal transparency in ownership of oil and gas projects. International companies can participate in joint ventures (JVs) or production sharing agreements (PSAs) with Turkmenneft for offshore oil and gas blocks in the Caspian Sea.[29]

III. Capital and Technology

Being landlocked, Central Asian countries face a number of challenges in bringing their resources to world markets. Uzbekistan and Turkmenistan are geographically far from end-use markets and lack sufficient pipelines to export more hydrocarbons, and also suffer from an inefficient and older energy infrastructure. They need large investments to expand capacity and bring them to diversified markets. Tajikistan and Kyrgyzstan have the potential to produce many times more electricity than what they are producing at the moment. Both are planning big investments in hydro-electric projects. Donors are pushing regional energy market integration and the construction of power lines that will allow Tajikistan and Kyrgyzstan to sell surplus summer electricity output to Afghanistan and Pakistan. The larger CASA-1000 power line project to link Afghanistan and Pakistan with Central Asia has been delayed by financing problems.[30]

IV. The Capabilities of Indian Companies

ONGC Videsh Limited is a wholly owned subsidiary and the overseas arm of India's largest corporation, ONGC Limited. From just one asset in Vietnam in 2000, Oil Videsh Limited had 32 assets by 2013.[31] During August 2008, ONGC, India's biggest exploration company bought Imperial Energy Plc for US$ 2.1 billion to tap Siberian deposits. Imperial energy is a UK-based petroleum exploration and production company operating in Russia. Imperial Energy is the biggest overseas acquisition by ONGC. Imperial has in place reserves of about 3.4 billion barrels of oil equivalent, and this takeover was to enhance ONGC's reserves by around 20 per cent.[32]

ONGC's Imperial Energy and Russian Sistema have merged their oil and gas business in Russia under a joint venture, in no-cash deal in December 2010. ONGC would have 25 per cent share of merged entity, but with a say in the management. The merger of three companies – Bashneft, Russneft, both Russian companies and Imperial Energy – would give ONGC a share in the Russian firm's 25-million-ton annual oil production and 20 million-ton refinery output in new oil fields, Trebs and Titov. The fields have an estimated 200 million tonnes of recoverable reserves, equivalent to 35 per cent of ONGC's total oil reserves.[33]

India has been making investments in Sudan, Russia, Libya, Vietnam, Iran, Syria, Lebanon, Kazakhstan, Indonesia, Iraq, Myanmar, Bangladesh, Sri Lanka, Angola and Burma. ONGC Videsh has spent over US$ 10 billion to acquire over three dozen assets in about 16 countries. It is engaged as an operator in 19 projects, including eight jointly operated projects.[34]

ONGC Videsh's model of energy engagement in Russia can be instructive. Since pipelines can take a long time to materialize due to economic, political or security reasons, investment in exploring and developing energy fields is an important option. This can be done by buying stakes in existing companies that are already active in the energy sector, or bidding for stakes in energy fields on its own. This has been done in Russia, and is being tried in Central Asia. The energy extracted can be swapped or be sold in the international market. Cheaper energy can be purchased from other sources.

V. Decline in European Energy Demand

According to scholars, OECD countries are now "no growth markets" for oil due to climate change policy, shifting of transport market and substitute fuel from agribusiness. Oil demand for transport sector (over half of consumption) in the US and EU is projected to fall by 30 per cent between 2009 and 2035 or from 17 mbpd (million barrels per day) to 11.5 mbpd. At the same time, demand from Asia is projected to rise in the same period from 7.5 to 13.5 mbpd.[35] In terms of natural gas, European markets, which are major buyers of oil and gas from Eurasia, are undergoing transformation due to unconventional gas technologies. The shift towards globalization of gas markets (LNG) and the growing potential for exploitation of unconventional reserves elsewhere places less premium on supplies to European markets over and above ongoing projects. Due to fall in European gas demand, Russia has reduced gas purchase from Turkmenistan. Sales of Turkmen gas to Gazprom – which buys Turkmen gas to sell on to Europe – fell from 42.3 bcm in 2008 to 10.7 bcm in 2010. According to the latest BP Statistical Review of World Energy, Turkmenistan reduced its gas output from 66.1 bcm in 2008 to 42.4 bcm in 2010.[36] Thus, there is a need to look beyond the European markets to key Asian markets for global energy consumption growth, which are mainly China and India.

VI. India's Benign Geopolitical Engagement

In the early 1990s, when India was facing severe economic problems, it extended credit lines ranging from US$ 5 million to US$10 million for the newly independent states in Central Asia. India's assistance needs to be appreciated given the difficulties the country itself was faced with in 1991, when it had to mortgage its gold reserves for foreign exchange. Later, the common threat of terrorism resulted in a growing convergence of views on the need to cooperate and jointly fight this menace. India also provided financial assistance to the anti-Taliban Northern Alliance, which was backed by Russia and some Central Asian states.

In the past few years, India has signed a Strategic Partnership Agreements with three Central Asian States – Kazakhstan, Uzbekistan and Tajikistan. India and Kazakhstan have established a forum not only to cooperate on fight against terrorism, but also for 'early action' finalising agreements in military and technical cooperation. It has given special attention to defence co-operation between the two countries, which envisages joint production of military hardware such as torpedoes and heavy machine-gun barrels. Kazakhstan also co-operated in India's space programme by allowing the launch of Indian satellite from its territory (Baikanour cosmodrome operated by Russia).

India's approach to regional organisations in the region has changed in recent years. It has joined the Shanghai Cooperation Organisation (SCO) as an Observer after years of hesitation, and has been an enthusiastic participant in Conference on Interaction & Confidence-building Measures in Asia (CICA), which was initiated by Kazakhstan.[37] Within the CICA framework, India now acts as a Co-coordinator for a CBM on Securing Secure and Effective Transportation Corridors and a CBM on Energy Security.

Before India decided to give up its hesitation in joining the SCO, Central Asian leaders, particularly President Nazarbayev, had been persuading India to join the Shanghai Cooperation Organisation (SCO). As a result, during the February 2002 visit of President Nazarbayev to India, the Joint Declaration stated that India's membership in SCO "would add to the strength of that organization".[38] Their initiatives indicate a strong desire to involve India in a more integrated security framework as a stabilizing force in Central Asia.

Afghanistan's stability is also on top of the agenda of India and Central Asian states. India has been proceeding along a strategy that looks beyond simply linking the country with Afghanistan through either Pakistan-Afghanistan or Iran. The objective is to make Central Asia and Afghanistan a region of greater international cooperation, and not a theatre of a "New Great Game". In the process, India wishes to have greater economic engagement with the broader Eurasian region that would also help in Afghanistan's development agenda.

Afghanistan's stability depends on a development paradigm in which energy and infrastructure would play an important role. India's stronger economic engagement with the Eurasian region would also help in Afghanistan's reconstruction and stability. While geopolitics will remain relevant, a development model could benefit India, Central Asia and Afghanistan. The TAPI and Kazakhstan-India pipeline would be strong vectors in that process.

Central Asia and India are interested in the North-South axis in their engagement with each other. With this in mind, India has pursued sea-land corridors and pipeline projects that embody this vision. The International North-South Transport Corridor (INSTC) and Chabahar projects are going to provide India access to Afghanistan, Central Asia and Russia. The proposal to extend/link TAPI pipeline to Kazakhstan – and beyond to Russia – will lend a strong basis to India's "Look North" vision. Apart from Russia, India, Iran (founding members since 2000 Agreement), Central Asian states like Kazakhstan and Turkmenistan are part of the INSTC.

The Eurasian integration processes, especially the creation of the Customs Union (CU), has opened up huge opportunities for India in Eurasia. With the two key transportation links, India has positioned itself well to take advantage of the Eurasian integration process. India is working on a Comprehensive Economic Partnership Agreement (CEPA), an omnibus free trade agreement with the Customs Union.

Any pipeline to India evokes a no zero-sum narrative, like it does in the case of other pipeline projects like the BTC (Baku-Tbilisi-Ceyhan), Southern Gas Corridor, Nabucco, etc., which are meant to take oil and gas to Europe. In fact, Russia, the US and Asian financial institutions like the ADB have been supportive of TAPI pipeline project. The idea of another pipeline, from Kazakhstan to India, was put forth during Kazakhstan's Foreign Minister's visit to India in March 2013. Similarly, during India's Foreign Minister's visit to Moscow in May 2013, Russia favoured the idea of extending the proposed pipeline to Russia.

Conclusion

India's emergence as a global economic power is going to make huge demands on the Central Asian energy sector. At the same time, its economic potential could make it an attractive partner. The need to diversify by both sides could facilitate energy partnership between Central Asian states and India. While pipelines will create strong connectivity, India's investment in the Central Asian energy sector is equally important for India's future energy security. Given the fact that Indian companies have the capital and technology to contribute to expansion of energy production in the region, India's role is likely expand in the region. In that sense, investment in Kashagan and in the Uzbek and Turkmen fields can deepen the energy partnership. India and Central Asia have an extremely close political and diplomatic relationship. The relationship needs to be based on solid economic foundation, in which energy can play a pivotal role. Similarly, India's capital and technology could contribute to the electric power sector in Tajikistan and Kyrgyzstan. In the nuclear energy sector, while Kazakh and Tajik uranium would help India's power plants, India can help build nuclear power plants in Central Asia. In short, there are enough opportunities for both sides to look forward to in the energy sector.

Endnotes

1. Manzaruzzama, "Indo-Kazakh relations: Time to act", *Central Asia's Affairs*, Kazakh Institute of Strategic Studies, 2(26), 2009.
2. *The Economic Times*, April 16, 2011.
3. Sandeep Dikshit, "Nuclear Cooperation, key to multiple projects: Kazakhstan", *The Hindu*, 27 March 2013, p. 10.
4. *Press Trust of India News Agency*, 26 April, 2006.
5. *Press Trust of India News Agency*, 26 April, 2006.
6. "Uzbekistan, India sign a raft of deals in New Delhi In June 2011", universal news wire, 18 May 2011, http://www.universalnewswires.com/centralasia/viewstory.aspx?id=4072; "India and Uzbekistan Signed 34 Agreements during the visit of Islam Karimov", Jagran Josh, 2 June 2011, http://www.jagranjosh.com/current-affairs/india-and-uzbekistan-signed-34-agreements-during-the-visit-of-islam-karimov-1307016886-1
7. *Ministry of External Affairs*, Government of India, http://www.mea.gov.in/Portal/ForeignRelation/Uzbekistan-January-2012.pdf
8. Wintershall and Maersk Oil have 34 per cent and 36 per cent participating interest respectively (India Atlantic Shipping Private Limited, November 30, 1999); (*Embassy of India in Ashgabat*, December , 2012).
9. Siddharth Varadarajan, *The Hindu*, July 11, 2005.
10. Rollie Lal, Central Asia and its Neighbours. Security and Commerce at the Crossroads, Rand Paper, Rand, Santa Monica, 2006; Sudha Ramachandran, "Indian forays into Central Asia", *The Financial Express*, New Delhi, 15 August 2006 Lal, 2006.
11. Address of the Tajik President to Tajikistan's parliament in April 2008, cited in Uddipan Mukherjee, "Presidential Visit to Tajikistan: India among the Pamirs?", Article, #2972, 22 September 2009, Institute of Peace and Conflict Studies, http://www.ipcs.org/article_details.php?articleNo=2972
12. *US Energy Information Administration* (Henceforth, EIA), updated on Jan. 25, 2012, http://www.eia.gov/countries/cab.cfm?fips=TX)
13. Sandeep Dikshit, "India proposes hydrocarbon pipeline from Kazakhstan, *The Hindu*, 6 March 2013, p. 1.
14. Sandeep Dikshit, "India-Kazakh pipeline can extend to Russia", *Ibid*, p. 10.
15. Gulshan Sachdeva, "India's ONGC Plans To Bring Russian Hydrocarbons To South Asia", *The Central Asia Caucasus Analyst*, 15 May 2013.
16. *EIA Analysis Briefs, Kazakhstan*, Last updated September 18, 2012.

17. *EIA, Country Analysis Briefs, Uzbekistan*, Last updated Jan. 19, 2012.
18. *EIA Country Analysis Briefs, Turkmenistan*, Last updated January 2012.
19. Global Security.Org, http://www.globalsecurity.org/military/world/centralasia/tajik-energy.htm
20. *EIA, Country Analysis Briefs, Kyrgyzstan*, Last updated February 12, 2013.
21. *EIA, Country Analysis Briefs, Uzbekistan*, Last updated January 19, 2012.
22. *EIA Country Analysis Briefs, Turkmenistan*, Last updated January 2012.
23. *EIA, Country Analysis Briefs, Kyrgyzstan*, Last updated February 12, 2013.
24. Manju Sahai, Two decades of India-Russia energy cooperation: Hydrocarbons and nuclear energy, 1991-2010, *Ph.D Thesis*, Department of Business Economics, University of Delhi, 2013, p. 287.
25. Manju Sahai, *Ibid*, p. 174.
26. Manju Sahai, *Ibid*, pp. 210, 278.
27. Manju Sahai, *Ibid*, pp. 125-126, 135.
28. *EIA, Country Analysis Briefs, Uzbekistan, op. cit.*
29. *EIA Country Analysis Briefs, Turkmenistan*, Last updated January 2012.
30. Global Security.Org, http://www.globalsecurity.org/military/world/centralasia/tajik-energy.htm
31. *ONGC Videsh Ltd.* Web site. http://www.ongcvidesh.com/(X(1)S(mxmpgd45ifv1ql55dfv0lxbq))/company.aspx
32. "ONGC to take over Imperial Energy", *The Financial Express*, 5 January 2009, http://www.financialexpress.com/news/ongc-to-take-over-imperial-energy/406564); Dadan Upadhyay, "Falling oil output makes Imperial Energy a liability for ONGC in Russia", *Russia & India Report*, 31 January 2013, http://indrus.in/economics/2013/01/31/falling_oil_output_makes_imperial_energy_a_liability_for_ongc_in_ru_22001.html
33. "ONGC, Sistema may soon merge assets in Russia", *The Economic Times* Bureau, 30 July 2011 http://articles.economictimes.indiatimes.com/2011-07-30/news/29833165_1_imperial-energy-bashneft-sistema
34. "ONGC to invest $ 20 bn on assets abroad", *Thaindian News*, 14.3.2010, http://www.thaindian.com/newsportal/business/ongc-to-invest-20-bn-on-assets abroad_100334560.html; and, ONGC Videsh Ltd. Website, http://www.ongcvidesh.com/company.aspx
35. Michael Denison, "Game over? Shifting energy geopolitics in Central Asia", *Central Asia Policy Brief*, No. 5, October 2012, The Elliot School of International Affairs, George Washington University, USA .
36. Murat Sadykov, "Turkmenistan Draws Attention to Gas-Expansion Plans", *Eurasianet.org*, March 28, 2013 http://www.eurasianet.org/node/66756?utm_source=Turkmenistan+News+Brief&utm_campaign=de02c28b3c-my_google_analytics_key&utm_medium=email
37. Kazakh President Nazarbayev first put forward the proposal for such a conference during UN General Assembly in 1992. The first Conference was held in Almaty in 2002. India participated in all CICA Conferences.
38. Rahul Bedi, "India and Central Asia", *Frontline*, Vol. 19, Issue 19, 14-17 September, 2002

11
India and Central Asia: Trade Prospects

Pradeep Agrawal and Seema Sangita

Introduction

The year 1991 has a special significance in the economic history of the five nations of Central Asia (CA5) – Kazakhstan, Kyrgyzstan, Tajikistan, Turkmenistan and Uzbekistan. The Union of Soviet Socialist Republics (USSR) was formally dissolved in December 1991, and the Central Asian countries veered towards a market economy, while India adopted economic reforms in the same year. Up until 1991, the economies of these countries were primarily determined by national planning. After that, as the economies became more market oriented and many industries were privatized, these nations stepped into a globalizing world. Coincidently, India, too, initiated economic liberalization and globalization in 1991. While there have been differences and similarities in the growth experience of these countries since 1991, in the last four years all these countries have been affected by global recession. One of the ways of coping with recession in the West is looking for diverse trade and investment partnerships and to develop stronger South-South ties. In this paper, we examine the current trade and business relationship between the Central Asian countries and identify potential for improvement.

The central Asian region was part of the erstwhile USSR, and the economic activities of these countries were determined by the central planning framework. In 1991, the USSR collapsed and the Central Asian nations were born. In the initial phase of transition, this region faced severe economic downturn. There were several factors behind this downturn, including disruption in production network with the former USSR, loss of subsidies from former USSR, inexperienced private sector, insufficient infrastructure and lack of institutions for a market economy, including well-functioning capital and labour markets (also see Dowling and Wignaraja, 2006a). The manufacturing sector experienced severe breakdown of supply of raw materials and lack of markets. At the same time, the Central Asian countries, now much smaller both in terms of geography and economy, were forced to create foreign trade ties with other countries, since self sufficiency in commodities had collapsed.

Concurrently, India adopted structural reforms, including liberalization policies in 1991. The economy entered into a period of transition from a semi-socialist planning oriented economy to a much more market oriented open economy. India and Central Asia faced one common challenge in 1991 – how to integrate into the world economy? Each country, however, had a different set of resources and different circumstances and encountered varied degrees of success in this challenge. The Central Asian countries and India have geographic proximity; however, the distance is enhanced due to the unfavourable political relationship between India and Pakistan. Yet, despite these problems, trade in goods between India and Central Asia has increased many-fold over the last decade.

However, this increase is hardly enough, since Central Asia's exports to India remained at a level that averaged only about one per cent of their total exports, and did not exceed two per cent for any of the five countries. Also, imports from India to Central Asia remain similarly small (see Section 3 below). In fact, India does not feature in the list of key trading partners in any of the five countries in Mogilevskii (2012). A good trade relationship with the Central Asian countries is of high strategic importance for India, since the Central Asian countries are located strategically, sandwiched between major powers like Russia, China, Iran and Europe. Further, these nations have enormous amounts of energy resources that would be of considerable importance to India, which needs more energy resources to sustain its high economic growth. Given the volatile global economy, there is a greater need to forge trade relationships with a range of countries in the developing world. Also, several major and regional powers, including the Western countries, have been giving importance to a strategic relationship with Central Asia due to its location at the crossroads of Eurasia. This cooperation is essential to maintain peace and harmony in the region, and acting as a bulwark against terrorism and illegal activities like drud trafficking, so that mutually beneficial economic trade and investment ties can be promoted (Rakhimov, 2010).

I. The Economies of Central Asian Countries and India

In the first half of the 1990s, the Central Asian countries were dealing with the aftermath of the dissolution of the USSR. When these countries were a part of the erstwhile USSR, their role in the economy was mostly to supply raw materials and energy to the USSR. For example, Hiro (2010) discusses how Uzbekistan had a "cotton monoculture". It produced cotton, but had no textile industries. It processed barely 15 per cent of the total cotton output.[1] Similarly, Hiro (2010) also documents that Turkmenistan was planned to function as a cotton producing area, before natural gas was found here. Most manufacturing industries were located elsewhere. As a result, this region never developed an independent industrial sector or managerial skills. International trade was planned and executed in Moscow (Dowling and Wignaraja 2006a). As a result, after the collapse of the Soviet Union, these nations were stranded with an undermined manufacturing sector and lack of easy access to traditional trade. Even from a geographic perspective, the countries were land locked and isolated from trading routes. The self sufficiency of the economy disappeared, and the supply chains of goods and raw materials destroyed. The lack of access to resources resulted in increasing poverty, making it even more difficult for the economies to focus on industrial growth.

The growth rates of the economies were mostly negative due to the collapse of existing economic relations. However, turnaround occured towards the end of the 1990s, and most of the Central Asian economies moved into a positive economic growth trajectory. Since then, the five economies have evolved in different ways, but the growth rate of the GDP has been quite high. Further, all the economies have experienced structural changes, with an expansion of the services sector and a relative decline in the agriculture sector.

Table 11.1 compares the average annual growth rate of the Central Asian economies across the decade of 1991-2000 and 2001-2011. There is a dramatic turnaround in the average annual growth rates in every country of Central Asia from negative values in the nineties to positive in the following decade. Further, the magnitude is high, except in the case of Kyrgyzstan, which experienced a political crisis – the Tulip Revolution – in 2005.

Table 11.1: Average GDP Growth rate

Year	*Kazakhstan*	*Kyrgyzstan*	*Tajikistan*	*Turkmenistan*	*Uzbekistan*	*India*
1991-2000	–3.35	–3.46	–8.39	–1.82	–0.08	5.59
2001-2011	8.25	4.32	8.69	8.43	7.07	7.46

Source: World Bank (2012).

One main reason behind the turnaround of the Central Asian Region is the beginning of a transition to a market economy. New economic arrangements were made, market institutions were developed and efforts were made towards restoration of faith in the new economic arrangements. These reforms, along with a large petroleum and minerals resource base, triggered a huge increase in foreign direct investment in the region, particularly in Kazakhstan. Clark and Naito (1998) document that a substantial part of the FDI was in mining sectors due to demand for oil and natural gas, and other metals. As can be seen in Figure 11.1, there has been a dramatic increase in FDI inflows in Kazakhstan between 2005 and 2008. This was followed by a sharp decline in 2009 and 2010, but FDI flows were beginning to pick by 2011. Turkmenistan is a distant second in terms of FDI inflows; however, the inflows have been increasing and there was a substantial increase in 2009, followed by a decline. Uzbekistan and Kyrgyzstan also have experienced increasing inward

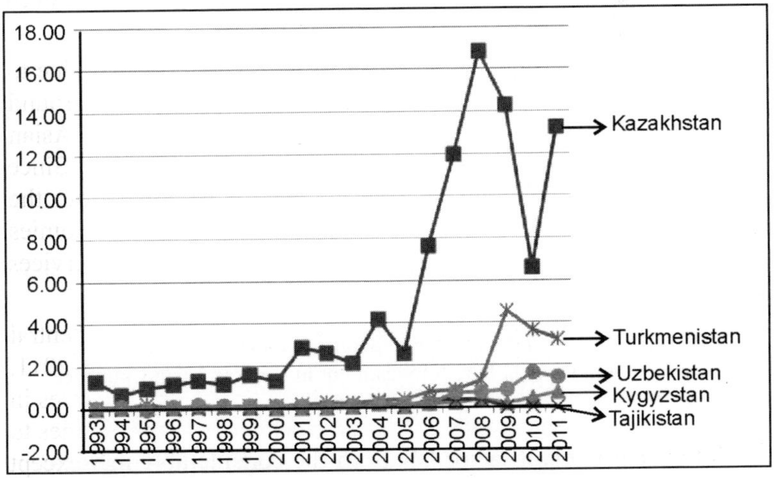

Source: World Bank (2012).

Fig. 11.1: Foreign Direct Investment, net inflows (current billion US$)

FDI flows, albeit at a much lower rate; however, in Tajikistan, there is a decline in the magnitude of FDI inflows. It is likely that the FDI inflows fell after during 2009 and 2010 due to the global financial crisis and recession beginning in September, 2008. However, as there are signs of improvement in the global economy, we see some upward trends in FDI coming into Central Asia toward 2011.

The FDI inflows increased investments in the manufacturing sector. Policy reforms, stabilization of new regimes and FDI inflows also helped in the revival of domestic investment. Thus, manufacturing and the economy as a whole revived gradually. Figure 11.2 demonstrates clearly, at least in the case of Kazakhstan, Kyrgyzstan and Uzbekistan that in the span of last one decade, there has been a concomitant increase in foreign direct investment, domestic investment and manufacturing value added. In Tajikistan, there has been a decline in FDI inflows since 2008, but this has been made up by a sharp rise in the domestic investment.[2]

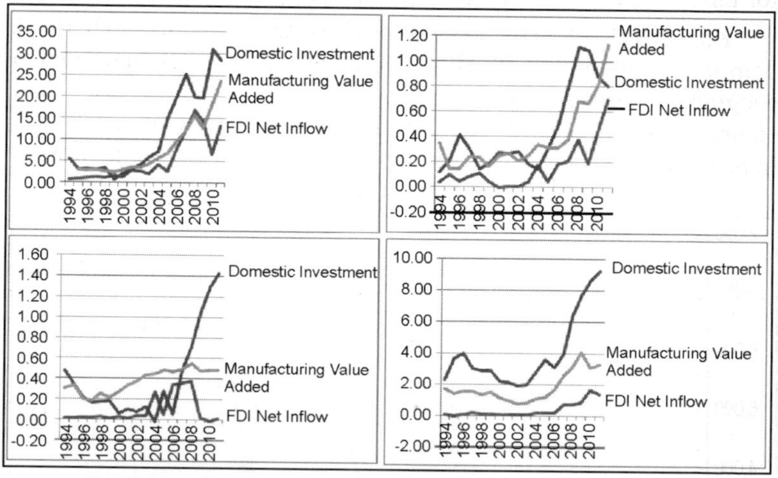

Source: World Bank (2012)

Fig. 11.2: Relation between Manufacturing Value Added, Domestic Investment and Foreign Direct Investment in Central Asian Countries (billions US$)

Another important factor has been the considerable increase in international crude oil and commodity prices. Many countries in this region are richly endowed with commodities such as crude oil, natural gas, minerals and metals. There was an increase in international crude oil prices as well as other commodity prices. In order to capitalize on their natural resources, especially in the context of the high international prices, there was large foreign investment flow into the oil and gas-rich countries of Central Asia, especially into the oil and gas exploration and production sector. The FDI was remarkably higher in the oil and gas sectors due to rising prices as a result of increasing demand for oil and gas from rapidly growing emerging economies like China and India. The large deposits of minerals also created an interest amongst newly industrializing countries like China that required raw materials. This improved income and consumption levels of the people, the fiscal situation improved and investments were made in transport and infrastructure. In this decade, there was considerable political stability in all the countries vis-à-vis the previous decade. Also, the agriculture sector saw an upturn in some cases due to favourable weather conditions and buoyant international commodity prices. This helped in boosting international trade, even for the non-oil exporting countries of the region.

Kazakhstan has had the highest GDP per capita in the region, as demonstrated in Figure 11.3. Kazakhstan also has the largest geographical area as well as a relatively small population. (Table 11.2 compares the population and land area statistics for Central Asia and India). The country is rich in oil, Uranium and also has a strong

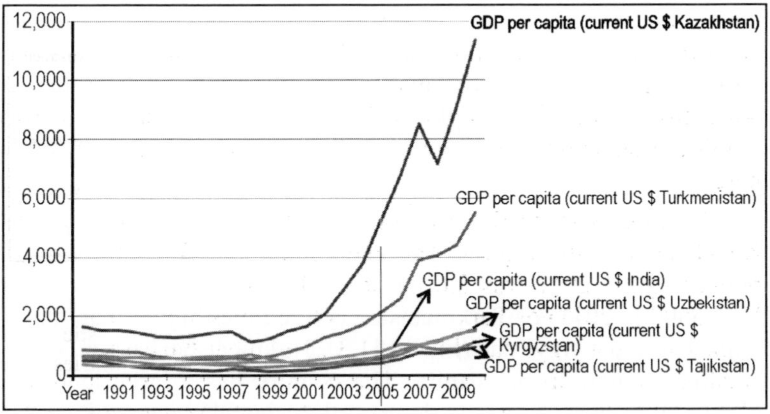

Source: World Bank (2012).

Fig. 11.3: GDP per capita of India and Central Asian Countries (current US$)

Table 11.2: Population and Land Area

Year	*Population (2011)*	*Land Area (sq kms)*	*Population Density (population per sq km)*
Kazakhstan	16,558,676	2,699,700	6.13
Kyrgyzstan	5,514,600	191,800	28.75
Tajikistan	6,976,958	139,960	49.85
Turkmenistan	5,105,301	469,930	10.86
Uzbekistan	29,341,200	425,400	68.97
India	1,241,491,960	2,973,190	417.56

Source: World Bank (2012).

agriculture sector. As observed in Table 11.1, the average annual growth rate of Kazakhstan in the decade of 2001 to 2011 is high at 8.25 per cent. In contrast, Kyrgyzstan is the least developed country of this region. The average growth rate of GDP of Kyrgyzstan between 2001 to 2011 is 4.3 per cent, which is much lower in comparison to range of 7.0–8.6 per cent observed in the other countries of the region.

Tajikistan is the other relatively poor country in this region. Although growth rate has been increasing, the GDP per capita was still the lowest among the five central Asian countries, as shown in Figure 11.3. The average growth rate of Tajikistan moved up from a negative eight percent in the decade of 1991-2000 to a positive 8.6 per cent in the following decade – 2001-2011. This rapid increase is primarily due to a very high growth rate of more than 20 per cent in 2006 and 2007. However, the oil price shock and global recession have affected Tajikistan after that. Tajikistan is the smallest nation in terms of geographical area, and has a relatively higher population. Apart from Uzbekistan, Tajikistan has the highest population density in this region, and the per capita GDP has consistently remained low here.

Turkmenistan is the second most developed economy after Kazakhstan in the region. The average annual GDP growth rate between 2001-2011 was 8.6 per cent. The GDP per capita (about US$ 5500 in 2011) of Turkmenistan is five times higher than that of Tajikistan and Kyrgyzstan (Figure 11.3). Turkmenistan has a relatively smaller population per capita. The country has a large land area (Table 11.2), but it is mostly desert. While the GDP per capita fell in 2008 after the oil price shock, the magnitude of the fall was not as much as in the rest of the region.

Uzbekistan is the most populous country in Central Asia, and also has the most population per square kilometer area (Table 11.2). There has been a steady increase in the GDP growth rate since 1991. In the decade of 1991-2000, Uzbekistan had an average growth rate of negative 0.08 per cent (Table 11.1). Although negative, Uzbekistan had the highest average growth rate among the five central Asian countries. There has been a respectable rise in the average growth rate to seven per cent in the subsequent decade of 2001-2011. The GDP per capita of Uzbekistan, however, is much lower than Kazakhstan or Turkmenistan.

The region's economy is primarily dependent on international exports of primary goods, and the economy is growing following increase in exports and their international prices. The heavy dependence on foreign trade also leads to vulnerability to events like the global financial crisis.

While the higher international prices of oil benefitted Central Asia, they were not very favourable to India, which imported oil in large quantities, leading to problems of increased inflation and slowdown in growth for the Indian economy. The dissolution of USSR and disruption in the economies of member states countries (including Russia), which were a major trading partner of India, also contributed to the trade imbalance. It led to a balance of payments crisis in 1990, and prompted the structural reforms policies at the behest of IMF. Thus, around the same time as the creation of the Central Asian nations, India adopted policies of liberalization that ended industrial licensing, opened many sectors (telecom, banking, infrastructure, etc) to private sector participation, and also opened up the economy to foreign trade and investment. The average growth rate of the Indian economy was around 5.6 per cent in 1990s, and that increased to an average of 7.5 per cent in the decade of 2001-2012. India also has a large geographical area, which is comparable to Kazakhstan, and a large population (about 1.2 billion in 2012) and a huge supply of manpower. The population density of India is six times higher than Uzbekistan, the most populated country in Central Asia, and about 65 times that of Kazakhstan (Table 11.2).This reflects the potential of India as a trading partner in labour intensive commodities, and a market for Central Asia and the world.

India's foreign trade increased dramatically since the liberalization of the economy. The value of India's imports and exports increased by 20 and 16 times, respectively, from 1992 to 2011. India's primary exports are processed fuels, jewelry, organic chemicals, electrical machinery and equipment, vehicles etc. and the primary imports are mineral fuels, gold, machinery and parts of machinery, electric machinery, organic chemicals etc.

II. Merchandise Trade between Central Asia and India

Over the last decade or so, the exports and imports of Central Asia have steadily increased for most parts. In Kazakhstan, one sees a rapid increase in exports between 2003 and 2008, followed by a decline in 2009 and 2010 (see Table 11.3). The likely cause for this phenomenon is decline in crude oil prices in 2009 and the recession in Europe and the USA. Similarly, in the other four countries – Kyrgyzstan, Tajikistan, Turkmenistan and Uzbekistan – there has been an increase in exports till 2008, and subsequently, a decline. The total imports, in contrast, have increased more or less steadily over time, including after 2008 for Central Asia, as can be seen in Table 11.4. The only exception in this case is Kazakhstan, where imports rise consistently till 2008, and fall thereafter. In 2008, the imports by Kazakhstan were at their peak at USD 37.80 billion, and this declined to a little over half by 2011.

Table 11.3: Total Exports of Central Asian Countries and India (billion US $)

Year	*Kazakhstan*	*Kyrgyzstan*	*Tajikistan*	*Turkmenistan*	*Uzbekistan*	*India*
2000	9.88	0.50	0.77	2.51	2.18	42.63
2001	9.09	0.48	0.65	2.56	2.09	43.32
2002	9.67	0.49	0.74	2.82	1.55	50.52
2003	12.93	0.58	0.80	3.45	2.02	61.13
2004	19.94	0.71	0.91	3.53	2.74	75.39
2005	27.69	0.63	0.91	4.95	3.61	98.21
2006	38.01	0.80	1.40	5.64	5.25	120.55
2007	46.98	1.13	1.47	6.30	6.29	153.78
2008	71.17	1.62	1.44	10.14	7.48	177.70
2009	43.19	0.90	1.01	3.08	4.77	165.19
2010	57.24	1.05	1.19	3.23	5.55	222.93
2011	80.19	1.14	1.00	7.59	5.59	307.11

Source: International Monetary Fund (2013).

Of the five central Asian countries, India has had most trade with Kazakhstan, which is also the largest economy in Central Asia.

Table 11.4: Total Imports of Central Asian Countries and India (billion US $)

Year	*Kazakhstan*	*Kyrgyzstan*	*Tajikistan*	*Turkmenistan*	*Uzbekistan*	*India*
2000	5.05	0.55	0.67	1.79	2.07	50.34
2001	6.48	0.47	0.69	2.21	2.29	50.14
2002	6.58	0.59	0.72	2.13	2.08	58.91
2003	8.41	0.72	0.88	2.51	2.48	74.08
2004	12.64	0.94	1.19	2.68	3.16	99.84
2005	17.47	1.11	1.33	2.61	3.57	139.89
2006	23.70	1.71	1.73	2.53	4.48	176.67
2007	32.60	2.42	2.54	3.36	7.02	235.03
2008	37.80	4.07	3.25	5.46	10.11	281.47
2009	28.36	8.22	2.51	6.54	9.04	257.67
2010	24.02	7.23	2.66	5.64	9.26	350.78
2011	21.42	9.08	4.77	7.68	10.75	465.13

Source: International Monetary Fund (2013).

Kazakhstan's exports to India rose sharply after 2005, as can be observed in Figure 11.4. In 2011-12, the total exports of Kazakhstan to India stood at USD 166 million. Uzbekistan is a distant second, at a little over USD 60 million. The other nations of Central Asia have exported commodities valued at less than USD 20 million for most

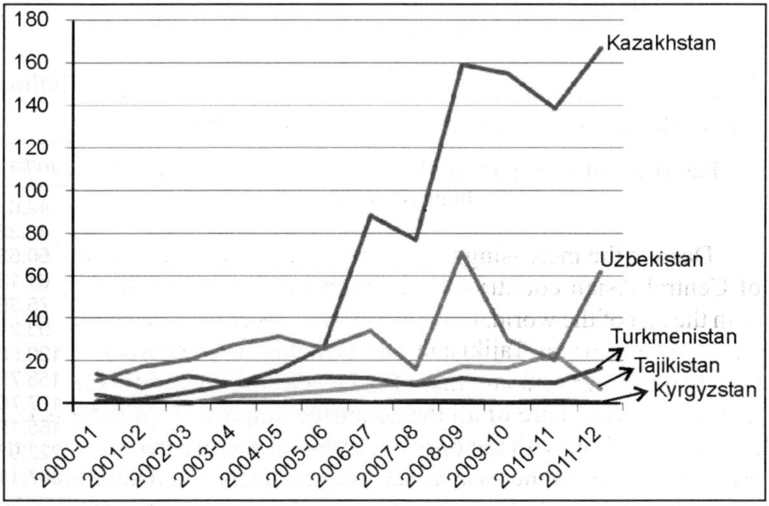

Source: Ministry of Commerce, Government of India (2013).

Fig. 11.4: India's Imports from Central Asian Countries/Central Asia's Exports to India (Million US$)

parts of the last decade (Figure 11.4). The value of Kazakhstan's imports from India has been consistently increasing from USD 50 million in 2000-01 to about USD 250 million in 2011-12, as can be seen from Figure 11.5. The imports of Uzbekistan have also been increasing, but the rise is not as sharp as that of Kazakhstan. The rest of the Central Asian countries have not observed much of an increase, but in general, imports of Central Asia from India are higher than the corresponding exports (Figure 11.5).

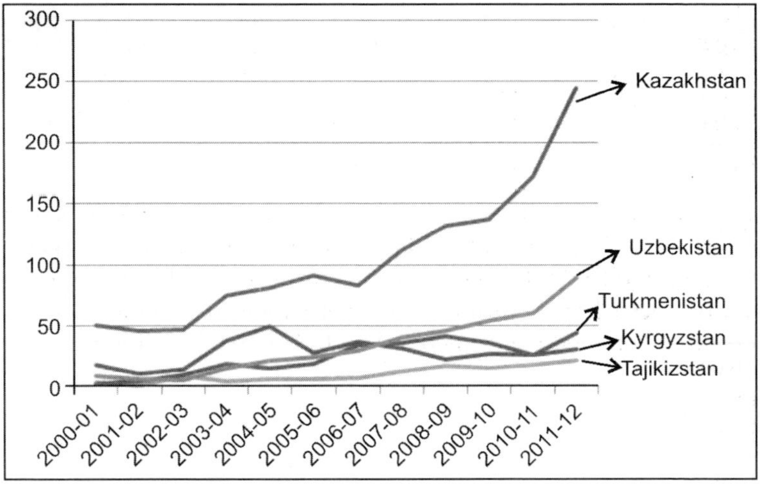

Source: Ministry of Commerce, Government of India (2013).

Fig. 11.5: India's Exports to Central Asia/Central Asia's imports from India (million US$)

Despite the increasing trade levels over the last decade, the share of Central Asian countries' trade with India, relative to their trade with the rest of the world, remains very low, as can be seen in Figures 6 and 7. The share of Tajikistan and Uzbekistan's exports to India is less than two per cent and that of the rest of the countries is less than .5 per cent. The share of all the countries' imports from India is less than 1.5 per cent, with the only exception of Kyrgyzstan in 2003 and 2004. However, in the case of Kazakhstan, there is a declining trend of total exports with the rest of the world, but an increasing amount of bilateral exports to India. This is a good sign of increasing importance of Kazakhstan trade with India. We should work towards

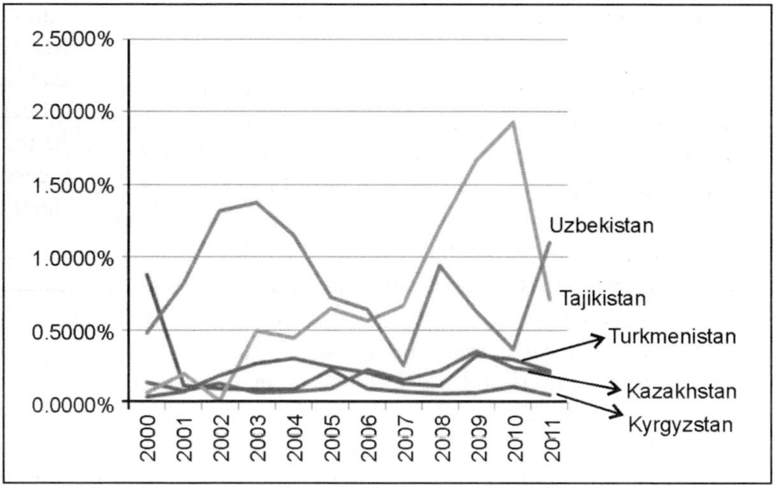

Source: Author's Calculations based on data from Ministry of Commerce, Government of India (2013).

Fig. 11.6: Share of Central Asia's Exports Going to India

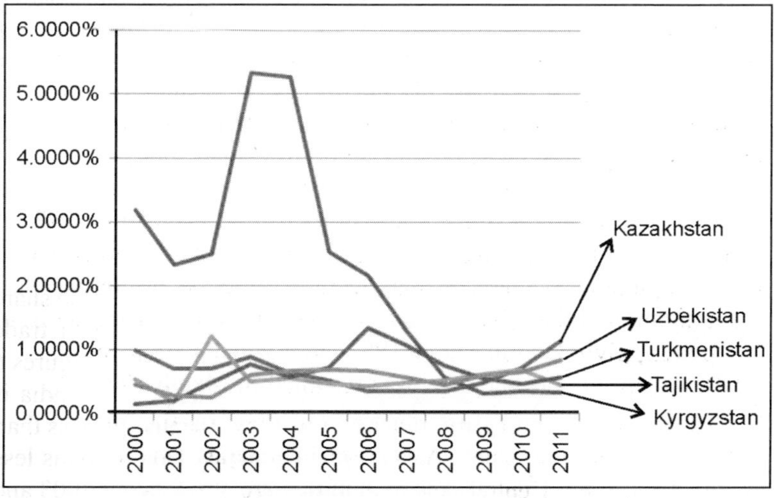

Source: Author's Calculations based on data from Ministry of Commerce, Government of India (2013).

Fig. 11.7: Share of Central Asia's Imports Coming from India (billion US Dollars)

a similar improvement in bilateral trade between India and the rest of Central Asia.

The popular exports of Central Asian countries to India are precious and semiprecious stones and jewelry (mostly unwrought and semi-processed silver), salt, sulphur, earths and stone. The other commodities that are purchased by India are in the category of chemicals; iron and steel; machineries; mineral oils; copper goods; plastic goods; wool and leather (Table 11.5). The main commodities that are imported by Central Asia from India include coffee, tea and spices; pharmaceutical products; electrical machinery and equipment as well as mechanical machinery (see Table 11.6). Apparel and clothing, both knitted and not knitted, is an important commodity that flows from India to almost every country in Central Asia. Processed meat products are another commodity category that is imported from India by almost all Central Asian nations. Other commodities that are imported include vehicles, ceramic products and mineral oils.

The trends in values of exports of Central Asia are heavily driven by prices of commodities in the international market. The export performance of Kazakhstan was driven by favourable energy prices (see Pomfret (2005)). In case of Uzbekistan, the world cotton prices were increasing till 1996 and dropped since then, and this correlates with the value of exports from the country. Pomfret also mentions the following regarding Turkmenistan – "Turkmenistan's exports are dominated by energy products, and the 1995–1996 values are inflated by over-reporting of natural gas exports to CIS destinations which were not paid for (the invoice value was recorded as exports, while the accumulating payment arrears were recorded as foreign assets); recognizing that the bills would never be paid in full, Turkmenistan stopped supplying gas in March 1997, after which export values (and GDP) collapsed until the flow was resumed in March 1999."

India is an emerging market country in the process of industrialization, and Central Asia is rich in minerals and raw materials. At the same time, Central Asian countries are small economies and they depend on foreign trade for fulfilling their needs. This situation leads to a huge potential in trade between India and Central Asia.

On the whole, exports from India to Central Asian countries are rather low in magnitude. This, however, is an opportunity for India

Table 11.5: Central Asia's Major Exports to India (million US$)

HS Code	*Commodity*	*Kazakhstan*	*Kyrgyzstan*	*Tajikistan*	*Turkmenistan*	*Uzbekistan*
	Total	**166.35**	**0.67**	**7.09**	**16.89**	**61.58**
71	Pearls, Stones, Jewelry	48.48				29.62
28	Chemicals, Precious Metals, Rare-Earth Metals.	11.22	0.29		11.11	
72	Iron And Steel	5.31	0.08			0.11
84	Machinery And Mechanical Appliances	1.95	0.03	0.15	0.07	1.87
27	Mineral Oils, Etc	1.08		0.12		3.45
74	Copper Goods	0.75				0.7
39	Plastic Goods	0.5	0.09		0.04	0.48
85	Electrical Machinery And Equipment	0.36		0	0.01	0.38
51	Wool And Woven Fabric.	0.21	0.04	0	0.68	
41	Raw Hides And Leather	0.16	0.09		0.11	0.44

Source: Ministry of Commerce, Government of India (2013).

Table 11.6: Central Asia's Major Imports from India (Million US Dollars)

HS Code	*Commodity*	*Kazakhstan*	*Kyrgyzstan*	*Tajikistan*	*Turkmenistan*	*Uzbekistan*
	Total	**244.39**	**30.55**	**21.28**	**43.95**	**61.58**
9	Coffee, Tea And Spices.	54.50	1.75	0.37		
30	Pharmaceutical Products	43.81	5.65	8.14	11.35	
85	Electrical Machinery And Equipment	39.44	1.80	0.14	4.10	0.38
61	Apparel (Knitted)	34.83	9.42	3.54	0.05	0.01
62	Apparel (Not Knitted)	19.05	6.29	0.33	3.45	
84	Machinery And Mechanical Appliances	7.24	0.13	1.40	13.08	1.87
87	Vehicles	6.95			0.05	
69	Ceramic Products.	3.88			0.28	0.01
27	Mineral Oils, Etc	1.94			2.34	3.45
2	Meat	1.02	1.59	4.67	2.74	

Source: Ministry of Commerce, Government of India (2013).

to develop its trade relations and increase exports to the region. The Pharmaceutical exports seem to dominate the scene when it comes to major products that flow from India to Central Asia. Since a market for Indian medicines and vaccines has been established, this market can be deepened further. Another product of India that appears to be popular in the Central Asian markets is frozen and processed meat. Manufacturing of vehicles and their parts is emerging as a significant sector in India. However, Uzbekistan is the only country that imports vehicles or their parts. This signals that there is a huge potential for expanding India's exports in the automobile sector to the other four nations of Central Asia. India's major imports from Central Asia are various metals, minerals and other raw materials. Some examples are Gold, Silver, Lead, Zinc, Mercury and Aluminum. These imports are essential to sustain the Indian manufacturing sector. There are also some imports of machineries and agricultural goods; however, there is scope to expand this trade.

Textiles could be a tremendous opportunity for India as well as the Central Asian countries. India imports fabrics of various kinds from Central Asia, such as raw cotton fiber, wool of different kinds, raw silk, etc. India also imports machinery for textile processing, like machines for spinning and knitting. In turn, India exports finished goods such as T shirts, blouses, baby's garments etc. made of cotton, dresses made of synthetic fiber, etc. Central Asia is a major producer of cotton from the Soviet era. Processing the raw cotton and other fibers into fabric and clothes is, relatively, a labour intensive industry and is suitable for the demographic structure of India. Hence, there is a huge potential in strengthening this industry for mutual benefit from both perspectives.

III. Services Trade of Central Asia and India

There has been a dramatic increase in trade of services, both in the Central Asian region as well as in India. Table 11.7 and 11.8 demonstrate the increase in the total exports and imports of services of the Central Asian countries and India. In India, the export of services to the rest of the world has increased by over six times in the course of the decade of 2000-2010. The service sector dominates in India with more than 51 per cent value added as a percentage of GDP. As can be seen in Figure 8, this was mainly due to huge increases in exports of services in the computer and software sector.

Table 11.7: Total Services Exports of Central Asia and India to the World (Billion US Dollars)

Year	*India*	*Kazakhstan*	*Kyrgyzstan*	*Tajikistan*	*Uzbekistan*
2000	16.27	1.05	0.06	0.06	0.45
2001	14.99	1.26	0.08	0.06	0.46
2002	16.78	1.54	0.14	0.07	0.48
2003	21.67	1.71	0.15	0.09	0.54
2004	30.13	2.01	0.21	0.12	0.57
2005	39.76	2.23	0.26	0.15	0.66
2006	52.19	2.82	0.37	0.13	0.77
2007	86.93	3.56	0.68	0.15	0.96
2008	107.23	4.43	1.00	0.18	1.20
2009	93.04	4.24	0.86	0.14	1.04
2010	124.31	4.25	0.69		1.19
2011		4.51			

Source: United Nations (2012).

Table 11.8: Total Services Imports of Central Asia and India from the World (Billion US Dollars)

Year	*India*	*Kyrgyzstan*	*Tajikistan*	*Uzbekistan*	*Kazakhstan*
2000	14.58	0.15	0.06	0.25	1.85
2001	14.48	0.12	0.07	0.32	2.63
2002	15.04	0.15	0.10	0.29	3.54
2003	17.42	0.15	0.12	0.30	3.75
2004	25.20	0.22	0.21	0.42	5.11
2005	32.55	0.30	0.25	0.43	7.50
2006	40.39	0.46	0.24	0.40	8.76
2007	47.78	0.60	0.59	0.39	11.73
2008	56.17	1.01	0.46	0.43	11.12
2009	53.73	0.87	0.29	0.42	10.04
2010	82.69	0.92		0.41	11.33
2011		1.14			10.92

Source: United Nations (2012).

The services sector has expanded in the Central Asian nations as well. As suggested by Dowling and Wignaraja (2006a), it is likely that the oil and gas sector-led growth has led to the development of the services sector. In order to exploit opportunities that emerged out of the increase in oil prices, there is a need to generate a huge ancillary services sector like construction, finance etc. Turkmenistan and Uzbekistan have a relatively smaller service sector in terms of value added as a percentage of GDP, but the service sector dominates in

Kazakhstan and is fairly high in Tajikistan and Kyrgyzstan. Yet, the demand for services is so high that there are high and continuously increasing imports of services in these countries, as is seen from Table 11.8. Table 11.7 shows that the exports of services are also increasing in these countries. With the exception of Uzbekistan, the imports of services are much higher than the exports of services in Central Asia. In case of Kazakhstan, the imports are more than two to three times as much as their exports in services. Tajikistan also has a substantially higher imports of services compared to exports.

We assess the potential for trade in services between India and Kazakhstan in Figure 11.8. We look at the case of Kazakhstan's imports in services in greater depth, and find that the largest component of services is other business services. This category

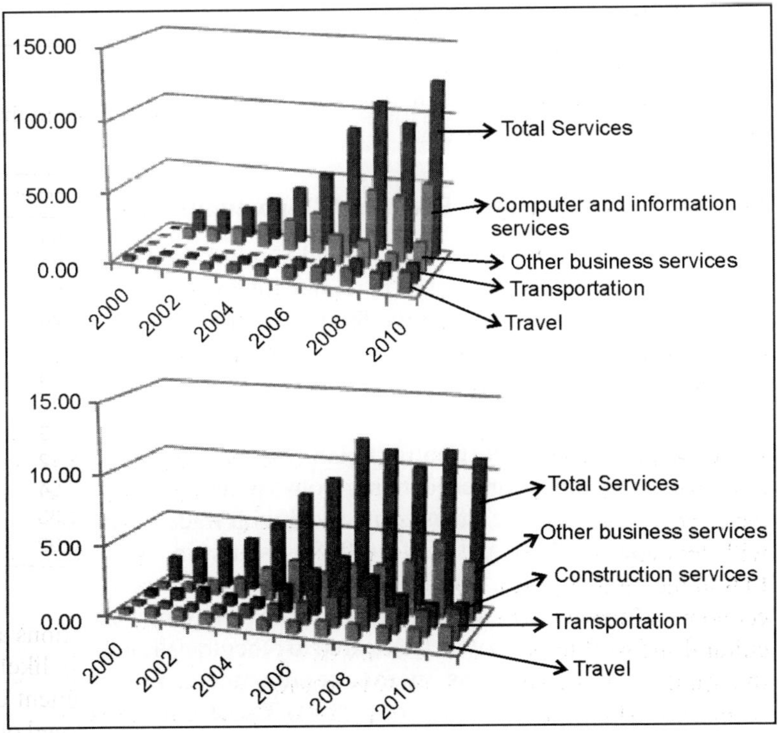

Source: United Nations (2012).

Fig. 11.8: India's Exports (left)and Kazakhstan's Imports (right) of Services to the World

includes merchant and trade related services; professional and technical services; legal accounting, management consulting and public relations; market research; research and development; architectural, engineering and other technical services; agriculture and mining processing services; etc. At a time when the oil and natural gas industry has been expanding, there has been a huge inflow of foreign investment in these industries, and consequently, demand for engineering and technical services on a large scale. Also, all the associated services with respect to foreign trade were demanded. One can also observe from the figure that there was a rise in import of construction services till 2007, which declined thereafter. Transport and tourism are also major service exports of India and service imports of Kazakhstan. Transport is a key aspect of foreign trade, and would rise with increase in trading and other business activities. However, Kazakhstan is not a large importer of computer and other software services. As the process of modernization of trade and services sectors in general takes place, there is an increasing need for the software sector – and this may well be a major opportunity for trade in services between India and Kazakhstan.

IV. Concluding Remarks: Risks and Opportunities for India

As seen above, trade between India and Central Asia is relatively small. However, there is a huge potential for increasing trade, and this provides a large opportunity for gains from trade for all the countries involved. In this section, we conclude with some thoughts regarding the risks and opportunities involved for India with this proposition.

Given the fact that the Central Asian countries are in the process of transitioning into a market economy from a planned economy, there tends be a higher degree of risks involved with trade or investment with this region. Clark and Naito (1998) discuss, in the context of FDI in the mining sector, that the major risks involved were political, economic, financial, infrastructural, contractual, environmental, socio-cultural and workforce related. Compared to other transition countries, the quality of institutions in this region needs improvement (Melnykovska and Schweickert (2009)).These countries lack a comprehensive legal framework that honours contracts, provides rule of law, ensures creditworthiness, etc. that is essential for foreign business initiatives. A more efficient infrastructure would be helpful for international trade. Clark and Naito (1998) and Hiro (2010) point out the need for higher levels of governance to control corruption. Some of these issues pose a problem in India, too. There is a need to improve transparency in the system to create an enabling environment for foreign trade and investment. This situation presents an opportunity for Central Asian countries and India to work collaboratively in finding efficient governance techniques that can create an efficient system that is conducive to international trade.

The economic ties between countries are, fortunately or unfortunately, deeply tied to political environment. This is more of a burden in the case of land locked countries attempting to participate in foreign trade. The most ideal route of trade would be via Afghanistan and Pakistan in terms of geography. However, this is not a politically feasible solution. There is anarchy and rampant terrorist activities in Afghanistan and Pakistan. The relationship between India and Pakistan continues to be volatile. In this scenario, it is a risky proposition to invest heavily in developing international trade infrastructure such as roadways or oil pipelines. So the alternative trade route is through Iran or China, and Iran is relatively shorter in terms of distance. Nevertheless, there is always a certain degree of risk of hold up of trade due to instability in international relations between these nations and Central Asian Nations or India.

However, there are two main solutions to this problem. One is a focus on foreign investment in each other's nation's, and the other is a focus on trade in services. In both these cases, there is no need for physical transportation of commodities. Creating a strong and secure internet connection would facilitate funds transfers as well as business process outsourcing activities. India is progressing as a country that is specializing in trade in services, while the Central Asian countries are rich in agriculture and natural resources. As an emerging market economy, India's need for agriculture and natural resources is growing, and as a newly industrializing region, Central Asia has a need for high technology services. This creates a huge potential for bilateral trade among these countries in future.

While Kazakhstan has already made substantial economic progress, the other Central Asian countries are on a growth trajectory. These economies currently depend heavily on agriculture and natural resources as a means for economic sustenance. While currently India may not be a major importer of goods from Central Asia, India's demand for natural resources such as oil and gas, Uranium and other mineral ores is increasing. There is also a huge potential for imports of agricultural commodities.

Health care is a core necessity for the welfare of citizens, and as the Central Asian economies develop, there is an expansion in the demand for better and affordable health care. One of the components of health care is pharmaceutical products, and India has the capability to supply low-cost medicines to the Central Asian countries. While this fact is being exploited already, there is a scope for strengthening trade in this sector. Another sector that can be expanded with bilateral cooperation is the textile industry, wherein Central Asia has lot to offer in terms of raw materials like cotton, while India has the capability to produce finished goods in the form of garments.

However, some import of machineries and equipment demonstrates an attempt to switch to mechanization and industrialization in these economies. The process would also require development of core infrastructure and transportation services. Given the nature of high technology involved in the process of developing manufacturing industry or infrastructure services, India is well placed to provide software and other technical support for these activities.

As can be observed in the data, Central Asian countries faced a huge dip in the value of international trade, particularly exports, in 2009 and for some time after that. This is a reflection of two factors. One is a crash in the price of oil in the global economy. Since oil is a major export of this region, the value of exports of oil fell in 2009. This calls for a need to assess the prospects for the future. It is likely that the oil-dependent economies will not be affected too much, since the demand for oil in the global market is likely to be strong. However, one cause for concern is that the primary market of the Central Asian region is Russia and European Union. The European Union has been facing an economic downturn since 2008, and the signs of recovery continue to be weak at best. It is, therefore, essential for emerging Central Asian countries to seriously consider diversifying their export market and develop trade relationship with other emerging market economies in order to mitigate the risk of economic collapse of the main trading partners. Strengthening the trade ties between India and Central Asia would help all the nations involved in diversifying their international trade market and thereby would benefit the economies of all the nations.

Acknowledgment: We will like to thank Piyush Mahajan for research assistance during the preparation of this study.

Notes

1. Hiro (2010), p. 139.
2. Turkmenistan is excluded in this analysis due to lack of adequate data on manufacturing value added.

References

1. Agrawal, Pradeep (2008), "Economic Growth and Poverty: Evidence from Kazakhstan," *Asian Development Review,* vol. 24, no. 2, pp. 90-115.
2. Arazmuradov, Annageldy (2012), "Foreign aid, foreign direct investment and domestic investment nexus in landlocked economies of Central Asia", *MPRA Paper No. 36881*, Online at http://mpra.ub.uni-muenchen.de/36881/
3. Asian Development Bank (ADB) (2006), *Central Asia: Increasing Gains from Trade through Regional Cooperation in Trade Policy, Transport, and Customs Transit*, Philippines: Asian Development Bank Publication Stock No. 030106
4. Clark, Allen L. and Naito, Koh (1998), "Risks and opportunities for foreign investment in the mineral sectors of the Central Asian Republics – Kazakhstan, Kyrgyzstan, Tajikistan and Uzbekistan, *Resources Policy.* Vol. 24, No. 2, pp. 105-114.
5. Dowling, Malcolm and Wignaraja, Ganeshan (2006a), "Central Asia: Mapping Future Prospects" Singapore management university economics and statistics working paper series – Paper No. 05-2006
6. Dowling, Malcolm and Wignaraja, Ganeshan (2006b), "Central Asia after Fifteen Years of Transition: Growth, Regional Cooperation, and Policy Choices" ADB Working Paper Series on Regional Economic Integration No. 3.
7. Hiro, Dilip (2010), *Inside Central Asia*, Noida: Harper Collins.
8. International Monetary Fund (2013), *Direction of Trade Statistics*, CD Rom, Edition: Feb 2013, Washington DC: International Monetary Fund.
9. Melnykovska, Inna and Schweickert, Rainer (2009), "Analyzing Bottlenecks for Institutional Development in Central Asia – Is it Oil, Aid, or Geography?" Private University of Applied Sciences Working Paper.No. 2009/02
10. Ministry of Commerce, Government of India (2013), *EXPORT IMPORT DATA BANK Version 6.0 – TRADESTAT.* Available at http://commerce.nic.in/eidb/Default.asp
11. Mogilevskii, Roman (2012), "Trends and Patterns in Foreign Trade of Central Asian Countries", University of Central Asia, Institute of Public Policy and Administration – Working Paper No. 1, 2012.

12. Pomfret, Richard (2005), "Trade policies in Central Asia after EU enlargement and before Russian WTO accession: Regionalism and integration in to the world economy" *Economic Systems,* 29 (2005) pp. 32-58.
13. Rakhimov, Mirzokhid (2010), "Internal and external dynamics of regional cooperation in Central Asia", *Journal of Eurasian Studies,* 1 (2010) pp. 95-101.
14. United Nations (2012), *United Nations Service Trade Statistics Database*, United Nations Statistics Division. Available at: https://unstats.un.org/unsd/servicetrade/default.aspx
15. World Bank (2012), *World Development Indicators 2012*, Washington, DC:World Bank. Available at: http://data.worldbank.org/data-catalog/world-development-indicators

12
India-Central Asia: Connectivity Issues

R.S. Yadav

The end of the Cold War and the consequent geo-political and geo-economic alignments and transformation has not only changed the very nature of international politics, but also led to re-orientation of foreign policies of the states as well. India and Central Asia are no exception to this phenomenon. It is because of convergence of interests in areas like the creation of a multi-polar world order; development of secular ethos that is against fundamentalism; retention of the plural social fabric; fight against non-traditional threats like terrorism, drug trafficking, smuggling of small arms, etc. on one hand and the emergence of economic compatibility amongst the two regions (of India and Central Asia) in the form of extraction and processing of important minerals; development of infrastructure; establishment of joint ventures; exploration of natural oil and gas, etc. and featuring in each others' foreign policy orientation. India's foreign policy initiatives in the form of 'Extended Neighbourhood' and 'Connect Central Asia' are manifestations of such change.

Simultaneously, since their inception, the Central Asian states have been keen to develop friendly relations with India, both at the bilateral and multilateral level. It is also true that during this time, Central Asia has also attracted attention of outside powers due its vast-resources of oil and gas reserves. The three states – Kazakhstan, Turkmenistan and Uzbekistan – possess some of the world's largest oil and natural gas fields. These states "are known to possess about 300 trillion cubic feet of gas and 90-200 billion barrels of oil (about same size as that of Saudi Arabia).[1] The Caspian Sea region is perceived as the region with the third largest reservoir of oil deposits after the Persian Gulf and Siberia. Kazakhstan is also described as being on the way of becoming another Kuwait. Besides, Kazakhstan also possesses a quarter of the world's known uranium reserves, while Uzbekistan holds the largest gold mines on Earth, with the capacity of mining 50 tonnes of ore a year. It is also the fourth largest cotton producing country in the world. Tajikistan, apart from holding the world's largest deposits of silver, possesses enormous gold and aluminium deposits. Turkmenistan is also the world's fourth largest producer of natural gas.[2] Moreover, the politics of oil in Caspian Sea after the Soviet disintegration has further enhanced the importance of this region in the eyes of the outside world.[3]

In this scenario, how can India acquire an important role for itself in Central Asian states is a moot question. To translate this into reality, there is an urgent need for India to develop connectivity with landlocked Central Asia. This chapter is a modest attempt to examine existing and alternative rail/road/gas and oil pipeline links connecting India and Central Asia, so as to explore prospects of bilateral and multilateral collaboration between these two regions. For convenience, this chapter has been divided into four parts. In the first part, inter-regional and intra-regional connectivity between India and Central Asia are presented, along with their limitations. In the second part, one alternative route and its future prospect has been suggested. In the third part, policy options for India and Central Asia have been presented, and in the end, a brief summing up has been attempted.

I

Before an evaluation of India-Central Asia linkages can be made, it must be made clear that old paradigms of like the 'Great Game' and the 'Silk Route' do not represent contemporary realities. In the 19th Century, 'Great Game' British and Russian foreign policies were designed to checkmate each others' moves in the Middle East and Central Asia. Today, there are new entrants and new contexts more than just the historical ones. Besides, in the bygone era, the role of indigenous states was negligible, whereas in contemporary times, these states are no longer just marginal players but are important actors in this region. Similarly, in the past, the 'Silk Route' represented a link between the states in the East with the Europe. It meant multiple routes connecting each other, starting from Hang Zhou and Guangzhou and ultimately reaching Constantinople. Though multiple products from different countries were exported along this route, the most important was nevertheless silk . As a result, this route came to be popularly known as the 'Silk Route'. But the present scenario is entirely different, especially with the discovery of natural gas and oil in Central Asia. Besides, while an earlier era, the trading routes were just a link between the East and the West in terms of a socio-economic and cultural sense and were devoid of power politics, whereas today, though the commercial links continue, political consideration amongst the states also influences the outcome or success of these routes.

The issue of India-Central Asia linkages can be addressed in terms of connectivity between them, both at the (a) Inter-regional and (b) Intra-regional level. A detailed analysis of the two is given below for a clearer picture.

(A) Inter-regional Connectivity

Three important rail/road/pipeline routes to link Central Asia and India – with broader links between Europe and Asia- are being explored. These routes are:

1. *International North-South Transport Corridor (INSTC)* – This Russian initiative linking Mumbai with St. Petersburg via Tehran and Moscow was signed in September 2000 by India-Iran and Russia. Later on 11 other countries- including all the states of Central Asia- joined the initiative, making it an ambitious project supported by 14 stake holders. The project envisages a multi-modal transport network that connects ports in India's West coast to Bandar Abbas in Iran by sea, then overland by road and rail networks to Bandar Anzali Caspian Sea port and thence through Rasht and Astara on Azerbaijan borders to Kazakhstan and further – towards Russia. A long road and rail stretch will run to St. Petersburg, the Russian port on the Baltic Sea, though Volvograd and Moscow.

Once completed, this initiative is expected to reduce transit time and costs of transportation of cargo significantly. Compared with the 16,129-kilometre route through the Suez Canal and Mediterranean Sea that is currently used, the North-South Corridor is just 6,245-kilometre long. It is going to reduce the time span by at least 15-20 days, and transport costs by about 30 per cent.

This corridor is much more than a link between three the countries of Russia, Iran and India. Through this route, if, on one hand, the Russian network of road and rail is connected to the entire Europe, then Iran's land links to Central Asia can be leveraged by India for commercial purposes.

2. *Turkmenistan-Afghanistan-Pakistan-India (TAPI) pipeline* – On 11 December 2011, Turkmenistan, Afghanistan, Pakistan and India signed a framework agreement to build the **TAPI** gas pipeline connecting the four states. In May 2012, the four states signed the gas sales and purchase agreement on the sidelines of the International Gas Conference held at the Caspian Sea Resort of Avaza (Turkmenistan). Three important companies – Turkmen gas (Turkmenistan), GAIL (India), ISGS (Pakistan) – signed this agreement. Work on this project is likely to start in 2015, and it is expected to become operational in 2018.[4] The 1,680-kilometres long pipeline is to be built at an estimated cost of US$ 7.6 billion, and also enjoys US support. The pipeline will begin from the Daulatabad (South Yalotan) gas field in Turkmenistan and will cover an area of 145-kilometres in Turkmenistan, 935-kilometres in Afghanistan and 800-kilometres in Pakistan. Turkmenistan, currently producing nearly 70 billion cubic meter (bcm) of gas per annum, is likely to enhance its production to 230 billion cubic meter (bcm) of gas by 2030. Out of the total production, at least 30 bcm of gas it is likely to be exported through the TAPI pipeline. After completion, this pipeline will have the capacity to transport nearly 90 million standard meters gas a day (mscmd), of which India and Pakistan would receive 38 mscmd gas each, while Afghanistan will receive the remaining 14 mscmd gas.[5]

3. *Iran–Pakistan–India (IPI) gas pipeline* – On 15 February 2002, construction of the 2,700- kilometres gas pipeline linking Iran's South Pars field in the Persian Gulf to Pakistan's major cities of Karachi and Multan – and further to New Delhi – was announced. The total length of this pipeline would run 1,100-kilometres in Iran, 1,000-kilometres in Pakistan and 600-kilometres in India, and will be completed with an estimated cost of US$ 700 billion. This project, if on time, is likely to be completed by December, 2015. Through this pipeline, an estimated 110 million cubic meter gas a day is envisaged to be supplied, starting initially with 30 million cubic meters.

It is thought that this pipeline will benefit all the three member countries. Iran is the main supplier, and supplies will be uninterrupted since it has 17 per cent of proven gas reserves in the world. Due to itslarge stake in exporting gas, Iran has also agreed to bear 60 per cent cost of construction of the pipeline. Similarly, Pakistan's two important cities of Karachi and Multan will be directly linked with gas supplies and will earn approximately US$ 200 to 500 million annually as transit fees from the pipeline. Finally, India will have access to 20 per cent cheaper supply of gas from this pipeline, and thus save around US$ 2 billion. Therefore, it is assumed that since the pipeline will benefit all the stake holders, there is a better likelihood of its completion despite the India-Pakistan imbroglio.

Out of these inter-regional linkages, the most important and viable is the INSTC. This corridor is not only an important link between India and Central Asia, it also is helpful in facilitating cooperation between India, Russia and the European Union. India visualizes the North-South corridor as "re-energizing an alternative route to Central Asia", which makes transportation costs 40 per cent cheaper and faster.[6] But the situation is not so rosy with other two initiatives of India, i.e., TAPI and IPI.

Due to the volatile nature of Afghanistan's political environment and the historical rivalry between India and Pakistan, the possibility of operationalizing these routes has become very difficult. This is why it has been rightly observed that "given the geopolitical complexities, security concerns in Afghanistan and Pakistan and issues related to finding a lead investor, the TAPI project could take some more time to become a reality……"[7]. Similar observations are true about IPI.

(b) Intra-Regional Connectivity

Before Central Asia emerged as an independent entity after the collapse of the erstwhile Soviet Union, all its transport and oil/gas pipeline infrastructure was directed towards Russia. Central Asia was not only land-locked, it was completely isolated even from its immediate neighbours outside the former Soviet space during that era.[8] Thus, the region as a whole had transport routes which were either Iran-centric or China-centric, besides the old Soviet routes.[9] Hence, all rail/road/pipelines are today oriented either towards China or Iran, but these can also serve as starting points from where they can easily be by linked to India.

1. *Turkmenistan–Uzbekistan–Kazakhstan–China gas pipeline* – Initially, construction of this pipeline began with the Kazakhstan-China gas pipeline – along with the oil pipeline- in June 2003. On 30 April 2006, China and Turkmenistan signed a framework agreement

on pipeline construction. On 30 April 2007, Uzbekistan and China signed a long-term gas supply agreement on the construction and use of pipeline's Uzbekistan section. In July 2007, it was formally announced that Turkmenistan would also join the original Kazakhstan-China pipeline project. Finally, on 14 December 2009, the Heads of States of four countries (Turkmenistan, Uzbekistan, Kazakhstan and China) inaugurated the 1,833-kilometre pipeline (188-kilometre in Turkmenistan, 530-kilometre in Uzbekistan and 1,115kilometre in Kazakhstan), connecting all of them. It was constructed with an estimated cost of US$ 7.3 billion, and is likely to transport 40 billion cubic meters of gas annually when it reaches capacity.[10]

This pipeline starts at Saman-Depe, carrying natural gas from the Bagtyyarlyu gas fields in Turkmenistan. It enters Uzbekistan at Olot, and runs across the country to Southern Kazakhstan, parallel to the existing Bukhara-Tashkent-Bishkek-Almaty pipeline. It then crosses the Kazakhstan-China border at Khorgos, where it connects with the second West-East-Gas pipeline. The pipeline is thus an example of important intra-regional cooperation amongst the three states of Central Asia in finding an alternative market in China.

2. *The Bukhara-Tashkent-Bishkek-Almaty gas pipeline* – This gas pipeline carries Uzbekistani gas to Kyrgyzstan and Kazakhstan. It was constructed during the Soviet era and commissioned in 1971. It is a West-East pipeline which links Bukhara to Almaty, passing through Tashkent, Shymkent, Taraz and Bishkek. This pipeline is the main source of gas supply to Northern Kyrgyzstan and Southern parts of Kazakhstan. It is possible that in the future, the pipeline may also connect with the Central Asia – China gas pipeline.

3. *The Mubarek (Uzbekistan)-Kelif (Turkmenistan)-Dushanbe (Tajikistan) gas pipeline; and the Mubarek-Shurabad-Dushanbe gas pipeline* – These are Soviet-era gas pipelines. The first runs along the Mubarek (Uzbekistan)-Kelif (Turkmenistan)-Dushanbe (Tajikistan) route, and is used to supply gas from Southern Uzbekistan and Turkmenistan to Tajikistan. The second pipeline is a bypass pipeline, completed in September 2003, and goes through Uzbekistan along the Shurtan-Shurabad route, avoiding the need to cross Turkmenistan. This pipeline is used to supply gas to Tajikistan from Uzbekistan.

4. *The Shiberghan (Afghanistan)-Kolkhozobod (Tajikistan) gas pipeline* – This pipeline, first initiated in 1993, was to supply natural gas from Afghanistan to Tajikistan, but could not materialize.

However, it was again revived in October 2007. It is an approximately 110-120-kilometre pipeline, connecting Shiberghan (Afghanistan) to Kolkhozobod (Tajikistan) to be constructed with an estimated cost of US$ 15-17 million. Since there already exists a gas pipeline connecting Shiberghan with Mazar-e Sharif in Northern Afghanistan, there is a possibility of using it as part of the project.

5. *Kazakhstan-Turkmenistan Corridor and Northern Distribution Network* – Through these two transit and transport networks from Central Asia, effort has been made to link Iran with India and other neighbouring states. One such corridor is the Kazakhstan-Turkmenistan corridor – a 677-kilometre railway line connecting these countries with Iran and the Persian Gulf. It will link Uzen in Kazakhstan with Gyzylgaya-Bereket-Etrek in Turkmenistan, and Gorgan in Iran's Golestan province. The second link comes in from Uzbekistan through Northern Afghanistan, known as the Northern Distribution Network. India also plans to extend this route to link up with the Zaranj-Delaram road that enters Iran.[11]

Thus, the effort of all these intra-regional linkages has been to develop larger connectivity amongst the Central Asian states and open up export markets for their gas and oil through China and Iran. Simultaneously, these states are conscious of utilizing Caspian resources and existing pipeline routes to Russia. These developments are keenly being observed by India, and it is making serious efforts in extending its reach to Central Asia through cooperation with Iran and Russia. However, India continues to ignore the alternative China route, which also needs to be explored more seriously.

II

Besides the above pipeline/transit routes, some experts have suggested more safe and viable route between India and Central Asia.[12] This route not only helps overcome the drawbacks and limitations of some of the above routes, but will also help consolidate regional cooperation, both in Central Asia and in India's neighbourhood. In this regard, Devendra Kaushik suggests the opening up of an overland route between India and Central Asia through the old Chang-Chenmo route, which passes through the Xinjiang region of China from Ladakh.[13]This route can be another option besides the already-operational Bandar Abbas sea and rail/road route through Iran, or the still-problematic and newly constructed link connecting the Iranian port of Chabahar by road to Zaranj-Delaram, which provides access to Central Asia. The old Chang-Chenmo trade route can be revived by India by building a small link road in Ladakh to join the Tibet-Xinjiang road built by the Chinese through the disputed Aksai-Chin territory of Ladakh in their possession.[14]

Similar suggestions were made by an Indian diplomat when he viewed a gas route running from Kazakhstan to Osh in Kyrgyzstan, then rerouted from Afghanistan and Pakistan through China's Xinjiang region, across the Karakoram and Himalayan mountain ranges, and finally into India's Jammu and Kashmir region at Rulog or Demchok in Ladakh. The pipeline can then be brought into the Indian heartland after bypassing Leh and Manali.[15]

However, Devendra Kaushik differs on the hazards involved in the Karakoram route. He is of the view that the route suggested through Ladakh has definite advantage over the Karakoram route, because of its lower height and better climatic conditions. Besides, the prospects of bringing Russian oil to India through this route have also increased with the completion of a new pipeline linking Russia and China. If the pipeline between Atasu in North-West Kazakhstan linking Alashankou in Xinjiang is joined by the already-existing Russia's Omsk-Chardzhou pipeline passing through Atasu, the possibility of Russian and Kazakh oil reaching India through Xinjiang region can become a reality.[16] Hence, there is a strong case made for India to explore the possibilities of reviving the old transit routes to Central Asia to access oil and gas from Kazakhstan and Russia.

Both these experts agree that this route can also be utilized for accessing hydro-electric power from Kyrgyzstan and Tajikistan. Sikri is of the view that in case it becomes very difficult to transport gas over such long distances, then Eurasian gas could be used to set up gas-fuelled power plants in Central Asia and Xinjiang, and the electricity thus generated can be transmitted to India.[17]This connectivity is going to bring India, China and Central Asia closer and could likely help ameliorate mutual suspicion between India and China. During the regime of Atal Bihari Vajpayee (1998-2004), such efforts were made, but follow-up did not happen later with the same vigour.[18]

Apprehensions about the India-China boundary dispute have been over emphasized to prevent cooperation in terms of pipeline, rail/

road linkages through Central Asia. However, cooperation between India's ONGC Videsh Ltd (OVL) and China National Petroleum Corporation (CNPC) was there for all to see when India's OVL mounted a successful US$ 573 million joint bid to acquire Petro-Canada's 37 per cent stake in the al-Furat oil and gas fields in Syria. Earlier, too, both organisations had collaborated in Sudan with the signing of an agreement between OVL and CNPC on 12 January 2006, during the visit of India's then – Minister of Petroleum and Natural Gas to Beijing.[19] Some scholars still view that "India and China may be cooperating in other areas, but when it comes to Central Asia energy, competition is fierce".[20] In this context, the example of acquisition of exploration sites in Kazakhstan is oft touted. It was in 2005 when China outbid India to acquire PetroKazakhstan, Kazakhstan's third largest oil producing area, with CNPC raising its bid to US$ 4.18 billion, though later, Kazakhstan reversed the bid. During the visit of Kazakhstan's President to India in January 2009, India's ONGC Mittal Energy Limited (OMEL) and KazMunaiGaz (KMG) signed an agreement for exploration of oil and gas in the Satpayev Block of Caspian Sea, which covers an area of 1,582 square kilometres and an estimated reserve of 1.85 billion barrels oil. The Indian company will have a 25 per cent share while the remaining 75 per cent will be with KMG.[21] Thus, there is an urgent need to consider this alternative possibility for larger connectivity with Central Asia.

III

After evaluating inter- and intra-regional connectivity and the alternative routes, it is possible to suggest some policy options for India and Central Asia. The following strategies can serve their mutual interest in a more appropriate manner.

First and foremost, both must realize the importance of Russia as a key player in terms of its bilateral and multilateral relations with Central Asian states in general and rail/road/pipeline connectivity in particular if they are to achieve their mutual goals of transport and pipeline connectivity. This is because Central Asia is not only the soft underbelly and in the neighbourhood of Russia, but also because most oil and gas pipeline of earlier Soviet era are still important and continue to remain so in terms of linkages with Moscow and the oil and gas terminals of Central Asian Republics. Even today, the supply of oil and gas from Moscow or Central Asia to the outside world has to be through either the Russia-Iranian or Russia-Chinese route. For India, Russia has always been a friendly country with plenty of mutual goodwill and cooperation. The need is not only to revitalize those ties, but to give practical shape to their strategic partnership, especially since the relationship does not have any negative baggage or irritants.

Secondly, India should give more importance to its engagement with China in its strategy for Central Asia – or the larger Eurasian space. Revival of the old Chang-Chenmo route from Ladakh and Xinjiang to Central Asia is the shortest route available between India and Central Asia, passing through only one state- China. Besides, routes passing through Pakistan and Afghanistan are volatile, unstable and unsafe given the contemporary politico-military environment in both the states. Moreover, despite the initiation of large scale CBMs between India and Pakistan, the scope of improvement in relations between them is limited. The exploiting of the Central Asia-China route offers great possibility for transporting Russian and Kazakhstan oil through the same pipeline. Also, here roads upto Ladakh are well maintained by the Border Roads Organization in India. There is only the necessity to build a small segment to join the already-existing Tibet-Xinjiang road passing through the disputed Aksai Chin region. Contemporary cooperation between the oil companies of both India and China (OVL and CNPC) has made the task easier. This will not only enhance India-Central Asia solidarity, but is also likely to have a spill-over effect on the resolution of the border issue between the two countries.

Thirdly, India's connectivity with Central Asia has to be factor in Kazakhstan. It is not only the largest producer of oil and gas in the region, but also a hub of all transit routes amongst Central Asian states and the outside world. Geographically, it enjoys geographical advantage since all routes in the North-South and East-West direction pass through Kazakhstan. Moreover, it is well connected in terms of oil and gas exports to China, Russia, Iran and the Caspian region. India's access to Central Asia through INSTC or Chabahar made possible merely by enjoying goodwill with Kazakhstan. It can even access gas and oil from Central Asia through swapping at Iranian . The alternative route through China can also be facilitated through linkages with Kazakhstan. Similarly, oil imports from Russia can also be accessed very easily. Currently, Kazakhstan is vigorously upgrading its ties with China and simultaneously, through active cooperation with Russia, also strengthening linkages with China. Therefore, it is high time India began to explore alternative routes for connectivity to Central Asia through increased cooperation with Kazakhstan.

Fourthly, Iran is an important factor for consolidating inter and intra-regional connectivity. Its ports of Bandar Abbas and Chabahar are important transit points for landlocked Central Asia with the outside world. Similarly, India can play a crucial role in this region by linking its exports and imports to Central Asia through facilities in Iran. Bandar Abbas is crucial for the success of INSTC as well as the India-Iran-Turkmenistan agreement. Chabahar, a free trade port and industrial zone with a periphery of 140 square kilometres, is also being developed by Iran into nine functional industrial zones. India is very interested in the development of this port. Consequently, during the recent visit of India's Foreign Minister to Iran, India committed to developing this port with an investment of US$ 100 million.[22] India is also exploring possibilities investing in the Chabahar Container Terminal Project and the proposed Chabahar-Faraj-Bam railway corridor upto the Afghanistan border. India looks at leveraging this railway network to link the already-built 200 km long Zaranj-Delaram road that hooks up with Afghanistan's 'Garland Highway', linking all major cities.[23] This link with Iran is not only going to consolidate bilateral economic ties, but will also strengthen its own developmental interests in Afghanistan. For India, it is going to assume greater importance after the post-2014 withdrawal of US forces from this region. The only problem is the strained US-Iranian ties, which may restrain India's role. But given the larger picture of India's foreign policy objectives and its role in Central Asia, it has to balance its relations with USA on the Iranian question.

Finally, India can make its presence felt in the region through its 'soft power' by enhancing infrastructural capabilities of Central Asian states and strengthening cooperation at bilateral and multilateral level. Besides trade and economic linkages, India should also make efforts to enhance cooperation in projects like health, medicine, information technology, energy, education, railways, hydroelectricity, culture, tourism, agriculture, etc. Especially, India can help the Central Asian states in setting up IT hubs and universities in the region. India should also play an active role in multilateral agencies like the Shanghai Cooperation Organization (SCO) and conference on Confidence-Building Measures in Asia (CICA) to boost larger connectivity with these states.

IV

It can be seen that given geo-economic developments at the global level in general and Central Asia in particular, it is imperative that existing rail/road/pipeline connectivity both at intra-regional and inter-regional level be strengthened to enhance mutual cooperation among the states of Central Asia. India can be an important partner in this outreach by utilizing its 'soft power' capabilities. Besides, emerging Russia-China-India cooperation can also be used to explore additional routes for the benefit of Central Asian states with Russia, China and India. In this context, India has to engage with regional institutional arrangements like SCO and CICA in a more visible manner. At this juncture, it must be clear that despite prevailing geo-politics and geo-economic realities, one must not forget that mere geography is not going to be the sole determinant in the evolution of inter-regional cooperation; rather, it can be realized through political willingness on the part of both India and Central Asia. Therefore, there is a need for India to invoke, like its 'Look East' policy, a comprehensive policy of 'Look North' to Central Asia, while the Central Asian states need to reciprocate such gestures in a more coordinated and concrete manner. Hence, both regions should work as partners in the peace and development of Central Asia.

However, everything is not perfect in establishing connectivity between India and Central Asia. To explore oil and natural gas, Central Asia is in great need of FDI and technological inputs. India's own FDI needs may prevent it from becoming a significant investor in the region. Besides, issues like prices and taxes are going to be another problem area amongst the producer states of Central Asia. These problems can be resolved only if the three important states of this region- Kazakhstan, Turkmenistan and Uzbekistan- come together to frame the rules regarding import and export of oil and gas. Nevertheless, prospects of India-Central Asia connectivity are bright because of their proximity, technological and infrastructural needs of Central Asia and India's rising energy demands.

Notes

1. Devendra Kaushik, "Caspian Cauldron: New Geopolitical Game", *Contemporary Central Asia*, Vol. 9, Nos. 2-3, 2005, p. 1.

2. R.S. Yadav. "India and the Central Asian Republics: Challenges and Opportunities", in B.G. Gafurov: *Dialogue of Cultures and Civilizations, Embassies of India and Tajikistan in the Russian Federation*, Moscow, 2000.
3. R.S. Yadav and Suresh Dhanda, "Oil Politics of Caspian Sea and Central Asia: Policy Options for India", *Contemporary Central Asia*, vol. X, no. 2, 2006.
4. Meena Singh Roy, "Turkmenistan – Afghanistan – Pakistan – India Pipeline" in Rashmi Doraiswamy, ed., *Energy Security: India, Central Asia and The Neighbourhood*, Manas, New Delhi, 2013, p. 128.
5. Atul Aneja, "India and Afghanistan: The Way Ahead", The Hindu, 4 January 2011.
6. Ajay Bisaria, "India Defence: Connect Central Asia Policy", MEA Press release, 4 September 2012 at http://www.security_risks.com
7. Singh Roy, n. 4, p. 140.
8. Edward C. Chow and Leigh E. Hendrix, Central Asia's Pipelines: Field of Dreams and Reality, National Bureau of Asian Research, Special Report no. 23, September 2010, p. 31 at csis.org/files/publication/1009_E Chow_L Hendrix_Central Asia.pdf.
9. For details see, Michael Fredholm, "The World of Central Asia Oil and Gas: Power Politics, Market Forces and Stealth Pipelines", Asian Cultures and Modernity, Research Report No. 16, December 2008.
10. For details see, Martha Brill Olcott, International Gas Trade in Central Asia: Turkmenistan, Iran, Russia and Afghanistan, Stanford Institute for International Studies, May 2004, working paper no. 28 at http://www.rice.edu/energy/publications/does/GAS_internationalGasTrade.in CentralAsia pdf. Also see, Chow, Edward, "Central Asia's Pipelines: Field of Dreams and Reality" in Pipeline Politics in Asia: The intersection of Demand, Energy Markets and Supply Routes, National Bureau of Asian Research, 2010 at http://www.nbr.org/publications/element.aspx?id=456.
11. Indrani Bagchi, "India to Spread Tentacles into Central Asia via Iran", *Times of India*, 13 March 1012.
12. Katherine Foshko, *India in Central Asia: Time for a New Strategy*, Gateway House: Indian Council on Global Relations, Mumbai, 2012, p. 47.
13. Devendra Kaushik, "India and Central Asia: Revitalizing Traditional Ties", *International Studies*, vol. 47, nos. 2-4, pp. 323-331.
14. *Ibid*., p. 329.
15. Rajiv Sikri, "The Geopolitics of Energy Security and Implications for South and Southern-Asia", ISAS Working Paper, 11 February 2008.
16. Kaushik, n. 13, p. 330.
17. Sikri, n.15.
18. Kaushik, n.13, pp. 330-331 (n.2). Also see, Foshko, n.12, p. 48.
19. R.S. Yadav, "India's Energy Security Policy", in R.S. Yadav & Suresh Dhanda, eds., *India Foreign Policy: Contemporary Trends*, Shipra, New Delhi, 2012, p. 214.

20. Gulshan Sachdev, "Regional Economic Linkages", in Nirmala Joshi, ed., *Reconnect India and Central Asia*, Central Asia-Caucasus Institute Silk Route Studies Programme, Singapore, 2010, p. 13.
21. "ONGC Mittal Signs Deal take 25 Stake in Kazakh Oil Field", *Times of India*, 24 January 2009.
22. "India to Develop Iranian Port", *The Hindu*, 5 May 2013.
23. "India Considering More Investments in Iran", *The Hindu*, 5 May 2013.

13

Commercial and Economic Linkages between Central Asia and India: Perspective From Kazakhstan

Gulnara Bekmagambetova

Development of transport and other sectors of the economy are closely interlinked. The level of development and trade determine the demand for transport services. On the other hand, transport is a backbone that has a significant impact on factors like living standards and production and trade of goods. Kazakhstan is a leading trade partner of India in Central Asia. However, trade turnover between these two countries has touched around US$ 500 million only. The overall trade turnover between India and CA countries does not exceed US$ 800 million (see Fig. 13.1 and 13.2).

At the same time, commercial relations between India and Russia, Kazakhstan's partner in the Customs Union, are well developed. According to information made available by India, in 2012 the trade turnover between these two countries exceeded US$ 6 billion. Trade turnover between India and Ukraine is also significant – about US$ 3 billion.

According to expert assessment, commercial and economic cooperation between CA countries and India has significant prospects. India is strong in areas that are of serious interest for CA countries and, in particular, for Kazakhstan: information technology and software, pharmaceuticals and medical equipment, machine building, chemical industry, textile, tea. India is one of the most dynamic countries in the world, accounting for increasing growth in consumption of a range of resources and expansion of markets. CA countries - known for their huge deposits of various natural resources-

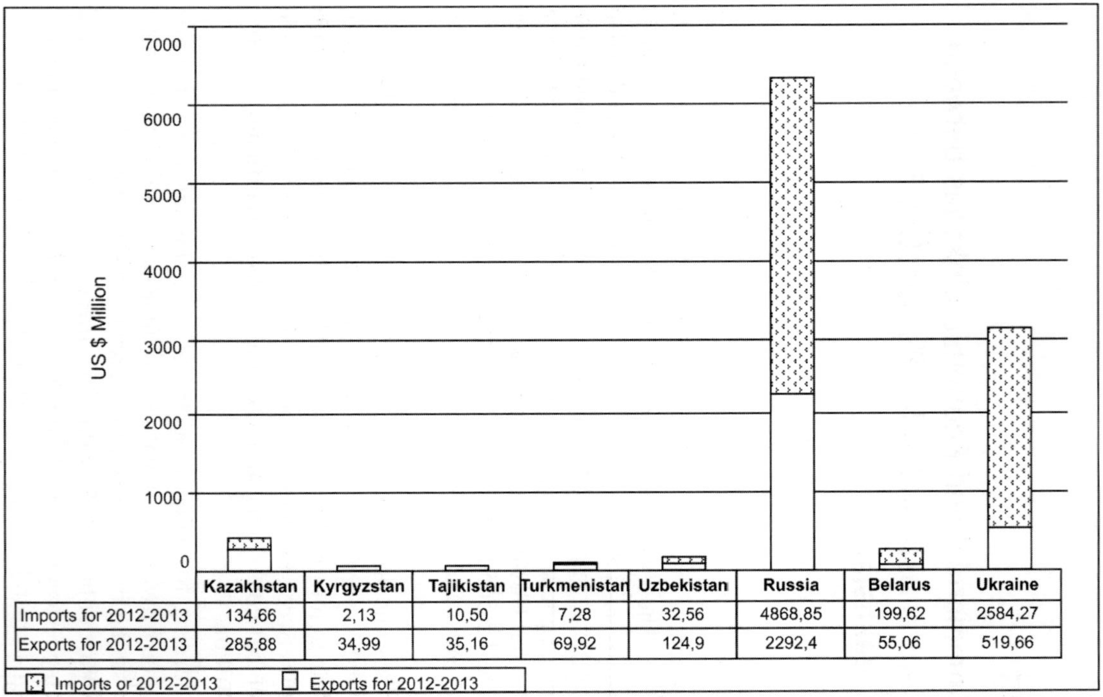

	Kazakhstan	Kyrgyzstan	Tajikistan	Turkmenistan	Uzbekistan	Russia	Belarus	Ukraine
Imports for 2012-2013	134,66	2,13	10,50	7,28	32,56	4868,85	199,62	2584,27
Exports for 2012-2013	285,88	34,99	35,16	69,92	124,9	2292,4	55,06	519,66

Source: Department of Commerce, India, Export Import Data Bank.

Fig. 13.1: Foreign trade in India with CA countries, Russia, Belarus and Ukraine.

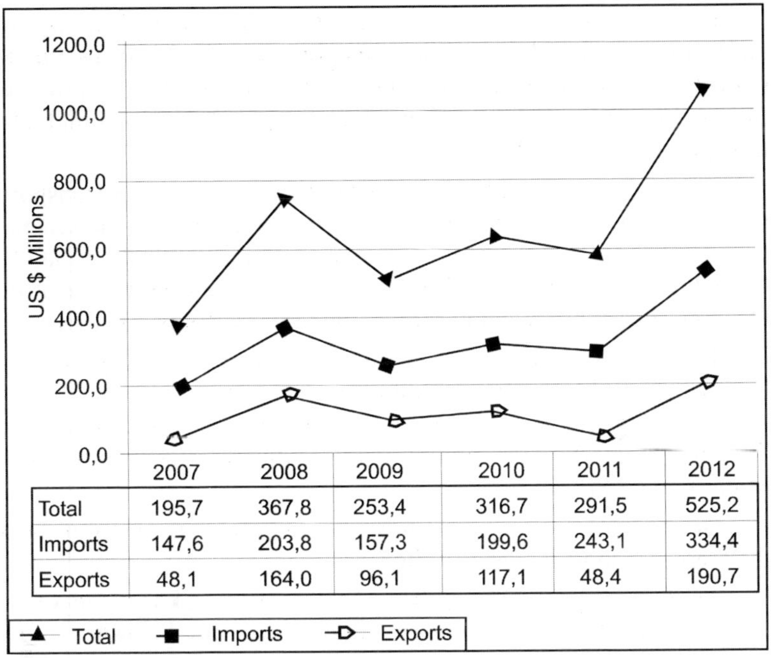

	2007	2008	2009	2010	2011	2012
Total	195,7	367,8	253,4	316,7	291,5	525,2
Imports	147,6	203,8	157,3	199,6	243,1	334,4
Exports	48,1	164,0	96,1	117,1	48,4	190,7

Source: Statistical Yearbook "Kazakhstan in 2012", the Agency of Statistics of the Republic of Kazakhstan.

Fig. 13.2: Dynamics of trade between Kazakhstan and India

can satisfy many demands of the Indian economy and also support the transit of Indian goods to other CIS countries and Europe.

Perhaps, one of the reasons for the less than potential development of commercial and economic relations between the two countries is the transport and communications bottleneck due to lack of common border, the complicated military, political and economic situation in some parts of Asia, and the landlocked geography of CA countries.

Closest distance from the sea:

Kazakhstan : 3,750 km,
Kyrgyz Republic : 3,600 km,
Tajikistan : 3,100 km,
Uzbekistan : 2,950 km,
Turkmenistan : 1,700 km

Ex-Soviet republics have made efforts to establish transport corridors to South and Southeast Asia For example, the North–South Corridor and the Trans-Afghanistan Transport Corridor can provide this region access to seaports by setting up railway, road and sea transportation networks.

The Intergovernmental Agreement on the International Transport Corridor (ITC) was signed by Russia, Iran and India at the second Eurasian Transport Conference on 12 September, 2000, in Saint-Petersburg. In April 2001, this Agreement was ratified by India; in October 2001 by Iran and in March 2002 by the Russian Federation.

To date, the following states have acceded to the Agreement: Belarus, Kazakhstan, Oman, Tajikistan, Azerbaijan, Armenia, Syria, Bulgaria, Kyrgyzstan, Turkey and Ukraine. Observer states are Turkmenistan, Bahrain, Saudi Arabia, Kuwait, UAE, Indonesia, Malaysia and Sri Lanka.

Goods traffic along the international transport corridor uses different transport modes as follows:

Trans-Caspian: Through the ports of Astrakhan and Olya Makhachkala by rail for transport of goods to/from the ports.

Eastern branch of the Corridor: Direct railway link through Kazakhstan, Uzbekistan and Turkmenistan with access to Iran's railway network through the border crossing at Tedzhen–Sarakhs.

Western branch of the Corridor: It follows the Astrakhan–Makhachkala–Samur route, then across Azerbaijan to Iran through the border station at Astara. Alternatively, goods can be transported from Samur through Azerbaijan and Armenia, with access to Iran through the border station at Julfa.

According to expert assessment, goods traffic along the ITC North - South will reach 25-26 million tons by 2015.

Alternative scenario: On 16 October 2007, Tehran hosted a summit of the Heads of Caspian states, where Iran, Kazakhstan and Turkmenistan signed a memorandum for the construction of a new Caspian railway line - Uzen–Gyzylgaya–Bereket–Etrek–Gorgan. The total length of this line will be 929-km. Each of the states will fund construction of sections in their territory. The construction of the section to the Uzen–Turkmenistan border was completed in 2011. The new line will be 600-km shorter than the existing line through the Sarakhs.

On 18 June 2003, the Governments of Iran, Afghanistan and Uzbekistan signed a tripartite agreement for the **International Trans-Afghanistan Transport Corridor** to Iranian ports.

The Agreement provided for the construction and renovation of the following highways:

- Termez – Mazari Sharif – Shibirghan – Gerat – Dilaram – Milak – Chabahar, with a total length 2298 km;
- Termez – Mazari Sharif – Shibirghan – Gerat – Daharan – Bandar Abbas, total length 2258 km;
- Tashkent – Termez – Mazari Sharif – Shibirghan – Gerat – Daharan – Tehran – Bazargan, total length 2812 km; and
- Railway line on the Termez – Hairatan Mazari Sharif – Gerat – Sangan – Khaf route, and facilitating traffic on the Uzbekistan – Afghanistan border through Afghanistan and Iran to Bandar Abbas, and further by train-ferry to UAE ports or ports in India and South East Asia.

Currently, the total length of highways connecting Afghanistan with neighbouring countries is 1,153 km, of which 1,119 km have already been rehabilitated, 34 km are under renovation and work is scheduled for completion by the end of 2013.

However, implementation of a major project like the Trans-Afghanistan Railway Corridor is delayed, primarily due to lack of funding.

Despite efforts by all countries to develop the transport infrastructure, the volume of goods being carried across borders between CA countries and India remains insignificant.

Most goods are transported between Kazakhstan and India via rail (Figure 13.3). Virtually all export and import routes cross the Russian territory or its ports. A very small proportion of exports to India (ferroalloys; about 2,000 tons in 2012) are shipped through China to its Eastern ports, and further by sea.

Underdevelopment of railway routes through Iran is due not only to a weak railways network (primarily in Iran) and the need to transship cargo/containers in Iranian ports, but also to logistical problems like different rail gauges across countries (rail tracks in CIS are 1520mm guage, in Iran - like in China, North America and

Turkey - they are 1435mm guage, while India, Pakistan and some other countries have the widest railway guage in the world (1600 mm or 1676 mm); reissue of shipping documents, etc.

However, most barriers are found in transportation by roads.

This region has a relatively developed highway network, some

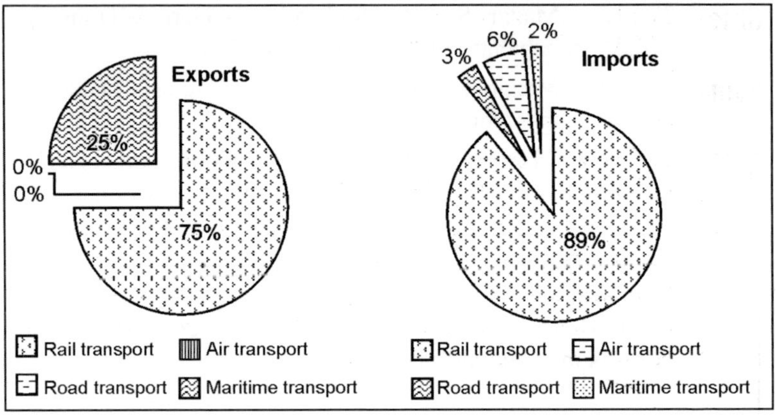

Source: NII TK, Kazakhstan.

Fig. 13.3: The role of modes of transport in trade between India and Kazakhstan

of which also are part of the highway network of the CIS, EurAsEC, Asian Highways and category E highways.

Nonetheless, as demonstrated by the International Road Transport Union (IRU), the development of the transport sector is greatly affected by issues like safety and existence of support infrastructure and services, such as motels, vehicle maintenance stations, fuel stations, etc.

Recent surveys of highways in Central Asia under the IRU Modal Highway Project show that highways in Kazakhstan generally have enough fuel stations, cafes and shops. However, these facilities often do not match the levels of quality and convenience needed for road users. Maintenance stations are located mostly in big cities and, as a rule, provide services for light vehicles. There is a lack of parking areas- trucks have to park at the roadside or roadside rest areas. With overall increase in number of service facilities, small and medium-size businesses ignore the needs of truck transportation since the construction and operation of servicing facilities for trucks requires larger capital expenditure. The situation in other CA Republics is even more distressed.

Currently, the development and operation of all modes of transport internationally is based mostly on bilateral agreements and multilateral conventions.

The Table 13.1 presents bilateral agreements with the Republic of Kazakhstan.

Table 13.1: Bilateral road transportation agreements with the Republic of Kazakhstan

Islamic Republic of Iran	Agreement between the Government of the Republic of Kazakhstan and the Government of the Islamic Republic of Iran on international road transport, signed on 12 May 1993 in Tehran. Since the Agreement of 1993 does not cover application of regulatory authorization system for the passage through the territory of the parties, a new draft Agreement has now been developed, 10 June 2011 it was provided to the Iranian side for review and further discussion in the 4th quarter 2011 in Astana. No reply thereto has been received from Iran as yet.
Kyrgyz Republic	Agreement between the Government of the Republic of Kazakhstan and the Government of the Kyrgyz Republic on international road transport. The Agreement provides for the permit-free system, except irregular passenger transportation.
Republic of Tajikistan	Agreement between the Government of the Republic of Kazakhstan and the Government of the Republic of Tajikistan on international road transport. Provides for the permit-free system of freight transportation in bilateral and transit communication, and to/from third countries, except passenger transportation.
Turkmenistan	Agreement between the Government of the Republic of Kazakhstan and the Government of Turkmenistan on international road transport. Provides for permissive system for export/import transportation, transit and transportation to/from third countries.
Republic of Uzbekistan	Agreement between the Government of the Republic of Kazakhstan and the Government of the Republic of Uzbekistan international road transportation of freight and passengers. Provides for the permit-free system for export/import transportation and transit. Transportation to/from third countries are carried out on a permission basis.
Republic of India	No
Islamic Republic of Afghanistan	No

Overall, countries worldwide are parties to more than 120 international treaties and conventions governing various aspects of transport activity. Almost half of them – 55 treaties and conventions – have been signed under the aegis of the United Nations Economic Commission for Europe (UNECE).

As early as 1992, UNESCAP passed special resolution 48/11 on road and railway transport to establish the legal basis for land transportation. Asian countries acceded to seven basic conventions and treaties:

1. Convention on Road Signs and Signals of 8 November 1968;
2. Convention on Road Traffic of 8 November 1968;
3. International Convention on the Harmonization of Frontier Controls of Goods, 21 October 1982;
4. Convention on the Contract for the International Carriage of Goods by Road (CMR) of 19 May 1956;
5. Customs Convention on the International Transport of Goods under Cover of TIR Carnets (TIR Convention) of 14 November 1975;
6. Customs Convention on Containers of 2 December 1972;
7. Customs Convention on the Temporary Importation of Commercial Road Vehicles of 18 May 1956.

For status of accession of states in the region to these and other international agreements, please see UNECE website at: http://www.unece.org/trans/conventn/intro.html

Accession to any international agreement(s) means the state will ensure that the rules, standards, requirements, rights and obligations of road users contained therein will be respected within their territory. It raises confidence in such state, raises their international reputation and forms one of the key conditions requisite for the development of international transportation.

India and Iran are not parties to the UNECE. However, they have acceded to some agreements developed within this organization.

All of the above just proves that there is a need to develop an integrated approach to cooperation between Central Asian states and India in the area of transport, based on key mechanisms of bilateral and multilateral partnership in the short and medium term.

14

Central Asian Countries and Trans-boundary River Basins: Energy Security and Water Resources Management

Tulegen Sarsembekov

General Overview of the Regional Water Basin and Energy Resources

The geopolitical unit of Central Asia including Kazakhstan, Kyrgyzstan, Tajikistan, Turkmenistan and Uzbekistan emerged after the collapse of the Soviet Union in 1991. The region's environment and geography account for a particular pattern of stream flow in river basins, while its political and economic conditions specify stream flow use patterns. The landlocked location of the countries dictates the need for enhanced trade and economic ties and better integration.

All major Central Asian rivers are trans-boundary rivers, which implies that political boundaries divide the sources of water flow located in one country and the water basins used in other ones. Changing climate and specificity of water resources of Central Asia, such as increasingly recurrent and long-lasting dry and high-water periods enhance water-related disasters such as flooding, land sliding, mud flows, drought, etc.

Regional environmental concerns related to water issues in Central Asia include air and water pollution, flooding and drought, hazardous waste from the mining industry and degradation of land and mountain ecosystems. Altogether, they determine the sustainability of river ecosystems and safety of water usage by underlining the need for integrated water resources management, both at the national and regional level.[1]

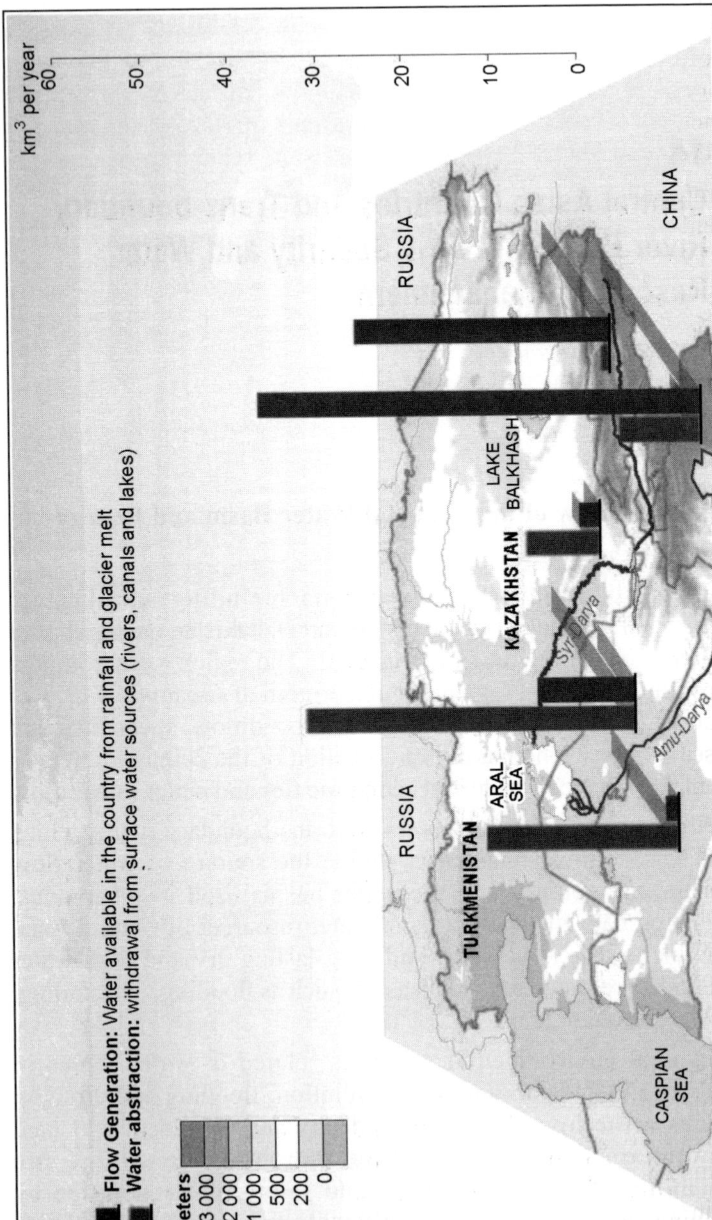

Source: Environment and Security: Central Asia-Ferghana/Osh/Khujand Area. 2005.

Fig. 14.1: Water Withdrawal and Availability in Aral Sea basin

The Aral Sea basin includes the basins of Amu Darya and Syr Darya, two continental rivers located in the Northern and Western parts of the Sub-Aral region. The Aral Sea basin covers the whole territory of Tajikistan, Uzbekistan, a major part of Turkmenistan, four provinces of Kyrgyzstan, the Southern part of Kazakhstan and the Northern part of Afghanistan and Iran.

Water resources of the Aral Sea basin are intensively used for different purposes. The water diversion rate was the highest during 1960-1990; later, this factor became crucial in aggravating the shrinking of the sea and environmental degradation.[2]

According to demographic estimates, by the year 2050, the population of Uzbekistan will grow to 35 million, Kazakhstan to 22 million, Tajikistan to 11 million and Kyrgyzstan and Turkmenistan to eight million. Despite structural changes in Central Asian economies, agriculture still consumes the bulk of water, and agricultural demands for water supply will continue to grow while there will be lack of renovation and upgrade of water and irrigation facilities. All these factors will have a decisive effect on the interstate division of water usage, and will determine water needs in the future; meanwhile, current rates of water usage already exceed the available water resources.[3]

Low levels of regional interaction and trade and economic integration, unresolved water and energy issues, along with sharp increases in fuel and food prices imported from neighbouring countries are the main factors for the growing demand for water resources needed for energy and irrigation in Central Asian countries. Furthermore, the construction of new heat power station (HPS) reservoir and structures, main canals and irrigation systems are often in violation of basin principles, and do not comply with environmental requirements in terms of maximum withdraw of trans-boundary flows. There is no due attention paid to consequences of water resource usage in the short and long-term; while erecting new structures on trans-boundary rivers, countries do not notify their counterparts about their intentions to do so. Under such circumstances, the changes in the role of the water reservoir and other regulating structures on trans-boundary rivers complicate solving energy, water, food and environmental safety problems for both neighbouring parties and the region as a whole.

Joint management of water bodies and sharing of trans-boundary river resources is one of the biggest challenges in Central Asia. While addressing this and other challenges like food, energy and environmental security, developing transport infrastructure etc., mutual investments should be seen as a key area of integration between the countries of the region.

The Central Asian countries have set up a legal and institutional framework for interstate and regional cooperation, such as inter-Governmental agreements and regional organizations for implementing coordinated water and energy policies. Sharing of information on measures taken and planned to prevent, control and mitigate trans-boundary impact on water resources, along with information on the quality and quantity of water resources is an important area of cooperation in Central Asia. The region's economy is strongly affected by natural disasters and extreme water-related events. Mitigation of their consequences calls for perfect forecasts that would underlie the development of warning and early response measures. Use of new equipment and devices – including satellite telecommunications to collect, process and transmit data – makes it possible to develop more reliable forecasts and make early warnings about hazardous weather and hydrological phenomena in trans-boundary river basins more effective. Timely dissemination of these forecasts amongst the region's countries is an important stage in disaster response readiness. River basin management should be aimed at a balanced use of surface and ground waters, which makes the role of planning and protection of water resources at all levels of Government, i.e. local, national or interstate, more important. It is instrumental to meet the goals of efficient use of water resources, efficient water distribution at the local, national and interstate levels and environmental sustainability of river basins. The limited and vulnerable nature of water resources has necessitated a new approach to their assessment, development and management. This approach is based on integration of water management plans, and programmes within the framework of regional, national, economic, social and environmental policies.

Solution of the water problem in the Central Asian countries should be based on a number of priorities set by the international community, including the principle of reasonable and equitable use of trans-boundary river resources, which is fundamental to regional cooperation. Protection of water quality and reduced consumption of water are regarded as the most urgent problems in the water resources management in Central Asia.

Central Asia has sufficient fuel and energy resources to allow the countries not only to provide for their own energy needs, but also to cater to foreign markets as well. There are considerable reserves of energy resources, although these vary significantly in value and type amongst the states in the region. Kazakhstan, for example, has large reserves of oil, gas, coal and Uranium, many times larger than the potential hydropower resources in the country. Uzbekistan is also a oil, coal and Uranium-rich country, but its hydropower resources are assessed as moderate. Turkmenistan has some of the world's largest gas fields, but almost no hydropower resources. Stockpiles and the distribution of primary energy resources determine the structure of the fuel and energy balance of Governments. Central Asia is considered as a region with some of the world's largest oil and gas reserves; however, it is also a transportation hub, a place for some of the most important transportation routes. One of the main Central Asian Central (CAC) gas pipelines that allow Uzbek and Turkmen gas to be delivered to Russia, Ukraine and the Caucuses is routed through Kazakhstan. Uzbekistan is a transit country for Turkmen gas and Kazakhstan – for Uzbek gas. Regional gas transport infrastructure was created during the Soviet period, and gas transportation routes out of Central Asia are largely set up in a centralized system to supply fuel to European countries. Four routes from the main gas pipeline run from Turkmenistan through Uzbekistan (and further through Kazakhstan), and one route runs along the coast of the Caspian Sea through Kazakhstan. There are also additional branches of the CAC, from which two are highlighted: between Turkmenistan and Kazakhstan and between Kazakhstan and the Russian Caucasus. Two lines from the Bukhara – Ural gas pipeline begin in Uzbekistan near the city of Gazli (Bukhara Province), cross Karakalpakstan (Uzbekistan) and then proceed through Kazakhstan to the Southern Urals. In addition, there are two other gas pipelines that cross Kazakhstan (Orenburg – Novopskov and Soyuz), which transport gas from Siberian reservoirs to Europe.

New oil and gas routes from Central Asia are being established in a competitive global energy market, and with the growing influence of world powers in the region. In the hierarchy of primary energy resources, gas, coal and oil occupy a special place in Central Asia. 81 per cent of total production and 83.5 per cent of energy resource consumption happen in Kazakhstan and Uzbekistan. If Kazakhstan is the largest producer of primary energy resources, then, according to demographic factors, Uzbekistan is a leader in consumption. Kyrgyzstan and

Tajikistan have great potential for hydropower resources, but they do not have sufficient reserves of hydrocarbons, which determine the development of energy in these countries, based on the use of hydropower resources.[4]

Specificity of Power Plant Capacities in Central Asia

The total installed power generating capacity of Kazakhstan is 19,892.1: 17,252.4 MW from HPS (86.7 per cent) and 2,639.7 MW from HPP (13.3 per cent), including small HPP and other renewable energy resources. 70 per cent of the total production of electricity is generated using local coal. There are gas turbine power plants operating in the West and South of the country. Kazakhstan is facing a deficit of electricity, which is covered by the Russian market. The reduction and subsequent elimination of the deficit is planned, and will be carried out by constructing new power plants and modernizing existing ones. Electricity production in 2010 reached 82.26 billion kWh.

Table 14.1: Structure of CA power plants' installed capacity

	Installed Capacity (MW)					
	HPS	*%*	*HPP*	*%*	*Total*	*%*
Kazakhstan	17,252.4	86.7	2,639.7	13.3	19,892.1	100
Kyrgyzstan	716	18.9	3,070	81.1	3,786	100
Tajikistan	318	5.8	5,121	94.2	5,439	100
Turkmenistan	4,536	99.8	9	0.2	4,545	100
Uzbekistan	10,643	85.5	1,810.7	14.5	12,453.7	100
Subtotal for CA	33,441.4	73.2	12,259.7	26.8	45,701.1	100

Note: as of 01.01.2012. HPS = Heat Power Station; HPP = Hydroelectric Power Plant.

Source: World Bank, 2010; CASA, 2011; Data from government bodies of energy management of CA countries.

The electric power system in Kyrgyzstan works in parallel with the Central Asian power grid, and is supported mainly by hydropower facilities (3070 MW, 81.1 per cent), which provide additional energy in summer and cover the periods of peak load by the unified energy system of Central Asia (UES-CA). Thermal power stations (716 MW, 18.9 per cent) are designated for handling increased load during winter. Hydropower plants are located mostly in the Naryn river cascade in the Southern part of the country. Electricity production in 2010 was 12.06 billion kWh. Kyrgyzstan has the ability to export up to 2.5 billion kWh of electricity during the periods of high irrigation releases from the Naryn HPP cascade.

The total installed capacity of power stations in Tajikistan is 5,439 MW: 5, 121 MW are from HPP (94.2 per cent) and 318 MW from HPS (5.6 per cent). Hydropower plants are mainly located on the Vakhsh cascade in the Southern part of the country, with the generating capacity of the HPP in the Northern region being only 126 MW. The annual production volume cannot meet the demand for electricity in the winter. From the beginning of October to the end of April, there is a deficit in electricity supply of about 4 billion kWh. In winter, Tajikistan is forced to limit demand for electricity. In summer, the country has a surplus of electricity, the volume of which depends on the amount of water released from the reservoir and the hydrological conditions of the particular year. In 2010, electricity produced from Tajikistan's HPP exceeded 16.4 billion kWh with its highest excess in recent years at 4.5 billion kWh. As Tajikistan has been shut off from the main UES-CA network, it cannot export electricity outside the country and for this reason faces great economic losses.[5]

Turkmenistan's generating capacities is mostly in its HPS, which use natural gas as the primary fossil fuel. The total installed capacity of Turkmenistan's power system is 4,525 MW: 4,536 MW is from HPS (99.8 per cent) and 9 MW comes from HPP (0.2 per cent) Turkmenistan has a surplus electricity generating capacity. Electricity production has reached 10.5 billion kWh and greatly exceeds the demand for it, which allows electricity to be supplied to other countries. Prior to Turkmenistan leaving the UES-CA in 2003, excess electricity was 50 per cent and its main importers were Kazakhstan and Tajikistan. As there was no transit agreement with Uzbekistan, Turkmenistan had to leave the UES-CA. Currently, electricity exports of 2.6 billion kWh go from Turkmenistan to Afghanistan, Iran and Turkey. According to Turkmenistan's Strategy for Economic Development up to 2020, electricity production will reach 26.4 billion kWh a year, with six billion kWh exported annually.

Uzbekistan's power system, which is geographically situated in the centre of the unified energy system and has about 50 per cent of the UES-CA's total capacity, plays an important role in ensuring a reliable power supply to consumers in the region by facilitating the transit flow of electricity exports to other countries. Uzbekistan's power system has an installed capacity of more than 12,453.7: 10,643

MW from HPS (85.5 per cent) and 1,810.7 MW from HPP (14.5 per cent). Electricity production in Uzbekistan in 2010 was 51.7 billion kWh a year. Almost the entire amount of electricity in Uzbekistan is produced by thermal power stations that use natural gas as the primary fuel. As operating thermal power stations are more effective in their base-load regime, regulating capacity in terms of lack of hydropower potential is a serious challenge for the country's power grid. It is worth mentioning the seasonal nature of the import and export of electricity: Uzbekistan imports electricity from Kyrgyzstan and Tajikistan in the summer, and delivers it in winter to various parts of Northern Tajikistan, based on bilateral agreements between the countries. Uzbekistan also exports electricity to Afghanistan. Of all hydropower plants in Uzbekistan, only the Charvak HS (620 MW) and the Khodzhikent HPP (150 MW) can provide regulation, but the required capacity is more than 2,500 MW. The economically and technologically appropriate solution to the problem of regulating frequency and capacity is the use of advanced interstate power lines with neighbouring countries that have significant hydropower potential, such as Kyrgyzstan and Tajikistan.

The demand for electricity in Central Asian countries is predicted to grow annually until 2030 at a rate of 1.6-2.6 per cent. One feature common for all Central Asian countries is the outdated power station equipment of all types and power lines, which together contribute to a large loss of primary energy resources and electricity generated. Therefore, one of the priorities for investment in the regional electricity sector should be to cut technical losses of electricity and modernization of the existing generating stations, so the bulk of the forecasted demand in Central Asia could be covered. Bringing online new generating capacity necessary for scheduled socio-economic enhancement could also be considered as an investment priority. Central Asia's hydropower potential was valued as early as the beginning of the 19th century. The German publication "Deutsche Wasserwirtschaftkrafte" printed an article titled "The Earth's Water Power", which gave a brief inventory of the world's water resources, including an overview of hydropower reserves in the former USSR. The numbers bear witness to the fact that Central Asia has the richest reserves of water energy (after the Caucasus) in the former USSR. It follows that Central Asia occupied first place in the USSR in terms of quantity and total capacity of the largest water energy resources.[6]

Hydropower Resources in Central Asia

A current assessment of Central Asia's hydropower potential is presented in Table 14.2.

The total gross hydropower potential of Kazakhstan is theoretically 170 billion kWh a year, of which 27-30 billion kWh is cost effective and viable for use. Accounting for the changing river water levels, the gross energy potential in Kyrgyzstan accumulating in 268 rivers (linear accounting), 97 of the largest canals, and 18 reservoirs explored is 249 billion kWh of electricity produced a year, at average water levels. Production of 99 billion kWh a year is economically justified for utilization. Tajikistan has significant hydropower resources. An assessment of its reserves, based on direct observations of 530 (from a total 947) rivers in the country, and on primary data from the Hydro Meteorological Service, shows that the gross hydropower potential is 527 billion kWh, while technical potential – also accepted as economic – is more than 317 billion kWh a year. Turkmenistan has no hydropower resources that are sufficient for use. Nonetheless, Turkmenistan has had experience in making use of rivers hydropower. The oldest hydropower plant in the CIS – the Hindu Kush HPP – is located here. At the end of the 19th – beginning of the 20th centuries, three dams were built on the Murghab River (Turkmenistan) for irrigation: the Yoloten, Syltanbent and the Hindu Kush; the last two had hydropower plants constructed on them. The Murghab River is a trans-boundary river that originates in Afghanistan. The Hindu Kush HPP was the largest power station in pre-revolutionary Russia. There are three hydro turbines installed in the power plant with a total capacity of 1.35 MW. Power equipment was supplied by the Austro-Hungarian company, Hans. Celebrating its 100th anniversary, the Hindu Kush HSP is still in operation, annually producing an average 0.8-0.9 million kWh of electricity. Potential hydropower resources in Uzbekistan have been adequately studied and compared to other forms of renewable energy resources. The gross potential of 656 rivers and their tributaries is 107 billion kWh a year. Uzbekistan's hydropower resources were estimated taking into account the potential of both large and small rivers; existing, under construction and project reservoirs, master irrigation canals and main trunk canals with a discharge between 50-158 m3/s and which have a possible drop of 2 to 120 m. The technical potential of hydropower resources

Table 14.2: Central Asian Hydropower Resources

Countries	*Hydropower Resources (potential, billion kWh annually)*							
	Gross		*Technical*		*Economical*		*Utilized*	
	Total	*share in CA (%)*	*Total*	*share in CA (%)*	*Total*	*share in CA (%)*	*Total*	*share in CA (%)*
Kazakhstan	170	15.8	30	6.3	23.5	5.71	9	17.7
Kyrgyzstan	249	23.1	99	20.9	55	13.3	14	27.6
Tajikistan	527	48.9	317	67.1	317	76.86	19.5	38.4
Turkmenistan	24	2.2	5.8	1.2	2	0.48	0.1	0.18
Uzbekistan	107	10.0	21.1	4.5	15	3.65	8.2	16.12
Total	1077	100	472.9	100	412.5	100	50.8	100

Source: UNESCO, 2010; Molodtsov, 2010.

Note: 1. Gross hydropower potential: energy equivalent of hydropower energy reserves concentrated in sources of potential hydropower at full usage;
2. Technical hydropower potential: part of the gross hydropower potential that can be used by modern technology to meet requirements of a socio-environmental nature;
3. Economic potential of hydropower: part of the technical hydropower potential whose use under current conditions is economically effective to meet requirements of a socio-environmental nature;
4. Utilised potential of hydropower: hydropower that is used.

is estimated at 21.1 billion kWh a year.[7] The geographical distribution of primary fuel and energy resources objectively stipulates the structure of the Central Asian states' generating capacity as well as the need for, and feasibility of, regional energy integration on the basis of exchange (export-import) of electricity and various other forms of energy.[8]

Unified Energy System of Central Asia: Challenges and Opportunities

During the Soviet era and accounting for territorial particularities, Central Asia saw the creation of a fuel and energy complex that had a high level of regional integration. The unified energy system of Central Asia provided a stable mode of operation, reliable interstate supply of hydro resources and a water use regime that was regulated by hydropower plants in the region. The UES-CA, including Uzbekistan, the Southern regions of Kazakhstan, Kyrgyzstan, Tajikistan, and Turkmenistan was designed based on a unified criterion for the system to operate at the lowest cost. The regional electricity infrastructure of Central Asia, being a part of the UES of the USSR, was built to be an integrated system, optimally using available fuel, energy and hydropower resources in the region. The UES-CA is a set of electricity facilities, exploitable resources and their management, linked by a single process of electricity production, transmission and distribution. One of its most important advantages was the ability of participating states' electricity systems to operate parallel to one another – i.e. electricity systems working together on a common frequency. The parallel operation of electricity systems is a prerequisite for reliable operation and forms the basis for mutually beneficial cooperation in the electricity industry. The main principles of parallel operating power systems are:

- to satisfy the demand for electricity and capacity in each power system at all times through either their own power stations or energy delivered from other states on a contractual basis;
- to maintain the standard frequency within the agreed range in every power system through either its own sources of energy and/or through cross flows from power systems in other states; and

- to maintain the required reserves in every power system and supply the missing amount of reserve on a contractual basis from the power systems of other countries.

After the collapse of the USSR, in order to maintain parallel operations, the Central Asian countries signed an agreement in 1998 on the parallel operation of the energy system. All technical issues for the operation of existing 500 kW network and the 220 kW power lines were placed under the control of the Coordinating Council of UES-CA. It consists of the following national operators for the generation, transmission and distribution systems. In Kazakhstan: JSC KEGOC – network operator; Uzbekistan: State JSC UzbekEnergo – vertically integrated state energy company for production, transmission, and distribution; Tajikistan: JSC Barki Tochik – vertically integrated state energy company for production, transmission, and distribution; Kyrgyzstan: JSC NESK – network operator; JSC Power Plants – generation; Turkmenistan: State Corporation Kuvvat – vertically integrated state energy company for production, transmission, and distribution.

The Coordinating Council of the UES-CA established "Energy", a Coordination Dispatch Centre (CDC-Energy), located in Tashkent and functioning as the first hierarchical level of the power system's dispatch of Central Asia. The second level dispatch centres in the CA countries are performed by separate organizations that are involved in the dispatch of the national power system. CDC-Energy is funded on the principle of shared costs between the parties involved. As a regional system operator, CDC-Energy shall ensure compliance with the principles of parallel operation and operational coordination based on the information received daily from the national dispatch centres. These centres make use of instructions and recommendations from CDC-Energy.

However, not all countries in the region support joint operations, which significantly reduce opportunities for regional energy security and interstate water use in the trans-boundary river basins. Uzbekistan has limited its participation in parallel operations and the power systems of Tajikistan and Turkmenistan function in isolation from the UES-CA. Moreover, Turkmenistan's power system has changed in configuration, and in order to restore the technical parameters and lines connecting it to the other countries in the region, significant investment is needed. The economic losses from isolated power system operations are considerable. As a result of a fragmented UES-CA and its unstable parallel operations, CDC-Energy is not fully exercising its functions. Instead, it has been reduced to mostly monitoring capacities (the flow and production from large hydro and thermal power stations, and the demand for electricity in the separate units); the operating of automatic load-frequency control, the distribution of delivered and needed amounts of electricity for balancing; and to providing analytical and advisory services.

The effectiveness of the CA's power system control mechanism and corresponding HPP operations have fallen sharply with the loss of its regulatory functions as a result of national power systems leaving this system. The bulk of electricity exports and imports amongst countries in the region is maintained in the summer, when water releases from reservoirs are needed for irrigation in Uzbekistan and Kazakhstan. But this regime is fraught with difficulty because of the abeyance of mutual commitments and the conditions for fulfilling them. The volume of regional electricity trade has decreased from 25 GWh in 1990 to 3.7 GWh in 2008. As noted in the World Bank 2010 Survey "Analysis of cnergy management and the reciprocal exchange of energy between nation power systems in the Central Asian region", Kyrgyzstan, Tajikistan, Uzbekistan and Southern Kazakhstan can fulfil their own electricity needs, but in order to do so, energy systems working in parallel is a necessity. The same study also emphasizes that Central Asian countries are trying to increase their energy independence and export capabilities beyond the region. However, not having sufficient funds to upgrade their energy infrastructure, they are reducing the amount of regional energy cooperation. To achieve the criteria for a reliable, national power system is only possible through creating a unified energy system. The results of the World Bank's SWOT analysis and a modulation of the Central Asian power systems shows the significant benefits of the regional power systems working in parallel, one of which is an increase in the reliability of the supply. According to the results, parallel operation of Central Asian power systems could save more than $1.6 billion in the first three years of a fully-functioning unified system. Given that losses due to an undersupply of electricity by users reached no less than $200 for 1 MW, a stable and operational power system can have a positive economic effect of more than $0.5 billion. Thus, in the first stage of transition of Central Asian power systems to this mode of operation, expected savings will exceed $2.1 billion. In general, the benefits of a unified power system outweigh any possible shortcomings. The UES is beneficial to all participants from both a technical and an economic viewpoint (*see* Table 14.3).

Energy Sources in the Region: Prospects for the Future

The current economic environment is forcing every country to exercise its own energy policy, often conflicting with the prospect of developing a regional power framework. In the structure of Kyrgyzstan's generating capacity, for example, 81.1 per cent is contributed by hydropower and 18.9 per cent by thermal power; in Tajikistan, hydropower accounts for 94.2 per cent and thermal for just 5.8 per cent. With a limited transit flow of electricity within the UES-CA, this type of generating capacity ratio makes energy supply in winters difficult for these countries. They are, therefore, implementing plans to bring new HPP generating capacities online.

Table 14.3: Results of the SWOT analysis for the unified energy system

Strengths	**Weaknesses**
Optimal use of natural resources. Optimal scheduling. Efficient use of thermal generation. Decrease in necessity of investments. Use of advanced regional network. Reduction in undersupplies of energy. Improved reliability of supply. Decrease in the need for secondary reserves.	Potential risk of violation of agreements by other participants. Potential risk of emergency situations in neighbouring countries (which are compensated by the ability of neighbouring countries to offer support). Lapse in energy supply, leading to social and economic harm.
Opportunities	**Threats**
Ability to resolve: Issues of electricity and water resources (complex solutions). Issues with transit and customs duties. Issues related to import-export of electricity. More incentives and better conditions for the development of regional projects.	Issues of national energy security, primarily, independence from external energy resources. Could lose priority access.

Source: World Bank, 2010.

However, these solutions do not fully take into account impact on the short-term energy security and interstate water use for the whole region. Energy development is seen more from the position of being able to export excess capacities outside the region without sufficient regard for their own or regional needs in the future. Forecasts show that Central Asia is expecting an increased demand for electricity between 2020-2050 due to the dynamics of economic development and population growth. This period coincides with forecasts for climate change and a stable reduction in water levels in the Sir Darya and Amu Darya basins. With insufficient storage in the reservoirs, drawdown for electricity needs could lead to numerous negative consequences such as reduction in the production of electricity, deficit of water during the vegetation season, loss of long-term regulation of reservoir capacity and worsening conditions in interstate water management. As international practice shows, the policy of individual countries of the region for developing hydropower facilities alone does not provide appropriate amount of energy and water security for the region.

It is therefore necessary for all Central Asian Republics to diversify their energy sources and ensure reliable electric power. Coal could play an important role in raising the sustainability of energy supply and combating the rise of regional power imbalances. Creating transportation corridors for the delivery of coal to thermal stations, adopting preferential tariff regimes for this type of energy, and the use of clean coal technologies will enhance its competitiveness in comparison to other types of fuel, and ensure reliable energy supply. The production of energy from renewable sources such as the wind or sun or from the use of small hydropower plants is still quite expensive, but this sometimes is the cheapest means of providing electricity to rural populations. It is necessary to quickly develop new and effective technologies for the use of renewable sources of energy. However, the most reliable and guaranteed source of electricity for cities and major settlements is still coal. In general, the region is considered to have an overabundance of coal, allowing for wider scope of use of coal in building new TPP. Incidentally, this is a worldwide trend: according to forecasts, by 2025 coal will provide 31 per cent of the world's electricity. By 2025, coal will account for 50 per cent of the total energy production in the US. China's use of coal in electricity generation will increase from 72 per cent in 2001 to 73 per cent by 2025. Coal is a flexible source of energy, and although today it is mainly used for electricity production, it can also be processed into synthetic gasoline, diesel, hydrogen or other types of transport fuel. New technologies imply the potentiality of coal to reduce oil consumption. Kazakhstan is one of the large coal-mining countries of Central Asia (3.5 per cent of the world's coal reserves). The presence of large reserves and the reliability of the supply could help eliminate in a relatively short time the disparities in the generating capacity structure in Kyrgyzstan and Tajikistan, thereby increasing their energy security.[9]

Energy production using coal is also competitive in terms of price. To overcome negative environmental effect of using coal will require the development of new technologies and applying them on an industrial scale. Upgrading existing and construction of new facilities using modern technologies that increase the efficiency ratio will make a positive difference in the volume of emissions and control of greenhouses gas emissions.

Another promising source of electricity in the region is Uranium. 17 per cent of the world's reserves are located in Central Asia, with Kazakhstan and Uzbekistan amongst the top ten in the world in terms of overall reserves of Uranium and possession of advanced technologies for its extraction. Kazakhstan has 1.6 million tonnes of proven uranium reserves, which makes it second in the world. There are six uranium-rich deposits in Kazakhstan: Shu-Sarysui, Syr Darya, North Kazakhstan, Caspian, Balkhash, and Ili. Uzbekistan is seventh in the world in uranium reserves and fifth in its extraction. Uranium mining and processing also takes place in Kyrgyzstan and Tajikistan, and the prospects of a nuclear industry are tied to the development of earlier-proven ore deposits.

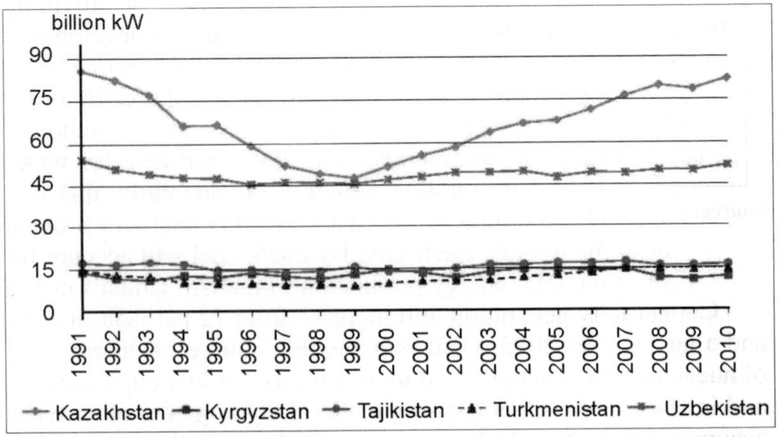

Source: CIS Statcommittee, 2012.

Fig. 14.2: Dynamics of electricity production in Central Asian countries

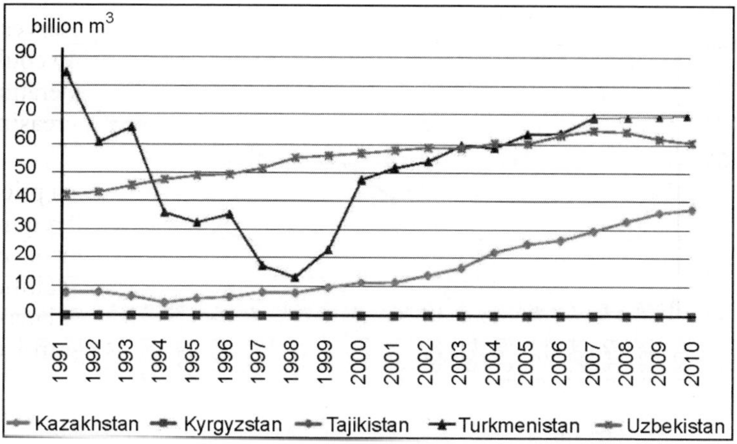

Source: CIS Statcommittee, 2012.

Fig. 14.3: Natural gas production

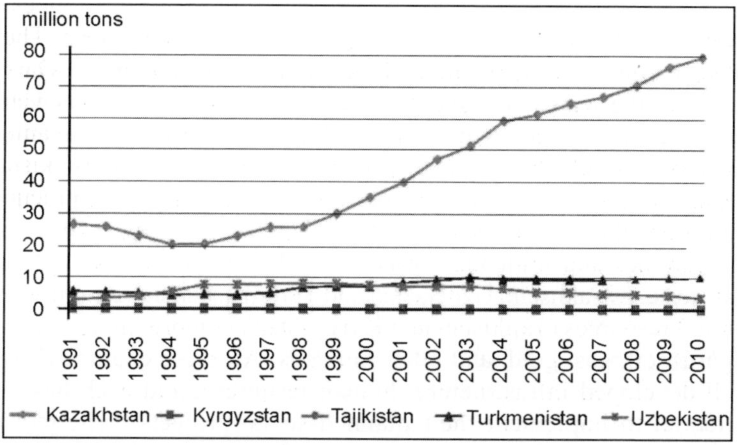

Source: CIS Statcommittee, 2012.

Fig. 14.4: Oil drilling, including gas condensate

Countries of the region that have sufficient reserves of uranium and a nuclear industrial complex can cooperate in the development of nuclear energy. It should be noted that as a result of the prolonged and intensive mining and processing of uranium ore, the region has accumulated a large amount of radioactive waste stored in tailing ponds. Many of them are located near tributaries of the trans-boundary

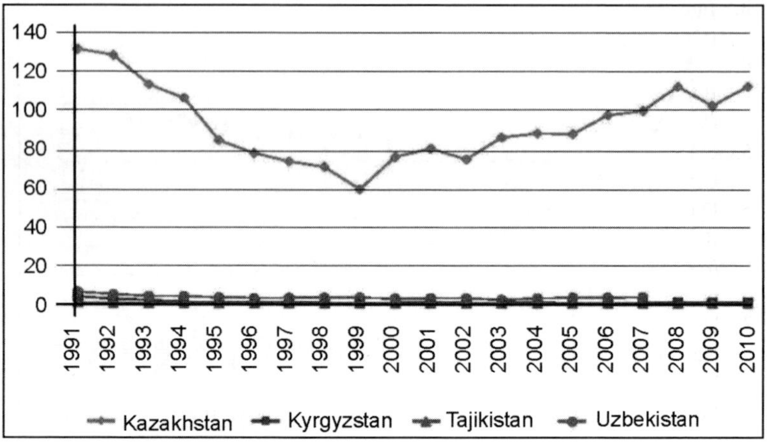

Source: CIS Statcommittee, 2012.

Fig. 14.5: Coal mining (million tons)

rivers. Because of the unsatisfactory state of the tailing ponds, they present a threat to the public and the environment, and in case of an accident, the waste may seep into the rivers and spread over large territories. Tailing ponds are in need of major repairs and preventative measures should be taken to prevent the release of radioactive substances into surface and ground water. The problem is regional in nature, and the Central Asian countries could work together to develop programmes and implement practical solutions to dispose tailings and waste. Kazakhstan, Uzbekistan and Turkmenistan have significant natural resources (Tajikistan and Kyrgyzstan are more limited in this regard): oil, gas, gold, and other minerals. All these countries have well-developed infrastructure, human resources, and each has the potential to implement their planned social projects.[10] The global situation in terms of raw minerals, especially energy, is also conducive to enhancing economic development in the region.

Endnotes

1. Sarsembekov T. *et al. Ispolzovanie i okhrana transgranichnykh rek v Tsentralnoy Asiy* (Use and Protection of Transboundary Rivers in Central Asia) (Almaty: Atamura, 2004), p. 272.
2. Environment and Security: Central Asia-Ferghana/Osh/Khujand Area. UNEP, UNDP, OSCE, NATO 2005: Geneva. ENVSEC. p. 21.

3. Interstate Statistical Committee of the Commonwealth of. Independent States (CIS Statcommittee). Moskow. 2012. www.cisstat.org
4. World Bank. Load Dispatch and System Operation Study for Central Asian Power System. Report. Mercados – Energy Markets International (Spain). (World Bank. 2010. October).
5. CASA (2011) Central Asia – South Asia Electricity Transmission and Trade CASA -1000). Final report. SNS Lavalin International Inc. February.
6. Davydov Yu. (1925) Water Energy Reserves in Central Asia. Water Resources Management in Central Asia. *Vestnik Irrigatsii*. no. 7. *Monthly journal*. Central Asian water resources publication. Tashkent. July. pp. 91-93.
7. UNESCO. Use of Renewable Energy Sources in Central Asia. United Nations Educational, Scientific and Cultural Organization. (Almaty. 2010)
8. Molodtsov S. *Regional Concept of Fuel and Energy Resources Use Efficiency Improvement Policy in Central Asia for 2011-2015*. (Moscow: Center for Energy Policy, 2010).
9. Yassinskiy V., Mironenkov A., Steklov Y., Sarsembekov T., Mezhdunarodnay praktika sotrudnichestva i problemy razvitiya gidroenergetiki v basseinakh transgranichnykh rek (*International Practice of Cooperation and Problems of Hydropower Development in Transboundary River Basins). Eurasian Development Bank*. (Almaty: RUAN, 2011). p. 192.
10. Yassinskiy V., Mironenkov A., Sarsembekov T.. *Priorities for Cooperation in Central Asian in Transboundary River* Basins. *Eurasian Development Bank*. (Almaty: RUAN, 2012). p. 232.

15
Regional Interactions: South Asia and Central Asia

Yelena I. Rudenko

Introduction

Politico-strategic interaction of individual states and Central and South Asia is of critical significance, yet it is complicated by issues faced, in particular, by their cooperation in the economic sphere. Being stable and sustainable in character, the relationship includes aspects of both positive complexity and diversity. Thus, on the domestic policy front, one can speak of a meaningful list of similarities in mutual priorities and so on. The foreign policy sphere encompasses numerous issues of both indirect and direct cooperation like security, approaches to the solution of the Afghan problem, participation in supra-regional organizations, etc. Nevertheless, there are certain problematic aspects to the political-strategic involvement of the states and regions under consideration, which should be dealt with. It should also be noted that so far as Kazakhstan in Central and India in South Asia are the leading states in their regions, it is their relationship that deserves special attention.

Antecedences of Interaction: An Overview

Researchers have looked at the early priorities in the relationship between the newly-independent republics of Central Asia and India and Pakistan. Some Indian experts believe that the political aspect related to intra-and inter-regional security was of primary importance. Others are inclined to say that the economic aspect prevailed over the political: India has been interested mainly in trade and economic cooperation with Central Asian states, and only on the basis of its own economic interests has formulated its political and economic policy towards these states.

In any event, it can be argued that India felt a clear convergence of interests between its own achievements and the needs of the Central Asian states. This included, above all, the ability of Central Asian states to cooperate with India in more or less all possible fields, and to learn from its experience in the economic sphere. India's Central Asian partner states, for a certain period of time proved these mutualities correct. However, over time, such an "all-embracing" interest by Central Asian states has given the way to a more rational and balanced approach. Sometimes, it was seen that interest shown in India by one of the Central Asian countries, like Uzbekistan or Tajikistan, was immediately projected by India as proof of its acceptability to the entire region, which India (erroneously) perceived as being a uniform one. This led to a number of erroneous conclusions largely due to the overconfidence displayed by India in reading its unquestionable importance to the region. The results of this miss-step can be seen even today and must be mutually reconsidered.

In addition, two major South Asian states from the very beginning acted as rivals in Central Asian region, even though there were also perceptions about the importance and even the necessity of Indo-Pakistani cooperation in Central Asia. Both India and Pakistan closely monitored the activities and successes of each other in consolidating their positions in the region. Due to the fact that the premises and consequent activities of these two South Asian countries were quite different, none of them could make full use of each others' experience and only highlighted each others' success or failures. All this left a negative impact on the nature of interaction between South and Central Asian countries, especially since the CA countries were not interested in the rivalry but in cooperation with the two neighbouring rivals. To some extent, one can even accept the assertion that the Indian policy with regard to Kashmir, Afghanistan and Central Asia has a pronounced anti-Pakistan character. And while India and Pakistan fight each other for expanding their influence in Central Asia, other states actually stand to gain actual economic and political power in this region.

Nevertheless, one cannot but admit that if not the similarity in domestic and foreign policy concepts of CA states, then at least mutual understanding between them in the political sphere is of great importance for successful cooperation and collaboration with the international community. In this respect, political support to development of Central and South Asian states is definitely a positive factor in the current interaction between the two regions.

As correctly noted by many researchers, at the political level India has a significant relationship with Central Asian countries. Indeed, in the political aspect, there have been – from the very beginning – areas of mutual contact between India and the Central Asian republics. The Indian side leveraged its advantages in the domestic and political system (democracy, secularism, combination of pluralism with multi-faith and multi-ethnicity, etc.) and their participation in international fora. And while Pakistan did not have the same overall recognition in the Central Asian region as compared to India (except for the ambiguous though still favourable factor of common religious affiliation), it nevertheless also sought to support the CA republics in their political endeavours.

Initially, if at the initial stage the Indian and Pakistani sides did not have full confidence in the direction foreign policy in the newly-independent Central Asian states would move, over time they received their answer. The Central Asian Republics have chosen, in principle, to be part of the international community facilitated to some extent by India (and in a slightly lesser extent, by Pakistan) by moving to identify the most promising areas in Central-South Asian political engagement.

Perception of Supra-regional Units

As a positive factor, it should be noted that though natural, both Indian and CARs had considerable convergence of views on the role and the nature of activities of international organizations. Thus, both India and the countries of Central Asia have always emphasized a decisive role of the UN in world affairs and, in addition, sought to actively participate in the activities of this organization. It is within the framework of the UN that similarities in positions of India and Central Asian states over major issues of world order have manifested most vividly. Besides, Central Asian republics constantly and unequivocally support Indian claims to become a permanent member of the UN Security Council, as well as her appeal for a more diversified, resolute and fair UN.

Central and South Asian states also work together in a number of other fora as well. Thus, Uzbekistan is party to the Non-Aligned Movement, one of the founders of which was India, and which includes other countries of South Asia. Of no less importance is Indian and Pakistani participation in CICA, created on Kazakhstan's initiative, as well as their partial membership in SCO. Besides, India has regularly expressed its support for the candidacy of Kazakhstan and other Central Asian states for their full membership in the Regional Forum of ASEAN, where the Indian side has a strong position, which is also quite positively perceived by Central Asian side.

However, some analysts believe that there is some divergence in opinion on international and regional supra-state actors between Central and South Asian states, which arc both history-specific and on current politico-economic conditions.

Thus, there is a difference in view on the activities of some organizations in which Central Asian states and India cooperate with each other, including the UN. In general, the difference lies in the fact that India is trying – and actually does play – a more active and visible role in these fora than the Central Asian Republics. The latter, as a rule, accept the rules of the game already established within these organizations, while India, when necessary, seeks to adjust these rules to her own interests. This, in fact, indicates the leading position of India on the world stage, which should ideally be of significant interest to the Central Asian states.

Within CICA, Kazakhstan attaches most priority to declarative strategic-cultural cooperation aimed to the enhancement of peaceful relations, without special attention to bilateral tensions, while India wants economic relations supported by peaceful political initiatives to be more active within CICA; Kazakhstan wants CICA to enter into disarmament talks in the Asian sub-continent, while India in principle a supporter of disarmament, believes that these can only take place on a global scale rather than within individual regions.

A very interesting situation emerged in the Indian perception of Central Asian countries' membership of the OIC. It seems that India, being initially anxious about OIC's extended influence in the neighbouring region, later declared its comfort in dealing with the OIC after the Central Asian Republics joined it and India was convinced that Islam did not pose any threat to her interests in these republics. In addition, India is also convinced about the fact that it is the "Central Asian factor" that, to certain extent, weakened the position and the anti-Indian stance of Pakistan within the OIC.

Not without interest is the fact that while the activities of the "Muslim" ECO were previously strongly criticized by India, later it changed its stance and a number of Indian experts even started speaking about the appropriateness of India's possible accession to the organization, since it may expand the geographical area of its economic presence and contribute to the resolution of transportation issues between States.

Hence, while the interaction of the States of Central and South Asia within the framework of various inter-national and inter-regional organizations is generally positive, at the same time further convergence between the political and economic ideologies between the states of these two regions must also take into account due respect towards their mutual points-of-view.

Security Issues as a Background for Deeper Interaction

One of the most significant components of political cooperation between Central and South Asian countries is their many-sided engagement in the maintenance of security: the fight against terrorism, Islamic extremism, drug trafficking, transnational organized crime, illegal migration, etc. – all that constitutes a threat to the welfare of both regions. Between almost all the countries of Central and South Asia, many joint agreements on these issues have been entered into. However, it should be noted that India's cooperation with Central Asian Republics in Indian strategic circles in the sphere of security evolved over the time; in the beginning, while it was discussed as a possibility, it was not seen as something that was urgently required.

An important Declaration – the Kazakhstan-India Joint Declaration of 12 February 2002 – reflects the convergence of views between the two States on the situation in Afghanistan, threat of terrorism as well as regional initiatives to combat various threats global and regional in character.

On the basis of this Declaration, there has been an Agreement on Establishment of Joint Working Group on Combating International Terrorism and Other Crimes in June 2002, between India and Kazakhstan. It states that the purpose of creating such a Group lies in sharing experiences and coordinating approaches in the fight against international terrorism, organized crime, illicit traffic in narcotics, weapons, and exchange of information with respect to terrorists and organized crime and curbing their activities. It is also envisaged to improve mechanisms of sharing experiences and information, provide mutual technical assistance, including training, as well as coordination and expansion of cooperation on issues related to the global campaign against these threats.[1] Kazakhstan also has a bilateral Agreement on Cooperation in Combating Terrorism and International Crime with Pakistan.

In December 2002, Kazakhstan approved a Memorandum on Military-Technical Cooperation between the Government of the Republic of Kazakhstan and the Government of the Republic of India, which was floated on 3rd June, 2002. This Memorandum stipulates mutual provision of military-technological goods and services, implementation of joint projects related to military techniques and technologies; cooperation between defense enterprises, including technology transfer, technical assistance, training and co-production; cooperation in the field of military science and technology through the exchange of information and experts, as well as mutual learning.[2]

India has similar strategic or/and diplomatic agreements with other Central Asian republics as well. The provisions of, for example, Kazakhstani-Indian Memorandum show that an important aspect of interregional cooperation between Central and South Asia in the field of security lies in the training of military personnel. A number of military personnel, including those from Kazakhstan, have been trained in Indian military institutions (National Defense Academy, Command-Staff College and others), mainly under the ITEC programme. However, because of the relative remoteness of the two regions and lack of sufficient interest, joint military exercises are still to begin.

Central Asian States and India share views on the principles and methods to combat the above-mentioned threats. Both sides note the need for mutual coherence of activities: "the fight against terrorism is essential. Equally important are the coordinated joint actions by all countries". Also recognized is the need to exchange experiences in this area: "We know that India has a wealth of experience in the fight against terrorism, using a variety of methods and technologies".[3]

Unfortunately, with regard to ongoing cooperation between Kazakhstan and India in the field of security, it should be accepted that, by now, this cooperation is, unfortunately, more in a declarative nature (with the exception of interaction within CICA). At the same time, it should be noted that a very important feature is the substantial similarity – not only in the views of the two states on the priorities for cooperation in the field of security but also in their perception of this cooperation and their role in it. Here, both India and Kazakhstan tend to play a leading role in their respective regions, and hence show increasing sensitivity to both direct threats to their own security and threats to their general areas of interest as well. Therefore, in this area at least, the two countries have the potential not only for cooperation on specific aspects of security, but also in the overall coordination of this agreement and cooperation at the inter-regional level.

Afghanistan as a Crucial Aspect of Inter-Regional Convergence

The countries of South Asia, especially India and the Central Asian Republics – attach great importance to cooperation in post-war management of Afghanistan. Here, while the Central Asian states consider such cooperation as happening at the international level, India, however, eyeing Afghanistan as a buffer between Central and South Asia, sees this cooperation happening at the inter-regional level. The Indian side believes that states adjacent to Afghanistan (which, besides Central Asian countries, also includes China, Iran and Russia) are, more than the others, interested in the complete elimination of conflict and in the stabilization of the situation in Afghanistan. Therefore, India is not simply talking about the need for such cooperation in the way the Central Asia Republics do, but often insists on it categorically. India and the countries of Central Asia (as, indeed, most other states and international organizations) share similarity in the ways to solve or at least mitigate the Afghan problem. Thus, both sides are inclined to believe that stabilization of the situation in Afghanistan should be done, as far as possible, based on a non-military approach. The representatives of both India and the Central Asian states also have sought to rebuild the economy of Afghanistan not only through external sources of funding, but also through the development of country's own agricultural and industrial base, training of local personnel, improved education and healthcare systems, women's empowerment, environmental initiatives, etc.

A number of Central Asian and Indian experts and official representatives support the "Greater Central Asia" idea proposed by the U.S., which comprises the political and economic unification of South and Central Asia through Afghanistan. However, it has also been observed that the presence of U.S. military bases in Central Asia has not eliminated the threat of terrorism in the region, but rather, the U.S. invasion of Afghanistan and Iraq has contributed to the fact that the Taliban, which was earlier concentrated largely in Afghanistan, has expanded beyond Afghan borders into Iraq, Iran, Pakistan, and Indian Jammu and Kashmir. As reality has shown, the Afghans themselves had much better control of the situation and had ensured the stability of the Wakhan Corridor area than what the US has been able to achieve. Moreover, as the US fight against terrorism is focused mostly against al-Qaida and the Taliban, India, Kazakhstan and other Central Asian Republics should not rely on its help in dealing with such threats, but should independently participate in regional and interregional anti-terrorist fora.

India is currently stepping up the level of its involvement in all aspects of life in Afghanistan, and is actually ahead of Pakistan, not only in its economic presence but also in terms of political influence on the religiously moderate sections of Afghan population. At the same time, India unobtrusively wants the Central Asian Republics to participate in the economic and political reconstruction of not only by cooperating with India but also on the basis of their own interests and preferences. Fortunately, India's desire to see Afghanistan as an economically liberal and, if possible, secular state is what the Central Asian states also seek – not only in Afghanistan but also in relation to their own socio-political and economic development.

One should, however, note while there is general similarity of views and approaches to the Afghan problem, there are also some differences in the interpretation and in the peculiarities of individual perceptions by Central and South Asia states. Moreover, these differences exist both intra-regionally but also inter-regionally as well. Nevertheless, regional benefits of the joint resolution on the situation in Afghanistan seems to be obvious and very significant. This, above all, can promote the possibility of constructing across Afghan territory a convenient, cheap and politically acceptable transport and pipeline network from Central to South Asia. In addition, the buffer zone separating Central and South Asia, Afghanistan could become a zone of all-round cooperation between the two regions. The mitigation of radical Islam in Afghanistan could remove religious tensions in

Kashmir as well as in the Central Asian states, particularly those neighbouring Afghanistan, which could also facilitate mutually beneficial intra- and inter-regional cooperation.

Of particular significance is a speedy but reasonable and balanced solution to the problem of drug trafficking. According to UN data, only 21 per cent of drug traffic passes through the states of Central Asia while more than 50 per cent passes through Pakistan. However, India believes that this problem is largely faced by the Central Asian republics. And although the Central Asian states are well aware of this issue and make a strong and manifold effort to deal with it (it is worth mentioning, for example, the formation in 2007 of the Central Asian Regional Information and Coordination Centre for Combating Illicit Trafficking in Narcotic Drugs), India, for its part, consistently keep a focus on this threat as well. Hence, Central Asian states may consider India as a reliable partner and a valuable source of experience in the management of drug trafficking in the region.

It should be specially noted that depending on the degree of remoteness of each State from the abovementioned threats, the states of Central Asia have different opinions and evaluation of its relative seriousness to their security. If the problem of illegal migration is more relevant for Kazakhstan, then for Uzbekistan the problem of Islamic extremism is more acute, while the threat of drug trafficking is equally serious for the entire Central Asian region.

However, some overall inconsistency in the perception of certain threats by individual Central Asian states cannot be compared to the disagreement primarily between India and Pakistan. India accuses Pakistan in fomenting trouble on almost all the issues listed above, while Pakistan – also a victim of many of these problems – but also suffers – directly or indirectly – loss of credibility in the eyes of its neighbours and the international community, though it says it is also making efforts to address these issues. As far as the overall terrorist threat is concerned, it makes no sense to look for a "guilty" state. In contrast, the countries of neighbouring regions and world community as a whole should be engaged and intensively cooperate with each other, including the epicenters of terrorism like Pakistan and Afghanistan, as a common threat. Moreover, participation in such a struggle that involves Pakistan, Afghanistan and the Central Asian Republics – officially being Muslim states – is especially important since about it is not perceived as a "clash of civilizations" but a clash within a single Muslim civilization – between progressive and radical

Muslims. It is also important to note that no matter how great is the actual responsibility of Pakistan for the emergence and spread of these threats, an but attitude of mistrust and prejudice by India and some Central Asian states clearly prevents overcoming these threats together. This is obvious to the Kazakhstani side, and, in the joint fight by the Central and South Asian states against terrorism, extremism, drug trafficking and other threats, it actually makes no distinction between India and Pakistan.

As for differences in perception of common threats that exist between the two regions, it should be noted that there is an element of exaggeration of these threats in relation of one region to another. Assessing the degree of responsibility of Pakistan for facilitating and exacerbating various regional problems, the states of Central Asia are of the opinion that the threat is both from the South – from within Pakistan – as well as a result of the long-festering Indo-Pakistan rivalry in the region. India, on the contrary, seeing Afghanistan as part of the Central Asian region in many aspects, sees the periphery of instability extending to the Central Asian states, especially those that directly border Afghanistan. Hence, this point needs to be seen based on mutual perceptions. However, in terms of security cooperation with Central Asian countries, India follows the same approach as in other spheres of interaction: that inter-regional cooperation will be more effective if there is effective intra-regional cooperation within the Central Asian region and the CIS. In this regard, India highly appreciates the role of regional organizations such as CSTO and the SCO, which work in areas that are also of concern to India.

Home-Policy Priorities: Advantages of Approximation

Mainly, there is similarity in the domestic socio-economic situation in the Republics of Central Asia and India in relation to the multi-ethnic, multi-religious and multicultural composition of their populations. This very aspect is not only socially indispensable internally, but also acts a like a common link between the two regions, since all states of the two regions have, in principle, a similar approach to addressing the needs of their populations as also supporting each other. In fact, the Republics of Central Asia regularly acknowledge the success of the Indian State in managing its "unity in diversity". The Indian side is also very positive about the socio-political initiatives of Central Asian leaders in this sphere.

It should be especially noted that until recently, there was an aspect of domestic policy where mutual understanding between the countries of Central and South Asia was not complete– the question of ensuring a functioning democracy in the Central Asian Republics in accordance with standards accepted by the global community and India itself. India, as the most populous and vibrant democracy in the world, has traditionally paid considerable attention to the extent and nature of domestic developments and democratic reforms in the Central Asian states. In doing so, Indian experts, from the beginning of the 1990s, began to voice their concerns about the insufficient democratic standards in the Central Asian region, even without making appropriate distinctions between individual states.

From the very beginning, thus, India began to offer sharing its own experience in democratic reforms as a model for the newly-independent states of Central Asia. Indian businessmen from both the public and private sectors also pointed to democratic development as an important factor in successful economic cooperation between the two regions. The Central Asian states, while generally agreeing with such opinion, were however in no hurry to borrow from the Indian experience. However, over time India began to accept that the question of political and democratic maturity reached by each individual state in general was not essential, and that the level of democracy practiced in the Central Asian region as a whole did not have to correspond to the Indian political viewpoint. Indeed, it was clear that success in adapting the Indian model of democracy would depend not just on the desire, but on the need, for Central Asian states to adopt this very model, which in its turn was conditional on their internal social and political situation. Kazakhstan, being primarily focused towards the West, was impressed by the West's recognition of India as the world's largest democracy, but its "Oriental specifics" was still a reason for the skeptical attitude of Kazakhstan to this fact. Equally important also was the factor of Kazakhstan's "national pride", which called into questioned the need to borrow democracy from anyone at all.

However, there actually are areas where, Kazakhstan in particular, displayed interest in the Indian socio-political experiences. These include Indian methods of managing the civil phenomenon of "multi-", interrelation between Executive and Legislative powers, developing certain institutional aspects, etc.[4]

Unfortunately, there are also certain problematic areas in the political-administrative component of economic cooperation of the two leading states of Central and South Asia.

For instance, in 2003, the Indian Ministry of Commerce and Industry launched a "Focus CIS" Programme, whose purpose was, in particular, to assist representatives of business circles in India and the CIS states to expand mutual economic contacts in various fields. As part of this programme, many visits of trade-industrial delegations, organization of trade exhibitions, etc.[5] took place on a reciprocal basis. However, officials, businessmen and academics note with sorrow that the full potential of the programme is still to be realized. In recent years, India has expressed interest in Kazakhstan and Central Asia under the "New Silk Road" Programme as well, with the possible hope that this initiative would be more viable and beneficial.

It should also be accepted that Kazakhstani and Indian Chambers of Commerce and Industry, Committees on various types of bilateral cooperation, etc. only work within their frameworks and in overly loose manner, while there is a need for industry-specific committees on specific aspects of cooperation. Despite Indian organizations like EEPC, ECS and others participating in various exhibitions in Kazakhstan and similar organizations in Kazakhstan as well, there is still a need to work more closely by both sides. Moreover, it should be pointed out that even large Indian organizations and important for a rarely are successful since they assign little time and resources on preliminary preparations.

Besides other reasons, political and economic interaction between Central and South Asian states is still largely determined by mutual perceptions between the two sides. Therefore, the mutual sharing of updated and objective information about each other, including people-to-people contacts between the Kazakhstani and Indian sides, is very essential. No less important is the tracking of how and in what form the information reaches its audience. One should also pay attention to other sources of information which may be used by each other. Thus, both Kazakhstan and India receive mainly distorted and biased information about each other from Western sources. The way to correcting this situation may be raising diplomatic representation (for official level), as well as mutual dissemination of information about each country at the popular level. In this context, India should more aggressively use its own experience in cultural diplomacy while Kazakhstan should more actively study the Indian experience.

Conclusion

In the closing, some points for consideration on the political-strategic cooperation between the two regions are presented here. First, it seems that despite some apprehensions in Kazakhstan, in the long term the countries of South Asia will have neither the capacity nor the desire to interfere in both the internal and international affairs of the Central Asian region, except for perhaps India or Pakistan. The two South Asian states' need to participate in the "Great Game" in the extended neighbourhood of Central Asia for over a decade are focused on the economic sphere, including the strategic hydrocarbon reserves and interregional transport infrastructure potential of CARs. The Central Asian republics also are likely to be only watching the India-Pakistan relationship, traditionally expressing support and respecting the opinions of both, while insisting on the need of these states to solve their problems on a bilateral basis.

Thus, a variety of minor contradictions between the regions of Central and South Asia could be settled easily enough, while dominant political-strategic issues can serve as a potential for deeper and wider cooperation. Meanwhile, it must be remembered that the global situation as seen by India can be summed up thus: "In the world of today there are two mutually contradictory trends – one towards integration of nations, through trade blocks and development of security communities... and the other – towards fragmentation". The first is directed to the developed and the second to the developing world.[6] Within this context, the prevention of political as well as economic "fragmentation" among the states and regions of Central and South Asia should be considered necessary for their security through unimpeded internal development and mutually beneficial interregional cooperation.

Endnotes

1. Agreement between the Government of the Republic of Kazakhstan and the Government of the Republic of India on Establishment of Joint Working Group on Combating International Terrorism and Other Crimes dated 3 June 2002, articles 1-3.
2. Memorandum on Military-Technical Cooperation between the Government of the Republic of Kazakhstan and the Government of the Republic of India dated 3 June 2002, articles 1-2.

3. Gulomov, K.G. "Threats from International Terrorism: A Central Asian Perspective," in K. Santhanam, R. Dwivedi (ed.) *India and Central Asia: Advancing the Common Interest* (New Delhi: Anamaya Publishers, 2004), p. 328.
4. See in more details: Rudenko, Yelena. "Current Status, Problems and Prospects of India-Kazakhstan Cooperation in Political Sphere," *Foreign Policy Research Centre Journal: India and Central Asia*, No. 10 (April-June 2012), p. 241-242. http://www.fprc.in/fprc_journal.php.
5. Trade Promotion Programme - Focus: CIS. http://www.commerce.nic.in/trade/international_tpp_cis.asp (Accessed May 7, 2013).
6. Subrahmanyam, K. "India and the Changes in the International Security Environment," in L. Mansingh et al. (ed.) *Indian Foreign Policy: Agenda for the 21st Century* (New Delhi: Konark Publishers Pvt. Ltd., 1997), Vol. 1, p. 70.

PART III

India-Central Asia: Bilateral Relations

Part III

16
Trade Potentials Between India and Kazakhstan: An Overview

Vijay Laxmi and Gurinder Kaur

In the era of globalization, economic ties are key to any bilateral, trilateral or multilateral cooperation. The economic and strategic significance of Central Asian countries considerably fuels India's still developing "forward" Central Asian policy. Amongst all five Central Asian Republics, Kazakhstan is very rich in hydrocarbons, wheat production and mineral and metal resources, and has 15 per cent of world's uranium resources. After Soviet disintegration, Kazakhstan holds a special place in India's foreign policy priorities. India and Kazakhstan are rapidly growing economies, which has opened up new vistas for bilateral cooperation between the two nations. Amongst all the Central Asian countries, Kazakhstan remains the largest trading partner of India.

The purpose of this chapter is to present an overview of trade data between India and Kazakhstan, and to highlight future possible cooperation potentials for enhanced trade between the two countries.

Over the year, the two countries have been involved in bilateral trade of various goods and materials. Major items of import by India include silver and silver-gold, asbestos, steel, aluminium, wool, raw hides, etc. Major commodities of export from India are tea, pharmaceuticals, medical equipment, machinery, tobacco, consumer items, etc. Presently, about 280 companies are engaged in conducting business between India and Kazakhstan, with India's investment in Kazakhstan reaching US$ 38 million.[1] Hence, it becomes significant to observe the existing trends in trade between the two countries.

Table 16.1 depicts the export and import values (in US$ million)

Table 16.1: Import and export values of trade between India and Kazakhstan

S. No.	Per Year	2007-2008	2008-2009	2009-2010	2010-2011	2011-2012
1.	**EXPORT**	111.99	131.68	136.54	172.16	244.39
2.	%Growth		17.58	3.69	26.09	41.95
3.	India's Total Export	163,132.18	185,295.36	178,751.43	251,136.19	305,963.92
4.	%Growth		13.59	–3.53	40.49	21.83
5.	%Share	0.07	0.07	0.08	0.07	0.08
6.	**IMPORT**	76.78	159.03	154.91	138.42	166.35
7.	%Growth		107.11	–2.59	–10.64	20.18
8.	India's Total Import	251,654.01	303,696.31	288 372.88	369,769.13	489,319.49
9.	%Growth		20.68	–5.05	28.23	32.33
10.	%Share	0.03	0.05	0.05	0.04	0.03
11.	**TOTAL TRADE**	188.77	290.70	291.44	310.59	410.74
12.	%Growth		54.00	0.25	6.57	32.25
13.	India's Total Trade	414,786.19	488,991.67	467,124.31	620,905.32	795,283.41
14.	%Growth		17.89	–4.47	32.92	28.08
15.	%Share	0.05	0.06	0.06	0.05	0.05
16.	**TRADE BALANCE**	35.21			33.74	78.04
17.	India's Trade Balance	–88,521.83	–118,400.95	–109,621.45	–118,632.94	–183,355.57

Source: Directorate General of Foreign Trade, Government of India.

between India and Kazakhstan from 2007 to 2012. This data has been obtained from the Directorate General of Foreign Trade, Government of India.

The Table 16.1 shows that India's total exports grew by 13.59 per cent from 2007-2008 to 2008-2009. India's total exports in 2007-2008 were US$ 163, 132.18 million, which increased to US$ 185, 295.36 million in 2008-2009. In the same period, India's exports to Kazakhstan were US$ 111.9 million (2007-2008), which grew by 17.58 per cent and reached US$ 131.68 million in 2008-2009. In this phase, India's export growth vis-a-vis Kazakhstan was higher than India's export growth in totality. India's total share of exports to Kazakhstan was 0.07 per cent in 2007-2008 and 2008-2009 of the total exports of India.

In 2009-2010, India's total exports were US$ 178, 751.43, falling significantly in the negative quadrant of growth to –3.53 per cent, as compared to the exports in 2008-2009. However, India's exports to Kazakhstan remained in the positive quadrant of growth, at 3.69 per cent. India's exports to Kazakhstan were US$ 136.54 million in 2009-2010. There was an increase in exports from India to Kazakhstan in this year, but with less overall growth as compared to previous year. India's total share of exports to Kazakhstan, out of her total exports, increased to 0.08 per cent from the previous 0.07 per cent. This was a phase of economic turmoil not only in India, but all over the world. Major economies of the world like the US, the UK and some other European countries were on the brink of recession. The overall market sentiment in this phase was low. In spite of this shrinking in trade at the global level, India saw an increase in its exports to Kazakhstan, howsoever low they may have been.

2010-2011 saw the revival of global economies and an end to economic turmoil and uncertainty. This phase saw significant growth in India's exports, which reached 40.49 per cent, to US $ 251,136.19 million. This was a significant increase from the previous year's dismal export values. With respect to Kazakhstan, too, India's exports witnessed a growth of 26.09 per cent to US$ 172.16 million. As compared to previous years wherein India's exports to Kazakhstan were higher than its overall export growth, this phase saw India's exports growth to Kazakhstan less than her overall export growth. Again, India's share of exports to Kazakhstan as part of its overall exports reverted to 0.07 per cent from the previous 0.08 per cent.

The value of India's total exports increased to US$ 305,963.92 in 2011-2012, as compared to the previous year, but there was a fall in its growth of exports to 21.83 per cent. With reference to Kazakhstan, India's export increased to US$ 244.39 million, with a growth of 41.95 per cent, the highest ever in the last five years, and also significantly more than the overall export growth of India. The share of India's exports to Kazakhstan increased to 0.08 per cent out of its total exports. These observations are presented in the following Graph 16.1.

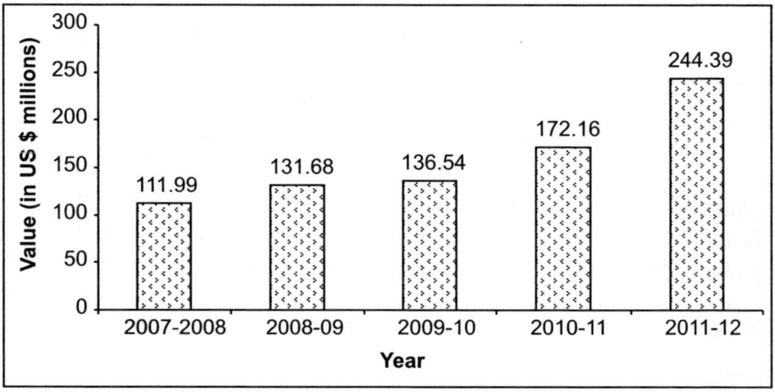

Graph 16.1: Export trends: India and Kazakhstan (2007-2012)

The top five export products from India to Kazakhstan include coffee, tea, spices; pharmaceutical products; articles of apparel and clothing (knitted or crocheted); articles of apparel and clothing (not knitted or crocheted); electrical machinery. The export values from 2009-2010 to 2011-2012 have shown a constant increase in the trading of these top five items of export. There is rise in the total export value from US $ 136.54 million in 2009-2010 to US $ 172.16 million in 2010-2011 to US $ 244.39 million in 2011-2012.

As can be observed from the Graph 16.2, there is a constant increase in the export of top five products from India to Kazakhstan since 2009, except pharmaceuticals. This sector, ideally, could have been a major export market for India due to its nascent stage and increasing requirements. There have been many expert-level visits in the field of health care from India to Kazakhstan. India is also trying to encourage pharmaceutical companies to invest in Kazakhstan. However, due to the impending finalisation of the agreement on

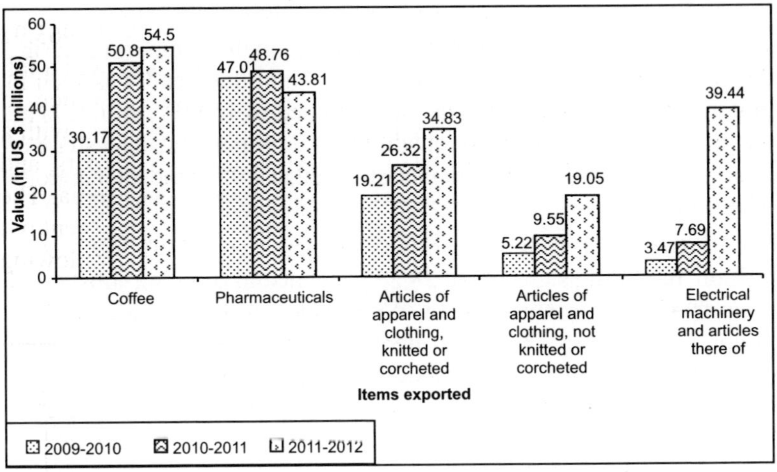

Graph 16.2: Top five exported items to Kazakhstan from India

pharmaceuticals between the two nations, the extent of these exports is decreasing. Also, exports in general, and pharmaceuticals in particular, have been hampered due to ad hoc implementation of customs codes, regulations and rules, excessive and unclear documentations, etc.[2] The dip in exports in this sector needs to be analysed more thoroughly, and efforts should be made to increase the trend in the future. In terms of exports of electrical machinery, a significant jump is observed in the trade.

Though India's exports to Kazakhstan have been increasing over the years, never falling in the negative quadrant of growth of exports, the share in comparison to India's overall exports is almost nonexistent. Kazakhstan ranks number 82 (as of December 2012) in list of first 100 trading partners of India. There is ample scope of improving this scenario provided the right opportunities are created and grasped in this.

As seen from Table 16.1, India's total imports in 2007-2008 were valued at US$ 251,654.01 million, which increased to US$ 303,696.31 in 2008-2009, showing a growth of 20.68 per cent. In the same period, India's imports from Kazakhstan were valued at US $ 76.78 millions in 2007, and increased to US$ 159.03 million in 2008-2009, showing an excellent growth of 107.11 per cent, much higher than India's total import growth. The share of India's imports from Kazakhstan was 0.03 per cent of its total import in 2007-2008, and 0.05 per cent in 2008-2009.

In 2009-2010, India recorded a drop in imports from the previous year to US$ 288,372.88 million, with the growth of imports entering the negative quadrant to –5.05 per cent. A similar trend was seen in imports from Kazakhstan. The value dipped to 154.91 million, with the growth entering negative quadrant at –2.59 per cent. The share of imports from Kazakhstan remained stagnant at 0.05 of the total imports from India.

In 2010-2011, India's imports again increased to US$ 369,769.13 million, recording a growth of 28.23 per cent and showing substantial jump from prior import growth. With respect to Kazakhstan, India's imports at US$138.42 million depicted a regression not only from previous decreasing import value but also way behind the trend in overall import scenario of India. The growth again registered a negative value of –10.64 per cent. India's share of imports from Kazakhstan decreased to 0.04 per cent.

In 2011-2012, overall imports again saw an increase as compared to the previous year, totalling US$ 489,319.49 million. Imports from Kazakhstan entered a positive quadrant after a gap of two years, showing a growth of 20.18 per cent and valued at 166.35 million. However, India's share of imports from Kazakhstan again decreased to 0.03 per cent of its overall import trade.

India's imports from Kazakhstan have been showing a consistent decrease from 2008 to 2011. An increase in imports was seen in FY of 2011-2012. The share of imports from Kazakhstan is of very little value as compared to India's overall import trade value. The trends in India's imports from Kazakhstan are shown in Graph 16.3 below.

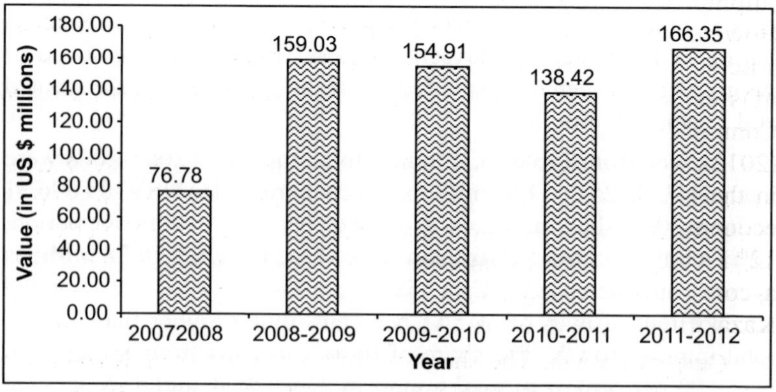

Graph 16.3: Import trend of India with Kazakhstan (2007-2012)

The top five items of import include zinc and articles thereof; iron and steel; natural or cultured pearls, precious or semi-precious stones, etc.; salt, sulphur, earth and stone, plastering material, lime and cement; inorganic chemicals, organic or inorganic compounds of precious metals. Unlike the constant increase seen in export values over the last three years, import values show a fluctuation from US$ 154.91 million in 2009-2010 to US$ 138.42 million in 2010-2011, while again increasing to US$ 166.35 million in 2011-2012.

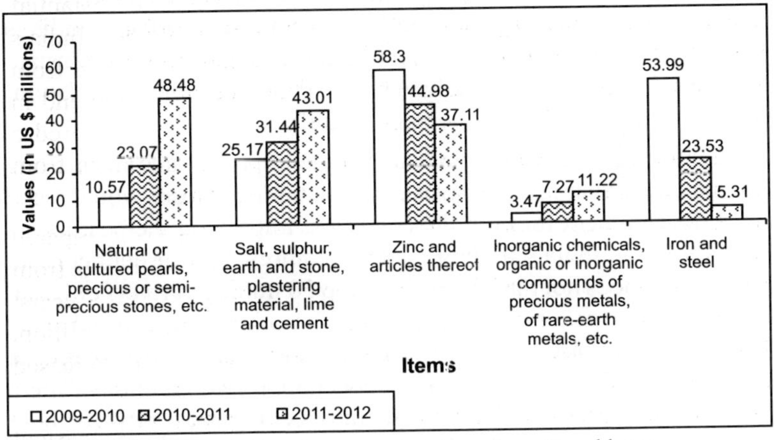

Graph 16.4: Top five imported items from Kazakhstan

Graph 16.4 shows there has been an increase in imports of natural or cultured pearls since 2009, reaching a very high value of US$ 48.48 million in 2012. The same trend is seen in the import of salt, sulphur, earth and stone, plastering material, lime and cement. However, lower trends are seen in the import of zinc and related articles and iron and steel. There is a steep decline seen in the import of steel over the past three years since 2009. The Planning Commission Report on the steel industry for the 12th Five Year Plan (2012-2017) has attributed the decline in domestic demand for steel in the 11th Five Year Plan to economic slowdown in the country's economy. The Planning Commission predicts the similar trend in the 12th Five Plan as well. As a result of the economic downturn in India, a consequent decline is seen in import of iron and steel from Kazakhstan.[3]

Currently, Kazakhstan ranks 94 in terms of India's import trading partners. A lot of other significant items like Uranium and other energy resources, which are necessary for the developmental and energy needs of India, could be included in the priority list of imports from Kazakhstan. India's growing energy sector requires more raw materials. The cost of importing raw material due to high transportation costs makes it economically unfeasible. It becomes economically difficult for India to import raw material and unprocessed products from Kazakhstan. Joint ventures between the two countries could be set up within Kazakhstan to process raw materials into finished goods and then export them to India. India is particularly interested in importing rare earth metals from Kazakhstan. This has also been acknowledged by the then Petroleum and Natural Gas Minister of India, Mr. Veerappa Moily.

Effort could be made from both sides to improve trade and moving it to a much higher level. Improvement in trade relations would mean more development for both the countries. Improving the position of Kazakhstan as India's trading partner requires a lot of deliberation. Kazakhstan does not rank even in the top 50 trading partners of India. Efforts must be maintained to improve this ranking and strive to bring Kazakhstan in India's top ten leading trade partners by creating a conducive environment for trade between the two countries. There are several barriers in the way of trade cooperation between both countries, as enumerated below.

Hindrances in Mutual Cooperation in Trade

Both India and Kazakhstan share common perceptions about the need to have friendship and mutually advantageous economic relations. However, there are several hindrances that need to be addressed before any meaningful commercial relations with each other can be established. Some significant factors that are a hurdle in this are:

1. Language barrier
2. Lack of direct connectivity: Kazakhstan is a landlocked country and a lack of coastline increases cost of transportation by sea or land, thus increasing the costs of goods imported or exported. As an alternative to this, India is collaborating with Russia and Iran for furthering the North-South corridor. The opening of this corridor would enhance the ease of trade between the two countries.[4]

3. The banking sector experienced major problems during the global economic downturn, and continues to be one of Kazakhstan's major weakness. Due to this, a major impediment is non-availability of foreign currency and lack of conversion facilities.
4. Inadequate marketing through major media outlets/newspapers by respective Governments.
5. Intense power play by neighbouring countries like Russia, China, USA and other Western countries in the strategic arena of Central Asia.

Emerging ties between India and Kazakhstan clearly show that despite several roadblocks to the growth of relations, there are also immense prospects for future cooperation which can help enhance trade and investments between India and Kazakhstan.

Potential Areas for Future Cooperation between India and Kazakhstan

In order to improve the possibilities of trade between India and Kazakhstan, it is important to take note of some potential areas:

Agriculture

Central Asia could possibly gain from India's own experience in increasing food productivity as well as enhancing agricultural technology. India could possibly share its experience with the Green Revolution with Central Asian countries for increased agricultural productivity.

India and Kazakhstan could cooperate in the field of agriculture. Indian companies could render assistance to Kazakh farmers in the scientific-methods plan. The agronomic science is well developed in India. The country has about 50 agrarian universities. There is a state organisation – the Indian Council of Agricultural Research- which monitors more than 100 scientific-research establishments throughout country. They work in different thematic areas on various crops, in accordance with climatic and natural conditions of their regions.[5] Kazakhstan, on the other hand, is one of the world's largest grain producers and exporters. Both climate and soil fertility provide ideal conditions for growing wheat, barley, rice, corn, millet and buckwheat.

Around 220 million hectares are under cultivation in the country. Nevertheless, lack of scientific techniques regarding sustainable farming methods has resulted in declining soil fertility and a reduction in productivity and biodiversity.[6] Kazakhstan would prefer that its farmers and agricultural companies bring in new, environment-friendly technologies. India has the man power, excellent scientists and farmers with rich experience as well as well developed agricultural technologies to enhance agriculture-based exchanges with Kazakhstan.

The Punjab Government in India is set to explore land leasing opportunities for its farmers in the Central Asian countries, especially in Kazakhstan and Uzbekistan. Kazakhstan is a potential market for export of fruit, vegetables and potato seeds from India. The Confederation of Potato and Seed Farmers Association representative, Jang Bahadur Singh Sangha, from Jalandhar in Punjab says there is a lot of scope for selling potato seeds to Central Asia, especially to Kazakhstan and Uzbekistan.[7]

Energy

India is the one of the largest importers of energy resources in the world, and her needs are still growing. In Central Asia, Kazakhstan occupies a leading position in the energy sector. To continue their economic modernization and sustained growth, India and Kazakhstan rely strongly on energy imports and exports, respectively. India also looks to Uranium-rich Kazakhstan to feed its growing nuclear industry as it seeks to meet its immense energy needs. India may, in fact, require up to 8,000 tonnes of Uranium per year, since its demand for nuclear fuel is expected to grow tenfold by 2020.[8]

Mr. Doulat Kuanyshev, the Ambassador of the Republic of Kazakhstan to New Delhi, said in an exclusive interview with *Mediakhabar* that considering five-fold increase in volumes of output of Uranium in Kazakhstan and a 10-fold increase in the power generation capacity of nuclear power stations in India by 2020 could open up cooperation in this field, with long-term benefits to both.[9]

Micro, Small and Medium Enterprises (MSMEs)

Kazakhstan is a potential market for Indian Micro, Small and Medium Enterprises (MSMEs). There is a need to increase awareness about this region in India, and vice versa, to fulfill this potential. The Confederation of Indian Industries (CII) has, over the years, been organising "Enterprise India" shows in order to serve as a forum for Indian Small and Medium Enterprises (SMEs) in Kazakhstan. Kazakhstan topped the list of countries with the most improved business conditions in 2011.[10] Kazakhstan's former Deputy Foreign Minister, Kairat Umarov, said that in diversifying its economy with the coming of least 140 new manufacturing projects, Kazakhstan is keen to see investments by Indian businesses.[11] In India, the top MSME clusters in Punjab are located in the districts of Jalandhar (10), Ludhiana (8), Amritsar (4), Sangrur (3), and Faridkot (3). Punjab has many MSMEs who have the potential and willingness to go global. The two countries must create a platform for bringing together these prospects for the mutual benefit of each other.

Information Technology

Cooperation between India and Kazakhstan in high technology holds immense promise. Kazakhstan faces challenges in the IT sector, such as limited public-private dialogue, lack of soft skills amongst its employees, limited human capital capabilities and low levels of innovation. India has a pool of highly trained manpower in this field and is also at the forefront of advanced technologies like bio technology, nano-technologies and space. Both countries could also carry out joint research in advanced technology and explore possibilities of setting up joint projects. For furtherance of bilateral cooperation with Kazakhstan, an Indo-Kazakh Joint Working Group on Information Technology has been formed. TCS, NIIT and Shree InfoTech have their presence in Kazakhstan, and are involved with its banking sector. In the field of communication and information technology, both countries can cooperate in research in high-end computing and in training and education of personnel in Kazakhstan in advanced computer technologies.[12] India would also be happy to work with Kazakhstan in setting up Software Technology Parks in the country.

Apart from these above-mentioned potential areas of cooperation in trade and investment between India and Kazakhstan, there are other two major sectors – banking and healthcare – for an enhanced relationship in trade and investment.

Conclusion

In spite of huge potential in exploring new areas of cooperation with each other, these potentials have not been explored to their maximum. Thus, to conclude, in order to make India's "Connect Central Asia" policy a reality, some strong and rigorous steps need to be taken, such as:

1. Develop specific instances of joint ventures in business, agriculture, industry and essential services
2. Language is the main barrier between India and Kazakhstan, which needs to be solved through cooperation by both sides. However, this, too, could be turned into an important venture, wherein India could set up training and coaching centres on English which could help in capacity building and human resource development of Kazakhstan.
3. To develop trade and investment relations, there is an enormous need for developing new transport routes (rail, roads and airways) and improving connectivity between both the countries. There is a need for more Indian investment to strengthen bilateral economic cooperation between India and Kazakhstan.
4. To improve the current scenario, the two nations must not confine themselves to only Government-to-Government undertakings in trade and investment, but also involve their private sector to participate in enhancing trade ties and investment opportunities.
5. Bilateral exchange visits between the two countries by trade and industry delegations would increase awareness and enhanced cooperation further.

Endnotes

1. Roman Muzalevsky , India and Kazakhstan Bolster their Strategic Partnership, *Eurasia Daily Monitor*, Volume 8, No. 91, May 11, 2011,
2. www.pib.nic.in/PrintRelease.aspx.
3. Report of the working Group on Steel Industry for the Twelfth Five Year Plan (2012-2017), planningcommission.nic.in.
4. Gulshan Sachdeva, Economic Changes in Central Asia and India Response.

in J.N. Roy and B.B. Kumar, eds., *India and Central Asia: Classical to Contemporary Period,* 2007, New Delhi: Concept Publishing Company, pp. 251-272.

5. Muratbek Makulbekov, 2011.
6. Dirk Meganck, 2011.
7. Uzbekistan, Kazakhstan offer Land on Lease to Punjabi Farmers, *The Tribune*, August 24, 2010.
8. Roman Muzalevsky, India, Kazakhstan Bolster Ties, *Asia Times Online*, May 13, 2011, http://www.atimes.com/atimes/South_Asia/ME13Df03.html
9. http://mediakhabar.com/interview-doulat-kuanyshev-the-ambassador-of-the-republic-of-kazakhstan-to-new-delhi/, October 26, 2011.
10. Doing Buisness: Kazakhstan, 2011.
11. Sarwar Kashani, Kazakhstan seeks Indian investment in its Rapid Industrialisaion, April 16, 2011, http://_two circles.net/2011apr16/ kazakhstan_secks_indian_investment_its_rapid_industrialisation.html
12. PM's interview to Kazakhstanskya Pravda and Egremen Kazakhstan, April 15 2011, Ministry of External Affairs, Government of India.

17
Technological Development of Kazakhstan: Drawing Lessons from India

Farhad Dnishev

In today's world, the development paradigm took shape in the context of global technological shifts. Technological advances, particularly in areas like information and communications technology, biotechnology and nanotechnology, have greatly expanded the possibilities of solving the problems of economic development, welfare and quality of life and protection of the environment. Globalization has opened up new ways of overcoming the global digital divide; more and more countries now have access to new technologies and their applications. The geography of technological development or the technology leaders, which until recently only included the industrialized countries, is beginning to embrace developing countries as well. In particular, it impacts China and India. Around the world, there are new centres that are working on network technologies, and the most famous is Bangalore.

The link between globalization and technology has led to the formation of a global technological space. The production and promotion of new products in the world market now requires building global networks of specialized suppliers, major producers and consumers in a technological supply chain. There is growing internationalization of research and development, implementation of which increasingly involves foreign partners. These activities often go beyond the borders of the home country or of the innovator.

The setting up of global production chains, global centres of industrial production and the subsequent Research & Development centres have all had an effect on the development of the global innovation and technology sector. Transnational corporations are the driving force behind these changes.

First, the relocation of production has affected low-tech industries, such as mining and the primary natural resources processing industries. For example, large steel companies have shifted to resource-rich countries, in particular to areas where timber is harvested. This is because of the policy followed by multi-national corporations (MNCs) to be closer to resource bases and major ports to simplify logistics, therefore ensuring faster shipment of goods to customers. Currently, the most attractive countries for the transfer of resource industries are the BRICS countries (Brazil, Russia, India, China and South Africa). Petrochemical and gas production is located in areas rich in raw materials, which include the aforementioned BRICS nations as well as countries in the Arab world, Pakistan, Vietnam, and, increasingly, Africa.

In recent years, changes in the distribution of global industry are affecting the tech sector as well. Developing countries are acting as ideal locations for outsourcing and off-shoring for many corporations, including automotive, shipbuilding and aircraft construction, precision engineering, electronics and information technology. For example, the release in 2006 of Apple's new iPad created 41,000 jobs, and only 14,000 of them were in the United States.[1] It is expected that these processes will continue to gain momentum. For example, the automotive industry will be more focused on BRICS countries and other centres of large-scale civil shipbuilding, reflecting a shift from Europe and Japan to Korea and China. Over the last 20-30 years, these countries have seen a surge in the development of large industrial and technological parks or clusters in areas including - but not limited to - shipbuilding, automobile manufacturing and power engineering.

Changes in the distribution of industry have been accompanied by the movement of innovation and technology centres. The global innovation strategies of large MNCs now include transferring research and development programmes to developing countries. Of course, MNCs have their own economic interests, like need for MNCs to adapt products and technologies to local markets, proximity of research and development centre to large and fast-growing markets, expanding the scope to attract qualified and relatively cheap manpower and qualified staff, and access to a rapidly developing innovation infrastructure.[2]

The art of politics requires that countries involve themselves in this process for their own benefit. A relevant example for Kazakhstan in this respect is India.[3] India skilfully took advantage of the decision of MNCs to shift innovation and technology centres to emerging markets. Many MNCs have opened offshore innovation centres in the country. More than 300 TNCs have invested in offshore software development divisions in India. Companies in the Fortune 500 (the largest US companies) have opened 63 research centres in India. In India, one of the world's largest MNCs – General Electric – has hired more than 2,400 people to work in areas like aircraft engines, durable consumer goods and medical devices. Pharmaceutical companies such as Astra-Zeneca, Eli Lilly, GlaxoSmithKline, Novartis, Pfizer and Sanofi-Aventis have conducted clinical trials in India.[4]

All this contributes not only to the process of technology transfer to these countries, but also to creating their own technological platforms that enable them to attain competitive positions in the global technology market. Production centres for emerging technologies are beginning to focus not so much on domestic consumption but on the global market. As a result, India's competitive position in the global technology markets has increased significantly. Thus, India is the global market leader in offshore software development and is ranked third in the world pharmaceutical market.

Foreign technology transfer is a widespread international practice; it is carried out by most developed countries, and is even more important for developing countries. Other countries should follow this approach. It is important that countries learn from each others' success and emulate successful approaches. They should avoid merely "following the foreign technology." In order to have favourable, long-term impact, the import of technology must be followed by the recipient country building on – and improving it, followed by becoming an exporter of these products. To be successful requires a movement away from simple goods to sophisticated ones. The gradual accumulation of knowledge, experience and capital can eventually cover markets for goods and services with technologically sophisticated products.

The Indian example shows that such an approach to the spread of modern technology, along with modernization of its own technical base, leads to extensive self-innovation as well. This gives rise to self-perpetuating, modern approaches to science and technology. The result is self-reliance in scientific and technological development, which is reflected in the nature of economic development, the structure of the national economy and of exports.

The mobilization and strengthening of existing scientific and technological capabilities for the industrial modernization of Kazakhstan has received much attention in recent years. At the same time, external factors in technological development also played a crucial role. Kazakhstan, taking its lead from India's experience, can take advantage of technological development helped by external factors. In this regard, one can identify a number of technology policy priorities for external sources of technology. These include foreign technology transfer, engagement with MNCs other than those from the oil sector, the use of the "raw materials in exchange for technology" paradigm, and Research & Development outsourcing.

In Kazakhstan, these engagements are on the rise, but more work needs to be done. For example, technology transfer has so far been dominated by the supply of machinery and equipment, but the acquisition of know-how and licenses has developed so far. In 2011, the country's enterprises and innovators acquired a total of 38 patents abroad, and concluded six know-how and technology transfer agreements. The payment for services under these licenses has been only 1.2 per cent. [5]

Kazakhstan has almost no MNCs involved in non-primary production. And if they are present, they are largely limited to marketing links. MNCs are mainly concentrated in the resources sector. A special policy is needed to convince MNCs to implement innovative projects in Kazakhstan. They should be encouraged to transfer their latest technologies in exchange for access to resources and the opportunity to work in the country. The Kazakhstan 2050 Strategy emphasizes the need to "allow investors to obtain and use our raw materials in exchange for the creation of new industries in our country."[6] In other words, a series of "raw materials in exchange for technology" projects must be initiated. Elements of such a mechanism were laid out in the Programme of 30 Corporate Leaders, but it has not been developed. At the same time, for example, China has introduced an all-new "rules of the game", forcing foreign corporations operating in the country to share their technology with Chinese state-owned enterprises, particularly in industries such as air transport, energy, high-speed railways and IT.

It is important to bear in mind that movement of technology is affected not only by economic factors, but also by cultural ones. In particular, China and India are attractive because of the use of the English language in education, research and technical documentation, which significantly reduces communication barriers.

However, this does not mean that Kazakhstan cannot follow this path of integration into the global technological space. It can start with the arrival of leading international companies in the domestic market, such as equipment suppliers and service companies, which generally tend to place their service centres closer to their customers. In Kazakhstan, for example, it could be major suppliers of petroleum and mining equipment. A number of foreign companies are also involved in the drilling of oil in west Kazakhstan.

In the next stage, with the growth of technologically sophisticated products for the consumer market, Kazakhstan is expected to become a centre for outsourcing in high-tech industries. We are talking about industries that use domestic labour and foreign technology platforms. Academic centres that can develop viable high-tech products and research can evolve in proximity to industries. Kazakhstan already has a number of these centres, including the Kazakh-French Center for Technology Transfer and the Kazakh-Korean Technology Transfer Center.

We also need special measures aimed at increasing the attractiveness of Kazakhstan to foreign companies seeking to implement research programmes. For example, the introduction of special economic zones in Nazarbayev University can play a major role. A combination of emerging infrastructure and qualified personnel may become a huge motivating factor in the creation of facilities for major multinational companies in fields such as information, communications and biotechnology.

When people talk about strengthening economic cooperation between Kazakhstan and India, the limiting factor is often viewed as logistics. In the field of science and technology, logistical obstacles can fade into background. Therefore, science and technology should be the object of special attention in the realm of cooperation between Kazakhstan and India. This is particularly true in areas including, but not limited to, nuclear technology, space research, information and communication technology, green economy and irrigation technology.

Endnotes

1. Portnoff André-Yves “Le retuar a l’industrie” *Futuribles*. P., №364, 2010, p. 5-23.
2. Eroshkin A., Petrov M. Novye tendentcii vzaimodeystvya razvytyh i razvivayushihsya stran v innovatsionnoy sfere [New trends of interaction amomg developed and developing countries in innovation sphere] (*Myrovaya economica I mezhdunarodnye otnoshenya,* 2012, №12) - pp. 3-20.
3. The Global Innovation Index 2012. Stonger Innovation Linkages for Global Growth. http://www.globalinnovationindex.org
4. World Investment Report 2005: Transnational Corporations and the Internationalization of R&D. - United Nations New York and Geneva, 2005. http://unctad.org/en/docs/wir2005_en.pdf
5. Balance of Payments of the Republic of Kazakhstan. http://www.national bank.kz/?docid=343
6. N.Nazarbayev. Address to a Nation “Strategy Kazakhstan-2050”: New Political Course of the Established State”, Astana, 2012. http://www.akorda.kz/en/page/page_poslanie-prezidenta-respubliki-kazakhstan-lidera-natsii-nursultana-nazarbaeva-narodu-kazakhstana-

18
Transportation Linkages between Kazakhstan and India

Dudar Zhakenov

According to the World Trade Organization, there has been a recession in European Union countries, which account for a third of world trade. This has adversely affected the dynamics of global export-import, in particular exports to Europe from Asia and America.

According to statistics, the volume of world trade in 2012 increased by two per cent than in 2011. In this context, the development of India's foreign trade is largely determined by the general trends in world trade and the global markets. Today, the Government of India is working to diversify the regional structure of Indian exports through the expansion of markets in Asia and Africa. Amongst the leading trading partners of India are China, the UAE, Saudi Arabia, the United States, Germany, Switzerland, Indonesia, Singapore and Hong Kong.

As reported by the Ministry of Commerce and Industry, Government of India, the volume of foreign trade in 2012 amounted to US$ 809.4 billion, of which exports accounted for US$ 309.1 billion. Despite the trade deficit, the Indian economy remains one of the most dynamic in the world. Over the past 10 years, India has achieved 50 per cent growth in industrial output and a 65 per cent increase in exports of high-tech products.

In the country's development strategy, great importance is attached to "India: Vision-2020" Programme, which spells out the strategic direction of the development of the Indian economy in the medium and long term: energy (including nuclear), information technology clusters, strategic industries (defense industry, aerospace, aviation, telecommunications, etc.). In these circumstances, energy is a top priority for India, because three per cent of India's energy needs are covered by nuclear power and in the future, it is planned to increase this to 20 per cent. There was a time when the country was unable to obtain enriched Uranium for political and economic reasons. However, today India can deal with both the manufacture of nuclear power stations and nuclear technology, but also generate energy from its nuclear power stations; there are 20 atomic units in India today.

India is one of the most dynamic of developing countries. Along with China, India has positioned itself as a future great power, and its foreign policy is characterized by the global reach of major economic and political contributions. However, as one of the leading regional powers, India's policy under the slogan "Look East", and "Connect Central Asia" is regarded as one of the priority areas. This policy is because of India's desire to secure its national interests, to enhance its international status and not to lag behind its main rival in Asia – China.

As one of the major regional powers, the country pays special attention to the further enhancement of its role in the international arena. In the early 1990s a new direction – Central Asia – appeared in the foreign policy strategy of India.

Within the framework of the "New Silk Road" initiative of India's foreign policy, India attaches great significance to the development of relations with Central Asia, through whose territories have run political, economic, trade and cultural routes since ancient times. The factor of rapprochement has also become important due to shared interests and readiness in tackling threats to India and Central Asia states – Islamic extremism, terrorism, drug trafficking, the situation in Afghanistan and regional security.

Due to its industrial development, India and China are huge importers and one of the largest consumers of natural resources in the world. India openly acknowledges that countries of Central Asia are a huge potential market for Indian industrial products, as well as a promising source of fuel-energy and mineral resources. This means that India can become a permanent and reliable importer of oil, gas and Uranium.

Interests in the field of energy, along with ensuring political stability, are the main driving factors encouraging India to strengthen its presence in the region. Energy consumption in India is expected to grow between 3.6 and 4.3 per cent per year, and more than double by the year 2030. This will make India the third largest oil importer by 2025. Hydrocarbon security depends on the country's stable economic development, and therefore, national security. Currently, approximately 70 per cent of oil and gas imports of India are from the Persian Gulf. The conflict in Iraq, which has led to rising oil prices, has pushed the Indian Government to seek alternative sources of raw materials. Central Asia is viewed as promising in this respect.

This implies that today, India seriously looks at convergence of its energy security with the Central Asia states, and the issue of global energy security in the long term will be even more crucial for India.

In addition, the Central Asian region is a very convenient corridor for the transportation of Indian goods to Russia, the CIS countries – and further to Europe. The trade turnover of India with Europe today has reached US$ 57 billion, and is expected to further increase in 2015.

Currently, trade and economic cooperation with the Central Asian states is far below satisfaction, and India's share is less than one per cent of the total turnover. One reason for India's trade imbalance is the weakness of the transport and logistics component. Under such circumstances, India needs to search for new markets and suitable transport routes. Already, existing transport corridors can be a solution for this sector.

The weak presence of Indian companies in the Central Asian markets is attributable to transportation and communication constraints because India does not share borders any country of the region, since all the Central Asian countries are landlocked. As a result, the Indian Government has had to make great effort to enable Indian companies to compete and invest in the Central Asian markets. Its primary concern is the development of transport infrastructure, which is also in the interests of all countries in the Asian region since it will undoubtedly facilitate the expansion of trade between them.

To implement trade and economic plans, the International Transport Corridors (ITC) is of great importance. For example, in the "West-East" and "North-South" direction, container traffic on the Eurasian route in 2000-2010 – and prospectively in 2015 – has increased.

Today, the main corridors connecting Europe with Asia are the Trans-Asian Railway, TRACECA and the "North-South" ITC.

International organizations, represented by the European Union and the United Nations, like ECE and ESCAP, have developed their own strategies regarding corridors from Europe to Asia, like the pilot projects – TRACECA and SPECA. At the beginning of 2013 in Geneva, the UN Office in Europe signed a joint statement on the future development of Euro-Asian transport links. In addition, this issue was on the agenda of the 16th International Conference – "TransBaltica-2013" – held in Riga on June 6-7, 2013, with participation of 20 European countries and the CIS.

To date, the main trade traffic to and from Europe to Asia is by sea, valued at several billion dollars. The freight traffic is constantly growing, while the capacity of the Suez Canal in Egypt is shrinking. If cargo through the Suez Canal from South Asia to Europe is delivered in 35 days, it would take about 20-25 days to be delivered using the "North-South" corridor. Today, companies from Europe and countries in the Asian region have to search for alternative routes for delivery of goods. The "North-South" ITC could be the way out.

The Treaty for establishment of the "North-South" ITC corridor was signed in St. Petersburg on 12 September 2000, between Russia, Iran and India. In May 2002 in St. Petersburg, a Protocol on the opening of this corridor was signed by the Ministers of Transport of the participating countries. Later Azerbaijan, Armenia, Belarus, Kazakhstan, Oman and Syria joined the Treaty. Turkey and Ukraine have applied for accession. The "North-South" ITC is meant to provide transport links between the countries of Eastern, Central and Northern Europe – including the CIS – with the Persian Gulf and South Asia (India, Pakistan via Iran), as well as countries that have expressed their willingness to participate in this project. The main advantages of the "North-South" ITC against other routes (primarily via the Suez Canal) are two-fold: reduction in distance and reduction in cost of transportation of containers, compared to transportation by sea.

The idea of development of transit potential of the "North-South" ITC through Central Asia is determined by the region's geography and history. Making Central Asia a bridge between Europe and Asia for transit of goods, of course, would be beneficial for the region itself, and transport companies from different parts of the continent could participate in the project.

In turn, Kazakhstan is ready to facilitate the passage of goods by land and by using the sea port of Aktau, which has modern sea terminals and developed infrastructure. The trial run showed that transporting cargo using the new corridor was 20 per cent cheaper than via the Suez Canal, and India could annually save up to US$ 16 million. According to experts, the transport of cargo by the "North-South" route is expected to reach 20-25 million tons per year, without taking into account the transportation of raw crude and petroleum products. The "North-South" ITC will bring tangible financial benefits to India. It will also contribute to increasing the competitiveness of Indian products in the world market, as well as low-cost and quick imports.

The Indian weekly magazine "India Today" believes that the "North-South" transport corridor will not only broaden trade by India with Central Asia, the Caucasus, the Baltic States, Scandinavia but, according to New Delhi, also help bring stability to the domestic market through "the axis of goodwill".

If Indian companies join the "North-South" ITC, its benefit will be guaranteed to all involved, provided they ensure its legality, safety and profitability.

The joint effort by India and the countries of Central Asia in developing transportation links will enhance their ability to better confront the global challenges of our times, and help promote understanding between countries of the large region – Asia.

19
India-Kazakhstan: Socio-Economic Engagements

Punit Gaur

Introduction

The twentieth century witnessed a wave of independent states. Revision of European borders after the unification of East and West Germany revived the desire for independence, which led to a surge in self-affirmation by dozens of large and small ethnic groups. In this context, the disintegration of the Soviet Union also led to the formation of 15 new independent states. The newly independent countries not only had to re-build their domestic politics and seek their place in the international arena, but they were also faced with the foreign policy challenge of defining their relationship with other countries. Kazakhstan was also one of the countries that faced these challenges twenty years ago.

It is well-known that a nation is not marked by territory alone but also by its developed political system and civic consciousness. An important component of the nation is national (civic) identity, which is formed by the man in the street, through an imaginary opposition to the common "stranger" or taking pride in one's country. In this context, Kazakhstan – like India – also proved itself as a powerful nation and emerged on the international scene twenty years or so ago. When talking about relations between India and Kazakhstan, the two important aspects which are very similar to both the countries is the high degree of diversity (in India it is religious and cultural diversity while in Kazakhstan it is about ethnic diversity), and the "youthfulness" of these states, despite the fact that India and

Kazakhstan have historical and cultural links that go way back in history. These two aspects are also very important to understand prospects of cooperation in the coming years. This paper helps to explore the different perspectives on cooperation in Kazakhstan with India.

Historical/Cultural Perspective

As Cummings (2005) states, Kazakhstan (which celebrated its twentieth anniversary of independence in 2011) was born by default from the breakup of the Soviet Union in 1991, and this was neither the result of secessionist demands by its leadership nor a national liberation movement; it just resulted from the decision by Moscow to end the Soviet edifice . But historically, present-day Kazakhstan also is the result of centuries-long existence of various ethnic tribes in the vast steppes between the Altai and the Volga. In this context, the emergence of a separate statehood was long in the making due to both the nomadic lifestyles of these tribes and the many external invasions, ethnic migration and, last but not the least, due to the inner struggle for power amongst various Kazakh tribal groups (Kazakh society itself is divided into three *zhuz,* which are further divided into so many clans and tribes), which are still important in modern Kazakh society.

The fundamentals of Kazakh culture can be traced back to the country's rich history and geographical location in Eurasia. Throughout its history, Kazakh lands were at the centre of major trade routes like the Silk Road, which gave significant geopolitical advantage to civilizations that developed in the region. Thus, Kazakh culture evolved as a fusion of a diverse group of ethnic and social influences. The present Kazakh culture carries rudiments from both the country's original Turkic characteristics and its Soviet inheritance. In this background, India and Kazakhstan have both profound influences of history and culture, and both can contribute not only to each other but also to building and preserving world culture as well.

Geographical Perspective

Independent Kazakhstan is situated at the centre of the Eurasian continent, with an area of 2,724,900 square km. In terms of area, it is the second largest amongst the CIS states, and occupies ninth place in the world after Russia, China, USA, Argentina, Brazil, Canada, India and Australia. Kazakhstan borders China (1,460 km of common border), Kyrgyzstan (980 km), Turkmenistan (380 km), Uzbekistan (2,300 km), and the Russian Federation (6,477 km). Kazakhstan's borders stretch from the low reaches of the Volga in the West to the foothills of the Altai Mountains in the East for some 3,000 km (a distance that spans two time zones), and from West Siberian lowlands in the North to the desert of Kyzyl Kum and the mountain range of Tien Shan in the South for some 2,000 km. According to the 2009 Census, the population of Kazakhstan was 16,036,6000. The population density is 5.9 persons per square km. There are more than a hundred nationalities and ethnic groups, such as Kazakh (63.1 per cent), Russian (23.7 per cent), Uzbeks (2.9 per cent), Ukrainians (2.1 per cent), Uyghurs (1.4 per cent), Tatars (1.3 per cent) and Germans (1.1 per cent). More than 70 per cent of the population practices Islam (Sunni Muslims) while about 26 per cent practice Christianity. Astana has been the capital of the country since 1997. Kazakhstan has a harsh continental climate and its diverse landscape consists of steppes, desserts and forests along with various rivers and lakes. It possesses rich deposits of minerals and numerous oil and gas fields. It can be said that geographically, Kazakhstan is very significant for India for strategic and security reasons, as both countries can collaborate on issues like religious fundamentalism, drug trafficking, military training, counter-terrorism coordination and consultations on Afghanistan.

Political Perspective

Economic restructuring by Kazakhstan after independence were accompanied by reforms in the political arena. Kazakhstan became a constitutional republic with a strong accent on the principles of national identity, political stability and democracy. Distinct from other Central Asian countries, Kazakhstan is now stable both politically and socially due to its enormous political maturity. The political leaders of the country have been quite successful in sharing their vision of the country with their people . Moreover, the emphasis on social and ethnic diversity by the political leadership also contributed to the current political climate where civil organizations also find representation. The country also accepted the political opposition, the right to assemble and encouraged freedom of civil institutions.

Further amendments to the political and social landscape further supported economic growth in this emerging market by providing a stable business environment for foreign investors.

In this context, India recently declared its "Connect Central Asia" policy to strengthen its relationship with Central Asian countries. Frequent visits by diplomats in the last 4-5 years, India's invitation to the Kazakh President its the Republic Day celebrations, continued high-level meetings with officials of Kazakhstan are all significant steps for improved cooperation between India and Kazakhstan in the political sphere.

Economic Perspective

The Kazakh economy has achieved a remarkable growth rate in recent years. This is expected to continue in the next decade as a result of economic reforms and strategic expansion plans, which attract foreign direct investment to Kazakhstan. Furthermore, the wealth of natural resources along with oil and gas fields bodes well for future the economy of Kazakhstan.

Kazakhstan's economic strength depends on mainly gas and oil deposits; the economic stability has had an enormous effect on social and political life in the country. The future of the economy is closely connected to its further amalgamation with international economic institutions, judicious use of its hydrocarbon and mineral resources , export of industrial and agricultural products and training its highly qualified human resources. During the Soviet period, Kazakhstan was an agrarian country and raw-material supplier. During the 20 years since independence, Kazakhstan has transitioned from a centrally-planned economy to a market economy. Kazakhstan has made substantial progress in implementing composite political, economic and social reforms to establish a politically stable environment. The first 10 years of Kazakhstan's independence were characterized by numerous economic, social and environmental challenges.

Since 1992, Kazakhstan has vigorously pursued a programme of economic reforms for a free market economy through privatization of state enterprises and economic decentralization. Successful implementation of reforms resulted in recognition of Kazakhstan in 2001 as the most market-oriented country in the CIS. Western countries have praised Kazakhstan's reforms in areas like currency convertibility, inflation, foreign investment policy, de-monopolization and reallocation of ownership of enterprises. Being the most successful reformer in Central Asia – and based on its macroeconomic performance and financial health – Kazakhstan became the first former Soviet Republic to repay all its debt to the International Monetary Fund (IMF) in 2000 (seven years ahead of schedule). This helped the nation receive investment-grade credit rating from major international credit rating agencies. The global financial crisis, which began in the end of 2007, had multiple implications for Kazakhstan's economy and exposed its underlying vulnerabilities. With lower oil and commodity prices and adverse international capital markets, new challenges for the emerging economy surfaced – declining public revenue, liquidity shortages, dependence of financial institutions on external funding, negatively investors confidence and capital outflows.

In these circumstances, the Government quickly stepped in to regulate and stabilize the situation. A set of policies were introduced under the Anti-Crisis Programme to help mitigate economic vulnerabilities, and establish a basis for strong growth. As a part of the policy, Kazakhstan devalued its currency and vastly expanded its role in the monetary sector. With important reserves of oil and gas, coal and Uranium, Kazakhstan is an important energy provider to the world. However, bearing in mind recent fluctuations in the world commodities market, the Government's energy policy focuses on further diversification of energy resources, efficient energy use, stimulation of R&D in renewable energy and environmental awareness. Today, investments in natural resources constitute 77 per cent of all investments in the economy. 75 per cent investment in natural resources come from overseas, and the rest from local sources. Key to the energy sector is a system of pipelines and infrastructure. Kazakhstan's counterparts (United States, EU, China and Russia) have shown strong interest in cooperating with Kazakhstan in this area, particularly in building trans-continental oil and gas transportation systems. Kazakhstan has made it clear that this fully meets its own vision of development of multiple energy transportation routes from and through Kazakhstan.

The international economic crisis strengthened Kazakhstan's economy by ridding it of companies and economic institutions that placed all their bets on high profits and showed no interest in long-term industrial growth. It also corrected the over-evaluated real estate market and channelled it in more economically stable and productive sectors. The crisis demonstrated that Kazakhstan's overall financial system is stable enough to deal with a market collapse. Further diversification of the economy, social and political stability, sizable natural resources, foreign capital, implementation of international technical, financial and business standards, accession to the WTO as a member of the Customs Union, promotion of corporate governance, education and administrative reforms are all driving Kazakhstan in achieving its strategic objectives .

The most important challenge before Kazakhstan is to trounce its principal reliance on natural resources and diversify into sectors such as telecommunications, financial services, transport, construction, pharmaceuticals, food processing. With the possibility of developing (including value addition) of many key industrial segments and modernisation of the services sector, Kazakhstan offers great opportunity for trade and investment. Despite this fact, India has no any direct access to Kazakhstan, this is why it is time for India to have greater cooperation with Kazakhstan, especially since the country is opening up other sectors of its economy apart from the oil and gas sectors.

Thrust Area of Cooperation in the Future

Defence, civil nuclear energy and hydrocarbons are three major areas where India can collaborate with Kazakhstan. The extent of bilateral trade between India and Kazakhstan is, however, insignificant. It is characterized by two features: one, Kazakhstan is the principal trading associate of India amongst all Central Asian countries, approximately accounting for more than 70 per cent of total trade between India and the CARs. Second, trade has recently registered faster growth than it was earlier. Kazakhstan's main exports consist of mineral products, leather and raw materials while imports from India include tea, pharmaceuticals, chemicals, plastic, machinery and equipment.

Kazakhstan has also shown keen interest in strengthening military ties with India, particularly enhancing arms exports and aerospace alliance. In its 2006 defence policy document, Kazakhstan focused on the Indo-Pacific region – including India – as its export market. Besides this, Kazakhstan's largest crop is wheat, which is exported. It ranks as the sixth largest wheat producer in the world. During the visit of Vice President of India to Kazakhstan in April 2008, where agriculture was identified as a promising area of cooperation, both sides recommended signing an agreement on cooperation in agriculture and allied sectors as an important step in this direction.

Indian Small and Medium Enterprises, after making their presence felt in the pharmaceutical and tea markets of Kazakhstan, are now planning to venture into the country's Information Technology (IT) sector. In addition to Government initiatives, Indian SMEs could also tap Kazakhstan's IT market by offering new technologies like IP technology, Linux for critical applications and formulating databases for their domestic IT firms. It is one of the important sectors where India can take the lead.

Kazakhstan has sought India's assistance in setting up industrial clusters in textiles, and is also seeking cooperation in areas of hi-technology and financial services. There is great scope for trade in textiles between the two countries, since Kazakhstan has a good resource base in cotton, coupled with good logistics and a sound banking infrastructure . The pharmaceutical industry in Kazakhstan provides a market of US$550 million. This is thus an appropriate time for Indian pharmaceutical industry to invest there on a large scale.

Conclusion

Soon after the collapse of the Soviet Union, Kazakhstan was considered the most unstable post-Soviet state. Despite certain difficulties in the first few years, Kazakhstan has managed to ensure economic and social development based on democratic principles. Barring a few incidents of inter-ethnic strife, it has managed to preserve stability in the country and unite its people.

In the recent years, Kazakhstan has appeared as a large market with evidence of economic growth. This economic progress demonstrates the country's success in its transition to a market economy. The changes in trade policies are encouraging for other countries that would like to invest in the Kazakh market. Yet, there linger challenges in cooperating with Kazakhstan because of the shadow if its earlier political, economic and social systems. Therefore, the strength of post-Soviet Kazakhstan and prospects of cooperation with India will depend on mature leadership and a civil society that is mindful of common interests and democratic principles. There is no doubt that both the countries have potential for cooperation in various fields.

Notes

1. Akiner, Shirin (ed.) (1991), *Cultural Change and Continuity in Central Asia,* London: Kegan Paul International.
2. Akiner, Shirin, (ed.) (1992), *Economic and Political Trends in Central Asia*, New York: Routledge & Kegan Paul.
3. Brass, Poul R., (1996) *Ethnicity and Nationalism: Theory and Comparison*, New Delhi: Sage Publications.
4. Collins, Kathleen, *Clan Politics and Regime Transition in Central Asia*, New York: Cambridge University Press, 2006.
5. Cummings, Sally N. (2005), *Kazakhstan: Power and The Elite*, London: I.B. Tauris Publishers.
6. Cummings, Sally N., 'Politics in Kazakhstan: the constitutional crisis of March 1995', *FSS Briefing Paper*, London: Royal Institute of International Affairs, August 1995.
7. Dave, Bhavna, 'A new parliament consolidates presidential authority', *Transition* 2, 6, 1996, pp. 33–7.
8. Gleason, Gregory (2001). Foreign policy and domestic reform in Central Asia. Central Asian Survey, 20:2, pp 167-182 (http://dx.doi.org/10.1080/02634930120073488).
9. Griffin, K. (1999). Social policy in Kazakhstan during the economic transition. *International Journal of Social Economics, 26* (1/2/3), pp. 134-152.
10. Gros D. and Steinherr, A., 2004, *Economic Transition in Central and Eastern Europe: Planting the Seeds*, Cambridge University Press, Cambridge.
11. International Monetary Fund, "Kazakhstan: Making the Most of Its Oil Wealth," August 16, 2011, http://www.imf.org/external/pubs/ft/survey/so/2011/int081611a.htm (accessed June 5, 2012).
12. Joint Statement on PM's visit to Kazakhstan, 16 April 2011, Accessed at http://meaindia.nic.in/mystart.php?id=530517550.
13. Kathleen Collins, Clans, Pacts, and Politics in Central Asia, *Journal of Democracy* Volume 13, 7: 2002.
14. "Kazakhstan," The Economist.
15. M. Terterov (ed.), *Doing Business in Kazakhstan*, Sterling, VA: Kogan Page Limited, pp. 41-54.
16. Ministry of External Affairs, Government of India, Accessed at http://meaindia.nic.in/meaxpsite/declarestatement/2011/04/16js03.pdf.
17. Olcott, Martha Brill, *Kazakhstan: Unfulfilled Promise*, Washington, DC: Carnegie Endowment for International Peace, 2002.

18. Olcott, M. B., 2005, *Central Asia's Second Chance,* Carnegie Endowment for International Peace, Washington DC.
19. Oleynik, I. S. (Ed.). (2002). *Kazakhstan: Country study guide.* Washington, DC: International Business Publications.
20. Roy, Olivier, *The New Central Asia: the Creation of Nations*, London: I.B. Tauris, 2000.
21. Rumer, Boris, *Central Asia: A Tragic Experiment*, Boston, MA: Unwin Hyman, 1989.
22. Warikoo, K. (1995), *Central Asia: Emerging New World Order,* New Delhi: Haranand Publications.
23. World Bank, June 2005, *Republic of Kazakhstan, Country Economic Memorandum – Getting Competitive, Staying Competitive: The Challenge of Managing Kazakhstan's Oil Boom,* Washington DC.

20

Kazakhstan-India Cooperation: Regional Transport and Logistics System Security

Rafik Tairov

In today's globalised environment, transport and logistics networks play a key role in the industrial development of a state. Global markets in transport logistics is estimated at US$ 2.7 trillion, i.e. about seven per cent of world income. In developed countries, the share of transport logistics is 13-14 per cent of GDP. For example, in Ireland it is 14.2 per cent, in Singapore 13.9 per cent, in Hong Kong 13.7 per cent, in Germany 13.0 per cent, etc. This shows that the development of the transport sector is critical for these countries as a source of national income. In Kazakhstan, the share of the transport logistics sector is approximately eight per cent.[1]

If we examine the world map of movement of capital, labour, goods, technology, finance and investment, we find it coincides with an extensive network of highways enveloping the globe.

Kazakhstan, located at the crossroads of international transport corridors, has a developed transport and logistics network. During the 25th plenary meeting of Foreign Investors' Council (May, 2012), the President of Kazakhstan, Nursultan Nazarbayev, emphasized that Kazakhstan has the potential to become a major business and transit hub for the Central Asian region, and a bridge between Europe and Asia. This implies the creation of international hubs (trade and logistic, finance and business, innovation and technology as well as tourism) in the key transport corridors of Kazakhstan.

Taking into account the process of globalization, Kazakhstan defined its strategic goals based on current realities, future opportunities, challenges and threats. This requires understanding and creating new forms of mutually-beneficial partnerships between regions and countries in transport and logistics development, and security.

Kazakhstan-India relations based on constructive engagement become even more important a factor in regional and bilateral cooperation.

For India, Central Asia is important as a huge market for industrial goods; source of fuel and energy resources; source of natural resources (nonferrous and precious metals and gold – India is world's largest gold consumer); and as a 'corridor' for transport of Indian goods to Russia, CIS countries and Europe.

Kazakhstan, in turn, perceives India as a supplier of quality textile products; a potential market for natural resources; a gateway to South Asia's market; and a potential supplier of new technologies, particularly IT.

India and Kazakhstan are countries with rapidly developing economies. Despite the fact that Kazakhstan is a major trading partner of India in Central Asia (it accounts for over 70 per cent of total Indian trade with Central Asian countries), bilateral trade between the two countries, less than US$ 400 million, is below potential. There are about 280 companies involved in business between India and Kazakhstan.

As one of the world's largest energy consumers, India has to augment its nuclear power generation to meet future energy needs. This needs Uranium as a raw material, and Kazakhstan ranks second in the world in terms of Uranium reserves (21 per cent of world reserves), and plans to mine 20,000 tonnes of Uranium in 2013. This means that in the near future, Kazakhstan could become a permanent and reliable exporter of Uranium to India.

Petroleum is one of the most strategically important areas of our cooperation. Bilateral cooperation in the field of exploration, production, refining, transportation and marketing of petroleum products is considered as potentially huge. However, under-developed transport and logistics infrastructure impacts the economy of Kazakhstan and as well as cooperation between India and Kazakhstan.

The logistics costs in our country are enormous and are several times the level of developed countries. Thus, today, the share of logistic expenses in Kazakhstan go up to 25 per cent of the final products' value, while the world average is 11 per cent, in China 14 per cent, in EU countries 11 per cent, and in USA and Canada 10 per cent.[2] As a result, Kazakhstan has to face pressure as a result of its transport system in comparison with developed countries.

Kazakhstan requires the shortest transport corridor to ports on the Black and the Mediterranean Seas, and to access routes to Indian and Pacific Oceans. This is due to obvious economic advantage – the cost of sea transport is lower than that of the road and rail transport. In a view to this, cooperation between the two countries aims to establish transport corridors that will connect India with Central Asia, Kazakhstan, and Russia, and, accordingly – with Europe – which has promising prospect.

For example, the North-South transport corridor from Aktau through the Caspian Sea to Iran and the Arabian Sea offers good opportunity. The North-South transport project also incorporates railways and other transport modes from Europe through Russia, Azerbaijan and Iran to India and other South Asian countries. Kazakhstan is interested in creating a system of warehouses and distribution services in Aktau to transform it into a major hub for transportation of goods between Kazakhstan and South Asia, as well as the Persian Gulf. Indian companies may also be interested in participating in this project.

According to experts' opinion, if India clarifies its position in the Central Asian and Caspian regions, current global players (Russia, China, USA and the EU) will no longer be seen as exclusive by Kazakhstan since it would now have a serious alternative – a rising India. However, they may also not object to this scenario since, first of all, their interaction with India is much stronger than Kazakhstan-India cooperation and, secondly, strengthening the partnership between Kazakhstan and India can be beneficial for global players. Under these circumstances, it is very important to find a solution to the problem of the legal status of the Caspian Sea as one of the conditions for establishing a secure and reliable regional transport and logistics hub in the region.

Another promising project involves the creation of a road transport corridor between India-Pakistan-China-Kazakhstan. Currently, a large-scale transportation project – the construction of the Turkmenistan-Kazakhstan section of the Kazakhstan-Turkmenistan-Iran – railway has been implemented. This presents a great opportunity in the optimization of traffic flow in Eurasia. The project gives to European countries a route from ports on the Baltic Sea to the commodity markets of the Middle East and on to the countries around the Indian Ocean, significantly reducing distance and travel time.

It also provides an alternative to connect the transport infrastructure to the South and East with huge economic centres such as India, China, Pakistan and the Asia-Pacific, which also means creating a new, more ambitious canvass of cooperation based on truly innovative thinking in the global geo-economics and strategic vision. It also addresses the problem of transition of Indian goods through Iran. However, this also has its own difficulties today – the West's economic embargo against Iran.

Of course, taking into account the current international situation Kazakhstan, we could initiate a discussion on this problem and its possible solutions with all interested parties through diplomatic and other channels (including mechanisms as the SCO, CICA etc.).

Energy dialogue between the two countries provides great opportunity. Energy cooperation between the two countries is an essential element of national security. Kazakhstan supports major regional projects, which are still under development: TAPI gas pipeline (Turkmenistan–Afghanistan–Pakistan–India), CASA–1000 (high-voltage power transmission line from Central Asia-South Asia), as well as a project to expand the railway network in and around Afghanistan.

A pilot project aimed at the economic rehabilitation of Afghanistan – and supported by the USA – is the New Silk Road. But not all experts agree. One group believes that the project will contribute to the economic development of the region, with Afghanistan as the main transport hub between Central and South Asia. The project will link India and the Central Asian Republics into a single transport and logistics chain. Currently, the movement of freight between Afghanistan and India through Pakistan is limited because of poor relations between Islamabad and New Delhi.

According to other experts' opinion, the project is intended to justify the retention of NATO military bases in the region and reduce the role of Iran, China and Russia. In addition, the prospects of trans-Afghanistan transport raises concerns amongst member states since – the region is too volatile, and thus their disinterest in the trans-Afghanistan corridor in its current orientation.

Thus, there is dilemma – the simultaneous interest of external players in the promotion of its influence in the region – and the intent of Central Asian states to get external support for their own interests, including relations with their neighbours. This creates opportunities for various alliances based on mutual interests, both for intra-regional and non-regional actors.

Continued tension in the Caspian region and political instability in neighbouring countries of Afghanistan can provide an opportunity for extremists – including the Islamic Movement of Uzbekistan and the Taliban – to mobilize efforts and go north to attack the main hydrocarbons transport routes.

Today, there is a need for joint collaboration to strengthen pipeline safety through better control of the pipeline industry and ensuring its security. Practices across the world show that pipelines are easy targets for terrorist organizations aiming to damage the international gas and oil infrastructure and the economic and security environment of the transit country.

The need to ensure security of transit of goods and people is also important thus. Transport infrastructure has always been a soft target for terrorist attacks. After 9/11, the safety of transit transport has become even more critical. To ensure security, it is necessary to take into consideration how terrorists view it:

- for organizing an act of terrorism by using it to transport and/or transfer explosive material, or as a weapon (as in terrorist attacks of September 11, 2001);
- target of terrorism (destruction of bridges, tunnels, railways and highways); and
- as an object located in the damage area.

The threat of transit terrorism is probably not universal; most attacks in the developed world have been in the cities and aimed at destroying g major road junctions. In addition, in the age of cybernetics, new types of threats related to cyber-terrorists have emerged. Today, even the most developed nations of the world are not immune to these threats or to be defeated by them even. Within a short span of time, information systems – providing logistical support to transport and energy systems – may fail under the control cyber-terrorists, or be destroyed. And this can lead to tragic consequences.

Thus, the imperative is to find interstate solutions to the problem of critical infrastructure cyber security – automated control systems for regional transport and logistics networks and pipelines.

India has great potential in the fight against international terrorism and religious extremism, as well as cyber threats. Therefore, further expansion of the Kazakhstan-India partnership in this field could be a focus of bilateral cooperation.

India as an Observer to the SCO – and as a leading international donor – has invested heavily in the reconstruction of Afghanistan. India and Kazakhstan are interested in the stabilization and post-conflict reconstruction of Afghanistan. Both states believe that the Afghan problem has no military solution, and attach particular importance to rehabilitation of the Afghan economy and infrastructure.

The stabilization of the situation in Afghanistan will not only strengthen regional security but also create conditions for the implementation of promising international projects in the field of energy and transport. That is why it would be rational to support India in its striving to become a full member of the SCO. This would not only involve India in large-scale regional projects (particularly in energy) but also for a new power balance in the organization.

The positions of Astana and Delhi with respect to complex issues related to Iran are similar. Both Kazakhstan and India are interested in the implementation of projects with Iran, invest in the country and are thus not interested in a military solution to Tehran's nuclear programme.

Military cooperation, which is one of the most important focus areas of the Kazakhstan-India partnership, also involves:

1. joint counter-terrorism exercises aimed at ensuring security of transport and logistics lines, and dealing with environmental disasters
2. sharing experiences in peacekeeping
3. countering cyber threat
4. establishing a joint centre for cyber security research

Thus, Kazakhstan is interested in optimizing balance of power in Central Asia and the Caspian region. India's increasing presence in all areas of cooperation (including energy) may have far-reaching geo-political and geo-economic repercussions. This is especially important in the context of the global financial and economic crisis, when inflow of new foreign investment is so required, and it is important to show that Kazakhstan remains open to foreign investors.

Reference

1. Iskaliev Erkhat. Transport Logistics Today is a Key Component of National Programme of Enhanced Industrial and Innovative Development. In http://www.kazlogistics.kz/analytics/95/708/.
2. Transport logistics today is a key component of National Programme of forced industrial and innovative development – Elkhart Iskaliev. http://www.kazlogistics.kz/analytics/95/708/

21
Cultural Relations between Tajikistan and India

Habibullo Rajabov

Before speaking generally about the future of bilateral relations where there were no previous obstacles at some point in history, we should first take into account several factors:

First, what is the level of the relationship between the two countries currently? Second, do they share borders, or are they far from each other? Third, what are the land, air or sea lines of communication possible between the two countries? Fourth, what is the political system in these countries, and what role does it play in the development of bilateral relations? Fifth, what is important in the rapprochement between the two countries geographical location, reasonable well-established communication, community links, contacts at the Head of State level, or other similar phenomena? Sixth, the situation regarding stability of the political and economic situation in the region and around the world. Seventh, do the two countries have historical cultural relations or roots with each other?

The answers to these questions seem easy, but they still play a significant role in establishing various contacts, not excluding cultural relations.

On Complex Relations between Our Two Countries

Talking about this and other similar issues, we should first take into account the fact that not only the Republic of Tajikistan but also the entire Asia, including Central Asia, bears the stamp of Indian culture. Close contacts between the peoples of Central Asia, including Tajikistan and India in the past, were well written about in various accounts by Tajik and Indian scholars about their history, philology, archaeology, and art, and also proven by written sources and archaeological sites. Today, we live in a different era: the era of huge changes not only in the political map of the world, but also in the spiritual world of humanity. Cultural relations always precede all other relationships, or accompany them. Thus, to talk about the nature and importance of cultural relations at every opportunity is relevant and useful, because their essence – the love of man and mankind – to create, if possible, a milieu to facilitate contacts in other areas of the relationship.

Since independence, the Republic of Tajikistan as well as all the other republics of the former Soviet Union, have, in a very short time, established contacts with various countries of the world, and this is independent of the many problems associated with the effects of the civil war, which caused serious damage to the economy. On August 28, 1992, India formally recognized the independence of Tajikistan. In the historical sense, this is a short period of time for big transformation, recovery, strengthening of positions on the international arena, establishing good contacts and cooperation with foreign countries, but we must also recall a few facts to make sure that in a short period of time, a lot can happen. During this period, President of Tajikistan, Emomali Rahmon, visited India six times. The Indian Prime Minister and the Indian President also visited our country. During these visits, and during the high-level talks, both sides called for expansion of bilateral cooperation and effective use of existing linkages, and signed a number of important agreements. For example, in May 2001 the following documents were signed:

1. Agreement between the Government of the Republic of Tajikistan and the Republic of India on cooperation in combating illicit trafficking of narcotic drugs;
2. Agreement between the Government of the Republic of Tajikistan and the Republic of India on air communication;
3. Agreement between the Government of the Republic of Tajikistan and the Republic of India on technical cooperation;
4. Agreement between the Government of the Republic of Tajikistan and the Republic of India on the principles of mutual relations;
5. Agreement between the Government of the Republic of

Tajikistan and the Republic of India on long-term trade and economic cooperation in industry;

6. Agreement between the Government of the Republic of Tajikistan and the Republic of India on mutual legal assistance in criminal matters.

According to these and earlier agreements, Indian will assist the Republic of Tajikistan in the reconstruction of Aini airport, provide training in a variety of areas – including the armed forces – in military training institutions in India. Though several joint ventures are registered in Tajikistan, their activity is not so significant. Contacts are also in place for a working group on counter-terrorism. In the development of bilateral cooperation, an important role is played by the Intergovernmental Commission on Trade, Economic, Scientific and Technological Cooperation. This commission – from December 2001 to May 2013 – held seven meetings in Delhi and Dushanbe. As a result of these meetings, various agreements on the economy, trade, science and technology were signed. While visiting India, the President of Tajikistan, Emomali Rahmon, signed a number of important bilateral documents. During a recent working visit of President Emomali Rahmon to India to the Republic of India, held from 1 to 4 September 2012, 12 important cooperation documents were signed, including a Memorandum of Understanding between the Main Department of Geology under the Government of the Republic of Tajikistan and the Indian company – Khoday Group – on scientific-technical cooperation. In accordance with the signed document, the Khoday Group is researching on obtaining artificial fuel from coal deposits, geological and technological research. In case of a breakthrough, the parties intend to continue cooperation in this regard.

During the visit, President Emomali Rahmon stressed: "The progressive strengthening of friendly relations and mutually beneficial cooperation with India is an important and fundamental part of Tajikistan's foreign policy towards Asia." Particular attention was paid to the development of cooperation in science, education and health care. During the press conference, Prime Minister of India, Mr. Manmohan Singh, said that "Tajikistan is a key partner of India in Central Asia". These examples demonstrate that now there are no barriers to cooperation.

The Relative Border

Tajikistan and India do not share borders but from Tajikistan, India is almost within handshaking distance. In other words, there is no great distance between the two countries. However, they do desire to work together for peace, development and prosperity, trusting each other. After all, history shows that being next door, two countries may still not find a common language to talk to each other and pressing problems can remain unsolved for decades.

Possibilities of Communications between the Two Countries

India is a naval power, but between Tajikistan and India there are no direct sea links; however, it does not at all mean that this reality should not be taken into account. However, land and air transport can be used without any constraint. However, if this issue is approached more seriously, it can be seen that land links between the two states depend on the stability and security in Afghanistan and Pakistan. It seems that this problem can be resolved. The economic cooperation between India and the Republics of Central Asia can leverage the use of Afghan territory to assist the peoples and economies of Afghanistan and Pakistan. But in any case, for the desired level of economic cooperation, emphasis on economic cooperation is the key – for mutual interest, mutual benefit and mutual understanding.

With Respect to the Political System

In this regard, there is no significant difference between Tajikistan and India. However, if it does exist, it does not affect the outcome of the interactions between these two countries at any level. India, after a long and hard fight, was finally able to drop the yoke of colonial oppression and then moved forward taking giant steps, strengthening its economy, completely getting rid of the unwanted legacy of the colonialists. The fate of the Republic of Tajikistan, during the last two centuries, has been a bit different, although there are similarities. It means that after becoming independent countries, Tajikistan and India want to stand "on their own feet." In this regard, India is undoubtedly a perfect example.

About What is Important in the Rapprochement between the Two Countries?

The answer to this question cannot be the same, and it is natural. But, above all, there must be stability, not only in a particular country, in this case in Tajikistan and India, but in the regions where these countries are located. Next, is the important role played by geographical location and reliable communication and, of course, a shared common tradition, when it is. One cannot ignore the fact that the existence of these factors can only have a positive result when the Governments of these countries are working for the well-being of their peoples. The case of India and Tajikistan is encouraging as can be easily seen the number of times the officials in the two countries repeatedly discuss it in their official meetings and conversations.

Stability of the Political and Economic Situation in the Region and the World

Friendship and cooperation between two states if only fully possible in an atmosphere of political and economic stability in both countries in the first place, and it should not be temporary. It can be safely predicted that in the next ten to twenty years, this fruitful cooperation does not face any serious threat. Of course, in our troubled age, it is hard to imagine perfect world peace, but the people should be optimistic.

One last question: **Do the two countries have historical roots in cultural relations?**

Note the presence of the common historical roots at all levels of relations between the two countries, including cultural relations. Cultural contacts between Central Asia and India, each of whom boast a distinctive culture, can be traced to ancient times. These contacts and cooperation in history played a useful role and had their own significance in learning between the countries for the future. In the Middle Ages, science, culture and literature flourished in the court of each Mughal Emperor of the Mughal Empire in India, which in turn attracted the attention of travellers and philosophers from Central Asia, which continued for many subsequent centuries. It began a synthesis of Indo-Muslim culture, which was reflected in literature, language, music, dance, painting, sculpture, architecture, and even in traditional customs and celebrations. A new language – Urdu –

with rich literature was born in Indi, and up until the twentieth century, Persian literature flourished in the country.

Therefore, based on these facts, it can be said that now cooperation in all spheres, including cultural, is open for each country to aspire for results. Culture should be used to further promote various forms of cooperation. It is believed cultural and scientific exchanges have a serious role to play in the development of relations in education. For this, it is necessary to exchange delegations of experts on higher education, as well as exchange of students and scholars. At this stage, basically only two universities in Tajikistan: in medical and technical training – have about 80 Indian students. In universities in India, Tajik students are currently enrolled. It is encouraging that the Indian Council for Cultural Relations (ICCR) in New Delhi annually provides 15 scholarships to students from Tajikistan. In recent years, the programme for Government employees at the Indian Technical and Economic Cooperation (ITEC) run by the Government of India, has more than 50 seats allocated to Tajikistan.

In the formation of relationships between countries, people play an important role. For several years now, the Tajik National University has been training specialists on Indian philology. Introduction to the basics of rich Indian culture from ancient times to the present day is taught at the Tajik National University as part of the study of Indian history, literature, art, ethnography and Hindi and Urdu. Similarly, the works of Indian writers and poets can be translated directly from Hindi and Urdu to Tajik language, and vice versa. Earlier, some works were translated but the translations were primarily from the Russian language. Excellent scientific works in various fields by Indian scholars are still unknown for the Tajik people. Tajiks are familiar with the names of prominent Indian writers and poets such as Mirza Ghalib, Altaf Hussain Hali, Muhammad Iqbal, Ravindranath Tagore, Premchand, Yashpal, Surykant Tripathi Nirala, Sumitranandan Pant, Upendranath Ashok, Krishan Chandar, Mohan Singh, Mohan Rakesh, Mannu Bhandary, Rajendra Ydav and other masters of poetry and prose. India's famous epic, Ramayana, was translated from Russian to Tajik. A few works of Tajik writers and poets have been translated in Hindi, Urdu and some other languages of India. However, all this is just a drop in the ocean. The rich and ancient Indian medieval literature is still little known to Tajikistan. Books like Mahabharata and works of Kalidasa need to be translated. The works of Mahatma Gandhi (1869-1948), Swami Vivekananda (1863-1902), Jawaharlal

Nehru (1889-1964), Kamtaprasad Guru (1875-1949) and Shivadansinh Chauhan (born. 1918) are very popular amongst Tajik scholars. In 2009, the book by President of the Republic of Tajikistan, Emomali Rahmon, called 'Tajiks in the Mirror of History', was translated into Hindi. Thanks to the generosity of the Indian Embassy in Tajikistan, all the works of Mahatma Gandhi were presented to the scientific academic library named after Indira Gandhi.

Another possibility of cultural cooperation is in the study and promotion of the cultural heritage of India. There are published works of Amir Khosrow Dehlavi, Hasani Dehlavi, Zebunnisa, Ghani Kashmiri and other famous Persian poets of India. And so, until recently, all this was limited to Persian literature of India. With the arrival of Muslims in India, in line with the Bhakti movement, the time was ideal for Sufism. The study of Sufism and Sufi literature and Sufi poetry is important not only for scholarship, but also for the spiritual rapprochement of the peoples of India and Central Asia, including Tajikistan, in the Middle Ages. In academic libraries, there are stacks of books and thousands of manuscripts in Persian on history, philosophy, mathematics, astronomy, literature, and culture of India and the Muslim East. This golden treasure is almost untouched.

Prior to Tajikistan's independence, in 1968 in the city of Dushanbe, on the proposal of Academician, Bobojan Gafurov, then-director of the Institute of Oriental Studies of the Academy of Sciences of the USSR, an international scientific conference dedicated to the archeology and culture of Central Asia Kushan era was organised. This conference saw participants discuss several issues, amongst which was present a formidable delegation of India's most famous scientists, and it was a unique event in the cultural history of Soviet Tajikistan.

In 1987, the year of the fortieth anniversary of India's independence, the National Library named after Firdausi in the Tajik capital Dushanbe, held an exhibition of "The Indian book". The exhibition included more than four thousand books on various branches of science. These books were a mirror into the history of India, of its advanced medicine, industry, agriculture, fine arts, literature, technical progress and the lives of prominent Indian figures, like freedom fighters, for example. This was the first such exhibition in the history of Tajik-Indian relations. It should be noted that all the books for exhibition were presented to Firdausi National Library.

During the years after independence, India has made great progress in all spheres of life – economy, technology, education, science, etc. It would be useful in the coming years to organize such an exhibition or a national exhibition of India in the Republics of Central Asia, including Tajikistan.

Art – this is an area of human activity where there is no place for enmity and hatred. The art of ancient times still serves world peace and understanding, and its role has increased significantly today. This should be widely talked about and used. After all, the whole world is familiar with Indian movies, songs and dances. However, artists travelling abroad from India are not a very common phenomenon.

Thus, for the coming together of two different people, one can find dozens of ways and paths, and hundreds of methods and reasons. Cultural relations are the desired caravan which, for the sake of something beautiful, useful and necessary, can travel through familiar and unfamiliar deserts and oasis to bring people together.

22
Configuring India in Kazakhstan's Foreign Policy

Kuralay Baizakova

Introduction

India occupies an important place in the multi-vector foreign policy of the Republic of Kazakhstan. India was one of the first countries to recognize the independence of the Republic of Kazakhstan. It also supported our country during the process of joining the UN. India has demonstrated its generosity and willingness to help Kazakhstan throughout. And that is not a random phenomenon. It is not only because India has long been advocating the freedom and peaceful cooperation with all countries. The root of our ties and friendship was laid centuries ago.

India's Role in the Global Community

Kazakhstan's interest in India is determined by its place and role in the modern world. India has always played a constructive role on the international stage. Currently, India is a rising and one of the most dynamic economies in the world, as also being one of the main global centres of influence, thus presenting itself as a global player.

The Republic of India continues to pay particular attention to further enhancing its role in South Asia, safeguarding its national security and the need to strengthen the region to play a more significant role in the world community.

The policy of non-alignment and peaceful coexistence of India has earned it the highest accolades and given it a moral authority in today's world; it also fits into the new philosophy of international relations in the 21th century. Kazakhstan highly appreciates India's foreign policy strategy based on the ideas of non-violence as put forward by Nehru, and the emphasis on cooperation with all countries of the world.[1]

Most Indian politicians hold the point-of-view put forth Father of The Nation, Mahatma Gandhi, whose philosophy was an embodiment of humanism as the universal principle of unity between the man and the world. His method of non-violent conflict resolution with emphasis on dispersal of the conflict situation instead of the dispersal of the enemy is highly regarded by many. The provision for peace and national security and defence of the sovereignty and territorial integrity of the nation were – and still are – the main challenges of modern India. Implementation of these requires the support of numerous countries across the world who are willing to support and work with India.

Kazakhstan welcomes the current military and political alliance of China, India and Russia. It is important that such an alliance is not directed against anyone. Only such politics has a future in the ever-changing world. In this dynamic world, there is a seed of peace and security finding root in the joint effort by Kazakhstan and India.

There is no doubt that "this power has its own geopolitical interests in the region determined by several factors. These include the partnership with Russia; Chinese presence in Central Asia; India's rapprochement with the West and the United States; India's rivalry with Pakistan; the threat of militant Islam; India's transport, energy, trade and economic interests in Central Asia and other neighbouring regions", etc.[2]

India is interested in Kazakhstan – and Central Asia – as part of the "New Silk Road of India's foreign policy", aimed at securing and further enhancing cooperation in our geopolitically important region with a wealth of strategic resources.

The Main Stages of Cooperation

As noted by the Plenipotentiary of Kazakhstan in India, D. Kuanyshev: "Over the past 21 years, Kazakh-Indian cooperation developed dynamically in all areas of political, economic and cultural life".[3] The dynamic development of the bilateral and equitable partnership, based on mutual respect and understanding, suggests a unified approach to the views and positions of the two countries in various areas of this cooperation.

Since 1992, when the Declaration of Principles and Directions of Co-operation between Kazakhstan and India was signed,[4] there have been no fundamental disagreements on key issues of international relations between two countries.

The first stage of our cooperation was defined in the 1990s, when the legal basis for this cooperation was given shape.

The next stage was characterized by a surge in India's geopolitical interests in Central Asia in 2002-2003, after anti-terrorist operations in Afghanistan brought about a change in the entire geopolitical situation in the region. India's interests can be divided into two groups: the geopolitical, which include competition between China and India and the partnership with Russia, and the economic interests, which primarily include energy as well as economic and trade interests.[5]

In 2009, Kazakhstan and India entered the third stage of their bilateral relations by signing the Strategic Partnership Agreement[6] during the visit of the President Nursultan Nazarbayev to India.

At this stage, it should be noted that relations between India and Kazakhstan were given specific direction and substance in the context of bilateral political, economic, scientific, technical and cultural ties.

Thus during the visit of Indian Prime Minister, Manmohan Singh, to Kazakhstan in 2011, the "Road Map" on the development of the strategic partnership was signed.[7] The visit gave new impetus to the development of bilateral cooperation; the 2011-2014 Strategic Partnership Development Plan was adopted, and seven agreements were signed in areas like energy, cyber security, space exploration, education, high-tech development and others.

During the visit of the Kazakh Minister of Foreign Affairs, Erlan Idrissov, to India in 3-5 March, 2013, the countries confirmed their willingness to build a constructive dialogue based on issues of regional and global security, reconstruction of Afghanistan and interaction within multilateral bodies like the UN, CICA and SCO.

During these visits, exchange of views on key issues on the international agenda and shared perspectives on bilateral cooperation have taken place. The growing intensity and the focus of these official visits prove the vigour this bilateral cooperation enjoys in both countries.

Main Areas of Cooperation

The predominant areas of cooperation between Kazakhstan and India are trade and economic cooperation, sustainable socio-economic development, political stability and strengthening of the security in the region.

There are no tensions or contradictions in the political space between Kazakhstan and India. Regular meetings are held at the inter-governmental and inter-state levels. Also, inter-parliamentary ties have developed successfully between the two countries. The Indian Parliamentary Friendship Group with Kazakhstan was created in October 2011.

Cultural ties develop more actively than economic ones. There are exchanges of musicians and actors, mutual yoga interests, visits of interesting people taking place. On May 2011, New Delhi successfully hosted the Days of Kazakhstan Culture in India. The scientific and academic contacts between these communities in both countries have become a regular affair as well. Tourism flourishes, too, and the 'Kazakhstan-India Tourism and Travel Fair' has been held annually since 2005.

Kazakh-Indian relations are based not only on cultural-historical and political ties, but also on economic aspect as well. Kazakhstan is the largest trading partner of India in Central Asia.

One should take into account the fact that the fast developing Indian economy requires more energy resources. No surprise that India keeps making attempts to enter and consolidate its position in Kazakhstan's hydrocarbon market. Production and sale of energy sources is a priority in economic cooperation between Kazakhstan and India.

The points of contact between India and Kazakhstan are not limited to cooperation in financial, economic, energy and transport sectors. India places importance to meet the needs of its nuclear industry. Kazakhstan and India signed an agreement for cooperation in peaceful uses of atomic energy[8]. The agreement to supply more than 2000 tons of Kazakh Uranium by 2014 to India may not be enough to meet India's growing needs in nuclear energy.

Leaders of the two nations have also discussed the joint construction of a nuclear reactor, which is a priority for Kazakhstan since it aspires to become a major global supplier of nuclear fuel and reactors as it seeks nuclear cooperation with Russia, Japan, China and India.

The framework of cooperation between India and Kazakhstan in outer space is also very significant. The leaders of the two countries agreed to boost cooperation in this area. However, Kazakhstan lacks the technological expertise and resources for the development of its space industry. The Indian space programme is strong and can provide Kazakhstan with the necessary technologies. Recently, India has become one of the most promising global leaders in the space industry, where the United States, Russia and China are leaders.

Kazakhstan, on the other hand, badly requires the technological know-how to build an innovative and vibrant economy. The two countries have signed the Memorandum of Understanding between the Indian and Kazakh Computer Security Incident Response Teams.[9]

Kazakhstan attaches great priority to enhancing cooperation in the field of defence and security. Since 1995, both countries have been maintaining military relations as well. The Memorandum on military-technical cooperation between the two Governments was signed in 2002.[10] Since 2011, agreements for cooperation between the Ministries of Defence in Kazakhstan and India are signed annually, allowing for cooperation in defence to go to higher and more structured levels.

As noted by Secretary (East) in the Ministry of External Affairs of India, N Ravi, "Kazakhstan and India, both being countries with multinational and multi-religious societies, share common values and common approaches on key international issues, including regional security".[11] Both sides actively oppose international terrorism, drug trafficking and aggressive fundamentalism.

Kazakhstan actively cooperates with India on multilateral forums, international and regional organizations, such as the UN, CICA and SCO. India has been very supportive on CICA since the initiative was launched by President Nazarbayev in October 1992.

India also supports Kazakhstan's initiative on holding the Congress of the World and Traditional Religions in Astana, and actively takes part in the activity of the Congress. Kazakhstan, in turn, supports India's goal to become a Permanent Member of the UN Security Council on all bilateral and multilateral meetings and negotiations.

Constraints on Bilateral Cooperation

Despite the positive external facets, the relationship between Kazakhstan and India has been developing slowly. If the level of cooperation with neighbouring Russia and China is already quite high, one cannot say the same about India, which is the fourth largest economy in the world and the second most populous country. However, there is a window of opportunity to change things for the better.

According to Kazakh experts, there are several factors complicating the development of Kazakh-Indian relations. There are objective and subjective reasons, chief amongst them being transport and communications, since India does not share a border with Kazakhstan or any other country in the region.[12]

Another factor is the lack of information on the perspectives and current trends in the development of our states in the expert community and amongst the people of the two countries.[13]

India is still seen as "latecomer" in Central Asia. Kazakhstan's multi-vector foreign policy can contribute to the further "awakening" of India in the region. First of all, one must consider the importance of strengthening the Asian side in Kazakhstan's foreign policy in general, and India in particular.

Perspectives of Bilateral Relations

What expectations countries of Central Asia – such as Kazakhstan – have for further development of relations with India? Here are a few recommendations.

Further impetus to cooperation should be on grounds of a sectoral approach, which is that existing cooperation mechanisms, such as working groups and dialogues, should be diversified at different levels.

It is important to disseminate the enhanced image of India as a rapidly developing country. In the post-Soviet public mind in Central Asian countries, India remains a country with rich cultural traditions, Bollywood movies and a developed textile industry. Hence, one can explain the poor ties at the level of small and medium-sized businesses.

Kazakhstan wants to attract Indian companies in the industrial sector as well as in establishing joint ventures in pharmacology.

Cooperation in the field of cyber security might become an important aspect of cooperation in the near future. Therefore, there is a need to further expand cooperation in information technology, particularly cyber security and the training of personnel.

Cooperation in the field of education has great potential, too. Targeted educational programmes should be developed to train area specialists that Kazakhstan requires.

Scientific cooperation between these communities, despite significant progress, has so far been of a limited nature. Thus, comprehensive long-term studies should mark the beginning of research between the two communities of these countries.

For Kazakhstan, it might be useful to study the Indian experience in developing domestic tourism.

Also, it is suggested to expand cooperation within the multilateral frameworks and study the rich experience of India in developing links in the joint fight against terrorism and drug trafficking.

Conclusion

In recent years, India has been interested in Kazakhstan and Central Asia within its "New Silk Road" initiative. India has potential to expand its economic, military, strategic and geopolitical presence in Central Asia, including Kazakhstan. It will depend on a number of factors – both economic and geopolitical – as well as the implementation of major communication and energy projects.

India does not wield strong economic or military influence in Central Asia, and partly relies on its technological capabilities. Recent bilateral deals and enhanced cooperation with Kazakhstan in technology, energy and space give a platform to India to expand its strategic presence and contribute to its goal of becoming one a leading power in the changing geo-political and economic landscape of Central Asia.

The common interests and goals between the two countries in the field of security and economic stability, as well as similarities in views on the root causes of emerging threats in the world present significant incentives for the development of Kazakh-Indian relations.[14]

India as a rising global player is already becoming a force to be taken seriously. Kazakhstan, being a dominant player in Central Asia, has a certain say in the general configuration of the balance of power in the region, too.[15]

Endnotes

1. Bulat Sultanov. *"Kazakhstansko-Indiyskie otnoshenya: sostoyanie i perspective* (Kazakhstan-Indian relations: state and prospects), In Tim Page (ed.) *India-Kazakhstan: perspective strategitsheskogo partnerstva* (India – Kazakhstan: prospects of strategic partnership). (Almaty, 2011), p. 46

2. A. Kazantzev *"Bolshaya igra" s neizvestnimi pravilami: mirovaya politika i Tsentralnaya Azia* ("Great game" with unknown rules: world politics and Central Asia of strategic partnership). (Moskou: Nasledie Eurasia, 2008), p. 236
3. *Proverennoe vremenem kazakhstansko-indiyskoe cotrudnichestvo na dnyax prazdnuet svoe 20-letie* (The Kazakhstan-Indian cooperation confirmed by time the other day celebrates the 20 anniversary) (Almaty, 2012). http://site.litera.kz
4. *Deklaratsia o printsipax vzaimootnosheniy mejdu Kazakhstanom i Indiyey* (The Declaration on the Principles of Relationship between Kazakhstan and India, 1992). http://online.zakon.kz/Document
5. Murat Laumulin. *Tsentralnaya Azia v zarubejnoy polotologii i mirovoy geopolitike, Tom V. Tsentralnaya Azia v XXI stoletii* (Central Asia in foreign politologie and world geopolitics. Volume V: Central Asia in the XXI century) (Almaty:KISI, 2009), p. 131
6. *Soglashenie o strategitcheskom partnerstve, 2009* (Agreements on Strategic Partnership, 2009). http://online.zakon.kz/Document
7. *Astana I Delhi prinyali "Dorojnuy kartu" strategitcheskogo partnerstva* (Astana and Delhi accepted "Road map" of strategic partnership). http://thenews.kz/2011/04/19/795269.html
8. *India I Kazakhstan usilivaut strategitcheskoe partnerstvo* (India and Kazakhstan strengthen strategic partnership). http://www.centrasia.ru/newsA
9. *Memorandum o vzaimoponimanii mejdu indiyskimi I kazakhstanskimi gruppami bistrogo reagirovaniya na narushenie komputernoy bezopasnosti* (The Memorandum of understanding between the Indian and Kazakhstan groups of fast response to violation of computer security). // http://www.centrasia.ru/news
10. *Memorandum o voenno-texnicheskom sotrudnichestve mejdu pravitelsrvami dvux stran, 2002* (Memorandum of Military and Technical Cooperation between the Governments of two countries, 2002). http://www.mfa.kz/ru/#!/foreign-policy/dogovorno-pravovaya_baza/dvustoronnie_mejdunarodnyie_dogovoryi-respubliki_kazahstan/indiya
11. *15 let sotrunichestva* (15 years of Cooperation). http:// www.kazpravda.kz
12. Bolat Sultanov. *"Kazakhstansko-Indiyskie otnoshenya: sostoyanie i perspective* (Kazakhstan-Indian relations: state and prospects), In Tim Page (ed.) *India-Kazakhstan: perspective strategitsheskogo partnerstva* (India–Kazakhstan: prospects of strategic partnership). (Almaty, 2011), p. 53
13. Adil Kaukenov. *Kazakhstan I Indiya: novii etap ekonomicheskogo sotrudnichestva* (Kazakhstan and India: New stage of economic cooperation). http// www. easttime.ru
14. *India-Kazakhstan: perspective strategitsheskogo partnerstva* (India – Kazakhstan: prospects of strategic partnership). (Almaty, 2011), p. 11
15. *Ibid.*, p. 19

23
Education in India and Central Asia: Building Bridges

Cholpon Turdalieva and Aizhamal Marat

Introduction

When we hear the word 'resources', the first thing we immediately think about are usually material goods, money and natural resources, while words like 'education' and 'knowledge' are the last things we would ever think of. Education and knowledge are also resources that transform society, nations and cultures. At this point, knowledge and education that have been accumulated through intellectual process of a nation for centuries become the base for building on local and national systems of education and knowledge. In this regard, India is an excellent example of knowledge production and dissemination, not only at the local but also international levels.

This chapter will looks at the influence of knowledge systems of India and Central Asia on each other at different historical periods. Therefore, in this historical and comparative narrative, we will see how knowledge was – and is – transformed and exchanged. So, what vectors of mutual partnership in the field of education that were established in the past would now become a source of large-scale collaboration in the framework of the 'Connect Central Asia' policy of the Government of India in 2012. In what ways should transportation systems and communications between these two subcontinents work in order to make mutual education programmes and projects become a base for production of effective and beneficial knowledge and skills.

Major facts and information presented in this chapter are based on data on Kyrgyzstan. However, some insights were also taken from other Central-Asian countries as well. In addition, faculty and Indian students from Kyrgyz Medical Academy and the Higher International School of Medicine in Bishkek were interviewed to understand contemporary trends in Kyrgyzstan-India relations in education.

India–Central Asia Educational Encounters

The first encounter with various genres of Indian philosophy, history and literature in Kyrgyzstan starts in the history, cultural studies and philosophy lessons in schools and universities. For example, students in school learn about Rig Veda, which means "praise, verse and knowledge". It gives knowledge about genesis and the role of human beings in this world. Gods, people, animals, plants, elements, seasons, sacrifices, etc. – they all attain a living embodiment that relates to – and transform – into each other through magic. History teaches students about ancient civilizations like Harappa, Ashoka, Maurya and the Mughal empires. Earlier, text books on Indian civilizations, particularly the Mughal empire, had limited information. Contemporary history books give more information about Babur, the Mughal empire and its influence on Indian architecture, art and science (Osmonov 2012:177-178).

Spiritual and ethical ideas of some mythological characters had an impact on Central Asian scholars, too. A Kyrgyz philosopher, K. Sadykov, made a comparative analysis of the Indian epic '*The Bhagavad Gita*' and the Kyrgyz epic '*Manas*' (Sadykov, 2012). He came to the conclusion that there are a number of similar aspects that appear in the two poems. These include:

1. The existence of certain types of "groups" or "schools" within ethnos, which transmits these sacred texts, keeping and making them sustainable;
2. The existence of a sustainable mechanism of transmitting these texts (Sadykov, 2012.p.2)

Thus, the mechanism of transmission of these two ancient works of wisdom lies in its stable and dialectical matrix and scheme.

Another scholar from Kyrgyzstan, Ch. Shamshiev, basing his findings on the French scholar, Georges Dumézil's triple Functional Hypothesis, stated that the epic Manas and Mahabharata belong to a large family of Indo-European epics, and have a lot of similarity in style and content. (Shamshiev, 2004)

Recently, Kyrgyzstan's scholars have developed a whole programme of translation, reproduction and promotion of small and large epics. It is a complex exercise that contains learning from the epic, Manas, in schools. Moreover, starting from 2012, in a decree by the President of the Kyrgyz Republic, the universities teach a mandatory subject called Manas Studies. The programme also includes epic retelling contests amongst epic tellers, who show their talents and interpretation skills.

The National Programme for study, research and popularization of Kyrgyz epics would be richer and more attractive if it contained an intercultural and, it can be said, an inter-epic dialogue between Kyrgyz and Indian researchers and epic tellers.

With the development of an independent state, the education system in Central Asia – and Kyrgyzstan – found an ethnocentric approach to the development of their curriculum and educational programmes. Another tendency in the educational system is predominance of works by Russian writers and thinkers, in subjects like foreign literature. For example, foreign literature as part of literature classes in schools comprises Russian writers by almost 80 per cent.

No doubt, learning about such Indian thinkers of the 20th century, like Rabindranath Tagore and Mahatma Gandhi, would have been essential and a key element of the development of humane pedagogy and education, of patriotism and nationalism based on non-violence, peace and tolerance. In this context, the Tolstoy School opened by Gandhi in 1910 can be an example of teaching and learning children without violence and depravation.

Probably, Indian students are not taught about the works of Central Asian scholars like Mahmud Kashghari, Zhusup Balasagyn, Al-Farabi and Firdausi or literature, philosophy and the art of later periods such as Kyrgyz poets of the 20th century like A Osmonov, A Tokombaev, O Suleimenov and other Central Asian poets and writers, who also highlight timeless human values like good versus evil, justice and love for the motherland. In this respect, a cross-cultural dialogue on the framework of adaptation and integration of the works of famous Indian and Central Asian scholars for educational programmes would have been a bridge not only in education, but economy, politics and international relations.

In general, a source for the introduction and adaptation of traditional knowledge about India in the region was the old Silk Road, which used to be an international transport corridor in 3rd BC. Ideas and ideologies, goods and technologies entered the region from India, and back through multiple branches of trade and economic networks.

However, the transmission of knowledge through this corridor did not have a steady, safe, and permanent method. For example, Buddhism as a religious and philosophical doctrine, which arose in India in the 6 century BCE, came to Central Asia in the 4th century BCE and became an important spiritual belief of certain nomadic tribes and sedentary peoples in the region (Roerich 1920:20, Goryacheva 2009). But not long away, with the advent of Islam, the role of Buddhism in Central Asia faded and was finally disappeared. Mahmoud al-Kashgari, a famous Central Asian thinker in the 11th century, elaborately wrote about the struggle of Muslims and Buddhists of that time (Elverskog, 2010:95).

> We came down on them like a flood!
> We went out among their cities!
> We tore down the idol-temples,
> We sat on the Buddha's head!

That is, the Great Silk Road, as an international transport link based on the infrastructure and security ecosystem typical of that period, facilitated the dissemination of knowledge and skills, ideas and technologies. But as history is witness, not all knowledge and skills that came from India were adapted and acculturated in local ethno-cultural spaces.

Today, the Silk Road can be a new branding in the advancement of political and economic cooperation between the two regions. Cross-border cooperation on transport of energy resources and a variety of goods may benefit from this branding. On the implementation of economic and political agenda, the New Silk Road diplomacy based on bilateral and multilateral cooperation between Central Asia and India can also be an undeniable strategic resource in the development of both educational and human capital.

Indian Consumers in the International Education of Kyrgyzstan

Currently, internationalization of education in Kyrgyzstan plays a significant role, both for the politics and the economy of the country.

According to some experts, benefit from international students from developing countries are seen in terms of increased income , cultural diversity and the prestige of the country (Altbach and Knight, 2009). In 2008, the export of educational services in higher and secondary education and language courses in Kyrgyzstan showed significant growth as compared to neighbouring Central Asian countries (Zhenish, 2012).

The main beneficiaries of the international character of education in Kyrgyzstan are students from Asian countries. The reasons include similar historical and cultural environment, geographic proximity, relatively low tuition fees and stress-free examination requirements. However, despite these factors, the countries that avail the educational services offered by Kyrgyzstan change frequently. For example, in 2004, the top five consumers of educational services and the volume of expenditure on education (in descending order) included Turkey, Uzbekistan, Kazakhstan, the USA, Russia and Pakistan (Jenish, 2012:14).

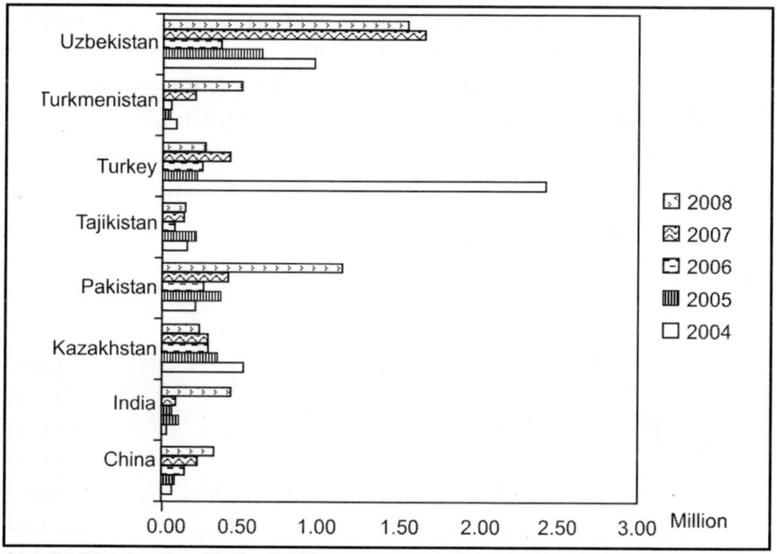

Source: UN Service Trade database.

Fig. 23.1: Major Importers of Kyrgyzstan's Education Services (USD millions)

In 2008, the picture changed: the top five customers included Uzbekistan, Pakistan, Turkmenistan, India, and China. Changes in the political and economic situation in the country certainly affects the ranking of exports in education and the income levels of the country. The 2005, the Tulip Revolution and the 2010 Revolution and Osh events in Kyrgyzstan led to a decrease in the number of international students in the country, while the number of students from Uzbekistan decreased sharply. (Jenish, 20)

Despite the social and political developments and local issues in the system of national education, the process of enrolling international students is still quite stable. Kyrgyzstan hosts about 20,000 international students out of an overall total enrolment of 230,000 students in the country. Students from the CIS countries – in numbers – exceed those from other countries in Kyrgyzstan.

Amongst the beneficiaries of educational services in Kyrgyzstan, India is perhaps the last in the list. In 2005, India was the last out of seven countries and in 2008, India was placed at the fourth place. Foreign exchange earned from Indian students increased from about US $ 85,000 in 2007 to about US$430,000 dollars in 2008, (Jenish, 2012:14), which is five times than in 2007. The influx of students from India became evident in 2007-2008 with the opening of the International Higher School of Medicine in the International University of Kyrgyzstan, with teaching in English and a more or less easy admission process (Jenish, 2012: 14).

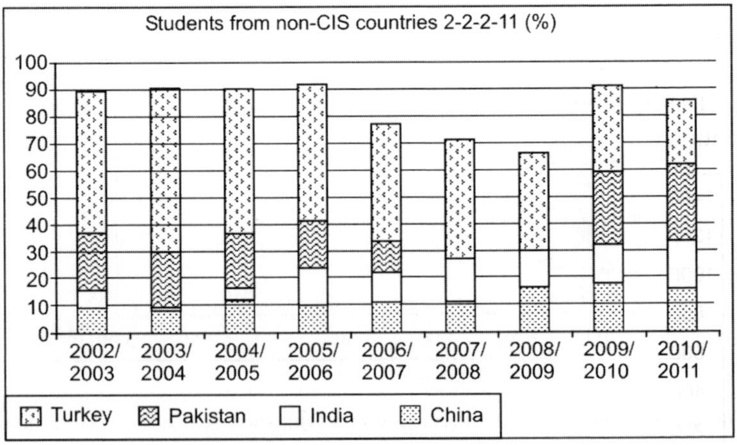

Source: National Statistics Committee of the Kyrgyz Republic

Fig. 23.2: India as a Consumer of International Education in KR in 2002-2011 (Table 2).

As of today, there are three tertiary institutions that are very popular universities for students from India. The Medical Academy (MA), the International Higher School of Medicine (IHSM) and the Asian Medical Institute (AMI) do offer medical courses for Indian students. The total number of students from India is 1,429. Out of these, 114 study in the KSMA (table 3)[1], 915 in IHSM (table 4) and 400 in AMI.

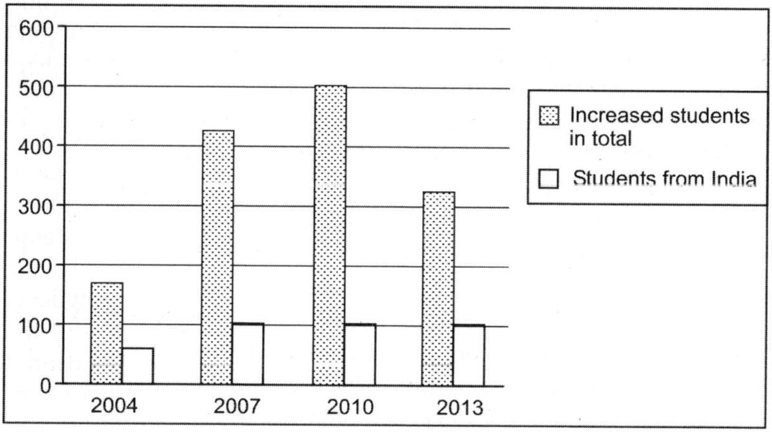

Source: Data from KSAM.

Fig. 23.3: International Education by the Particular Institutions: The Kyrgyz State Academy of Medicine (KSAM) (Table 3)

These students are all majoring in medicine, and almost all of them mentioned in interviews that it is prestigious to be a doctor in India.

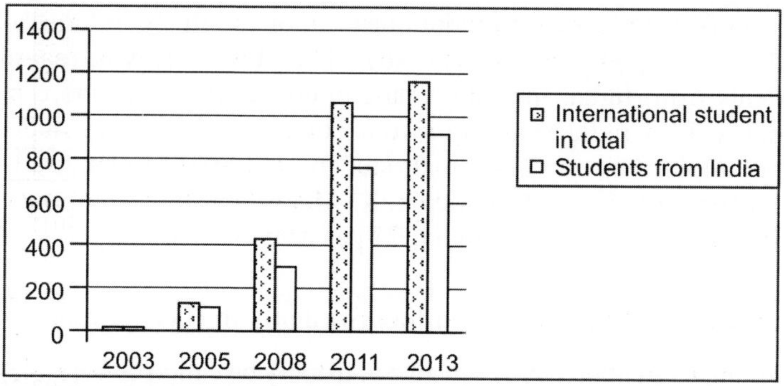

Fig. 23.4: International Higher School of Medicine (Table 4)

The admissions system for international students is not very harsh because of two reasons. First, unsatisfactory preparation of graduating students in Indian schools: 15 students interviewed from India said the main reason for their studying in Kyrgyzstan were low scores in their final exams. Second, medical educational institutions have moderate entrance requirements for international students because their tuition fees are crucial to the universities' budgets. These institutions send admission committees to India to organize Biology and English Language entrance exams. Applicants who received 50 per cent or more correct answers are enrolled in universities. Under these circumstances, factors such as competition and testing the knowledge of international students are not so important. Financial readiness and ability to pay tuition fees is the first criterion to enter any Kyrgyz University. To cope with these aspects, one solution could be to make entrance exams online. This step could increase transparency and lower costs, both for international students and the institutions.

As shown in tables, the proportion of students applying to Kyrgyz universities from India is not as large as that of Turkey, Pakistan and South Korea. Until recent times, Indian students used to go for international education mostly to Russia and the Ukraine.

For instance, in 2010-2011, the Peoples' Friendship University of Russia accounted for 16,616 students from Kazakhstan, the same number from China, 5,297 from Turkmenistan, 4,919 from Ukraine, 4,515 from India, 4,299 from Belorussia and 2,166 from Azerbaijan. Ukraine accounted for 2,500 students from India studying medicine, civil aviation and others subjects (Êitinov, Solodkova, 2010:20).

Female students are predominant amongst all the international students in Kyrgyzstan (Jenish, 2012:15). However, with regard to students from India, the ratio is the opposite: there are more male students from India studying in our country than female students. For example, there are 274 female students out of 915 Indian students at the Higher School of Medicine. KSMA's data shows that out of a total of 114 students from India, 75 per cent are male.

Paradoxes of Adaptation: Indian Students in Kyrgyzstan

Adapting to an alien environment can usually be called cultural shock. What kind of cultural shock did Indian students get when they first arrived in Kyrgyzstan? When they were asked "What things stood out when you first arrived in Bishkek?", they had different answers. Some of them remember small grey houses, drunk people or rainy days and cold winters. Any culture has its iconic structures, which helps people and gives clues to them on how to behave in daily situations. These signals unconsciously become part of everyone's lives. When this unconscious behaviour looks completely new, people experience profound shock. Therefore, in the beginning, Indian students experienced problems of adaptation and acculturation in Kyrgyzstan. We can understand this in the framework of Theory on Value Differences, called Stress of Acculturation, by J. Berry (Berry, 1997). The theory considers an encounter between different values when two cultures come together. The more these differences are evident and bigger, the longer lasting is the cultural shock.

The institutions in Kyrgyzstan try to minimize stress for its international students by organizing various events like Nowruz (New Year) and encouraging them to socialize by participating in other events as well. For example, in 2013, the Indian students took part in an event called the Night at the Museum held by the Kyrgyz State Historical Museum.

On the other hand, we should note that the level of social support and solidarity amongst Indian students is high. When asked about "What historical sites have they visited in Kyrgyzstan?", the students answered they had visited the historical museum, Ala-Archa and Kashka-Suu recreational areas.

Another way of coping with culture shock and adapting to an new environment is eating your own traditional diet. Students usually cook themselves and use Indian ingredients. 95 per cent of interviewed students answered they were vegetarians. Thus, cooking traditional food is a way to lessen culture shock and stress in a new environment.

It is believed that students who socialize both with their own group and the local population can more easily adapt to their new circumstances.

To the question "What kinds of Kyrgyz or Russian music do you like or listen to?", only two out of 15 mentioned Kyrgyz singers, and two others listen to famous local pop singers, Timati and Dima Bilan, while the rest prefer Indian music.

When asked about qualities that Kyrgyz people are known for, and whether the students have local friends, Indian students said that Kyrgyz people are usually friendly, fair and ready to help. But only two of those interviewed said they have local friends; one student had a roommate who was a local. From this, we can assume that the level of intermingling with local people and culture is not very common. One other factor that influences the acclimatisation of Indian students – and international students in general – is language. Knowing the local language can help students communicate with, and adapt to, Kyrgyzstan faster.

Thus, students take mandatory classes of Russian language. Interviewed students had good Russian skills and tried to speak in Russian during the interview. Another factor that enhances cultural stress is unfair – and sometimes criminal – behaviour of law enforcement agencies in relation to foreign students. International students, including students from India, can be extorted for money , abuse of power by representatives of law enforcement, and, as a consequence, turn to be a violation of basic human rights.

Stalbek Ahunbaev, the Vice President of the International School of Medicine, noted that the safety of international students has become a number one priority. In order to avoid the above mentioned situation, the school has assigned a security officer, who is responsible for the safety of students, and there are special buses that bring students from one building to another, and finally, there is absolute control over dormitories and places of living.

To sum up, we should note that educational collaboration between India and Kyrgyzstan is at a nascent stage today. However, the following circumstances can prevent wider cooperation in this sector:

First, traditional perceptions and stereotypes about India as a country of fairy tales learnt from the Great Silk Road, Indian mythology or Bollywood films. It seems that Kyrgyzstani people remember only just these historical and cultural images and are not so interested in knowing the other – modern India.

Second, Kyrgyzstan's national and international policy and public discourse about trans-regional security and politics somehow isolates India as an important geostrategic and geopolitical partner and collaborator;

Third, lack of educational and professional programmes for various levels of education in both Kyrgyzstan and India;

Fourth, lack of proper monitoring and supervision of quality of international education for students from India, and international students in general;

Fifth, poor access to educational services for Indians in India because of poor infrastructure in international education in Kyrgyzstan;

And lastly, lack of steps taken to establish an India-Central Asian University. In other words, there is a need for institutional orientation of competent professionals in the fields of medicine, telecommunications and languages who will take the lead in talking about new emerging social order and advocating for democracy.

Note

1. Statistics according to the foreign students of KSMA and IHSM was given by the administration of these institutions.

References

Altbach P., Knight J. (2007). The internationalization of higher education: Motivations and realities. Journal of Studies in International Education No.11, pp.290-305

Berry J. (1997) Immigration, Acculturation, and Adaptation Applied Psychology: an International Review.47, pp.5-68

Goryacheva V.D. (2009). Indo-buddiiskii component kul'turnogo nasledia in Problemy kul'turogeneza I kul'turnogo nasledia. SPB, 2009.

Elverskog J. (2010). Buddhism and Islam on the Silk Road. University of Pennsylvania Press.

Handi M. (1998). Moscow: The Publishing Housing by Shalva Amonashvili.

Kitinov B., Solodkova.(2010).RUDN e strany Azii. Moscow: RUDN.

Rerich Yu. (2002) Buddism e culturnoe edinstvo Azii. Sbornik statei. Moscow: MCR.

Shamshiev Ch. (2004) Indoevropeiskii miph i epos "Manas" at http://www.kyrgyz.ru/?page=247 2004, accessed on 1 May 2013.

Sadykov K. (2012) "Manas" è "Bhagavad – Gita" v svete problem translyatsii sakralnyh tekstov at http://www.edu.gov.kg/ru/presscentr/ accessed on 1 June 2013.

Part IV
Papers in Russian Language

24
К вопросу об открытии транспортных коридоров из Южной в Центральную Азию после 2014 года

Султан Акимбеков

Проблема развития ситуации вокруг Афганистана после 2014 года, помимо прочего, имеет важное измерение, связанное с вероятностью восстановления прежнего транзитного потенциала этой страны. Данный аспект имеет прямое отношение не только к развитию экономических отношений между Индией и Центральной Азией, но и к мирному урегулированию целого ряда давних конфликтов.

Во-первых, речь идет о том, чтобы Афганистан смог бы в перспективе самостоятельно зарабатывать деньги на транзите грузов из региона Центральной Азии в направлении Южной Азии – в Пакистан и далее в Индию. Это позволит частично снять часть расходов с международного сообщества, которые направляются на содержание государственных институтов этой страны.

Во-вторых, развитие транзита через Афганистан может стать важной составляющей обеспечения стабильности внутри этой страны, в том числе в связи с появлением заинтересованности местного населения и местных элит в доходах от транзита.

В-третьих, восстановление транзитного значения Афганистана позволит наладить сухопутную торговлю между двумя бурно экономически развивающимися регионами – Центральной Азией и Южной Азией. В Центральной Азии это может позволить снизить внутреннюю напряженность в отношениях между странами региона. В частности, она выражается в периодически закрываемых границах между

Узбекистаном и Таджикистаном. Уровень взаимной торговой проницаемости границ центральноазиатских республик крайне мал, особенно это характерно для отношений между Туркменистаном и Узбекистаном, а также двух этих стран с другими государствами. В Южной Азии развитие торговых отношений между указанными регионами автоматически превратит Пакистан в важную транзитную территорию, что может позволить также снизить известный уровень напряженности в пакистанско-индийских отношениях.

В целом данная идея выглядит, как один из возможных способов не только попытаться решить давний конфликт в Афганистане, но и способствовать урегулированию серии межгосударственных конфликтов в регионе.

Здесь стоит отметить, что прекращение торгово-экономических отношений между Центральной и Южной Азией не стало следствием конфликта вокруг Афганистана, начавшегося с апрельской революции 1978 года и вторжения советских войск. Исторически существовавшая торговля между данными регионами сократилась в момент начала конфликта между Британской и Российской империями в XIX веке. После же образования СССР и начала в этой стране масштабных преобразований ее граница с внешней Азией разделила советскую Среднюю Азию и Южную Азию.

Необходимо также подчеркнуть, что сухопутная торговля в Азии резко сократилась в размерах примерно с XVI века, когда торговые отношения между Азией и Европой переместились на море. Соответственно, Великий шелковый путь через Среднюю Азию потерял свое прежнее доминирующее экономико-политическое значение. Это сказалось также на ответвлениях данного пути, которые проходили из Средней Азии в Индию.

Конфликт в Афганистане закрепил взаимную изоляцию регионов Центральной и Южной Азии. Соответственно планы по развитию торгово-экономических отношений между ними являются весьма амбициозной задачей. Они способны в корне изменить ситуацию, как в вопросах экономики, так и в геополитике.

Однако, реализация данного глобального проекта весьма затруднительна по причине продолжающихся геополитических противоречий как вокруг Афганистана, так и в связи с борьбой за влияние в регионе в целом.

Существующий комплекс противоречий

В настоящий момент основные противоречия связаны с регионом Центральной Азии. В частности, США выступают за открытие данного региона с южного направления. С этим связана выдвинутая Вашингтоном идея создания Нового Великого Шелкового пути через Афганистан. Однако, Россия и Китай полагают, что за планами США скрывается их стремление установить свое влияние в стратегически важном для обеих стран регионе Центральной Азии. Москва и Пекин в принципе выступают против влияния третьих стран в данном регионе. Их опасения связаны с тем, что такие страны смогут оказывать давление на территории, уязвимые для обоих государств. Для Китая это Синьцзян, для России - семь тысяч километров границы с Казахстаном.

При этом Россия традиционно играет большую роль в Центральной Азии, чем Китай. Поэтому ее политика и внутри самого этого региона, и в отношении Афганистана является более активной. Если США выступают за открытие Центральной Азии и развитие торгово-экономических отношений между ним и странами Южной Азии, то Россия делает основной акцент на проблемах безопасности. С российской точки зрения после 2014 года ситуация в Афганистане может привести к обострению проблем с безопасностью. В том числе речь может идти об угрозе прихода к власти движения «Талибан». Соответственно, это потребует защиты интересов, с одной стороны, национальных меньшинств внутри Афганистана, с другой стороны, государств Центральной Азии от внешней афганской угрозы.

Здесь возможны два сценария. Один подразумевает восстановление в Афганистане ситуации, существовавшей до 2001 года. То есть, восстановления прежнего Северного антиталибского альянса, объединяющего национальные меньшинства. Второй исходит из идеи объединения государств Центральной Азии вокруг концепции противостояния угрозам безопасности.

Очевидно, что оба варианта развития событий

теоретически делают затруднительной идею восстановления торгово-экономических отношений между Центральной и Южной Азией. Таким образом существующие геополитические противоречия между великими державами за влияние в Центральной Азии, а также на подступах к этому стратегически важному региону напрямую влияют на будущее развитие событий. Поэтому все зависит от того, каким образом будут развиваться события в Афганистане после 2014 года.

Интересы стран Центральной Азии

Для независимых государств Центральной Азии вопрос Афганистана и любых будущих проектов вокруг него в первую очередь связан с проблемами безопасности. Вопросы экономического развития по своим приоритетам уступают возможным рискам, связанным с угрозами со стороны зоны длительного афганского конфликта. Кроме того, борьба за геополитическое влияние между великими державами также вынуждает страны региона проявлять максимальную осторожность в вопросах своей внешнеполитической ориентации.

В то же время, вопрос открытия транспортных коридоров на юг является одним из приоритетов политики таких приграничных с Афганистаном стран, как Туркменистан, Узбекистан и Таджикистан.

Туркменистан с середины 1990-ых годов выступает за строительство газопровода в направлении Пакистана. Любое руководство в Туркменистане стремится приобрести новые рынки сбыта для туркменского газа и снизить таким образом уровень зависимости от России. Сегодня ситуация для Туркменистана более благоприятная, чем в 1990-ых и начале 2000-ых. Часть газа с 2009 года туркмены отправляют в Китай по новому газопроводу через Узбекистан и Казахстан.

Узбекистан нуждается в открытии торговых путей на юг в связи с тем, что его промышленная политика в духе государственного капитализма требует снижения издержек. В то время как транспортировка грузов через Казахстан и Россию приводит к значительным затратам.

Для Таджикистана, у которого крайне сложные

политические отношения с Узбекистаном, в большей степени ощущает себя в экономической изоляции из-за трудностей в обеспечении перевозок через узбекскую территорию. Поэтому для таджикского руководства развитие отношений с северным Афганистаном - это не только вопрос местной торговли. Оно также хотело бы найти в Афганистане новые рынки сбыта, в частности для электроэнергии, вырабатываемой на таджикских ГЭС.

Все три указанные выше страны относятся к «прифронтовым», они непосредственно соседствуют с Афганистаном. Естественно, что любые глобальные процессы, которые будут происходить в региональном развитии, в первую очередь затронут именно их интересы.

В то же время, Казахстан находится вдали от Афганистана, он непосредственно не вовлечен в события в этой стране. Его экономическое положение позволяет чувствовать себя более уверенно. Кроме того, у него больше вариантов транспортировки различных грузов. Помимо российского направления, существуют также варианты транспортировки через Китай и через Каспийское море на Кавказ. В геополитическом плане Казахстан может поддерживать стабильно ровные отношения со всеми великими державами. Идеологически это обосновывается многовекторной политикой страны.

При этом для Казахстана непринципиально, какой именно вариант развития событий будет реализован во всем регионе, какая тенденция в итоге возобладает. Потому что, для Казахстана, с одной стороны, вполне приемлемо вероятное открытие транзитной торговли через Афганистан с Пакистаном и далее с Индией. Казахстан, несомненно, получит от этого выгоду с учетом достигнутого уровня его экономического развития, особенно в части инфраструктуры и финансовых институтов. С другой стороны, Казахстан не проиграет также и в случае, если сохранится статус-кво и основной акцент будет сделан на проблемах безопасности.

В целом все государства региона Центральной Азии находятся в положении land locked countries. Теоретически восстановление сухопутной торговли через центр континента, через Евразию, отвечает интересам всех стран региона и его непосредственных соседей. Вопрос по большому счету в исходе геополитического соперничества великих держав в регионе.

Индия и Пакистан

Очевидно, что у давних соперников Индии и Пакистана разные интересы в развитии ситуации вокруг Афганистана. Перед Пакистаном стоят две проблемы. Первая – необходимость открыть транспортные коридоры на север в регион Центральной Азии. Вторая – какую конфигурацию примет ситуация в Афганистане после 2014 года и кто именно окажется в итоге у власти в Кабуле. Последнее имеет значение с точки зрения не закрытого до сих пор вопроса о прохождении линии Дюранда, которая де-факто является границей между Пакистаном и Афганистаном.

Любое самостоятельное афганское правительство с преобладанием пуштунов, несомненно, будет ставить вопрос о линии Дюранда, законность прохождения которой пуштунские националисты традиционно оспаривают. Единственный приемлемый для Пакистана вариант был связан только с полностью подконтрольным ему правительством в Кабуле. Таким правительством до 2001 года было движение Талибан. В настоящий момент нет оснований полагать, что в условиях борьбы великих держав за влияние в регионе возможно простое повторение ситуации, которая была до 2001 года.

При этом, вопросы экономического развития все равно имеют приоритет для любого правительства в Пакистане. Поэтому можно ожидать, что интересам Пакистана будет отвечать идея открытия транспортных коридоров через Афганистан на север – в Центральную Азию.

Характерно, что интересы Индии больше связаны с вопросами геополитики и безопасности, гораздо больше, нежели, чем с задачами открытия транспортного коридора через Афганистан на север. В экономическом плане Индия, в отличие от Пакистана, может позволить себе просто сохранить статус-кво.

Этим позиция Индии в определенной степени близка к позиции Казахстана. Обе эти страны готовы согласиться с тем, что восстановление сухопутной торговли через Афганистан, а, значит, и транзитного значения и этой страны, и Центральной Азии является интересным проектом. Точно также оба государства могут согласиться с сохранением статус-кво в регионе.

25
Трансформация геополитических интересов Индии в Центральной Азии в экономическую дипломатию

Ибрагим Мавланов

Резюме

Уникальной особенностью индийской экономики является ее высокий стабильный рост, подтверждаемый мощью и устойчивостью. Экономическая дипломатия Индии со странами Центральной Азии и Южной Азии свидетельствует о продолжающейся положительной динамике. Взаимные визиты на высоком уровне осуществлялись регулярно. В статье предпринята попытка проанализировать, что Индия является сегодня не только надежным деловым партнером на двусторонней основе, но и одной из лучших по опыту стран в азиатском регионе, которая может своим экономическим потенциалом способствовать активному экономическому развитию между странами Центральной Азии и Южной Азии. Это показывается процессом смены геополитических интересов Центральной Азии (ЦА) в направлении экономической дипломатии Индии со странами ЦА. Кроме того, автор анализирует концептуальные подходы Индии и Узбекистана к вызовам мирового экономического кризиса. Автор рассматривает, как мировой финансовый и экономический кризис (МФЭК) 2008-2009 годах повлиял на индийскую экономику, и предложил сравнительный анализ подходов Индии и Узбекистана к вызовам МФЭК. Доказывается, что Индия достигла экономического роста в основном за счет роста ее внешней торговли. Действительно, было установлено, что применение инструментов внешнеэкономической деятельности ее экономической дипломатии сыграло решающую роль в урегулировании экспортной и импортной политики. Автор подчеркивает, что тенденции индийской политической и экономической дипломатии со странами Центральной Азии и Южной Азии являются стратегически важными в перспективе для межрегионального сотрудничества.

1. Экономическое развитие Индии после Мирового финансового и экономического кризиса (МФЭК) 2008 года

Индийская экономика является одной из самых быстрорастущих экономик в посткризисном периоде. Анализ процесса реформ показывает, что внешнеэкономическая политика Индии и ее двусторонняя и многосторонняя экономическая дипломатия позволила стране добиться значительных успехов в создании благоприятного инвестиционного климата и экономической либерализации экспортно-импортной политики.

В соответствии с последними данными, опубликованными Центральным статистическим управлением, рост валового внутреннего продукта (ВВП) по факторным издержкам составил 6,9 процента в 2011-2012 годах, в сельском хозяйстве со смежными видами деятельности – рост на 2,5 процента, в промышленности – на 3,9 процента и в сфере услуг – на 9,4 процента. Соответствующий рост ВВП в 2010-2011 годах составил 8,4 процента, в сельском хозяйстве и смежных отраслях, промышленности и сфере услуг на 7,0 , 7,2 и 9,3 процента соответственно.[1]

Несмотря на мировой финансовый кризис 2008 года, который сильно повлиял на глобальные потоки прямых иностранных инвестиций, анализ показывает их увеличение в 2011 году, когда роль развивающихся стран, в том числе Индии, возросла. По нашему мнению эти изменения были вызваны 2377 дополнениями, внесенными в законодательство по иностранным инвестициям за период с 1992 по 2008 год; 2650 изменений касались улучшения инвестиционного климата.[2] Таким образом, только с 2007 по 2009-10 годы количество ПИИ, поступающих в Индию увеличилось с 8,5 миллиардов до

19,791 миллиарда долл. США.[3]

Сегодня Индия является четвертой страной среди других развивающихся стран Восточной, Южной и Юго-Восточной Азии, по инвестициям из-за рубежа. Согласно данным ООН, Индия была второй в списке самых привлекательных стран для прямых иностранных инвестиций, после Китая и опережая США, Россию и Бразилию.[4] Индийский торговый дефицит был выше 85700 миллионов долл. США (9,4 процента ВВП) в течение 1-го квартала 2011-2012 против 68,9 миллиардов долл. США (8,9 процента ВВП) в первом квартале 2010-2011 гг.[5]

Изучая индийскую экономику, мы попытались проанализировать, как МФЭК 2008-2009 годов отразился на экономике, и было предложено провести сравнительный анализ подходов Индии и Узбекистана к вызовам МФЭК. Наш анализ показал, что МФЭК имел минимальное воздействие на Индию в связи с тем, что индийские банки непосредственно не пострадали от внешнего финансового кризиса, так как рост экономики Индии в значительной степени основан на внутреннем потреблении и внутренних инвестициях, при этом внешний спрос на экспортируемые товары был меньше чем 15% от ВВП. Тем не менее, правительство Индии предприняло три антикризисных пакета мер стоимостью 75 миллиардов долларов (7% ВВП).

Концептуальные подходы Узбекистана к вызовам МФЭК сформулированные Президентом Республики Узбекистан Исламом Каримовым, получили высокую оценку зарубежных ученых и аналитиков на международных конференциях. Однако, сравнительный анализ реакции правительств Узбекистана и Индии на вызовы МФЭК предполагает, что подходы обеих стран очень схожи. Это особенно заметно в таких областях, как необходимость разработки программы структурных экономических реформ, диверсификация производства, активная инвестиционная политика в целях реализации стратегически важных проектов, развитие социальной инфраструктуры в сельской местности и т.д. Эти шаги являются основными факторами стратегических двусторонних взаимных гарантий, межрегионального и международного экономического сотрудничества между Индией и Узбекистаном.

Анализ проблем финансового кризиса показал, что его

основные причины были связаны с сущностью экономических систем, общими и особенными чертами моделей экономической структуры каждой страны в отдельности. Таким образом, изучение модели экономических систем должно быть одним из первых задач экономической дипломатии для выявления возможных источников будущих кризисов. Анализ научных методов и показателей для оценки экономического кризиса позволил нам выявить недостатки существующих моделей и индикаторов раннего предупреждения экономических кризисов, что ограничивает их широкое распространение. Таким образом, данная работа продолжает проведение дальнейших системных исследований и разработку новых моделей показателей устойчивости экономических систем в целом. Одной из наиболее важных задач экономической дипломатии является необходимость перенаправления инвестиционных потоков в Узбекистан, эффективное использование "зеркального" эффекта динамики глобальных потоков ПИИ. Это требует радикального совершенствования и развития новых дипломатических инструментов и подходов к сфере инвестиций и необходимость работы над сложными проектами в строительстве межрегиональных торгово-экономических зон. Соответственно, экономическая дипломатия должна выполнить следующие задачи: разработать новые фильтры внутренних и внешних угроз экономической безопасности на ранних стадиях их появления, дальнейший мониторинг и анализ фундаментальных причин кризиса, совершенствование и разработка новых методов для диагностики текущего финансового кризиса, улучшение системного анализа и мониторинга экономической безопасности.

2. Геополитические интересы Индии в Центральной Азии

Прежде всего, следует отметить, что Индия имеет прочные исторические отношения с центрально-азиатским регионом (с Казахстаном, Кыргызстаном, Таджикистаном, Туркменистаном и Узбекистаном). Как Индия, так и Центральная Азия были мощными центрами древней восточной цивилизации с большой степенью взаимодействия. Историческое прошлое обоих центров составляет прочную основу обменов в культурной, политической и экономической сферах. Древний "Шелковый путь" крепко связывал Индию и Центральную Азию, была ли это торговля или межличностный контакт.

Во-вторых, в последние годы многие индийские и западные ученые пытаются проанализировать роль Индии в Центральной Азии. Так Б.Б. Кумар писал: «Индия и Центральная Азия имеют давнюю традицию социально-культурных, политических и экономических контактов с далекого прошлого. Два региона имеют общие и сопредельные границы, климатическую последовательность, подобные географические особенности и геокультурную близость"[6] В книге «Индия и Центральная Азия: культурные, экономические и политические связи»[7] многие ученые подчеркнули, что отношения Индии с центральноазиатскими странами превосходны, подкреплены глубокими историческими и культурными связями, особенно с обретением независимости этими странами. Анализируя индийцев в Центральной Азии в 16 и 17 веках и индийских торговцев в Узбекистане, Сурендра Гопал сказал: "Индийцы были в состоянии получить доступ к важным центрам торговли Центральной Азии...»[8] Исследуя экономические отношения между Индией и Центральной Азией, Девендре Каушик замечает: «...экономические отношения между Индией и Центральной Азией продолжают существовать, несмотря на многочисленные препятствия ...»[9]

В книге «Индия и Центральная Азия»[10] под редакцией Indranil Banerjie, многие ученые выразили мнение, что визиты на высоком уровне между Индией и странами Центральной Азии осуществлялись на регулярной основе. Их дополняют выставки промышленных и потребительских товаров, не считая визиты торговых делегаций . Indranil Banerjie в частности отметил: «... контакты Индии с ЦАР (Центральноазиатскими республиками) разрабатывались на различных уровнях»[11] Он также отметил: «Некоторые проекты последнего времени по крупнейшим нефтяным месторождениям, бурению и трубопроводам были подписаны в этом регионе ... Если эти контракты будут прибыльными, Индия может пожелать устроить больше энергетических проектов».[12]

При изучении индийской стратегии в Центральной Азии д-р Стефан Блэнк подчеркнул: «Растущий интерес Индии в Центральной Азии не ограничивается лишь общими угрозами терроризма, сепаратизма, торговли наркотиками и подстрекательства к гражданскому насилию. Он также имеет глубокие и давние стратегические и экономические корни».[13] Он также добавил: "Большие запасы газа и нефти Центральной Азии и растущий спрос Индии на энергоносители также подразумевают естественные взаимодополняющие отношения».[14]

При проведении анализа по индийской энергетической стратегии в Центральной Азии, генерал-майор (в отставке) SCN Jatar подчеркнул: "Центральноазиатский регион, с его скромными запасами углеводородов, по сравнению с Западной Азией, важен для Индии по геостратегическим и геополитическим причинам».[15] Он также заметил: «Появление Центральной Азию как региона с углеводородным потенциалом дает Индии возможность усилить свою энергетическую безопасность в краткосрочной перспективе до 2025 года».[16]

Исследуя перспективы торговли и инвестиций Индии в Центральную Азию, T.K. Bhaumik говорит: «Индийская промышленность может развивать долгосрочные партнерские отношения с регионом и помочь ЦАР в достижении их целей роста экспорта. Индийские компании могут сыграть важную роль, вкладывая в секторы, обладающие экспортным потенциалом. Некоторыми из выдающихся экспортных секторов региона являются алюминий, текстиль, химикаты машинного оборудования общего назначения, сельскохозяйственная продукция, нефть и газ и другие энергоносители. Кстати, они также являются потенциальными отраслями для иностранных инвестиций в этом регионе... Внося существенный вклад в экономический рост ЦАР, такая стратегия также позволит индийским компаниям изучить новые глобальные рынки... Стратегические инвестиции в этом регионе могут, таким образом, предоставить доступ к более крупным рынкам в будущем».[17]

В-третьих, в настоящее время Индия стремится развивать прочные отношения с каждой из стран Центральной Азии. Существует множество точек соприкосновения для построения этих отношений. Секуляризм и демократия – это две характерные черты, которые являются общими для стран Центральной Азии и Индии. Кроме того, Центральная Азия имеет положительное и очень доброжелательное отношение к

Индии. Недавний дипломатический акцент Индии в сторону Центральной Азии принимает во внимание ее будущую потребность в энергии и стратегической позиции, путем двусторонних визитов и торговли.[18] Очевидно, что нефть и газ продолжают быть основными экономическими факторами мотивации для Индии, чтобы играть свою роль в Центральной Азии.

В другой статье говорится: «В усиливающейся глобальной гонке за ограниченные ресурсы энергии, Индия все чаще обращается к Центральной Азии в качестве надежного источника нефти и природного газа и одновременно фокусируется на своих стратегических интересах в Азии. Кроме нефти, республики Центральной Азии, включая Туркменистан, Казахстан, Узбекистан, Кыргызстан и Таджикистан, имеют важное значение для Индии с точки зрения национальной безопасности, особенно в борьбе с терроризмом, исходящего со стороны радикального ислама. Потенциал для сотрудничества между Индией и Центральной Азии огромен и может охватывать такие области, как информационные технологии, биотехнологии, телекоммуникации, сфера услуг и образование. Туризм в живописных городах Центральной Азии представляет собой еще одну область, которая может привести не только к увеличению бизнеса, но и к более тесному контакту людей к народу Индии. Если Индия будет играть свою роль основной азиатской державы, ей придется углублять взаимодействие и повысить свою значимость в регионе».[19] Другой ученый заметил: "Индия потерпела огромный спад в торговле со странами Центральной Азии в 1991-94 годах, что подчеркивает ее неуверенную конкурентоспособность с уже реформированным Китаем».[20]

Профессор Мартин C.Spechler в своей книге[21] пытается проанализировать ситуацию в Центральной Азии после драматических терактов 11 сентября 2001 года, которые исходили от Афганистана; обратил внимание США и Запада в целом на Центральную Азию, а также ожидания одних и страхи других о том, что безопасность и экономическая ситуация там изменится.

Профессор Нирмала Джоши, изучая современные отношения Индии с Центральной Азией, сказала: «Сегодня, индийские интересы существенны и находятся в сфере стратегической, политической и экономической безопасности. Любая конкуренция между крупными державами за контроль и влияние в расширенной окрестности Индии будет иметь отношение к ее политике и дипломатии в данном регионе. Если элемент конкуренции в Центральной Азии станет доминирующей тенденцией, то Индии придется принимать трудные решения».[22]

Профессор SD Muni в работе «Геостратегическое положение Центральной Азии и ее богатые минеральные и углеводородные ресурсы», отметил: «Индия сосредоточена на трех основных сферах, представляющих взаимный интерес, а именно: экономическое сотрудничество, терроризм и проблема политической стабильности и вопросы региональной безопасности и стратегического порядка».[23] Он также подчеркнул: «Вновь возникшая Центральная Азия предоставляет огромные стратегические и экономические возможности для Индии, и индийские политики пытаются использовать эти возможности... Это правда, что Индия страдает от препятствий в освоении полного потенциала Индо-Центральноазиатского сотрудничества, но есть также много возможностей для Индии улучшить экономическое управление своей дипломатией».[24]

В-четвертых, на третьей Индо-Центральноазиатской региональной конференции, которая была организована совместно Институтом оборонных исследований и анализа (IDSA), Нью-Дели, и Институтом стратегических и межрегиональных исследований (ISRS) в Ташкенте, бывший министр иностранных дел Узбекистана доктор Садик Сафоев подчеркнул «необходимость более широкого сотрудничества между Индией и Узбекистаном на экономической и технологической аренах» и «...координация усилий в борьбе с терроризмом, религиозным экстремизмом, незаконным оборотом наркотиков и организованной преступностью в Центральноазиатском регионе . Бывший министр иностранных дел Индии г-н Яшванта Синха свое выступление сосредоточил на четырех направлениях, а именно: исторические связи между Индией и Центральной Азией, экономический и энергетический потенциал Центральной Азии, двусторонние инициативы между Индией и Центральной Азией в международной безопасности».[25]

Бывший министр иностранных дел и советник по национальной безопасности правительства Индии г-н Дж. Н. Дикшит на той же конференции дал «некоторые общие оценки и рекомендации по структуризации отношений Индии со странами Центральной Азии», заявляя: «Индия должна быть более активной в мероприятиях по новому экономическому сотрудничеству и региональной безопасности, которые инициируют республики Центральной Азии».[26]

Доктор Равшан Алимов, рассматривая «важную роль Индии в обеспечении региональной безопасности в Центральной Азии», отметил: «интерес Индии к реализации крупных транспортно-коммуникационных и гидроэнергетических проектов в регионе, в целях обеспечения стабильных поставщиков энергетического сырья, может также способствовать росту потенциала этих проектов на международном уровне». Он также подчеркнул: «Кроме того, рост индийской экономики может позволить Индии активизировать свою торговлю, финансовое и экономическое сотрудничество со странами региона, принимая во внимание, в частности, настоящую потребность республик Центральной Азии в иностранных инвестициях».[27]

В-пятых, учитывая потенциал, который может предложить центральноазиатский регион, и незначительное присутствие Индии на этом рынке, Министром торговли и промышленности, Правительством Индии была запущена Программа СНГ «Фокус»[28] в 2003 году во время оглашения политики EXIM 31 марта 2003 года. В рамках этой программы правительство Индии расширяет помощь экспортерам, торговым палатам и т.д. по посещению этих стран, организации ярмарок, приглашению торговых делегаций Центральной Азии посетить Индию и принятию других различных рекламных мер рынка. Инициативы, предпринятые в рамках этой программы получили обнадеживающий ответ от индийского торгового сообщества и, вероятно, еще больше увеличат объем двусторонней торговли в ближайшие годы.

В недавнем прошлом экономические меры по либерализации, принятые странами Центральной Азии и Индией, создание институциональных механизмов для взаимного взаимодействия и развития быстрых/прямых связей с Центральной Азией способствовали повышению экономического взаимодействия между странами Центральноазиатского региона и Индией. Однако полный потенциал еще не реализован. Признавая необходимость расширения торговли и стимулирования интереса у предпринимателей обеих сторон, был предпринят ряд визитов на высшем уровне, а также ряд инициатив.

Наконец, страны Центральной Азии имеют значительный экономический потенциал для сотрудничества с Индией. Потенциал для расширения торговли и инвестиций велик, так как данная область чрезвычайно богата минеральными ресурсами, которые должны быть задействованы, использованы и превращены в продукты с добавленной стоимостью.

3. Трансформация геополитических интерсcов Индии в Центральной Азии в экономическую дипломатию

Анализ официальных документов Индии и международных организаций, а также исследований индийских, западных и других политиков и дипломатов доказывает наличие геополитических, стратегических и экономических интересов Индии в Центральной Азии. Эти интересы нашли практическое отражение во внешней политике Индии и осуществляются при помощи экономической дипломатии, которая не ограничивается переговорами президентов, премьер-министров, министров и государственных учреждений, но характеризуется и деятельностью частного сектора.

Анализируя механизмы реализации экономической дипломатии, становится ясно, что они имеют положительное влияние на торговлю со странами Центральной Азии, где мы также можем заметить положительную динамику (табл. 1).

Существующие модели индийской многосторонней экономической дипломатии с Центральной Азией и тенденции ее развития показывают, как теоретические концепции и практические возможности многосторонней экономической дипломатии Индии эффективно реализуются в Центральной Азии, как это продемонстрировано на Совещании по взаимодействию и мерам доверия в Азии (СВМДА) и Шанхайской организации сотрудничества (ШОС).

Таблица 1
Товарооборот Индии со странами Центральной Азии и членами ШОС на 2001-2010 гг (млн долл.)[1]

Страны	Финансовый год					
	2001-02	2003-04	2006-07	2007-08	2008-09	2009-10
Кыргызстан	11,53	38,74	37,84	32,43	23,95	27,48
Таджикистан	2,56	8,42	15,41	22,21	34,18	32,56
Туркменистан	6,30	28,55	45,94	44,64	53,50	46,15
Узбекистан	23,80	42,84	63,60	56,52	116,27	84,00
Казахстан	53,09	84,07	171,48	188,77	290,71	291,45
В общей сложности со странами Центральной Азии	97,28	202,62	334,27	344,57	518,61	481,64
Китай	2988,34	7008,33	25796,89	38017,75	41850,52	42441,90
Россия	1333,69	1673,39	3312,74	3418,77	5424,62	4547,48
В общей сложности с членами ШОС	4413,01	8855,79	29397,96	41736,45	47740,25	47424,87
Общий товарооборот Индии	95240,02	141991,66	312149,29	414786,19	488991,67	467124,31

Наши исследования показали, что усилия дипломатии Индии со странами СВМДА направлены на развитие механизмов сотрудничества в экономической, экологической и гуманитарной областях, а также сотрудничества в области энергетической безопасности и развития транспортных коридоров.

Анализ официальных документов и статистических данных Индии дает понять, что индийская дипломатия в отношении ЦА в основном сосредоточена на торговле и инвестициях в силу следующих причин: богатые природные ресурсы ЦА;

1. It is made by the author on the basis of data of Department of commerce of the Ministry of commerce and the industry of India. http://commerce.nic.in/eidb/iecnt.asp

регион становится все более и более вовлеченным в геополитику, выступая и как ее объект и как субъект; Индия рассматривает страны Центральной Азии в качестве основных партнеров по региональной торговле и инвестициям, а также в области политики и безопасности, с приоритетом на Узбекистан.

Наши исследования также определили стратегические экономические интересы Индии в регионе ШОС, что определяется следующими факторами: 1). Страны ШОС обладают огромным экономическим и природным потенциалом, 2). два члена ШОС являются постоянными членами Совета Безопасности ООН и играют важную роль в мировой политике, 3). геоэкономическое пространство ШОС представляется Индии в качестве масштабного экономического рынка со стратегическим потенциалом, и 4). развитая система транспортных коммуникаций в регионе ШОС могла бы предоставить Индии доступ к соседним регионам и возможность эффективного торгово-экономического и инвестиционного сотрудничества. В период 2001-2010 гг индийская торговля со странами ШОС была увеличена более чем в 10 раз.

Наш анализ также показал, что Индия является стратегически важной страной для ШОС и Центральной Азии, что определяется следующим образом: 1). Индия активно участвует в обсуждении вопросов политического и экономического мирового порядка, 2). участие Индии в региональных экономических вопросах и вопросах безопасности увеличивается, 3). растущий экономический, научно-технический потенциал (особенно в области информационных технологий, фармацевтики, биотехнологии и т.д.) придает этой стране стратегическое значение , 4). Индия является перспективным рынком для экспорта и инвестиций.

Таким образом, я хотел бы заявить, что взаимные стратегические интересы определяют новые тенденции институционализации региональной экономической дипломатии Индии с Центральной Азией. Согласно моим исследованиям, одной из возможных тенденций в расширении экономического сотрудничества Индии со странами Центральной Азии в целях укрепления двустороннего и многостороннего формата, является, пожалуй, создание полномасштабной институциональной модели **«Индия + Центральная Азия»** (рис. 1). Дальнейшее развитие этой модели может быть **«Биполярная модель межрегионального экономического сотрудничества в Центральной и Южной Азии»** (рис. 2).

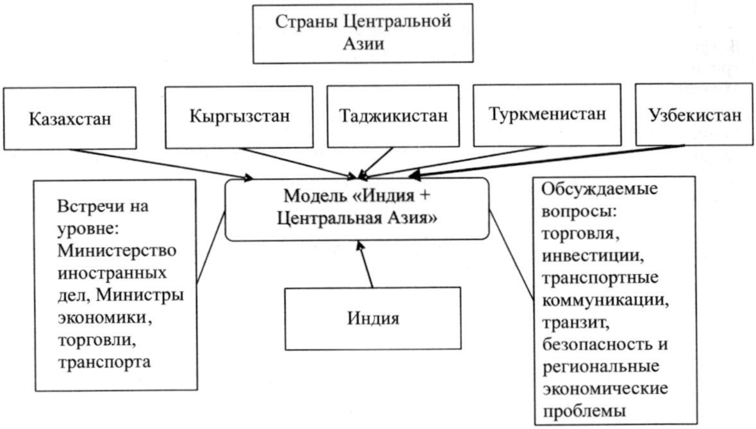

Рисунок 1. Институциональная модель «Индия + Центральная Азия» [2]

Эти прогнозы, на мой взгляд, могут быть реализованы в ближайшее время, так как образование новых структур в Центральной и Южной Азии является объективной реальностью в международных отношениях, особенно среди развивающихся стран.

Заключение

Экономическая дипломатия Индии видит в Центральной Азии перспективный экономический, инвестиционный и торговый рынок, который имеет стратегический потенциал для создания совместных предприятий в сфере малого и среднего бизнеса, которые могут составить ключевой сектор экономики Индии и дать ей преимущества в долгосрочной перспективе. Регион Центральной Азии является важной целью для Индии в

2. Разработана и предложена автором статьи.

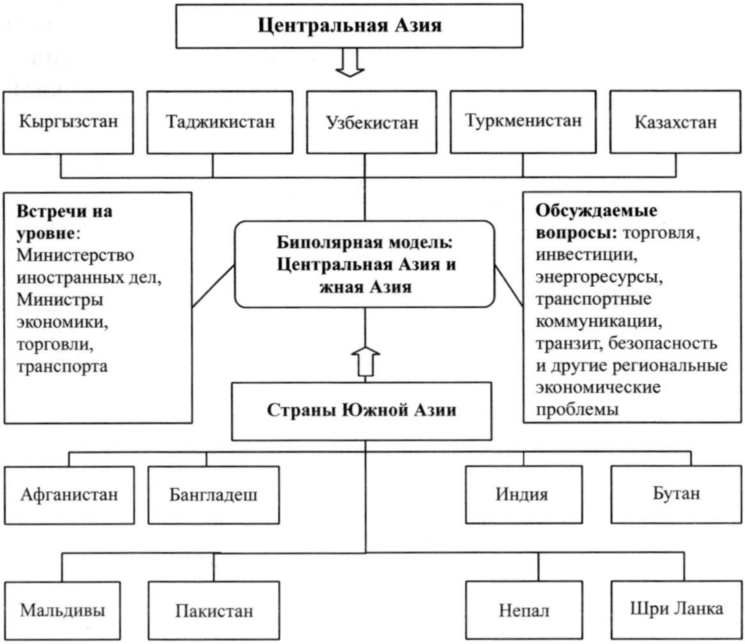

Рисунок *2*. «Биполярная модель межрегионального экономического сотрудничества в Центральной и Южной Азии» [3]

реализации транспортно-коммуникационных проектов, которые могут способствовать быстрому выходу из стран Центральной Азии на мировые рынки. Страны Центральной Азии обладают значительными запасами энергетических ресурсов (нефть, газ, сырье для атомных электростанций), возможностью развития газопроводов и разведки огромных запасов минеральных ресурсов, что открывает перспективы для их геологоразведки, добычи, переработки и транспортировки. Технически продвинутые страны Центральной Азии позволят Индии быстро развивать сотрудничество во всех сферах.

1. Индия будет в полной мере развивать свою многостороннюю дипломатию в регионе Центральной Азии и ШОС на основе имеющихся и создания новых

---

3. Разработана и предложена автором статьи.

моделей межрегионального экономического сотрудничества в Центральной и Южной Азии. С точки зрения нового видения роли Индии в мировой политике и экономике, ее присутствие в Центральной Азии является стратегически важным и необходимым фактором не только с точки зрения выхода Индии за пределы традиционной сферы влияния в Южной Азии, но и с точки зрения государства, претендующего на роль новых политических и экономических полномочий нынешнего столетия.

2. Инициатива модели экономического сотрудничества в формате «**Индия + Центральная Азия**», а в будущем – «**Биполярная модель межрегионального экономического сотрудничества в Центральной и Южной Азии**» будет служить интересам Узбекистана и будет служить в качестве основы для построения моста активного сотрудничества с регионом Юго-Восточной Азии.
3. Учитывая фундаментальные причины мирового финансового кризиса в связи с сущностью экономической системы, обращается внимание на решение следующих научных и практических задач : а) углубленное изучение индийской модели экономических систем в качестве возможного источника борьбы не только с текущими, но и с будущими кризисами, б)анализ моделей экономической дипломатии в ее устойчивости к Мировому финансовому кризису и возможное введение показателей устойчивости, в) своевременная диагностика мирового финансового кризиса г) совершенствование и развитие новых дипломатических инструментов и подходов к привлечению инвестиций во время кризиса.
4. На данный момент, как признают индийские аналитики, для экономической мощи Индии, пожалуй, наиболее важно создать в Центрально-Азиатском регионе стабильную экономику и экономическую безопасность. Экономический рост Индии показывает, что Индия является не только надежным деловым партнером, но и одной из лучших по опыту стран в

азиатском регионе, которые могут своим экономическим потенциалом способствовать активному экономическому развитию в регионе Центральной Азии, которая является одним из источников экономической безопасности и стабильности. Экономические факторы играют решающую роль в формировании экономической политики Индии в Центральной Азии.

Цитируемая литература

1. Annual Report 2011-2012. Ministry of Finance, Government of India. - New Delhi, 2012. pp. 1-3. http://www.finmin.nic.in/the_ministry/dept_eco_affairs/index.html
2. World Investment Report 2009: Transnational Corporations, Agricultural Production and Development. New York and Geneva: United Nations, 2009. p. xxii, 16, 31
3. Global Economic Crisis and its Impact on India., New Delhi: Research Unit (LARRDIS), Rajya Sabha Secretariat, 2009. p. 28; Annual Report 2009-10. New-Delhi: Ministry of Finance, Government of India, 2010. p. 33.
4. World Investment Report 2008: Transnational Corporations and the Infrastructure Challenge. p. 33.
5. Annual Report 2011-2012. Ministry of Finance, Government of India. - New Delhi, 2012. p. 3. http://www.finmin.nic.in/the_ministry/dept_eco_affairs/index.html
6. B.B. Kumar. Central Asia: Indian Literary Perception. Dialogue January-March, 2004, Volume 5 No. 3. http://www.asthabharati.org/Dia_Jan.04/central%20asia%20kumar.htm
7. India and Central Asia: Cultural, Economic and Political Links. Edited by Surendra Gopal. Shipra Publications. New Delhi. 2001. p. 200.
8. *Ibid.*, p. 25.
9. *Ibid.*, p. 71.
10. India and Central Asia. Edited by Indranil Banerjie. Brunel Academic Publishers Ltd., UK. 2004. p. 357.
11. *Ibid.*, p. xiv.
12. *Ibid.*, p. xv.
13. *Ibid.*, p. 262.
14. *Ibid.*, p. 264.
15. *Ibid.*, p. 304.
16. *Ibid.*, p. 325.
17. *Ibid.*, pp. 339-340.
18. India and Central Asia. Rahul Bedi. Frontline. Volume 19, Issue 19, September 14-27, 2002 http://www.flonnet.com/fl1919/ 19190600.htm

19. Central Asia, new focus of India's oil diplomacy. Manish Chand (IANS). New Delhi, April 6, 2005. http://www.hindustantimes.com/news/181_1308782,0002.htm
20. Richard Pomfret. The Economies of Central Asia. Princeton, NJ: Princeton University Press, 1995, p.155.
21. Martin C. Spechler. Economy and Security in Central Asia since 9/11: A Skeptical Look. http://www.ca-c.org/journal/eng-01-2003/05.speprimen.shtml
22. Central Asia: The Great Game Replayed.An Indian Perspective. Edited by Prof. Nirmala Joshi. New Centure Publications. New Delhi. 2003. p. 8.
23. *Ibid.*, pp. 97-110.
24. *Ibid.*, pp. 126-128.
25. Ramakant Dwivedi. 3rd India-Central Asia Regional Conference. Tashkent, November 6-8 2003. Strategic Analysis. Quarterly Journal of the IDSA. Oct-Dec 2003. Vol. 27. No. 4. p. 621.
26. India and Central Asia: Advancing the Common Interest. K.Santhanam, Ramakant Dwivedi. Anama Publishers. New Delhi. 2004. p. 20.
27. *Ibid.*, pp. 91-94.
28. FOCUS CIS – Programme 2004-2005. A Programme for Developing and Enhancing India's Trade with CIS. Government of India, Ministry of Commerce and Industry, Department of Commerce. New Delhi. 2004.

26
Сотрудничество Индии и ШОС: состояние и перспективы развития

Маруфджон Абдурахмонов

Кардинальнос изменение международной обстановки после окончания холодной войны не могло не повлиять на перемены и в индийской внешней политике. Распад Советского Союза и последующая почти тотальная ориентация России на Запад потребовали от Индии новых подходов к оценке ее безопасности. В своей внешней политике она не предпринимала резких ходов, противоречащих ее прежней политике и тем более отрицающих ее. В традиционном для нее духе спокойной, глубокой и детальной проработки внешнеполитической стратегии и тактики она гибко приспосабливалась к изменениям на мировой арене, исходя из принципиальных соображений защиты национальных интересов и безопасности. Для Индии эта задача облегчалась тем, что она не встала на путь отказа от прошлого. Вместе с тем и ей было непросто найти свое достойное место в мире в изменившихся условиях.

В современных условиях растущей глобализации, высоких темпов развития ее экономики и роста политического влияния в мире Индия не могла оставаться в стороне от развития международных процессов в регионе стран постсоветского пространства, где имеют свои интересы и другие державы. Став наблюдателем ШОС в июле 2005 г., Индия еще раз не только подтвердила исторические связи со странами-членами ШОС, которые базируются на глубоких корнях со времен Великого шелкового пути, но и подчеркнула, что она имеет стратегические интересы в данном регионе.

На встрече глав правительств 26 октября 2005 г. министр иностранных дел Индии подчеркнул, что цель Индии – «играть активную роль в ШОС..., увеличивать межрегиональное торговое и экономическое сотрудничество..., особенно в сфере энергетики,... развитии транспортных коридоров, что обеспечит более короткий и эффективный торговый путь в Россию и страны Центральной Азии». 16 сентября 2006г. на встрече глав правительств ШОС государственный министр Индии, отметив, что «ШОС превратилась в важную организацию, которая гарантирует безопасность, стабильность и экономическое сотрудничество в регионе», указал на огромные возможности для Индии «участвовать в проектах в области энергетики, транспорта, информации, коммуникации и сельского хозяйства». На встрече глав государств-членов ШОС 16 августа 2007г. министр нефти и газа Индии заявил, что интересы его страны в деятельности ШОС распространяются на сферы энергетики, развития экономики, борьбу с терроризмом и транзитом наркотиков. Отсюда очевидно, что, обладая геостратегическим видением своей региональной роли в Южной Азии, Индия, несомненно, имеет геополитические интересы в регионе ШОС.

Также большинство индийских ученых отмечают, что отношения Индии с Центральной Азией превосходны, подкреплены глубокими историческими и культурными узами. Так, индийский ученый, доктор наук Б. Кумар (редактор научного журнала «Диалог») отмечает, что «Индия и Центральная Азия имеют продолжительные социально-культурные, политические и экономические контакты с далеких прошлых времен. Оба региона имеют общую и смежную границу, климатическую целостность, одинаковые географические черты и гео-культурную близость»[1].

В 2008 г. статус полного члена ШОС имели упомянутые шесть государств. В число наблюдателей входили Индия, Пакистан, Иран, Монголия. При этом Пакистан и Иран проявляли наибольшую заинтересованность в получении статуса полноправных членов ШОС.

В июне 2009 г. в Екатеринбурге одновременно с саммитом

1. Kumar B.B. Central Asia: Indian Literary Perception // Dialogue. 2004 (January-March). № 5 (3).

БРИК проходила очередная встреча руководителей стран – членов Шанхайской организации сотрудничества. В ней приняли участие главы шести стран: России, Китая, Казахстана, Узбекистана, Таджикистана и Кыргызстана, а также лидеры четырех стран-наблюдателей – Индии, Пакистана, Монголии, Ирана и Афганистана. Было принято решение расширить торговые связи и инвестиции между государствами-членами ШОС и государствами-наблюдателями. Особенно большое внимание было уделено обсуждению масштабных проектов в транспорте, коммуникациях, торговле и туризме, инновациях, энергосберегающих и возобновляемых энергетических технологиях. Лидеры ШОС заявили, что их целью является превращение Центральной Азии в трансконтинентальный мост между Европой и Азией. Для этого должны быть созданы новые транспортные коридоры и модернизированы существующие железные дороги и шоссе.

ШОС одобрила ряд документов, направленных на усиление борьбы с терроризмом и экстремизмом в 2010–2012 гг. Особое внимание было уделено вопросам безопасности. Был принят документ о политико-дипломатических механизмах по реагированию на ситуации, угрожающие миру, безопасности и стабильности в регионе.

Как и на предыдущих встречах, было рассмотрено положение в Афганистане. ШОС выразила глубокую озабоченность ухудшившейся ситуацией в этой стране и приняла решение усилить сотрудничество со странами-наблюдателями ШОС и другими государствами и организациями для усиления борьбы против растущей угрозы терроризма и наркотрафика. Было объявлено о создании трехсторонней группы в составе России, Афганистана и Пакистана с целью решения проблемы терроризма в зоне племен. Россия заявила, что проблема Афганистана не может быть разрешена без нормализации положения в некоторых пакистанских провинциях и без уничтожения укрывшихся там террористов.

В свою очередь, Индия не была сторонним наблюдателем того, что происходило в Афганистане после начала контртеррористической операции, проводимой коалицией во главе с США. Она не принимала участия в военных действиях, но осуществляла масштабные работы по восстановлению гражданских объектов, на что ею было выделено более 1,2 млрд. долл. С этой целью в 2009 г. в Афганистане работало около 4 тыс. индийцев.

Дипломатические связи Индии с ШОС и ее странами-членами получают свое развитие как на двусторонней, так и на многосторонней основе. Двусторонняя дипломатия Индии со странами ШОС обеспечивается ее дипломатическими представительствами в каждой стране. Их деятельность в странах ШОС до принятия Индии в качестве наблюдателя этой организации была направлена на зондирование возможностей участия в ней Индии в качестве наблюдателя и на продвижение имиджа Индии в этих странах. Соответственно были активизированы двусторонние дипломатические контакты и визиты на различных уровнях, на которых Индия получала поддержку своих намерений вступления в ШОС в качестве наблюдателя. Активное сотрудничество Индии со странами-членами ШОС в течение последнего десятилетия проявлялось в форме взаимных визитов президентов, премьер-министров, министров иностранных дел и парламентских делегаций. Развитие отношений Индии со странами ШОС необходимо не только с точки зрения эффективной совместной борьбы с угрозами терроризма во имя стабильности и безопасности в регионе Азии, но и в плане решения ключевых вопросов мировой политики. Индийская дипломатия, не ограничиваясь указанными вопросами, активно действует во всех сферах, особенно экономической и торгово-инвестиционной. В рамках экономической дипломатии Индии были проведены многократные заседания торгово-экономических комиссий, бизнес-советов, ярмарок, выставок, поездок различных торговых и промышленных делегаций, заключено множество контрактов и т.д. Такая активность экономической дипломатии Индии в последние годы позволила ей значительно увеличить взаимный торговый оборот со странами ШОС, который обладает еще большим потенциалом для дальнейшего развития.

Стратегические экономические интересы Индии в регионе ШОС определяются следующими факторами. Во-первых, в ШОС входят страны, обладающие немалым экономическим потенциалом и природными ресурсами. Члены ШОС располагают и огромной территорией, и огромными демографическими ресурсами. Во-вторых, в ШОС входят два государства, играющих важную роль в мировой политике и являющихся постоянными членами Совета Безопасности ООН. В-третьих, регион ШОС, включающий и страны Центральной Азии, становится все более активным субъектом геополитики, что весьма важно и в продвижении экономических интересов, и в их защите. В-четвертых, Индия видит в странах-членах ШОС естественных партнеров по политическому и торгово-экономическому сотрудничеству, а также обеспечению совместной безопасности.

Исходя из этого, геоэкономическое пространство стран-членов ШОС предстает для Индии в будущем как новый огромный экономический рынок, обладающий огромным стратегическим потенциалом, включая следующее:

- занимая довольно обширную территорию, регион ШОС обеспечивает Индии геостратегический выход в Европу на западе и в Азиатско-Тихоокеанский регион на востоке. Развитая система транспортных коммуникаций на огромном пространстве ШОС предоставит Индии выход в смежные регионы и возможности эффективного торгово-экономического и инвестиционного сотрудничества;
- огромный инвестиционный и торговый рынок стран-членов ШОС, где создание совместных предприятий в сфере малого и среднего бизнеса представляет ключевой сектор, дает промышленности и экономике Индии в целом преимущества в долгосрочной перспективе;
- ШОС может быть действенным инструментом для Индии в реализации новых транспортно-коммуникационных проектов, которые могут способствовать быстрому выходу стран Центральной Азии к мировым рынкам;
- часть членов ШОС располагает внушительными запасами энергетических ресурсов (нефть, газ, сырье для атомных электростанций); перспективно и развитие трубопроводного транспорта
- освоение огромных запасов минеральных ресурсов открывает широкие перспективы для проведения их геологической разведки, добычи, переработки и

транспортировки;

- развитый и достаточно оснащенный в техническом отношении регион ШОС позволит Индии ускоренно развивать сотрудничество во всех сферах экономики на взаимовыгодных условиях, успешно реализовывать свои потенциальные интересы;
- страны ШОС проводят активную политику по реформированию своих экономик во всех сферах, что способствует нарастанию притока капиталов и из других развитых государств и значительно повышает роль данного региона;
- народы стран-членов ШОС и Индии хорошо знают продукцию и культуру друг друга, и это тоже создает огромный потенциал и действенный стимул для развития их взаимного сотрудничества.

Анализируя в целом перспективы участия Индии в качестве наблюдателя в ШОС и ее сотрудничества со странами этой организации, необходимо учитывать стратегическую значимость этой страны для региона ШОС, которая заключается в следующем: 1) Индия все активнее вовлекается в решение вопросов глобального политического и экономического миропорядка; 2) с годами возрастают ее роль и значение в решении региональных вопросов безопасности, борьбы с терроризмом; 3) растущий экономический и научно-технологический потенциал Индии (особенно в сфере информационных технологий, фармацевтики, биотехнологий и др.) выводит эту страну на уровень стратегической важности; 4) Индия – перспективный рынок для экспорта продукции стран ШОС.

Экономически стабильная и прогрессивно развивающаяся Республика Индия в последнее десятилетие уверенно укрепила свои позиции в мировой политике и экономике. Обладая огромным международным авторитетом, она способна сегодня оказывать позитивное воздействие и содействие в развитии других регионов мира, в том числе на пространстве ШОС. Эта страна с более чем миллиардным населением и крупным экономическим и научно-технологическим потенциалом уже является великой державой, проявляя заботу и ответственность за судьбы народов мира, активно участвуя в международных и региональных организациях. Все это свидетельствует о том, что Индия, ставшая ныне важным субъектом международных отношений, будет играть в ШОС весьма позитивную роль, особенно в вопросах экономической интеграции, азиатской регионализации и безопасности. Важно отметить, что ШОС и ее регион с годами будут все более укрепляться, создавая прочную основу развития экономической стабильности и безопасности в Азии, оказывая существенное влияние на характер геополитической ситуации в Азии, и роль Индии в этих процессах будет неуклонно возрастать.

27
Транспортное обеспечение торгово-экономических связей стран Центральной Азии и Индии: взгляд из Казахстана

Гульнара Бекмагамбетова

Развитие транспорта и других отраслей экономики тесно взаимосвязаны. Уровень развития производства и торговли определяют спрос на услуги транспорта. Вместе с тем, транспорт является системообразующим фактором, влияя на уровень жизни, развитие производительных сил и товарообмен.

Казахстан является ведущим торговым партнером Индии в ЦА регионе. Однако товарооборот этих двух стран колеблется только на уровне 500 млн. долларов США. В целом объем торговли между Индией и странами ЦА не превышает 800 млн. долл. США.

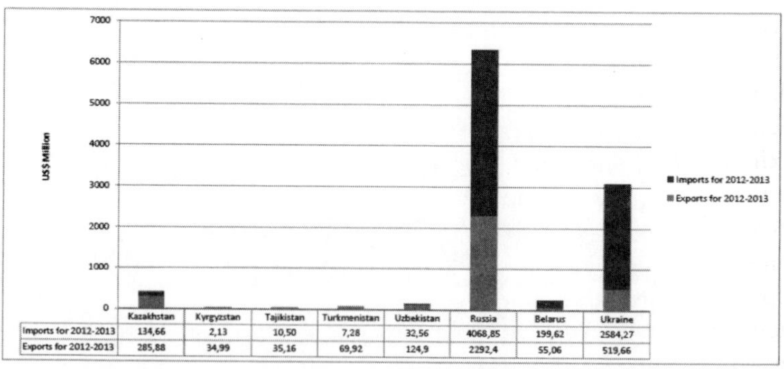

	Kazakhstan	Kyrgyzstan	Tajikistan	Turkmenistan	Uzbekistan	Russia	Belarus	Ukraine
Imports for 2012-2013	134,66	2,13	10,50	7,28	32,56	4068,85	199,62	2584,27
Exports for 2012-2013	285,88	34,99	35,16	69,92	124,9	2292,4	55,06	519,66

Picture 1 Foreign trade in India with CA countries, Russia, Belarus, and Ukraine

Source: Department of Commerce, India, Export Import Data Bank.

В то же время торговые отношения Индии с партнером Казахстана по Таможенному союзу – Россией достаточно развиты – в 2012 году по информации индийской стороны товарооборот этих двух стран составил более 6 млрд. долл. США. Достаточно велик объем торговли между Индией и Украиной – около 3 млрд. долл. США.

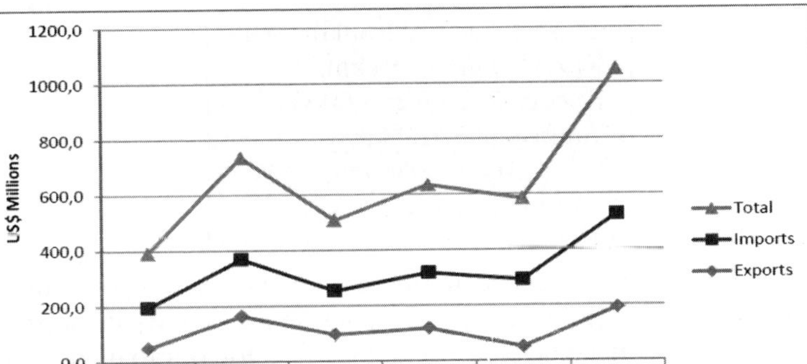

	2007	2008	2009	2010	2011	2012
Total	195,7	367,8	253,4	316,7	291,5	525,2
Imports	147,6	203,8	157,3	199,6	243,1	334,4
Exports	48,1	164,0	96,1	117,1	48,4	190,7

Picture 2 Dynamics of trade between Kazakhstan and India

Source: Statistical Yearbook "Kazakhstan in 2012", The Agency of Statistics of the Republic of Kazakhstan

По оценкам экспертов торгово-экономическое сотрудничество стран ЦА и Индии имеет значительные перспективы. Индия сильна в тех областях, которые представляют значительный интерес для центрально-азиатских республик, и, в частности, Казахстана - информационные технологии и программное обеспечение, фармацевтика и медицинское оборудование, машиностроение, химическая промышленность, текстиль, чай. Индия является одной их наиболее динамично развивающихся стран мира, что определяет рост потребления значительного спектра ресурсов и расширение рынков сбыта. Страны ЦА региона, известные своими природными богатствами, могут удовлетворить ряд таких потребностей, а также обеспечить транзит индийских товаров в другие страны СНГ и Европу.

Пожалуй, одной из причин недостаточного развития

торгово-экономических отношений двух стран можно назвать проблемы в транспортном обеспечении, обусловленные отсутствием общих границ и необходимых коммуникаций, сложной военно-политической и экономической обстановкой в некоторых частях азиатского региона, а также отсутствием у стран ЦА прямого выхода к морю.

Closest distance from the sea:
Kazakhstan: 3,750 km,
Kyrgyz Republic: 3,600 km,
Tajikistan: 3,100 km,
Uzbekistan: 2,950 km,
Turkmenistan: 1,700 km

В последние годы странами на постсоветском пространстве предпринимаются усилия по формированию транспортных коридоров в направлении Южной и Юго-Восточной Азии. Прежде всего, речь идет о коридоре «Север–Юг» и Трансафганском транспортном коридоре, которые могут обеспечить выход из региона к морским портам путем создания сети железнодорожного, автомобильного, морского сообщения.

Межправительственное Соглашение о международном транспортном коридоре "Север - Юг" было подписано Россией, Ираном и Индией в ходе второй Евроазиатской конференции по транспорту 12 сентября 2000 г. в Санкт-Петербурге. В апреле 2001 г Соглашение было ратифицировано Индией, в октябре 2001 г. Ираном, а в марте 2002 г. Российской Федерацией.

Сегодня странами-участницами Соглашения являются Беларусь, Казахстан, Оман, Таджикистан, Азербайджан, Армения, Сирия, Болгария, Кыргызстан, Турция и Украина. Страны-наблюдатели: Туркменистан, Бахрейн, Саудовская Аравия, Кувейт, ОАЭ, Индонезия, Малайзия, Шри-Ланка

Маршруты следования грузов по МТК «Север – Юг» с использованием разных видов транспорта:

Транскаспийский: через порты Астрахань, Оля, Махачкала. Участие железных дорог в этом варианте заключается в подвозе грузов в порты и вывозе их из портов.

По восточной ветви коридора: прямое железнодорожное

сообщение через Казахстан, Узбекистан и Туркменистан с выходом на железнодорожную сеть Ирана по пограничному переходу Теджен – Серахс.

По западной ветви коридора: направление Астрахань – Махачкала – Самур, далее по территории Азербайджана с выходом в Иран через пограничную станцию Астара. Или от Самура через территории Азербайджана и Армении с выходом в Иран через пограничную станцию Джульфа.

По экспертной оценке, товарный рынок МТК «Север – Юг» оценивается в 25-26 млн тонн к 2015 году.

Альтернативный вариант - 16 октября 2007 г. в Тегеране на встрече глав прикаспийских государств Иран, Казахстан и Туркмения подписали меморандум о строительстве новой прикаспийской железнодорожной линии Узснь - Гызылгая - Берекет - Этрек - Горган. Общая протяженность линии составит 929 км. Каждая из сторон финансирует строительство участков на своей территории. Строительство линии Узень – государственная граница с Туркменистаном было завершено в 2011 году.

Новая линия будет на 600 км короче существующего сообщения через Серахс.

18 июня 2003 года было заключено трехстороннее соглашение между правительствами Ирана, Афганистана и Узбекистана о создании **международного трансафганского транспортного коридора** к портам Ирана.

Соглашением было предусмотрено строительство и реконструкция автомобильных дорог:

- «Термез - Мазари Шариф – Шибирган – Герат – Дилорам – Милак -Чабахар» протяженностью 2298 км.;
- «Термез - Мазари Шариф – Шибирган – Герат – Догарун - Бандар-Аббас» протяженностью 2258 км.;
- «Ташкент – Термез - Мазари Шариф – Шибирган – Герат – Догорун – Тегеран - Базарган» протяжонностью 2812 км.;
- Железной дорогой «Термез – Хайратон - Мазари Шариф – Герат – Санган - Хаф», а также организация движения от узбекско-афганской границы через Афганистан и Иран в Бандар-Аббас и далее по

морскому железнодорожному паромному сообщению в порты ОАЭ, а также в порты Индии и государств Юго-Восточной Азии.

На настоящий момент времени общая протяженность дорог, соединяющих Афганистан с соседними странами составляет 1153 км., из которых 1119 км уже реабилитировано, 34 км находятся в процессе реконструкции, работы будут завершены к концу 2013 года.

Однако реализация такого крупного проекта, как Трансафганский железнодорожный коридор, тормозится, прежде всего, в виду отсутствия финансирования.

Несмотря на все усилия, предпринимаемые странами по развитию транспортной инфраструктуры, объемы перевозок в сообщении с Индией остаются незначительными.

Основной объем перевозок между Казахстаном и Индией выполняется железнодорожным транспортом (рисунок 3). Причем практически все маршруты транспортировки экспортных и импортных грузов пролегают по территории России и через ее порты. Незначительная часть экспортных грузов в Индию (ферросплавы, в 2012 г. около 2 тыс. тонн) перевозится через территорию Китая до его восточных портов и далее морем.

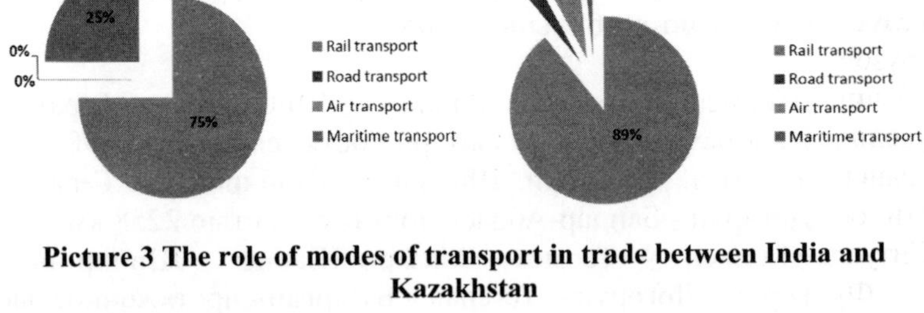

Picture 3 The role of modes of transport in trade between India and Kazakhstan

Source: NII TK, Kazakhstan

Слабое развитие железнодорожных перевозок через территорию Ирана вызвано не только недостатками технического состояния железнодорожной отрасли (прежде всего, Ирана) и необходимостью перевалки грузов/контейнеров в портах Ирана, но и организационными проблемами, связанными с перестановкой колесных пар (*нормальная колея на территории бывшего СССР—1520 мм, в Иране, как и в Китае, Северной Америке, Турции - 1435 мм. В Индии, Пакистане и некоторых других странах используется наиболее широкий в мире размер колеи (1600 мм либо 1676 мм)),* переоформлением документов и пр.

Однако больше всего барьеров существует на автомобильном транспорте.

В регионе имеется сравнительно развитая автодорожная сеть, отдельные участки которой входят в сеть автомобильных дорог СНГ, ЕврАзЭС, состав сеть Азиатских шоссейных дорог и, сеть дорог категории "Е".

Однако большое значенис на развитис перевозок, как показывают проекты, реализованные по линии International Road Transport Union (IRU) с участием автотранспортных компаний из стран региона, оказывает безопасность перевозок и наличие вспомогательной инфраструктуры и сопутствующих услуг – мотелей, СТО, АЗС и пр.

Недавние обследования автомобильных дорог в ЦА регионе в рамках проекта IRU «Modal Highway» показали, что трассы Казахстана, как правило, достаточно обеспечены АЗС, пунктами питания и торговыми точками. Однако эти объекты зачастую не соответствуют требованиям качества, удобства для участников дорожного движения. СТО преимущественно расположены в крупных городах и, как правило, предназначены для оказания услуг легковому транспорту. Ощущается нехватка стоянок, грузовые транспортные средства вынуждены останавливаться на обочинах или притрассовых площадках отдыха. При общем увеличении количества объектов сервиса, нужды грузового транспорта игнорируются малым и средним бизнесом, так как эти объекты более затратны в строительстве и эксплуатации. Ситуация в других республиках ЦА более плачевна.

Функционирование и развитие всех видов транспорта в международном масштабе в настоящее время практически полностью опирается на двусторонние соглашения и многостороннюю конвенционную основу.

В таблице представлены двусторонние соглашения Казахстана.

Таблица – Двусторонние соглашения Казахстана об автомобильных перевозках

Islamic Republic of Iran	Соглашение между Правительством Республики Казахстан и Правительством Исламской Республики Иран о международном автомобильном сообщении, подписанное 12 мая 1993 г. в г. Тегеране В связи с тем, что в Соглашении от 1993 года не урегулированы вопросы проезда по территориям сторон в части применения разрешительной системы, в настоящее время разработан новый проект Соглашения, 10 июня 2011 года направлено предложение об обсуждении данного проекта иранской стороне в 4-квартале 2011 года в Астане. До настоящего времени ответа от иранской стороны не поступало.
Kyrgyz Republic	Соглашение между Республикой Казахстан и Республикой Кыргызстан о международном автомобильном сообщении. Соглашение предусматривает безразрешительную систему, за исключением нерегулярных пассажирских перевозок.
Republic of Tajikistan	Соглашение между Республикой Казахстан и Республикой Таджикистан о международном автомобильном сообщении. Предусматривает безразрешительную систему перевозок грузов в двустороннем и транзитном сообщении, а также в/из третьи страны, кроме пассажирских перевозок.
Turkmenistan	Соглашение между Республикой Казахстан и Туркменистаном о международном автомобильном сообщении. Предусматривает разрешительную систему перевозок на въезд/выезд, транзит и перевозки в/из третьих стран.
Republic of Uzbekistan	Соглашение между Правительством Республики Казахстан и Правительством Республики Узбекистан о международных автомобильных перевозках грузов и пассажиров.

	Предусматривает безразрешительную систему на въезд/выезд, транзит. Перевозки в/из третьих стран осуществляется на разрешительной основе.
Republic of India	No
Islamic Republic of Afghanistan	No

В общей сложности страны мира являются участниками более 120 международных соглашений и конвенций, регламентирующих различные аспекты транспортной деятельности. Почти половина из их общего числа - 55 соглашений и конвенций - заключены под эгидой United Nations Economic Commission for Europe (UNECE).

В целях обеспечения правовой основы наземных перевозок еще в 1992 году ЭСКАТО ООН приняла специальную резолюцию 48/11 по автомобильному и железнодорожному транспорту. Государствам азиатского континента было рекомендовано присоединиться к семи базовым конвенциям и соглашениям:

- Convention on Road Signs and Signals, of 8 November 1968;
- Convention on Road Traffic, of 8 November 1968;
- International Convention on the Harmonization of Frontier Controls of Goods, 21 October 1982;
- Convention on the Contract for the International Carriage of Goods by Road (CMR), of 19 May 1956;
- Customs Convention on the International Transport of Goods under Cover of TIR Carnets (TIR Convention), of 14 November 1975;
- Customs Convention on Containers, of 2 December 1972;
- Customs Convention on the Temporary Importation of Commercial Road Vehicles, of 18 May 1956.

Статус присоединения государств региона к этим и другим международным соглашениям можно посмотреть на сайте UNECE http://www.unece.org/trans/conventn/intro.html.

Факт присоединения к тому или иному международному документу означает готовность государства гарантировать соблюдение в своих границах предусмотренных ими правил, норм и требований, прав и обязанностей участников перевозочного процесса. Это повышает доверие к государству, его международный авторитет и является одной из главных предпосылок развития международных перевозок.

Индия и Иран не являются членами ЕЭК ООН. Однако они присоединились к некоторым соглашениям, разработанным в рамках этой организации

Все вышесказанное свидетельствует о том, что назрела необходимость формирования комплексного подхода к развитию сотрудничества стран Центральной Азии и Индии в сфере транспорта, отражающего ключевые направления и механизмы дву- и многостороннего партнерства в кратко- и среднесрочной перспективе.

28
Перспективы казахстанско-индийского сотрудничества в сфере развития и обеспечения безопасности транспортно-логистической системы региона

Рафик Таиров

В современных глобальных условиях транспортно-логистическая сеть играет ключевую роль в индустриальном развитии государств.

Мировой рынок транспортной логистики оценивается в 2,7 трлн. долларов США, т. е. порядка 7% мирового ВВП. В развитых странах доля транспортной логистики составляет 13–14% от ВВП. Так, в Ирландии этот показатель достигает 14,2%, в Сингапуре-13,9%, Гонконге-13,7%, в Германии 13,0% и т. д. Это свидетельствует о том, что эти страны обращают особое внимание на развитие данного сектора как одного из источников национального дохода. В Казахстане этот показатель приблизительно равен 8%[1].

Если проанализировать мировую карту движения капитала, трудовых ресурсов, товаров, технологий, финансов и инвестиций, то можно обнаружить, что она буквально накладываются на густую сеть транспортных магистралей, опутавшую весь земной шар.

Казахстан, находясь на стыке международных транспортных коридоров, располагает достаточной транспортно-логистической сетью.

---

[1] Транспортная логистика сегодня - это ключевой компонент в реализации ГП ФИИР – Ерхат Искалиевhttp://www.kazlogistics.kz/analytics/95/708/.

На 25-м пленарном заседании Совета иностранных инвесторов Президент Казахстана Нурсултан Назарбаев отметил: «У Казахстана есть потенциал стать крупнейшим деловым транзитным хабом Центрально-Азиатского региона, своеобразным мостом между Европой и Азией… Это создание на ключевых транспортных коридорах Казахстана единого комплекса хабов международного уровня – торгово-логистического, финансово-делового, инновационно-технологического и туристического».

Учитывая процесс глобализации, охвативший весь мир, Казахстан сориентировал стратегические цели исходя из сегодняшних реалий, будущих возможностей, а также вызовов и угроз. А это потребовало осмысления и создания новых форм взаимовыгодных партнерских отношений между странами региона по развитию транспортно-логистических направлений и обеспечению их безопасности.

Немаловажное значение в региональном и двухстороннем сотрудничестве приобретают казахстанско-индийские отношения, основанные на конструктивном взаимодействии.

Это связано с тем, что для Индии ЦАР представляет собой:

- огромный потенциальный рынок сбыта промышленной продукции;
- перспективный источник топливно–энергетических ресурсов;
- возможный источник полезных ископаемых, прежде всего, цветных и драгоценных металлов, особенно золота (Индия - крупнейший мировой потребитель золота);
- «коридор» для транспортировки индийских товаров в Россию, страны СНГ и другие государства Европы.

Казахстан в свою очередь видит в Индии:

- поставщика качественной текстильной продукции;
- потенциальный рынок сбыта природных ресурсов;
- выход казахстанских товаров в Южную Азию;
- потенциального поставщика новейших информационных технологий.

Индия и Казахстан являются странами с быстро развивающимися экономиками. Несмотря на то, что Казахстан является крупнейшим торговым партнером Индии в Центральной Азии (на его долю приходится более 70% всего товарооборота со странами Центральной Азии), двусторонняя торговля между нашими странами, объем которой в настоящее время составляет менее 400 миллионов долларов, намного ниже потенциального уровня.

В настоящее время около 280-ти компаний задействованы в бизнесе между Казахстаном и Индией.

Будучи одним из крупных потребителей энергии в мире, Индия нуждается в увеличении атомной энергии для удовлетворения своих будущих потребностей в энергии. А для этого нужен уран.

Сегодня Казахстан находится на 2-м месте в мире по мировым запасам урана (21%). В 2013 году планируется добыть 20 000 тонн урана.

Поэтому, Казахстан может в ближайшем будущем стать для Индии постоянным и надежным экспортером урана.

Нефтегазовый сектор также выступает одним из стратегически важных направлений нашего сотрудничества.

В позитивном ключе рассматривается двухстороннее сотрудничество в области разведки, добычи и переработки нефти, транспортировки и сбыта нефтепродукта.

Вместе с тем, несмотря на потенциальные возможности, неразвитость транспортно-логистической инфраструктуры отражается на экономике Казахстана и взаимовыгодном сотрудничестве между Казахстаном и Индией.

Прежде всего, должен отметить, что расходы на логистику в нашей стране очень велики и в разы превышают уровень развитых стран.

Так, сегодня в Казахстане доля логистических издержек может достигать уровня 25% от стоимости конечной продукции. При этом среднемировой показатель находится на уровне 11%, в Китае 14%, в странах ЕС на уровне 11%, в США и Канаде – 10%[2].

В результате чего, экономика Казахстана вынуждена нести

---

[2] Транспортная логистика сегодня – это ключевой компонент http://www.kazlogistics.kz/analytics/95/708/

транспортную нагрузку в два раза больше, чем в развитых странах.

Казахстан нуждается в кратчайших транспортных коридорах к портам Черного и Средиземного морей, Индийского и Тихого океанов. Это связано с очевидным экономическим преимуществом – себестоимость морских транспортировок на порядок ниже, чем автомобильных и железнодорожных.

Поэтому перспективным направлением является сотрудничество двух стран по созданию транспортных коридоров, которые бы соединили Индию с Центральной Азией, Казахстаном и Россией и, соответственно – с Европой.

Так, реальные перспективы имеет транспортный коридор «Север-Юг» из Актау через Каспийское море в Иран и до Аравийского моря.

Проект транспортировки «Север-Юг» предполагает наличие железнодорожного и других видов сообщений из Европы через Россию, Азербайджан и Иран в Индию и страны Южной Азии. Казахстан заинтересован в создании системы складов и услуг дистрибьюции в порту Актау, с тем, чтобы он стал крупным центром для транспортировки товаров между Казахстаном и Южной Азией, а также странами Персидского залива. Индийские компании также могут быть заинтересованы в участии в данном проекте.

По мнению экспертов, в случае прихода Индии в Центральноазиатско-Каспийский регион нынешние глобальные игроки (РФ, КНР, США, ЕС) перестанут чувствовать свою исключительность, обнаружив, что у Казахстана и других стран региона имеется серьезная альтернатива в лице укрепляющейся Индии. Однако и возражать против этого они не станут, поскольку, во-первых, масштаб их взаимодействия с Индией многократно превосходит объем казахстанско-индийского взаимодействия; во-вторых, интенсификация казахстанско-индийского сотрудничества в ряде случаев может быть полезной и выгодной для глобальных игроков.

Поэтому в данной ситуации для наших стран актуально решение вопросов международного правового статуса Каспия, как одного из условий обеспечения безопасности транспортно-логистической системы региона.

Другой перспективный проект предполагает создание

автомобильного транспортного коридора Индия – Пакистан – Китай – Казахстан.

В настоящее время реализован один из масштабных транспортных проектов – строительство туркмено-казахстанского участка железной дороги по маршруту Казахстан–Туркменистан–Иран, что предоставляет огромные возможности в контексте оптимизации транспортных потоков на Евроазиатском пространстве. Проект открывает выход для европейских стран от портов на Балтийском море к товарным и сырьевым рынкам Ближнего и Среднего Востока и к государствам бассейна Индийского океана, позволяя значительно сократить расстояние транспортировки и время в пути.

Открывается перспектива подключения к транспортной инфраструктуре в южном и восточном направлениях, с выходом на такие мощные экономические центры, как Индия, Китай, Пакистан, страны Азиатско-тихоокеанского региона, что означает создание нового, еще более масштабного формата сотрудничества, являя собой пример подлинно новаторского мышления в глобальной геоэкономике, видения стратегических перспектив ее развития.

Это позволит решить вопрос транзита индийских товаров через Иран. Однако, здесь тоже не без сложностей, я имею ввиду эмбарго в отношении Ирана со стороны западных государств.

Разумеется, учитывая нынешнюю международную ситуацию, Казахстан мог бы инициировать обсуждение этой проблемы, путей ее решения со всеми заинтересованными сторонами по дипломатическим и иным каналам (в том числе в рамках механизмов ШОС, СВМДА и ДСА).

Большие перспективы имеются в сфере энергетического диалога двух стран. Вопросы энергетического сотрудничества наших государств являются важнейшим элементом национальной безопасности.

Казахстан поддерживает крупные региональные проекты, которые еще находятся в стадии проработки.

Среди них «ТАПИ» (газопровод «Туркменистан–Афганистан – Пакистан – Индия»), «КАСА-ТЫСЯЧА» (высоковольтная линия электропередачи «Central Asia-South Asia – 1000»), а также расширение сети железных дорог вокруг и внутри Афганистана.

Одним из пилотных проектов экономической реабилитации Афганистана, поддерживаемым США выступает проект «Новый Шелковый путь». Однако, не все эксперты однозначно разделяют эту точку зрения.

Так, по мнению одних, идея проекта – способствовать экономическому развитию региона, причем Афганистан выступает в качестве главного транспортного узла между ЦАР и Южной Азией. Проект позволит соединить Индию и страны ЦАР в единую транспортно-логистическую цепь. В настоящее время движение грузового транспорта между Афганистаном и Индией через территорию Пакистана ограничено из-за плохих отношений Исламабада и Дели.

По мнению других экспертов, проект призван оправдать сохранение военных баз НАТО в регионе и снизить роль Ирана, Китая и России. Кроме того, перспектива трансафганских перевозок вызывает у участников рынка сомнения – слишком беспокойный данный регион. Поэтому в своем нынешнем формате трансафганский коридор не представляет для них большого интереса.

Таким образом, дилемма складывающейся ситуации заключается в одновременной заинтересованности внешних игроков в продвижении своего влияния в регионе и стремлении государств ЦА получить внешнюю поддержку собственных интересов, в том числе и в отношениях со своими ближайшими соседями. То есть создаются возможности для появления самых разнообразных альянсов в интересах между внутри- и внешнерегиональными игроками.

Сохраняющаяся напряженность в Каспийском регионе, внутриполитическая нестабильность в ряде соседствующих государств с Афганистаном, по территории которых проходит или планируется проложить транспортно-логистическую магистраль, создадут условия для мобилизации и быстрого продвижения на север гипотетической армии экстремистских элементов, включая ИДУ, Талибан, а также диверсионных атак на магистральные и транспортные пути доставки углеводородного сырья.

Сегодня необходимо совместное сотрудничество по укреплению безопасности трубопроводов за счет улучшения контроля над трубопроводной отраслью и обеспечения ее безопасности.

Мировая практика показывает, что трубопроводы становятся легкой мишенью для международных террористических организаций, которые ставят своей задачей нанести ущерб международной газовой и нефтяной инфраструктуре и, помимо этого, экологический ущерб стране транзита.

Также возрастает необходимость обеспечения безопасности транзита товаров и пассажирских перевозок. Транспортная инфраструктура всегда оставалась местом проведения террористических актов. Особую актуальность безопасность транзитных перевозок приобрела после 11 сентября.

Обеспечения безопасности транзитной системы должно учитывать, что она рассматривается террористами как:

- средство организации теракта (*использование транспорта для перевозки и/или передачи взрывчатых веществ, использование транспорта в качестве оружия – атака 11 сентября*);
- цель теракта (*разрушение мостов, туннелей, железной дороги, шоссе*);
- объект, находящийся в зоне поражения теракта.

Угроза транзитного терроризма не одинакова для всех территорий, большинство атак происходят в крупнейших городах и направлены на разрушение крупных транспортных развязок.

Кроме того, в век кибернетики появились новые виды угроз связанные с кибертеррористами. Сегодня даже самые развитые государства мира не застрахованы от этих видов поражений.

В течение короткого времени информационные системы, обеспечивающие транспортную, энергетическую логистику могут оказаться под несанкционированным контролем кибертеррористов или быть выведены из строя. А это может привести к трагическим последствиям.

Таким образом, веление времени требует межгосударственного решения немаловажного вопроса по обеспечению кибербезопасности критической инфраструктуры – автоматизированной системы управления транспортно-логистической сетью региона и трубопроводами.

Индия сегодня располагает большим потенциалом в сфере борьбы с международным терроризмом и религиозным экстремизмом, а также киберугрозами. Поэтому одним из основных направлений двухстороннего сотрудничества может стать дальнейшее расширение казахстанско-индийского сотрудничества в сфере борьбы с международным терроризмом, экстремизмом и киберугрозами.

Сегодня Индия, являясь страной наблюдателем ШОС и одним из лидеров среди международных доноров, вкладывает значительные средства в восстановление Афганистана.

Как Индия, так и Казахстан глубоко заинтересованы в стабилизации и постконфликтном обустройстве Афганистана. Оба государства считают, что афганская проблема не имеет военного решения и придают особое значение вопросам восстановления экономики и инфраструктуры Афганистана.

Стабилизация ситуации в Афганистане позволит не только укрепить региональную безопасность, но и создать условия для реализации многообещающих международных проектов в сфере энергетики и транспортных коммуникаций.

Поэтому было бы целесообразно поддержать Индию в ее стремлении стать полноправным участником ШОС. Это позволило бы не только вовлечь Индию в масштабные региональные проекты (*особенно в сфере энергетики*), но и добиться нового баланса сил в данной организации.

Близки позиции Астаны и Дели и в отношении комплекса проблем, связанных с Ираном. Казахстан и Индия связывают с Ираном реализацию перспективных проектов, вкладывают в эту страну инвестиции и уже в силу этих факторов не заинтересованы в военном решении проблемы ядерной программы Тегерана.

Одним из важных направлений казахстанско-индийского сотрудничества является военное сотрудничество по следующим направлениям:

1) проведение совместных учений в контртеррористических операциях, направленных на обеспечение безопасности транспортно-логистического магистралей, ликвидации последствий ЧС после экологических катастроф;
2) обмен опытом в области миротворческой деятельности;

3) противодействие киберугрозам;
4) создание совместного центра передовых исследований в области кибербезопасности.

Таким образом, Казахстан заинтересован в том, чтобы, оптимизировать баланс сил в Центральной Азии и Каспийском регионе. Усиление присутствия Индии во всех сферах сотрудничества (в том числе в энергетике) может иметь далеко идущие геополитические и геоэкономические последствия. Это тем более важно в условиях мирового финансово-экономического кризиса, когда столь необходим приток новых иностранных инвестиций, когда важно показать всему миру, что Казахстан остается инвестиционно привлекательной страной.

29
Перспективные направления сотрудничества Казахстана и Индии в контексте совершенствования глобальной финансовой архитектуры

Владимир Додонов

Состояние казахстанско-индийского сотрудничества в экономической сфере

В условиях стремительно меняющегося геоэкономического ландшафта, перестройки фундаментальных принципов функционирования и развития сложных экономических систем, возрастания разрушительной силы финансово-экономических кризисов перспективные направления международного сотрудничества как на двух-, так и на многосторонней основе должны выходить за рамки традиционных сфер взаимной торговли и инвестиций, и охватывать системные вопросы совершенствования глобального экономического устройства, затрагивающего интересы заинтересованных стран. Для Казахстана и Индии тем более важен выход на новый уровень сотрудничества и иные его направления, учитывая тот факт, что в традиционных сферах двусторонних экономических взаимосвязей их уровень пока что весьма скромен.

Так, текущая ситуация в области казахстанско-индийского сотрудничества в инвестиционной сфере отличается крайне недостаточным уровнем. Индия, являясь одной из крупнейших экономик мира (третье место в 2012 году по размеру ВВП по паритету покупательной способности и десятое по номинальному размеру ВВП), занимает лишь 27 место по объему накопленных иностранных инвестиций в Казахстан (таб. 1), а в относительном выражении на Индию приходится лишь 0,14 % от общего объема привлеченных Казахстаном иностранных инвестиций.

Таблица 1: Позиция Индия среди основных стран-инвесторов казахстанской экономики по состоянию на 31.12.2012 г. (все инвестиции, млн. долл. США)[1]

1.	НИДЕРЛАНДЫ	49 564,8
2.	ВЕЛИКОБРИТАНИЯ	24 392,6
3.	КИТАЙ	18 985,6
4.	США	14 551,8
5.	ФРАНЦИЯ	8 753,3
6.	ВИРГИНСКИЕ ОСТРОВА (БРИТАНСКИЕ)	6 787,3
7.	РОССИЙСКАЯ ФЕДЕРАЦИЯ	5 930,8
8.	ЯПОНИЯ	5 071,3
9.	ЛИБЕРИЯ	4 042,4
10.	ШВЕЙЦАРИЯ	3 229,9
11.	АВСТРИЯ	2 626,7
12.	ОБЪЕДИНЕННЫЕ АРАБСКИЕ ЭМИРАТЫ	2 543,1
13.	ГЕРМАНИЯ	2 047,1
14.	КАНАДА	1 897,2
15.	РЕСПУБЛИКА КОРЕЯ (ЮЖНАЯ)	1 519,3
16.	КИПР	1 239,6
17.	КАЙМАНОВЫ ОСТРОВА (БРИТАНСКИЕ)	1 071,5
18.	ГОНКОНГ (СЯНГАН)	1 067,9
19.	ТУРЦИЯ	877,8
20.	БЕЛЬГИЯ	620,9
21.	РУМЫНИЯ	576,2
22.	БЕРМУДСКИЕ ОСТРОВА (БРИТАНСКИЕ)	570,7
23.	ШВЕЦИЯ	544,8
24.	МАЛАЙЗИЯ	509,6
25.	СИНГАПУР	419,6
26.	ГЭРНСИ ОСТРОВ	366,6
27.	ИНДИЯ	253,8
	ВСЕГО	**182 417**

Ежегодные объемы инвестируемых индийскими

компаниями в Казахстан средств нельзя охарактеризовать иначе как мизерные. На протяжении 2000-х годов (таб. 2) индийские инвестиции измерялись в лучшем случае десятыми долями процента от общего объема иностранных инвестиций, а как правило – не превышали даже нескольких сотых долей процента (исключением стал лишь 2011 год). Очевидно, что ежегодные объемы инвестиций, измеряемые несколькими сотнями тысяч долларов, не способны создать фундамент полноценного экономического сотрудничества между двумя странами.

Рассматривая двусторонние инвестиционные потоки, можно также отметить, что в последние годы существенно активизировались казахстанские вложения в индийскую экономику, которые во второй половине 2000-х годов превысили совокупный объем индийских инвестиций в Казахстан. То есть, тенденции последних лет свидетельствуют о росте интереса казахстанского бизнеса к индийскому рынку, что привело к переходу Казахстана из нетто-реципиента в нетто-инвестора индийской экономики – объем накопленных инвестиций из Казахстана в Индию составляет 280 млн. долл. против 254 млн. долл. в обратном направлении. Однако пока что и объемы накопленных казахстанских инвестиций в Индию также мизерны – Индия занимает лишь 30 место среди стран, в которые направляются средства казахстанского бизнеса (таб. 3), а доля этих инвестиций в общем объеме стремится к нулю и измеряется двумя сотыми долями процента.

Также низким уровнем отличается и сотрудничество двух стран в торговой сфере, которое в весьма малой степени реализует имеющийся потенциал: так, в 2012 году двусторонний товарооборот составил 525 млн. долларов, в том числе экспорт (из Казахстана) – 190,7 млн. и импорт 334,5 млн. Эти показатели составляют соответственно только 0,2 и 0,7 % от общих объемов казахстанского экспорта и импорта в 2012 году (92,1 и 47,4 млрд. долл. США – по данным Национального банка РК).

Таблица 2. Абсолютные и относительные показатели прямых инвестиций из Индии в Казахстан, млн. долл. США[2]

Страна	2000	2001	2006	2007	2008	2009	2010	2011	2012
ИНДИЯ	0,8	1,4	21,3	0,7	0,3	0,2	25,2	129,8	15,5
Всего ПИИ в Казахстан	2781,2	4556,6	10623,6	18452,6	19755,2	19017,3	19059	21056	22469
Доля индийских инвестиций в общем объеме ПИИ в Казахстан, %	0,028	0,031	0,201	0,004	0,001	0,001	0,13	0,62	0,07

Таблица 3. Позиция Индии среди основных стран – реципиентов казахстанских инвестиций по состоянию на 31.12.2012 г. (все инвестиции, млн. долл. США)[3]

1	США	48 287,6
2	ВЕЛИКОБРИТАНИЯ	17 080,6
3	НИДЕРЛАНДЫ	16 822,6
4	РОССИЙСКАЯ ФЕДЕРАЦИЯ	8 130,3
5	ГЕРМАНИЯ	6 843,3
6	ФРАНЦИЯ	6 201,7
7	ЯПОНИЯ	4 623,1
8	КАНАДА	3 162,8
9	ШВЕЙЦАРИЯ	3 114,1
10	КИТАЙ	2 659,7
11	РЕСПУБЛИКА КОРЕЯ (ЮЖНАЯ)	2 558,4
12	АВСТРАЛИЯ	2 532,7
13	ВИРГИНСКИЕ ОСТРОВА (БРИТАНСКИЕ)	2 408,3
14	АВСТРИЯ	2 179,0
15	МЕЖДУНАРОДНЫЕ ОРГАНИЗАЦИИ	2 166,5
16	ГОНКОНГ (СЯНГАН)	1 522,4
17	ИРЛАНДИЯ	1 442,8
18	СИНГАПУР	1 314,4
19	КИПР	1 162,6
20	ТУРЦИЯ	983,3
21	ДАНИЯ	940,6
22	СЕЙШЕЛЬСКИЕ ОСТРОВА	609,9
23	ОБЪЕДИНЕННЫЕ АРАБСКИЕ ЭМИРАТЫ	555,9
24	КЫРГЫЗСТАН	525,0
25	БЕЛЬГИЯ	501,3
26	ШВЕЦИЯ	423,7
27	УКРАИНА	392,7
28	ФИНЛЯНДИЯ	347,3
29	ГРУЗИЯ	320,5
30	ИНДИЯ	280,4
	ВСЕГО	**157 051**

Перспективные направления сотрудничества в финансово-инвестиционной и торговой сферах

На наш взгляд, высокий потенциал развития традиционных направлений сотрудничества может быть реализован посредством не только участия Индии в освоении сырьевых месторождений Казахстана (что, судя по всему, является приоритетом для индийской стороны), но и в других областях. Так, если рассматривать перспективные направления сотрудничества в финансово-инвестиционной и торговой сферах, то можно выделить такие его формы, как:

- активизация индийских кредитных институтов на рынке Казахстана;
- участие индийских финансовых институтов в реализации программ модернизации казахстанской экономики, таких, как ПФИИР, в том числе в рамках программ государственно-частного партнерства;
- использование механизма связанных кредитов, выдаваемых индийскими банками на льготных условиях (под низкие ставки и на длительные сроки) для приобретения индийских товаров казахстанскими компаниями и гражданами.
- сотрудничество Казахстана и Индии в области развития РФЦА: индийские финансовые институты могли бы более активно выходить на РФЦА в качестве инвесторов, а также вывод на Казахстанскую фондовую биржу (KASE) ценных бумаг компаний с участием индийского капитала;
- активное участие индийских инвестиционных институтов в приобретении ценных бумаг казахстанских эмитентов, включая инфраструктурные облигации и другие долговые бумаги, выпускаемые под программы индустриально-инновационного развития и инфраструктурные проекты, а также акции казахстанских предприятий;

Казахстанско-индийское сотрудничество по повышению стабильности мировой финансовой системы

В то же время, в контексте усиления глобальных кризисов, дестабилизации мировой экономики и системного несовершенства международной финансовой архитектуры, еще большее значение приобретают проблемы сотрудничества на многостороннем уровне, направленного на решение данных проблем. В связи с этим, вопросы сотрудничества Индии и Казахстана в современных условиях могут и должны включать соответствующую повестку – совместное влияние наших стран на идущие процессы реструктуризации глобальной экономики с тем, чтобы данная реструктуризация осуществлялась не только в интересах ведущих игроков финансового рынка – развитых стран, но и стран с развивающимися рынками. Развивающиеся государства в настоящее время играют все большую роль во многих аспектах глобальной экономики, в некоторых выходя на ведущие позиции, и их интересы должны быть отражены в концепциях и методах решения актуальных проблем реформирования глобальной финансовой архитектуры.

К числу ключевых из этих проблем можно отнести разбалансированность ответственности и последствий за принимаемые экономические решения между развитыми и развивающимися странами, диспропорции между реальным сектором экономики и финансовой сферой, искаженность инвестиционных критериев и обусловленных ими денежных потоков, растущая зависимость глобальной экономики от кризисов, генерируемых финансовым сектором преимущественно развитых стран, неустойчивость и непрогнозируемость экономического развития.

Для решения данных проблем необходимо проведение согласованной политики на многостороннем уровне, направленной на выправление существующих дисбалансов, в формулировании и реализации которой важную роль могут сыграть также и Казахстан с Индией, как в качестве инициаторов необходимых мер, так и используя имеющийся у стран экономический потенциал и рычаги влияния на ситуацию в отдельных сегментах мировой экономики и рынков. Сотрудничество наших стран могло бы осуществляться в следующих направлениях, способствующих повышению стабильности мировой финансовой системы.

1. Согласование позиций по реформированию мировой финансовой архитектуры, которое обсуждается на саммитах «двадцатки», в которых участвует Индия, но не участвуют Казахстан и другие страны Центральной Азии. Позиция Казахстана, как страны, сильно зависящей от колебаний конъюнктуры мировых товарных рынков, должна также быть доведена до стран-членов «двадцатки» и в этом может помочь обсуждение проблем мировой финансовой архитектуры на двусторонней основе. Ключевыми проблемами этой архитектуры, продуцирующими неустойчивость и кризисы, и нуждающимися в первоочередном реформировании, в том числе на уровне G-20, являются следующие:

- Растущая неконтролируемость мировых рынков вследствие несоот-ветствия объекта и субъектов регулирования. При уже сложившемся и ре-ально существующем едином глобальном финансовом рынке отсутствует единый глобальный регулятор рынка.
- Опережающее развитие «надстроечной» сферы финансов по сравне-нию с «базисным» реальным сектором мировой экономики, особенно – в развитых экономиках постиндустриального типа, ведущее ко все большей концентрации денег в системе глобальных финансовых рынков. Основной причиной этого явления стала отмена существовавшего ранее в рамках закона Гласса-Стиголла разграничения банковской и инвестиционной деятельности, после которого банки переключили свое внимание с кредитования реального сектора на операции на финансовых рынках либо их кредитование. Это привело к опережающему по сравнению с реальным сектором генерированию прибыли в финансовой сфере во многом за счет «эффекта пирамиды», когда прибывающие во все больших объемах средства толкают наверх цены финансовых активов и, тем самым, повышают норму прибыли на финансовых рынках, что, в свою очередь, привлекает новых инвесторов и т.д. В результате по

всем секторам организованных рынков надуваются «пузыри», сдутие которых (ведущее к очередному кризису) становится лишь вопросом времени.

- Существенные искажения и турбулентности на товарных рынках вследствие биржевого характера ценообразования. По мере возрастания роли биржевого оборота в международной торговле товарными активами, цены этих активов все более отрывались от реального базиса (себестоимости, объемов спроса и предложения) и становились производными от ликвидности на мировых финансовых рынках и настроений спекулятивных инвесторов.
- Наличие на глобальном финансовом рынке нерегулируемых внебиржевых сегментов деривативов, становящихся своего рода «черными дырами» неконтролируемой эмиссии и источниками как огромных объемов ликвидности, надувающей «пузыри» на рынках, так и очагами кризисов, когда эти «пузыри» начинают схлопываться, унося с собой триллионы инвестированных долларов.
- Деформированная система инвестиционных критериев, основанная на субъективизме кредитных рейтингов трех рейтинговых агентств – Moody's, Standard & Poor's, Fitch, а также на аудиторских заключениях «большой четверки» - KPMG, Deloitte Touche Tomatsu, PricewaterhouseCoopers и Ernst & Young.
- «Перекредитованность» хозяйствующих субъектов и домохозяйств развитых экономик и растущие затруднения с обслуживанием чрезмерных долгов, периодически выливающиеся в кризисы неплатежеспособности за-емщиков и череду банкротств.

2. На отдельных сегментах мировых товарных рынков, где сильны позиции Казахстана как продавца, а Индии – как покупателя (например, промышленные металлы, уран), в периоды сильных колебаний цен, вызванных учащающимися мировыми кризисами, возможны согласованные действия двух стран, направленные на стабилизацию ценовых скачков – от совместных заявлений до временного моратория на признание

мировых биржевых цен во взаимной торговле.

3. Совместное и согласованное влияние на процессы постоянно затягивающегося реформирования международных финансовых институтов (МВФ, ВБ) с целью повышения роли в управлении данными институтами развивающихся стран. В настоящее время остается актуальной проблема неадекватной представленности развивающихся стран в органах управления данных институтов и в количестве квот, соответствующих правам при голосовании. Несмотря на регулярные пересмотры квот, которые происходят обычно через пятилетний промежуток, и которых в истории МВФ было уже пятнадцать, США по-прежнему сохраняют фактическое право вето на ключевые решения МВФ, так как имеют более 17 % голосов, а важнейшие решения должны приниматься большинством в 85 %. Эту ситуацию не меняют и принятые в ноябре 2010 решения по «беспрецедентной» реформе МВФ, предусматривающие перераспределение голосов в организации в пользу развивающихся стран. Более подробно доли ведущих стран и их групп до и после изменений приведены в таблице 1.

Таблица 1. Распределение квот в МВФ между крупнейшими участниками до и после реформы 2010-2013 гг., %[4]

	Квоты		голоса	
	до	после	до	после
Группы стран				
Развитые экономики	60,5	57,7	57,9	55,3
Страны G7	45,3	43,4	43,0	41,2
ЕС-27	31,9	30,2	30,9	29,4
Развивающиеся экономики	39,5	42,3	42,1	44,7
Страны с переходной экономикой	7,1	7,2	7,6	7,7
Отдельные страны				
США	17,7	17,4	16,7	16,5
Япония	6,6	6,5	6,2	6,1
Германия	6,1	5,6	5,8	5,3
Франция	4,5	4,2	4,3	4,0
Великобритания	4,5	4,2	4,3	4,0
Китай	4,0	6,4	3,8	6,1
Италия	3,3	3,2	3,2	3,0

	Квоты		голоса	
	до	после	до	после
Саудовская Аравия	2,9	2,1	2,8	2,0
Канада	2,7	2,3	2,6	2,2
Россия	2,5	2,7	2,4	2,6
Индия	2,4	2,8	2,3	2,6

Однако и после этих изменений реальный расклад сил в МВФ не изменится, так как США по-прежнему будут иметь возможность заблокировать любое важное решение, а роль ведущих стран сохранится на максимальном уровне. Перераспределение всего 6 % квот не способно изменить процессы управления фондом. Кроме того, реализация принятых решений постоянно откладывается – если принципиальное решение было принято еще в октябре 2010 года, то фактическое перераспределение квот до сих пор не состоялось. В этих вопросах как Индия, так и Казахстан и другие государства Центральной Азии могли бы прилагать совместные усилия.

4. Координация усилий по повышению региональной экономической стабильности в условиях кризисов и формированию мер поддержки отдельных проблемных экономик региона, в том числе на институциональном уровне. В ходе борьбы с последствиями мирового кризиса в ряде регионов мира появились специализированные институты антикризисного характера, такие, как Европейский стабилизационный механизм, Антикризисный фонд ЕврАзЭС, обсуждается создание аналогичного института в рамках БРИКС. На наш взгляд, в случае продвижения интеграционных процессов в Центральной Азии Казахстан и Индия могли бы выступить в качестве инициаторов и ведущих акционеров такого рода антикризисных институтов для региона «большой Центральной Азии», что позволило бы в периоды будущих кризисов сглаживать внешние шоки и поддерживать макроэкономическую стабильность в проблемных экономиках региона.

Рассматривая ресурсы организаций, которые могут быть направлены на регулирование экономических процессов, необходимо учитывать еще и такую особенность современной экономики, как разные подходы к государственным финансам у развитых и развивающихся стран. Если первые традиционно финансируют свои экономические программы почти исключительно за счет государственных бюджетов и, в случае их нехватки – путем эмиссии долговых обязательств, то вторые имеют и значительные внебюджетные источники – резервы и суверенные фонды. В крупных развивающихся странах объемы резервов, суверенных фондов и (в некоторых случаях) активов государственных корпораций сопоставимы не только с размерами вышеперечисленных международных банков, но превышают и возможности крупнейших международных финансовых организаций, включая МВФ (таб.3).

Таблица 2. Крупнейшие суверенные активы в сопоставлении с ресурсами международных финансовых организаций, на январь 2012г.[5]

Страна	***Ресурсы, млрд. долл.***
Китай – резервы	3181
Япония – резервы	1342,5
ЕС – European Financial Stability Facility	1015
ОАЭ – Abu Dhabi Investment Authority	627
Норвегия – государственный пенсионный фонд	611
Китай – SAFE Investment Company	568
Саудовская Аравия – SAMA Foreign Holdings	532,8
Россия – резервы	506,3
Китай – China Investment Corporation	439,6
МВФ	**365**
Бразилия – резервы	355,1
Кувейт – Kuwait Investment Authority	296
Гонконг- Monetary Authority Investment Portfolio	293,3
Индия – резервы	**293,1**
Сингапур – Government of Singapore Investment Corporation	247,5
Сингапур – Temasek Holdings	157,2
Россия – Фонд национального благосостояния	149,7
Китай – National Social Security Fund	134,5
Катар – Qatar Investment Authority	100
Казахстан – Национальный фонд и резервы	**88,7**
ЕЦБ	88,3

5. Вследствие усиливающейся нестабильности мировых валютных рынков, затрудняющей процессы бизнес-планирования, целесообразно рассмотреть возможность отказа от расчетов во взаимной торговле от валют третьих стран.

Указанные направления сотрудничества как Казахстана и Индии, так и в более широком формате, с привлечением государств Центральной Азии и других партнеров, стали бы, на наш взгляд, весьма актуальным направлением международной кооперации в контексте совершенствования глобальной финансовой архитектуры, направленного на преодоление ее сегодняшних недостатков, не позволяющих нашим странам развиваться на стабильной и устойчиво-бескризисной основе.

Цитируемая литература

1. Источник: Географическое распределение инвестиций из Казахстана и в Казахстан по состоянию на 31 декабря 2012 года. Национальный банк Республики Казахстан. http://www.nationalbank.kz/?docid=680.
2. Источник: Валовый приток иностранных прямых инвестиций в Республику Казахстан по странам. Национальный банк Республики Казахстан. http://www.nationalbank.kz/?docid=680.
3. Источник: Валовый приток иностранных прямых инвестиций в Республику Казахстан по странам. Национальный банк Республики Казахстан. http://www.nationalbank.kz/?docid=680.
4. Источник: Quota and Voting Shares Before and After Implementation of Reforms Agreed in 2008 and 2010. IMF Finance Department. www.imf.org.
5. По данным из следующих источников: Time Series Data on International Reserves and Foreign Currency Liquidity. Official Reserve Assets and Other Foreign Currency Assets. IMF. **http://www.imf.org/external/np/sta/ir/IRProcessWeb/colist.aspx**; Sovereign Wealth Fund Rankings. **Largest Sovereign Wealth Funds by Assets Under Management**. **http://www.swfinstitute.org/fund-rankings/**. Данные по Казахстану приведены на апрель 2013 года.

Список использованных источников

1. Валовый приток иностранных прямых инвестиций в Республику Казахстан по странам. Национальный банк Республики Казахстан. http://www.nationalbank.kz/?docid=680.
2. Географическое распределение инвестиций из Казахстана и в Казахстан по состоянию на 31 декабря 2012 года. Национальный банк Республики Казахстан. http://www.nationalbank.kz/?docid=680.

3. Time Series Data on International Reserves and Foreign Currency Liquidity. Official Reserve Assets and Other Foreign Currency Assets. IMF. http://www.imf.org/external/np/sta/ir/IRProcessWeb/colist.aspx;
4. Sovereign Wealth Fund Rankings. Largest Sovereign Wealth Funds by Assets Under Management. http://www.swfinstitute.org/fund-rankings
5. Quota and Voting Shares Before and After Implementation of Reforms Agreed in 2008 and 2010. IMF Finance Department. www.imf.org.

30
Приоритеты экономического сотрудничества Индии с государствами Центральной Азии

Алишер Расулев

По данным Организации экономического сотрудничества и развития (ОЭСР) в Индии за последние годы отмечаются одни из самых высоких темпов роста макроэкономических показателей по сравнению с другими странами. Последствия глобального кризиса 2008-2009 гг. для экономики страны были менее выраженными, чем для большинства государств Азиатско-Тихоокеанского региона. В Индии создана мощная индустриальная база и накоплен научно-технический потенциал, имеющий по ряду направлений конкурентоспособный характер. Особенно следует отметить такие сферы как информационные технологии, медицина, фармацевтика, легкая промышленность и др.

В соответствии с прогнозными оценками на ближайшие 20 лет, темпы роста экономики Индии будут составлять в среднем 7–7,5% в год. Ее доля в мировом ВВП вырастет с 5,4 в 2010 г. до 7,2% в 2020 г. и превысит 8 трлн. долл. США (в ценах 2009 г.)[1]. В структуре экспорта страны, по оценкам экспертов, продолжится рост доли высокотехнологичной продукции, прежде всего информационно-коммуникационной сферы. Доля IT в экспорте товаров и услуг возрастет с 18% (70 млрд. долл. США) в 2012 г. до 30% в 2020 г.[2] Высокой конкурентоспособностью характеризуется и фармацевтический рынок Индии, на котором продолжают доминировать локальные производители лекарственных средств низкостоимостного сегмента. На долю Индии приходится около 8% мирового производства лекарственных препаратов.

Активизация регионального экономического сотрудничества между государствами Центральной Азии и Индией обуславливается необходимостью модернизации промышленной инфраструктуры, градостроительством, дорожным строительством и реконструкцией автодорог, развитием сельского хозяйства и других областей, связанных с их социально-экономическим развитием. Причем важно отметить необходимость выработки механизма ускорения их реализации, поскольку значимость и перспективность данных проектов для национальных экономик региона практически осознаются всеми.

Индия является одним из крупнейших в мире импортеров углеводородного сырья. Потребление энергии в Индии, как предполагается, будет расти от 3,5 до 4,5% ежегодно, и к 2030 г. более чем удвоится. От обеспеченности страны поставками углеводородов зависит ее устойчивое экономическое развитие.

Казахстан привлекателен для индийских инвесторов как главный поставщик нефти, на долю которого приходится более 96% доказанных запасов нефти региона. Узбекистан по добыче природного газа в настоящее время занимает третье (после России и Туркменистана) место среди стран СНГ и входит в десятку крупнейших газодобывающих стран мира. Ежегодно в республике добывается около 70 млрд м3 природного газа, часть которого идет на экспорт. Только в Устюртском регионе перспективные ресурсы по газу оцениваются почти в 2 трлн м3, по жидким углеводородам (нефти и газовому конденсату) - в 900 млн т. В долгосрочной перспективе (25 лет) прирост запасов газа на Устюрте ожидается в объеме свыше 1 трлн м3, что составит около 60% от общего прогнозируемого прироста запасов газа в республике.

Это обуславливает важнейший приоритет сотрудничества Индии с государствами Центральной Азии в данной сфере. Индия подключилась к казахстано-российскому проекту по разработке нефтяного месторождения «Курмангазы». В целом она планирует инвестировать 3,5 млрд. долл. в энергетические проекты региона, включая и Узбекистан. Для обеспечения устойчивых поставок углеводородов прорабатываются различные варианты строительства газопроводов от Туркменистана и Ирана до Пакистана и Индии.

Государства Центральной Азии представляют также интерес для Индии с точки зрения развития торгово-экономического сотрудничества, как рынок сбыта индийской продукции, а так же как транзитный коридор для транспортировки индийских товаров в страны СНГ и ЕС. В этой связи по инициативе индийской стороны организуются международные промышленные выставки, встречи представителей деловых кругов. Основной акцент страна делает на сектора экономики, где она традиционно сильна: информационные технологии и программное обеспечение, фармацевтика и медицинское оборудование, легкая и пищевая промышленность.

Одним из основных экономических партнеров Индии в Центральной Азии является Узбекистан, с которым сформирована устойчивая нормативно-правовая база двустороннего сотрудничества, включающая в себя 73 межгосударственных, межправительственных, межведомственных документа. В частности, вопросы двусторонних отношений регулируются в рамках созданной в 1992 году Межправительственной комиссии (МПК) по торгово-экономическому и научно-техническому сотрудничеству между Республикой Узбекистан и Республикой Индия. С 1993 по 2011 год состоялось девять заседаний МПК. В ходе последнего заседания, прошедшего 4 мая 2011 года в Ташкенте, стороны подтвердили значимость активизации политического диалога и проведения консультаций по расширению экономических связей, в частности в таких сферах как малый бизнес и частное предпринимательство, горная отрасль, машиностроение, текстильная промышленность, здравоохранение, наука, информационные технологии, сельское хозяйство.

Достижение конкурентоспособности и выход на мировые рынки производителей из Узбекистана может быть обеспечен за счет последовательного углубления структурных преобразований и диверсификации экономики, обеспечения опережающего развития новых высокотехнологичных производств, ускорения процессов модернизации и технического обновления действующих мощностей.

С этой целью в республике реализуется Программа «О приоритетах развития промышленности Узбекистана в 2011-2015 г.г.», которая предусматривает реализацию свыше 500 крупных инвестиционных проектов в промышленности общей стоимостью около 50 млрд. долл. США.

Ставится задача увеличить темпы роста объемов производства промышленной продукции не менее чем на 60%, увеличить долю отрасли в структуре валового внутреннего продукта в 2015 году до 28%. Опережающее развитие получат такие отрасли, как машиностроение и автомобилестроение, химическая, пищевая, фармацевтическая промышленность, промышленность строительных материалов и др. Важнейшим приоритетом для республики продолжает оставаться модернизация, техническое и технологическое перевооружение производства, ускоренное обновление ведущих отраслей экономики.

В соответствии с принятой Программой первоочередных мер по расширению объемов производства и освоению выпуска новых видов конкурентоспособной продукции предусматривается реализовать за 2012-2016 г.г. 270 инвестиционных проектов общей стоимостью 6,2 млрд. долл. США, а также отраслевых программ модернизации, технического и технологического перевооружения производства.

В Узбекистане для инвесторов создан во многом беспрецедентно благоприятный инвестиционный климат, система льгот и преференций. Убедительным свидетельством этого является рост от года к году иностранных инвестиций в экономику республики. За счет прямых иностранных инвестиций намечено реализовать свыше 70 инвестиционных проектов во многих отраслях экономики. Это, прежде всего, проекты по освоению месторождений Кандымской группы со строительством современного газоперерабатывающего завода, освоению месторождений Хаузак и Шады, проведению геолого-разведочных работ на перспективных месторождениях углеводородного сырья, строительству комплекса по производству аммиака и карбамида в Навоийской области, строительству цементного завода в Республике Каракалпакстан, организации производства готовых тканей и других швейных изделий в Ташкентской области, расширению системы коммуникаций, организации производства по выпуску готовых лекарственных препаратов.

Между Узбекистаном и Индией подписаны соглашения о торгово-экономическом сотрудничестве, защите и стимулировании инвестиций, избежании двойного налогообложения. В соответствии с Соглашением о торговом и экономическом сотрудничестве функционирует режим благоприятствования во взаимной торговле.

На сегодняшний день в Узбекистане аккредитованы представительства 18 индийских компаний и организаций, осуществляющие свою деятельность в разных сферах производства и реализации фармацевтической продукции. Число предприятий с участием индийского капитала, осуществляющих деятельность на территории Узбекистана, выросло до 62, из них 11 предприятий – со сто процентным индийским капиталом.

Активизации экономического сотрудничества послужил визит в Республику Индия Президента Республики Узбекистан И.А. Каримова в мае 2011 года, в ходе которого был подписан целый ряд документов, направленных на кардинальное расширение экономического и инвестиционного сотрудничества в газодобывающем комплексе, информационных технологиях, текстильной и фармацевтической промышленности, в банковской и торговой сферах. Так, предусматривается реализация более 30 проектов, в том числе направленных на совместный поиск, разведку и добычу углеводородного сырья с ведущей нефтегазовой компанией Индии «Ойл энд начурал гэз корпорэйшн»(ONGC), производство оптоволоконного кабеля в СИЭЗ «Навои», реализацию ряда проектов по производству субстанций и различных медицинских препаратов. С ведущими крупными текстильными компаниями подписаны документы по глубокой переработке хлопка, шелка и кожевенного сырья по производству и реализации готовых изделий.

Согласно Государственной инвестиционной программе Узбекистана, в 2007-2010 годах на 4 проекта привлечены инвестиции из Индии в размере 33,5 млн. долларов. В настоящее время реализуются 2 проекта с участием прямых инвестиций индийской компании «Spentex Industries» в текстильную отрасль Узбекистана на общую сумму 143,78 млн. долларов.

В сфере информационно-коммуникационных технологий

согласованы проекты по производству смарт-фонов, планшетных компьютеров и интернет-приставок, а также источников электропитания на основе солнечно-гибридных технологий. Для этих целей Национальным банком ВЭД Республики Узбекистан совместно с Экспортно-импортным банком Индии подписано соглашение о предоставлении кредитной линии на долгосрочных льготных условиях. Соответствующим соглашением оформлены крупные и долгосрочные поставки минеральных удобрений и других стратегических товаров. В целом общая стоимость экономического пакета, подписанного в ходе государственного визита Президента Республики Узбекистан, составляет более 2,2 млрд. долл. США.

По итогам 2012 года двусторонний товарооборот между Узбекистаном и Индией превысил 201 млн. долл. США, что превышает аналогичные показатели предыдущего периода.

Вместе с тем главным препятствием для активизации торгово-экономического сотрудничества Индии и государств Центральной Азии является крайняя недостаточность транспортных коммуникаций, обусловленная отсутствием общих границ. Именно поэтому для стран Центральной Азии особенно важна реализация проектов в транспортном секторе, поскольку данный регион благодаря благоприятному геополитическому расположению может стать связующим мостом между Европой и Восточной Азией. Это позволит не только увеличить доходы от роста объемов транзита через их территорию, но и органично интегрировать транспортный комплекс Центральной Азии в мировую транспортную систему. Несомненно, это приведет к снижению транспортной составляющей в стоимости продукции и услуг местных производителей и тем самым повысит их конкурентоспособность. Кроме того, реализация проектов в данной сфере позволит создать дополнительные рабочие места в системе транспорта и смежных с нею отраслях.

В настоящее время в Узбекистане реализуется Программа «Об ускорении развития инфраструктуры, транспортного и коммуникационного строительства в 2011-2015 годах» с общим объемом планируемых инвестиций 6935 млн. долл. США. Согласно договору между Индией с Узбекистаном, планируется строительство автодороги Заранж (Афганистан) – Чарбахар (Иран) с соответствующими подъездными путями из Индии и Узбекистана, что позволит сократить транзит на 1,5 тыс. км.

Современная геополитическая обстановка, важность проявления националистических и протекционистских тенденций в промышленно развитых странах, нарушение баланса интересов между странами-экспортерами и странами импортерами в рамках длительно действующих экономических блоков вызывают к жизни поиск новых возможностей регионального сотрудничества для обеспечения устойчивого развития и преодоления кризисных явлений мировой экономики.

Центральная Азия имеет огромные перспективы, которые без сомнения обретут реальные очертания и все вышеизложенное лишний раз убеждает в том, что жизнь несравненно богаче и сложнее любых теоретических исследований. Сумеем ли мы на древней земле Центральной Азии и Индии осознать свои истинные национальные интересы, выработать адекватную стратегию развития страны с мировой тенденцией экономического развития и его вызовов, преодолеть взаимное предубеждение? От этого в определенной мере зависит будущее Центральной Азии в XXI веке.

Notes and References

1. Strategicheskiy globalnyi prognoz 2030 / IMEMO RAN; pod redaktsiei A.A. Dynkina [Dynkin A.A. (ed.) Strategic Global Prognosis 2030 / IMEMO RAN] (Moscow: Magistr, 2011), p. 472.
2. India's International Trade. A Tech Segregated Perspective. India clocks US 69.7 billion IT exports during FY 2011–12.

31
Нефтегазовый комплекс Прикаспийского региона: проблемы межстранового экономического взаимодействия

Олег Егоров

Аннотация

В статье дан анализ современного состояния взаимодействия стран Прикаспийского региона в нефтегазовом комплексе. Рассмотрены направления транспортировки нефтегазовых ресурсов. Показана роль нефтяных компаний в реализации нефтегазовых проектов. Даны рекомендации относительно усиления межгосударственных связей в нефтегазовом комплексе Прикаспийского региона.

Ключевые слова: Прикаспийский регион, нефтегазовый комплекс, запасы углеводородных ресурсов, рациональное использование сырья, транспортировка нефти и газа.

В течение двадцати истекших лет Каспийский регион превратился в зону сосредоточения крупных запасов углеводородного сырья, что отразилось на перспективных планах развития нефтегазового комплекса пяти Прикаспийских государств. С другой стороны, это обстоятельство привлекло внимание крупнейших стран мира, чьи нефтяные корпорации проявили исключительно высокую активность в создании совместных предприятий и, тем самым, в инвестировании нефтегазовых проектов в Казахстане, Азербайджане и Туркменистане.

Каспийские нефтяные и газовые запасы, доставшиеся постсоветским республикам при территориальных разделах, распределились неравномерно между участниками этого процесса (таблица 1). При разделе Каспийского моря по национальным секторам согласно срединной линии самыми привлекательными для крупных иностранных инвесторов оказались Казахстан, Азербайджан и Туркменистан.

Временной период разработки нефтяных месторождений, залегающих на морских территориях, в мировой практике насчитывает ряд десятилетий. Достаточно отметить, что ведется она успешно американскими компаниями в Мексиканском заливе, на Аляске, в странах Южной Америки, Восточной Азии и Ближнего Востока.

Середина 70-х годов прошлого столетия стала периодом освоения крупнейшей нефтегазоносной зоны, расположенной в акватории Северного моря. Такие государства, как Великобритания, Норвегия, Дания стали обладателями достаточно крупных запасов нефти, что обусловило создание в этих странах многофункциональных нефтяных компаний, деятельность которых на текущий момент имеет тесную связь с нефтегазовой отраслью РК.

В контексте изложенного, необходимо иметь в виду и тот факт, что запасы нефтегазовых ресурсов в акватории Каспийского моря обнаружены многие десятки лет назад. Однако их извлечение сдерживалось недостаточной готовностью смежных производств к осуществлению необходимых операций на море. В этой связи начальный этап добычи и разработки нефтяных месторождений в этом регионе был приурочен к пятидесятым годам XX века, когда было введено в промышленную разработку первое месторождение углеводородов – Нефтяные Камни в Азербайджане.

С тех пор в шельфовой зоне Каспийского моря на территории всех пяти государств, расположенных вдоль его побережья, были обнаружены десятки структур, предположительно содержащих нефть и различающихся не только размерами прогнозируемых запасов, но также глубинами залегания продуктивных горизонтов, качеством содержащегося в них сырья.

Таблица 1: Ресурсы нефти и газа государств Каспийского региона, млрд. т условного топлива

Страны	Нефть			Газ		
	Доказанные запасы	Возможные ресурсы	Итого	Доказанные запасы	Возможные ресурсы	Итого
Азербайджан	0,7-2,0	5,4	6,1-7,0	0,4	1,3	1,7
Иран	0	2,4	2,4	0	0,4	0,4
Казахстан	2,0-3,2	17,0	19,0-20,0	2,0-3,1	3,3	5,3-6,4
Россия	0,04	1,0	1,0			
Туркменистан	0,3	6,4	6,7	3,7-5,8	5,9	9,6-11,7
Всего в странах Прикаспийского региона	3,0-5,7	32,0	35,2-37,9			
Всего в странах Прикаспийского региона (исключая Россию)	3,0-5,7	31,2	34,2	6,1-9,0	10,9	17,0-20,0

Современная ситуация, свойственная развитию нефтегазодобывающей промышленности во всех странах мира, свидетельствует о том, что период обнаружения и разработки легкодоступных месторождений завершился. Новые регионы сосредоточения крупных запасов углеводородного сырья характеризуются наличием продуктивных площадей либо в зонах, где залегающее сырье приходится извлекать с огромными финансовыми и материальными затратами, либо в шельфовой зоне некоторых морских территорий. Эта закономерность предопределяет всю сложность процессов обнаружения новых нефтегазовых месторождений и последующего их освоения как с позиции финансово-экономических, технико-технологических результатов, так и с точки зрения необходимости решения столь важной проблемы, какой является поддержание экологического равновесия, особенно в зоне такого столь уязвимого для интенсивного промышленного освоения, каким является Каспийское море.

В пределах его шельфа к настоящему времени уже начаты крупномасштабные работы поисково-геологического и эксплуатационного характера в российском, азербайджанском, туркменском и казахстанском секторах. В частности, в Азербайджане большие надежды возлагаются на структуры Азери, Шах-Дениз, Чираг, Гюнешли, в Казахстане перспективными в отношении нефтегазоносности считаются кроме Кашагана, такие структуры, как Актоты, Кайран, Каламкас, Тюб-Караган, Курмангазы, Жамбыл, Исатай, Абай и др.

Добыча нефти и газа остается одним из приоритетных и прибыльных направлений промышленности Казахстана. В настоящее время в Казахстане разведано более 200 месторождений углеводородов с общими извлекаемыми запасами около 2,8 млрд. тонн нефти и 1,7 трлн. $м^3$ газа. По прогнозам добыча сырой нефти Каспийского региона к 2015-2017 гг. достигнет 100 млн. т. Рост ее будет обусловлен, в первую очередь, разработкой месторождений Северного Каспия, в особенности одного из самых крупных нефтяных месторождений – Кашагана.

В настоящее время среди стран СНГ Казахстан является вторым после России производителем нефти, а из 90 стран мирового сообщества входит в первую тридцатку. По объему производства нефтегазовый комплекс Казахстана занимает заметное место среди других отраслей. Безусловно, и нефтяную промышленность затронул кризис, наблюдаемый во всей экономике, что проявилось, в частности, в снижении добычи нефти и газового конденсата. Из динамики, приведенной в таблице 2, видно, что с 2004 г. объемы добычи нефти, включая газовый конденсат, и природного газа существенно повысились, что было связано со структурной перестройкой экономики, дальнейшим развитием инвестиционных проектов в отрасли, внедрением новых технологий.

Разработанная в Казахстане «Государственная программа освоения казахстанского сектора Каспийского моря» представляет собой систему широкомасштабных проектов по вовлечению в промышленную разработку ряда перспективных месторождений углеводородного сырья. В соответствии с этой программой в том же году АО «Национальная компания «Казмунайгаз» учредила специализированное дочернее предприятие «АО «Морская нефтяная компания (МНК) «КазМунайТениз» для реализации нефтяных и газовых проектов в казахстанских секторах Каспийского и Аральского морей.

Основные функции вновь образованной компании состоят в разведке и оценке нефтегазоносности новых участков, разработке и вводе в стадию промышленной эксплуатации нефтяных и газовых месторождений, транспортировке и реализации углеводородных ресурсов.

Осуществляемая компанией разнохарактерная производственная деятельность концентрируется вокруг реализации следующих проектов:

1. Северо-Каспийский проект, включающий освоение месторождений Кашаган, Актоты, Кайран, Каламкас, Юго-Западный Кашаган, в котором доля АО «НК «Казмунайгаз» составляет 16,81%.
2. Два других проекта – освоение участков Тюб-Караган и Аташ находятся в стадии анализа и обобщения полученных геолого-геофизических данных. Их учредителями с 50-ти процентной долей участия являются АО «МНК КазмунайТениз» и «ЛукОйл Оверсиз Шельф Б.В.».

Таблица 2: Динамика добычи нефти, включая газовый конденсат, и природного газа в Казахстане

	2005 г.	2006 г.	2007 г.	2008 г.	2009 г.	2010 г.	2011 г.	2012 г.
Нефть и газовый конденсат, млн. т	61,5	65,0	67,0	72,0	76,5	79,5	80,5	79,2
Природный газ, млрд $м^3$	14,5	14,4	16,6	18,7	18,1	17.6	18,3	20,3
Примечание – Таблица составлена по данным НК «Казмунайгаз»								

3. Следующим перспективным проектом подготовки и последующего извлечения углеводородных ресурсов является месторождение Курмангазы, ориентировочные запасы которого могут составлять около 1 млрд т нефти. Участники этого проекта – АО «МНК КазмунайТениз» и ООО «РН-Казахстан», имеющие одинаковые 50-ти процентные доли участия, осуществляют в настоящее время комплекс геолого-разведочных работ, в том числе бурение ряда разведочных скважин.
4. Ряд других участков, считающихся перспективными в отношении содержания углеводородных ресурсов, таких, как Жамбыл, Абай, Исатай, находятся в стадии начального изучения путем проведения сейсморазведочных и гравиметрических работ.

Степень успешности выполнения столь внушительного объема работ, требующего освоения миллиардных инвестиций, использования новейших технических и технологических решений, создания разветвленной сети инфраструктурных объектов, зависит, прежде всего, от понимания той ответственности, которая возлагается на участников реализации проектов – иностранные и отечественные нефтяные компании, и, в этой связи, с выполнением всех необходимых работ в определенные документом сроки. Если говорить об ожидаемом результате в целом, то свести его надо не только к тем десяткам миллионов тонн извлекаемой на месторождениях шельфа Каспийского моря нефти и миллиардам кубических метров газа, но и к кардинальному решению проблемы сохранения окружающей среды, особенно уникального бассейна Каспийского моря.

Однако, несмотря на то, что реализация государственной программы уже продвигается в необходимом направлении, все же нельзя не отметить, что она сталкивается с рядом проблем, затрудняющих выполнение запланированных задач в установленные сроки. В этой связи следует, прежде всего, проанализировать ситуацию, сложившуюся на протяжении нескольких последних лет вокруг комплекса работ, относящихся к вводу в разработку месторождения Кашаган.

Неоднократное перенесение сроков начала его разработки

уже само по себе означает необходимость проведения кардинальной корректировки программы по всем ее разделам, так как прогнозируемое начало извлечения нефти, переносимое ориентировочно на 2012-2013 гг., соответственно влечет за собой изменение сроков и объемов поставки углеводородного сырья на экспорт, на переработку, на удовлетворение нужд социально-бытовой сферы.

При реализации программ столь крупного масштаба, требующих многомиллиардных вложений в строительство новых предприятий, оснащенных зачастую дорогостоящим оборудованием, в сооружение коммуникаций, создание необходимого задела в социально-бытовом секторе экономики, первостепенное значение должно иметь решение вопросов строгой и надежной координации, стыковки работ всех заинтересованных учреждений - министерств и ведомств, научно-исследовательских и проектных институтов, местных органов власти, в основу которой положен принцип достижения максимальных экономических результатов. Иными словами, должны быть реализованы главные элементы системного подхода при решении комплекса задач межотраслевого значения.

Наиболее результативным путем в этом отношении, способным обеспечить воплощение в реальных условиях принципов повышения экономической эффективности производства за счет решения таких задач, как оптимизация мощностей создаваемых предприятий, обоснования перечня необходимых для развития производительных сил производств, направления и способы использования сырьевых ресурсов и т.д., является стыковка интересов различных отраслей экономики на ранней стадии разработки проектных решений.

На фоне заметного проникновения крупных мировых нефтяных компаний в реализацию проектов освоения нефтегазовых месторождений Прикаспийского региона, происшедшего в 90-е годы XX века, в наши дни исключительную активность в этом направлении стали проявлять китайские нефтяные компании (таблица 3).

Аналогичная ситуация прослеживается и в нефтегазовом секторе Туркменистана. Финансовые институты Китая вместе с нефтяными компаниями проводят активную работу по вхождению в его нефтегазовую сферу. В конечном счете, область их интересов лежит в получении возможностей использовать туркменский газ в своих собственных интересах. И здесь они достаточно грамотно заняли свою нишу. Китайские компании, например, предложили Туркменистану целевой кредит на 3 млрд долларов для освоения газового месторождения Южный Илатань и сразу же приступили к строительству газопровода в КНР через территорию Казахстана, по которому будет подаваться от 30 до 40 млрд кубометров природного газа. Одновременно с реализацией этого проекта в Туркменистане был запущен еще один газопровод Давлетабад – Хангеран (Иран), что позволит увеличить поставки в эту страну природного газа с 8 до 14 млрд кубометров в год с последующим ростом до 20 млрд кубометров.

При всех тех положительных результатах, которые уже сегодня просматриваются в связи с освоением запасов нефти и газа в Прикаспийском регионе, все же одна проблема требует своего решения, а именно: как эти ресурсы эффективно использовать, как их доставить на мировые рынки? Вариантов решения этой проблемы обсуждалось много, вплоть до прокладки трубопроводов по дну Каспийского моря или создания технологий и оборудования для сжижения газа.

Однако, сегодня достаточно устойчиво работают только нефтепровод Баку - Тбилиси – Джейхан, принимающий нефть с азербайджанских месторождений, газопровод Туркмения – Казахстан – Западный Китай, нефтепроводы Атырау – Новороссийск, источником сырьевых ресурсов для которых служит нефть Тенгизского месторождения и конденсат Карачаганакского месторождения, и Узень – Самара, по которому прокачивается нефть месторождений Мангистау.

Туркменистан, обладающий крупными ресурсами природного газа, заинтересован реализовать их на мировых рынках на выгодных для себя условиях. Именно по этой причине он, не дожидаясь решения всех спорных вопросов относительно статуса Каспийского моря, активно принимает предложения иностранных компаний о строительстве с их помощью – финансовой и технической – газопроводов в различных направлениях.

Отмечая установившийся повышенный интерес в мире к газовым ресурсам, следует признать, что Прикаспийские государства сегодня относятся к зоне особого внимания, которое проявляют многие мировые нефтегазовые компании. Одной из таких зон является

Таблица 3: Участники реализации важнейших нефтегазовых проектов в Казахстане

ПРОЕКТЫ	ДОЛЯ СТРАН В ПРОЕКТАХ			
	США	КАЗАХСТАН	КИТАЙ	РОССИЯ
КАСПИЙСКИЙ ТРУБОПРОВОДНЫЙ КОНСОРЦИУМ	15%	19%	-	31%
Нефтепровод «ЗАПАДНЫЙ КАЗАХСТАН – КИТАЙ»	-	50%	50%	-
Газопровод «КАЗАХСТАН – КИТАЙ»	-	50%	50%	-
Разработка ТЕНГИЗСКОГО месторождения	50%	20%	-	5,0%
Разработка КАРАЧАГАНАКСКОГО месторождения	18,0%	10%	-	13,5%
Разработка месторождений «МАНГИСТАУМУНАЙГ АЗ»	-	50%	50%	-
Разработка месторождения КУМКОЛЬ	-	33%	67%	-
ШЫМКЕНТСКИЙ НЕФТЕПЕРЕРАБАТЫВА ЮЩИЙ ЗАВОД	-	50%	50%	-
Освоение ресурсов месторождения КАШАГАН	25,3%	16,81%	-	-

Туркменистан, ажиотаж вокруг его газового потенциала наблюдается в течение многих последних лет. Вполне возможно, что он поддерживается той информацией об объемах перспективных запасов, которая время от времени озвучивается на официальных мероприятиях и средствах массовой информации. Согласно этим данным оценочные запасы природного газа Туркменистана варьируют в пределах 4,5-14,0 трлн $м^3$. О чем может свидетельствовать столь значительная разница?

Объяснение этому может быть двояким. Во-первых, благодаря большим ресурсам возрастает политический вес государства на мировой арене, появляется реальная возможность устанавливать свои правила игры на газовом рынке.

Во-вторых, наличие столь впечатляющих объемов сырья может инициировать приток прямых иностранных инвестиций, за счет которых будет развиваться не только газовая отрасль, но и создаваться производства в иных секторах экономики, в производственной и социальной инфраструктуре.

На текущий момент в Туркменистане добывается около 80 млрд $м^3$ природного газа в год. Как же распределяются эти ресурсы? Согласно подписанным соглашениям в 2010 г. в Россию будет направлено 30 млрд $м^3$, 14 млрд $м^3$ – непосрсдственно в европейские страны, минуя Россию, определенный объем (возможно до 8-10 млрд $м^3$) будет направлен в китайский газопровод и 8,0 млрд $м^3$ газа транспортируется в Иран. Оставшаяся часть добываемых ресурсов, по-видимому, будет использована для собственных нужд. Как следует из этих количественных величин свободных объемов газа для участия Туркменистана в иных проектах, например в подаче углеводородного ресурса в лоббировании западными странами и США газопровод «Nabucco», практически нет.

Отмеченная нами ситуация, сложившаяся вокруг проблемы диверсификации использования газовых ресурсов в экспортоориентированных направлениях, позволяет сделать главный вывод – эффективность работы газопроводов имеет непосредственную зависимость от того, насколько обоснованно определен ресурсный потенциал на средне- и долгосрочный периоды, какой объем реально может извлекаться в течение всего периода, на который заключаются контракты.

Как следует из анализа предлагаемых сегодня проектных решений, направленных на увеличение экспортного потенциала Прикаспийских государств, предстоит достаточно сложный процесс выбора наиболее приемлемых направлений развития нефтепроводного транспорта. Сложность же заключается, прежде всего, в том, что кроме чистых экономических, коммерческих и конъюнктурных факторов следует принимать в расчет и факторы политического характера, деловых и торговых взаимоотношений с рядом государств, которые в определенной степени инвестируют многие производства и иные сферы деятельности республики.

Столь широкий спектр возможных направлений реализации нефти на внешнем рынке свидетельствует о том, что, несмотря на некоторую неопределенность относительно объемов углеводородов, которые будут извлекаться и экспортироваться в среднесрочной перспективе, оценка экономических, экологических, политических позиций должна быть осуществлена заблаговременно.

Национальная компания «Казмунайгаз» ведет работу по созданию Казахстанской Каспийской Системы Транспортировки (ККСТ), предназначенной для экспорта возрастающих объемов казахстанской нефти, которые будут добываться, в первую очередь, на месторождениях Кашаган и Тенгиз, через Каспийское море на международные рынки посредством системы Баку – Тбилиси – Джейхан и/или других нефтетранспортных систем, расположенных на территории Азербайджана.

В рамках ККСТ для обеспечения транспортировки казахстанской нефти на международные рынки планируется строительство нефтепровода Ескене - Курык и создание Транскаспийской системы, которая будет состоять из терминалов на казахстанском побережье Каспийского моря, танкеров и судов, терминалов на Азербайджанском побережье и соединительных сооружений до системы Баку – Тбилиси – Джейхан. Предполагается, что ККСТ обеспечит на начальном этапе транспортировку нефти в объеме 20млн. тонн в год с последующим увеличением до 35-56 млн. тонн в год.

Подключение Казахстана к действующему нефтепроводу Баку – Тбилиси – Джейхан будет осуществлено после ввода в разработку морских месторождений и, прежде всего, Кашагана. Известно, что на текущий момент сеть существующих нефтепроводов в стране не способна обеспечить планируемый объем транспортировки нефти северной части Каспийского моря при полном освоении месторождении Кашаган и Тенгиз. В этой связи сейчас разрабатывается проект строительства экспортного магистрального нефтепровода Ескене (Атырауская область) – Курык (Мангистауская область), который явится одним из главных звеньев созданной Казахстанской каспийской системы транспортировки (ККСТ).

В рамках реализации проекта ККСТ предусматривается создание специального танкерного флота и двух специализированных терминалов в Казахстане и Азербайджане, способных переваливать существенные объемы нефти – 60 и более миллионов тонн в год. Нефтепровод до нового порта и вся необходимая инфраструктура в портах Курык и Баку будет сооружаться на паритетных условиях – по 50% вложений придется на национальные нефтегазовые компании Казахстана и Азербайджана.

Следует учесть то обстоятельство, что трасса нефтепровода проложена через многочисленные горные участки, подверженные тектоническим воздействиям. Это обстоятельство увеличивает степень риска и предполагает в целях сохранности трассы и устойчивой работы ее объектов ввести в проект множество дополнительных технических решений, способных обезопасить как само сооружение, так и территорию, по которой оно будет проходить, от возможных осложнений в будущем.

Следует подчеркнуть, что Азербайджан, обладающий значительным потенциалом нефтегазоперерабатывающих производств, ресурсами нефти и газа на суше и на морских месторождениях, сегодня снабжает нефтепровод Баку – Тбилиси – Джейхан ресурсами только своих месторождений, так как несколько лет назад он отказался от поставок нефти из Казахстана. Вполне понятно, что с вводом в промышленную разработку шельфовых месторождений в Казахстане появятся некоторые излишки жидких углеводородов, которые необходимо будет реализовать. Одним из путей этого процесса может стать соглашение об экспорте казахстанской нефти в Иран, подписанное в августе 1996 года.

Согласно условиям этой сделки Казахстан ежегодно должен был доставлять в каспийские порты Ирана 2 млн. тонн нефти для переработки на заводах Тегерана и Тебриза. Иран, в свою очередь, должен быть отправлять аналогичное количество нефти казахстанским потребителям через свои порты в Персидском заливе по схеме замещения SWAP. Не исключено, что Иран в ближайшее время возобновит такой обмен и расширит объемы поставок казахстанской нефти до 5,5 млн. тонн в год. Для поставки нефти в Иран могут быть использованы казахстанские порты Актау, Курык и Атырау после его реконструкции.

Общее заключение о сотрудничестве стран Прикаспийского региона в нефтегазовом комплексе может быть следующим. На текущий момент их взаимодействие отчетливо просматривается только в реализации проектов по строительству нефте- и газопроводов. В реализации проектов, связанных с разработкой нефтегазовых месторождений, участвуют в основном европейские, американские и китайские компании. В области нефтепереработки и нефтехимии Азербайджан и Туркмения сотрудничают с западными корпорациями, Казахстан в этом направлении имеет связи с Россией, в частности имеет место тесное взаимодействие с Оренбургским ГПЗ, Омским и Орским НПЗ.

Думается, что в преддверии начала широкомасштабного освоения нефтегазовых ресурсов шельфа Каспийского моря в целях тесного взаимодействия при решении технологических, экономических и экологических проблем Прикаспийские государства должны найти те точки соприкосновения, которые будут способствовать достижению для каждого из них наибольшего экономического эффекта при использовании углеводородных ресурсов. Реализация этого направления развития вполне возможна в рамках разработки единой программы развития нефтегазового комплекса Прикаспийского региона.

32
Эволюция роли Индии во внешней политике Казахстана

Куралай Байзакова

Введение

В многовекторной внешней политике Республики Казахстан Индия занимает важное место. Индия одной из первых объявила о признании независимости Республики Казахстан. Она же оказала поддержку нашей стране, когда встал вопрос о приеме ее в ООН. Ее бескорыстие и желание помочь Казахстану ощущалось во всем. И это не случайное явление. Дело не только в том, что Индия издавна выступает глашатаем свободы народов и мирного сотрудничества со всеми странами. Корни наших связей и дружбы лежат в далеких прошлых веках. Еще до нашей эры и в первые века нашей эры жители Центральной Азии и Индии наладили торговые и духовные отношения.

Роль Индии в мировом сообществе

Интерес Казахстана к Индии определяется местом и ролью этой страны в современном мире. Индия всегда играла конструктивную роль на международной арене. Современная Индия входит в число восходящих и наиболее динамично развивающихся стран мира, являясь одним из главных глобальных центров влияния. Индия позиционирует себя как глобальный игрок.

В настоящее время Республика Индия продолжает уделять особое внимание дальнейшему повышению своей роли в Южной Азии, при этом учитываются как проблемы национальной безопасности, так и необходимость усиления позиций в регионе в целях обеспечения адекватного своему политическому весу места в мировом сообществе.

Политика неприсоединения и мирного сосуществования снискала Индии высокий моральный авторитет в мире в XX веке и вписывается в новую философию международных отношений в XXI в. В нашей стране высоко оценивают внешнеполитическую стратегию Индии, в основе которой лежат идеи Дж. Неру о ненасилии стран в отношении друг друга и необходимости сотрудничества со всеми государствами мира[1].

Большинство индийских политиков придерживаются взглядов, заложенных в свое время отцом нации Махатмой Ганди, чья деятельность представляет собой воплощение идеи гуманизма как универсального принципа единения человека и окружающего мира. Выдвинутый им метод неразрушительного, творческого разрешения конфликтов, суть которого заключается не в уничтожении противника, а в ликвидации конфликтной ситуации, очень многое значит для всего мира.

Обеспечение мира, национальной безопасности, защита суверенитета и территориальной целостности были и остаются основными задачами современной Индии. Обеспечение этих задач требует участия широкого круга взаимодействующих с Индией государств.

Наша страна приветствует складывающееся военно-политическое единство между Китаем, Индией и Россией. Важно, что оно не будет направлено против кого-либо и не имеет злых умыслов в отношении окружающего мира. Только такая политика обладает перспективой в современном мире, который меняется на глазах. И в этом изменяющемся мире есть добрый росток мира и безопасности, который выращивается совместными усилиями Казахстана и Индии.

Нет сомнений, что «эта держава имеет свои геополитические интересы в регионе, которые детерминированы рядом факторов. К ним относятся следующие: партнерство с Россией; китайское присутствие в Центральной Азии; сближение Индии с Западом и США; соперничество с Пакистаном; угроза распространения воинствующего исламизма; транспортно-энергетические и торгово-экономические интересы Дели в Центральной Азии и соседних регионах»[2].

Индия проявляет интерес к Казахстану и к Центральной Азии в целом в рамках программы «Новый Шелковый путь индийской внешней политики», направленной на проникновение и дальнейшее закрепление в нашем регионе, богатом стратегическим сырьем и занимающем выгодное геополитическое положение.

Основные этапы сотрудничества.

Как отмечал Чрезвычайный и Полномочный Посол Казахстана в Индии Д. Куанышев, «за прошедшие 20 лет казахстанско-индийское сотрудничество развивается динамично по всем направлениям политической, экономической и культурной жизни»[3]. Динамичное развитие двустороннего равноправного партнерства, основанного на взаимоуважении и взаимопонимании, свидетельствует о единых подходах, взглядах и позициях двух стран в различных сферах взаимодействия.

Очень важно, что начиная с 1992 г., с момента подписания Декларации о принципах взаимоотношений между Казахстаном и Индией[4], между двумя странами нет принципиальных разногласий по основным проблемам международных отношений.

Если условно выделить основные периоды нашего сотрудничества, то к первому этапу относятся 90-е годы, когда была создана правовая база нашего сотрудничества.

Следующий этап сотрудничества характеризуется всплеском геополитических интересов Индии в Центральной и Азии приходится на период 2002-2003 гг. после проведения антитеррористической операции в Афганистане и изменения всей геополитической ситуации в регионе. Интересы Индии можно разделить на две группы: собственно геополитические, которые включают в себя соперничество с Китаем и Индией, партнерство с Россией; и экономические, которые включают в себя в первую очередь энергетические интересы, а также торгово-экономические[5].

В 2009 г. Казахстан и Индия вступили в новый третий этап двусторонних отношений с подписанием Соглашения о стратегическом партнерстве между двумя странами[6] в ходе визита Президента РК Н.Назарбаева в Индию, и который продолжается по настоящее время.

В этот этап следует отметить, что отношения между Казахстаном и Индией наполнялись конкретным содержанием по линии межгосударственных политических, экономических, научно-технических и культурных связей.

Так, в ходе визит премьер-министра Индии Манмохана Сингха в Казахстан в 2011 г. была подписана "Дорожная карта" по развитию стратегического партнерства[7]. Этот визит придал новый импульс развитию двустороннего сотрудничества - был принят план развития на 2011-2014 гг. по укреплению стратегического партнерства между Индией и Казахстаном, подписаны семь соглашений в различных сферах, таких, как энергетика, кибернетическая безопасность, исследование космического пространства, образование, высокотехнологическое развитие, а также и другие направления.

Далее можно назвать визит министра иностранных дел РК Е. Идрисова в Республику Индия 3-5 марта 2013, в ходе которого стороны подтвердили заинтересованность в укреплении конструктивного диалога по вопросам региональной и глобальной безопасности, реабилитации Афганистана и взаимодействия в многостороннем формате, включая сотрудничество в рамках ООН, СВМДА и ШОС.

В ходе визитов проходит обмен мнениями по актуальным вопросам международной повестки дня, состоянию и перспективам двустороннего взаимодействия. Возросшая интенсивность и содержание официальных визитов свидетельствуют о динамичном развитии двустороннего сотрудничества.

Основные направления сотрудничества

Приоритетными направлениями взаимодействия Казахстана и Индии между собой являются торгово-экономическое сотрудничество, устойчивое социально-экономическое развитие, стабильность политической обстановки и укрепление безопасности в регионе.

В политической составляющей отношений между Казахстаном и Индией каких-либо трений, противоречий не имеется. Между странами проводились регулярные встречи на межправительственном и межгосударственном уровнях.

Необходимо отметить успешное развитие межпарламентских связей наших стран. Так, в октябре 2011 года была создана индийская Парламентская группа дружбы с Казахстаном.

Культурные связи у двух стран развиваются не в пример более активно, нежели экономические - здесь и обмен делегациями музыкантов и актеров, увлечение йогой, визиты интересных людей. Так, в мае 2011 года в Нью-Дели с успехом прошли Дни культуры Казахстана в Индии. Регулярно происходят научно-академические контакты между аналитическими кругами наших стран. Успешно развивается и туризм. С 2005 года ежегодно проводится казахстанско-индийская туристическая ярмарка.

Связи Казахстана и Индии основываются не только на культурно-историческом и политическом аспектах, но и на экономическом. Казахстан является самым крупным торговым партнером Индии в Центральной Азии.

В сфере экономического сотрудничества необходимо учитывать то обстоятельство, что стремительно растущая экономика Индии требует все больше энергоресурсов. В этой связи понятны попытки Индии войти и закрепиться в нефтедобывающем секторе казахстанской экономики. Производство и потребление энергоносителей — одно из главных направлений экономического сотрудничества Казахстана и Индии.

«Точки соприкосновения» между Казахстаном и Индией не ограничиваются сотрудничеством в финансово-экономической, топливно-энергетической и транспортной сферах.

Для Индии важно удовлетворение потребностей своей атомной индустрии. РК и Индия подписали пакт «О сотрудничестве в рамках мирного использования атомной энергии»[8]. Соглашения о поставках в Индию более 2 тыс. тонн казахстанского урана к 2014 году, возможно, будет недостаточно. Лидеры двух стран также обсудили вопрос о совместном строительстве ядерных реакторов, что является приоритетной задачей для Казахстана, стремящегося стать главным мировым поставщиком ядерного топлива и реакторов, поскольку он добивается ядерного сотрудничества с Россией,

Японией, Китаем и Индией.

Планы Индии и Казахстана по сотрудничеству в космическом пространстве также являются весьма значительными. Лидеры стран договорились об активизации сотрудничества в этой области. Казахстан не имеет технологической компетенции и ресурсов для развития своей космической промышленности. Космическая программа Индии достаточно сильна и может предоставить Казахстану необходимые знания и технологии. Недавно Индия стала одним из перспективных мировых лидеров в области космической индустрии, где заметно лидируют три державы: США, Россия и Китай.

Казахстану очень нужны технологические ноу-хау для создания инновационной экономики. Странами подписан меморандум о взаимопонимании между индийскими и казахстанскими группами быстрого реагирования на нарушение компьютерной безопасности для сотрудничества в области кибернетической безопасности[9].

Казахстан придает приоритетное значение активизации сотрудничества наших сторон в сфере обороны и безопасности. С 1995 г. оба государства поддерживают отношения в военной области. В 2002 подписан Меморандум о военно-техническом сотрудничестве между Правительствами двух стран[10]. С 2011 г. подписываются ежегодные Планы сотрудничества между министерствами обороны Казахстана и Индии, которые позволяют вывести оборонное сотрудничество между странами на более высокий и системный уровень.

Как в свое время отмечал заместитель министра иностранных дел Индии Н.Рави, «Казахстан и Индия как страны с многонациональными и многоконфессиональными обществами объединяют общие ценности и их позиции по актуальным международным вопросам, включая обеспечение региональной безопасности»[11]. Обе стороны активно выступают против международного терроризма, наркобизнеса, против агрессивного фундаментализма.

Казахстан активно сотрудничает с Индией в рамках многосторонних форумов, международных и региональных организаций, в том числе ООН, СВМДА, ШОС. Мы придерживаемся единых взглядов на глобальные и региональные процессы, сотрудничаем в важных сферах многосторонней дипломатии. Стоит отметить, что Индия оказала сильную поддержку СВМДА с того момента, как данная инициатива была озвучена Президентом Назарбаевым в октябре 1992 г.

Индия также поддерживает инициативу Казахстана в проведении форума мировых и традиционных религий в Астане, активно принимая участие в мероприятиях форума. Во всех двусторонних или многосторонних встречах и переговорах Казахстан поддерживает стремление Индии стать постоянным членом Совета Безопасности ООН.

Факторы, сдерживающие двустороннее сотрудничество.

Отношения Казахстана и Индии при всем их внешнем благополучии, развиваются сдержанно.

Если уровень сотрудничества с соседними Россией и Китаем у нашей страны уже достаточно высок, то с Индией — четвертой экономикой в мире и второй по численности населения страной — пока далеко не такой, как хотелось бы. Но возможность изменить ситуацию имеется.

По мнению казахстанских экспертов, есть ряд факторов осложняющих развитие казахстанско-индийских отношений. Это объективные и субъективные причины, главной из которых является транспортно-коммуникационная, поскольку Индия не граничит ни с Казахстаном, ни с какой-либо другой страной региона[12].

Другим фактором является определенный вакуум информации о состоянии и наиболее актуальных тенденциях развитии наших государств в экспертном и общественном сознании двух стран[13].

Индию всё еще считают «опоздавшим пришельцем» в Центральную Азию. Многовекторная внешняя политика Казахстана может поспособствовать дальнейшему «пробуждению» Индии в этом регионе. Прежде всего, надо учитывать важность усиления азиатского вектора во внешней политике Казахстана в целом и в отношении Индии в частности.

Перспективы развития двусторонних отношений

Какие ожидания могут иметь страны Центральной Азии, такие, как Казахстан, в отношении дальнейшего развития отношений с Индией. В качестве рекомендаций можно отметить следующее.

На наш взгляд дальнейшее развитие сотрудничества надо развивать исходя их уровнево-секторального подхода. А именно, существующие механизмы сотрудничества – мосты, рабочие группы, диалоги – надо диверсифицировать по уровням.

Необходимо шире демонстрировать имидж Индии, как динамично развивающейся страны. В общественном сознании стран Центральной Азии сохранилось оставшееся от советского периода представление об Индии как стране с богатой культурными традициями, кинофильмами, развитой текстильной промышленностью. Отсюда возможно и слабо развивается сотрудничество на уровне малого и среднего бизнеса.

Казахстан заинтересован в привлечении индийских компаний и в индустриальный сектор РК, в создании в нашей стране сети фармкомбинатов.

Сотрудничество в сфере кибернетической безопасности станет важным аспектом сотрудничества в ближайшем будущем. Поэтому необходимо дальнейшее расширение сотрудничества в области информационных технологий, а именно в области кибербезопасности и в подготовке грамотного персонала.

Сотрудничество в сфере образования имеет большой потенциал и надо развивать конкретные образовательные программы по специальностям, в которых нуждается Казахстан.

Научное сотрудничество академических сообществ, несмотря на значительные успехи, носит «точечный характер», следует начинать долгосрочные комплексные исследования, для выработки среднесрочных прогнозов.

В сфере развития туризма, следует изучить богатый опыт Индии по развитию внутреннего туризма.

Для развития сотрудничества в области борьбы с

терроризмом и наркотрафиком необходимо дальнейшее расширения взаимодействия в рамках многосторонних структур и изучение богатого опыта Индии;

Заключение.

В последнее время Индия проявляет интерес к Казахстану и к Центральной Азии в целом в рамках программы «Новый Шелковый путь». Потенциал Индии для расширения своего экономического, военно-стратегического и геополитического присутствия в Центральной Азии и в том числе в Казахстане существует. Как он будет реализован, зависит от ряда факторов, в том числе от объективных геополитических факторов, реализации ряда крупных коммуникационных и энергетических проектов.

Индия не имеет достаточного экономического и военного присутствия в Центральной Азии, и отчасти полагается на свои технологические способности. Недавние двусторонние сделки и активизация сотрудничества с Казахстаном в области технологий, энергоресурсов, космоса обеспечивают Индии платформу для расширения своего стратегического присутствия, и способствуют её цели стать одной из ведущих державой в меняющемся геополитическом и экономическом ландшафте Центральной Азии.

Совпадение интересов двух стран в области безопасности, общие цели по сохранению стабильности, а также схожесть взглядов на первопричины возникновения угроз миру являются важнейшими стимулами для развития казахстанско-индийских отношений[14].

Индия, как набирающий вес глобальный игрок, уже становится той силой, которую необходимо учитывать в будущем. Казахстан, в свою очередь, будучи доминантным игроком в Центральной Азии, оказывает на конфигурацию баланса сил в регионе серьезное влияние[15].

Цитируемая литература

1. См. Султанов Б. Казахстанско-Индийские отношения: состояние и перспективы // Индия – Казахстан: перспективы стратегического

партнерства. Материалы международного семинара. – Алматы, 2011. – С.46

2. Казанцев А.А. «Большая игра» с неизвестными правилами: мировая политика и Центральная Азия. – М.: Наследие Евразии, 2008. – С. 236
3. Проверенное временем казахстанско-индийское сотрудничество на днях празднует свое 20-летие // Сайт газеты «Литер»
4. Декларация о принципах взаимоотношений между Казахстаном и Индией, 1992 // http://online.zakon.kz/Document
5. См. Лаумулин М.Т. Центральная Азия в зарубежной политологии и мировой геополитике. Том V: Центральная Азия в XXI столетии – Алма-Ата: КИСИ, 2009. – С.131
6. Соглашения о стратегическом партнерстве, 2009 // http://online.zakon.kz/Document
7. Астана и Дели приняли «Дорожную карту» стратегического партнерства // http://thenews.kz/2011/04/19/795269.html
8. См. Индия и Казахстан усиливают стратегическое партнерство// http://www.centrasia.ru/newsA
9. Меморандум о взаимопонимании между индийскими и казахстанскими группами быстрого реагирования на нарушение компьютерной безопасности // http://www.centrasia.ru/news
10. Меморандум о военно-техническом сотрудничестве между Правительствами двух стран, 2002 // http://www.mfa.kz/ru/#!/foreign-policy/dogovorno-pravovaya_baza/dvustoronnie_mejdunarodnyie_dogovoryi-respubliki_kazahstan/indiya/
11. 15 лет сотрудничества // www.kazpravda.kz
12. См. Султанов Б. Казахстанско-Индийские отношения: состояние и перспективы // Индия – Казахстан: перспективы стратегического партнерства. Материалы международного семинара. – Алматы, 2011. – С.53
13. Каукенов А. Казахстан и Индия: новый этап экономического сотрудничества // www. easttime.ru
14. См. Индия – Казахстан: перспективы стратегического партнерства. Материалы международного семинара. – Алматы, 2011. – С.11
15. Там же, С.19

33
Сравнительная оценка уровня конкурентоспособности туристской сферы Казахстана и Индии

Галымжан Дуйсен

Индия – огромный субконтинент, расположенный в Южной Азии, где проживает более 1,2 млрд. человек. Она считается самой многонациональной страной мира. По физико-географическим признакам Индию можно разделить на три природных района: Гималаи, Индо-Гангская низменность и Деканское плоскогорье. В экономическом отношении Индию можно охарактеризовать как «ключевую развивающуюся страну», которая по макроэкономическим показателям сопоставима с крупными державами (размер номинального ВВП в 2012 год составил 1947,0 млрд. долл.)1. В аграрно-индустриальной экономике страны сочетается развитие базовых отраслей промышленности с многоукладным сельским хозяйством. Широкое распространение получила текстильная промышленность. Недра страны богаты разнообразными полезными ископаемыми (уголь, железные руды, алмазы, марганец и др.).

С точки зрения туризма наибольший интерес в Индии представляют крупнейшие города страны: Дели - столица Индии, Мумбаи, Калькутта, Ченнаи, бывший португальский анклав, а ныне 25-й штат Индии - Гоа; национальные парки Корбет, Сариска, знаменитый мавзолей Тадж-Махал. Калькутта - родина всемирно известного индийского писателя Рабиндраната Тагора. Здесь же находится «Дом Тагора». Самые популярные индийские курорты расположены на западном побережье Индии, в штате Гоа. Этот район считается наиболее развитым в туристическом плане и очень популярен среди европейцев. Здесь больше всего предпочитают комфортный, спокойный пляжный отдых с обедами в гостиничных ресторанах.

Известностью пользуется штат Керала - самый южный штат западного побережья и один из самых развитых штатов Индии. Классической поездкой в Индию считается тур по «Золотому треугольнику» с посещением всемирно известного Тадж-Махала – памятника индийской архитектуры, пятикупольного сооружения из белого мрамора с мозаикой из цветных камней, а также древнего города-призрака Фатихпур-Сикри и экзотического розового города Раджастхан. Индия является также центром религиозного паломничества. Основные центры общин индуистов находятся на территории этой страны. Индия привлекает экотуристов, мечтающих покорить горные вершины.

Республика Казахстан как страна с обширной территорией обладает большим разнообразием природных ресурсов. Наиболее неосвоенными являются рекреационные ресурсы, которые в свою очередь создают предпосылки для развития и культивирования многих видов туризма. В Казахстане расположены такие известные горные вершины, как пики: Хан-Танири (6995 м), Талгар (4973 м), Музтау (4506 м); уникальные озера: Каспийское море (северо-западная часть), Арал, Балхаш, Алаколь, Маркаколь, Тениз, Коргалжын, Бурабай, Кольсай; пустыни: Бетпакдала, Кызылкум, Сары-Есик-Атырау; примечательные памятники природы: Шарынский каньон, Тургенские водопады, Шалдайский ленточный бор, Поющий бархан, Шынтургенские ельники, Баянауылские, Каркаралинские, Ерейментауские, Кокшетауские, Мугалжарские, Улытауские горы и возвышенности, мавзолеи «Кожа Ахмета Яссауи», «Арыстанбаба», «Жошы хана», древние городища Отырар, Сауран, Тараз, курганы Есик, Берель и др.

На территории республики действуют 77 курортно-рекреационных зон, около 904 туристских маршрутов, в том числе конных – 27, приключенческих – 59, оздоровительных – 153, связанных с охотой и рыбалкой – 65, спортивных путешествий и маршрутов выходного дня – 344, экологических – 58, культурно-познавательных – 111, по маршрутам Шелкового пути – 67 и 20 паломнических туров[2].

Рекреационное значение страны обусловливается наличием запасов лечебных грязей, богатством минеральных и термальных источников, экологически чистыми и уникальными ландшафтами. Все это представляет собой благоприятные условия для многоцелевого использования туристско-рекреационных ресурсов.

Сравнивать Казахстан и Индию в географическом и экономическом плане является не совсем корректным в связи со многими различиями. Вместе с тем проведение общей оценки места двух стран в международном туризме и уровня конкурентоспособности туризма, характеристики деятельности туристско-рекреационных предприятий, использовании рекреационных ресурсов, представляется интересным. Это в свою очередь требует комплексное исследование всех факторов, индикаторов, определяющих развитие рекреационной сферы. Имеющийся набор базовой части показателей целесообразно дополнить как экономическими, социальными, так и экологическими, культурными и другими индикаторами, что позволит системно и более достоверно определять вклад рекреации и туризма в экономическое развитие рассматриваемых стран.

В настоящее время статистика туризма в Казахстане находится в стадии формирования, отдельные показатели не могут полностью отразить действительную картину сферы туризма и рекреации.

Согласно статистическому сборнику Агентства Республики Казахстан по статистике «Туризм Казахстана 2008-2012. – Астана, 2013 в Казахстане выделяются 59 основных индикаторов, характеризующих деятельность в области туризма, рекреации, особо охраняемых территорий, культуры, предпринимательства. Однако в странах с развитым туризмом таких показателей гораздо больше, и они охватывают все уровни рекреационной деятельности и совершенствуются по мере вовлечения новых форм и видов туризма.

Статистические исследования туризма должны основываться на достоверных источниках информации, получаемых специальным анкетным путем, а также с привлечением методов социологического анализа.

С экономической точки зрения, рекреационная сфера представляет собой феномен проявления потребительского спроса по месту временного пребывания человека. Объем и структура этого спроса, естественно, отличаются от этих параметров спроса в месте постоянного жительства: кроме продуктов питания, туристу необходимо то, к чему постоянные жители того или иного региона спроса либо вообще не предъявляют, либо, предъявляют его в малых объемах. Это услуги гостиниц и аналогичных средств размещения, сувениры, специальные помещения и оборудование для проведения мероприятий делового и интенсив-туризма, предметы, необходимые для отдыха и т.п. В этом проявляется мультипликативный эффект туризма, то есть способность благодаря инициации спроса вызывать необходимость развития многих, удовлетворяющих этот спрос производств на территориях, посещаемых туристами. Следовательно, оценка экономической роли туризма заключается в оценке его мультипликативного эффекта через долю в ВВП, занятости, инвестициях, доходах бюджета[3].

На наш взгляд, сравнительная оценка показателей развития туризма может варьироваться от сугубо статистических показателей до экспертных оценок. Для общего представления уровня конкурентоспособности туризма Казахстана и Индии следует обратиться к анализу статистических данных международных институтов, проводящих сбор и мониторинг информации по туризму стран мира.

Оценкой и анализом развития туризма и рекреации в мировом масштабе занимаются Всемирная туристская организация Объединенных Наций (World Tourism Organization (UNWTO), а также Совет по мировым путешествиям и туризму (The World Travel & Tourism Council (WTTC). Они как самостоятельные институты исследуют развитие и распространение мирового туризма, формируют и издают годовые рейтинги туризма. В частности, ЮНВТО обобщает и подводит итоги развития туризма по 215 странам и территориям мира. Основными показателями являются количество посетителей, доход государства от туризма, доля туризма в экспорте страны и другие. Помимо ЮНВТО, Всемирный экономический Форум (ВЭФ, Швейцария, Женева) ежегодно публикует Индекс конкурентоспособности туризма и путешествий (Travel & Tourism Competitiveness Index), который охватывает 140 стран мира. Он состоит из трех основных

компонентов, которые, в свою очередь, подразделяются еще на 14 подиндексов. Таким образом, в мировом масштабе достаточно четко ведется мониторинг туризма и рекреационной деятельности. С целью определения места Казахстана в глобальном туристическом рынке и уточнения критериев и индексов туризма и путешествий более подробно остановимся на этих моментах[4,5].

Как отмечалось, Индекс конкурентоспособности туризма и путешествий рассчитывается на основе трех компонентов:

а) подиндекс регулятивной структуры путешествий и туризма (T&T Regulatory framework);
б) подиндекс инфраструктуры и деловой среды путешествий и туризма (T&T Business environment and infrastructure);
в) подиндекс человеческих, культурных и природных ресурсов (T&T Human, cultural and natural resources).

При этом каждый из трех компонентов имеет следующие градации:

Подиндекс а): Политичсские правила и регулирование (Policy rules and regulations), Экологическое регулирование (Environmental regulation), Безопасность и охрана (Safety and security), Здоровье и гигиена (Health and hygiene), Приоритетность туризма и путешествий (Prioritization of Travel & Tourism).

Подиндекс б): Инфраструктура воздушного транспорта (Air transport infrastructure), Инфраструктура наземного транспорта (Ground transport infrastructure), Инфраструктура туризма (Tourism infrastructure), Инфраструктура интернета и телекоммуникаций (ICT infrastructure), Ценовая конкуренция в индустрии путешествий и туризма (Price competitiveness in T&T industry).

Подиндекс в): Человеческие ресурсы (Human resources), Восприятие национального туризма (National tourism perception), Природные ресурсы (Natural resources) и Культурные ресурсы (Cultural resources).

Анализ индекса конкурентоспособности туризма и путешествий показывает, что первое место в рейтинге занимает Швейцария со значением 5,66, следом располагаются Германия

(5,39), Австрия (5,39), Испания (5,38), Великобритания (5,38). Франция в рейтиге ВЭФ занимает 7 место со значением 5,31, но несмотря на это является абсолютным мировым лидером по числу туристов ее посетивших. К примеру Италия, входящая в пятерку мировых лидеров по прибытиям туристов, в рейтинге ВЭФ занимает 26 позицию со значением 4,90. Вместе с тем Италия славится своими туристскими достопримечательностями, имеет развитую инфраструктуру. Выше Италии по этому индексу оказались Республика Корея (25 место), Мальта (24), Люксембург (23), хотя они менее популярны и туризм развивается у них другими темпами (таблица 1).

Казахстан и Индия, как полноправные члены ЮНВТО, имеют большой потенциал для туризма и рекреации. В индексе конкурентоспособности туризма и путешествий по итогам 2013 года Казахстан находится на 88 позиции со значением 3,82, в 2011 году он был на 93 месте, что является с одной стороны продвижением, с другой достаточно низким показателем.

Индия по итогам 2013 года занимала 65 место со значением 4,11, в 2011 году находилась на 68 позиции, что также не является хорошим результатом, но в общем рейтинге опережает Казахстан на 23 пункта. В региональном рейтинге конкурентоспособности туризма и путешествий Индия занимает 11 позицию, а Казахстан 18 место.

Рассматривая индекс конкурентоспособности по его компонентам, можно отметить следующее. Компонент регулятивной структуры путешествий и туризма, включающий подиндексы - политические правила и регулирование, экологическое регулирование, безопасность и охрана, здоровье и гигиена, приоритетность туризма и путешествий - является важным в оценке туристской деятельности. Вместе с тем, он основывается на статистических данных и обследованиях, что может быть достаточно субъективным. США, являясь одним из главных генераторов туристских потоков и высокоразвитой страной, в рассматриваемом индексе занимает 44 место с 4.95 баллами. Менее развитые в туристском плане Сингапур по

Таблица 1 – Позиции Казахстана и Индии среди основных стран-реципиентов туристов по Индексу конкурентоспособности путешествий и туризма в 2013 году

Страна / Экономика	Общий индекс		Подиндекс регулятивной структуры путешествий и туризма		Подиндекс инфраструктуры и деловой среды путешествий и туризма		Подиндекс человеческих, культурных и природных ресурсов	
	место	значе-ние	место	значе-ние	место	значе-ние	место	значе-ние
Швейцария	1	5.66	1	5.94	1	5.42	2	5.63
Германия	2	5.39	8	5.57	6	5.29	7	5.31
Австрия	3	5.39	2	5.80	11	5.11	9	5.24
Испания	4	5.38	14	5.48	5	5.30	6	5.36
Великобритания	5	5.38	17	5.44	10	5.13	3	5.57
США	6	5.32	44	4.95	2	5.36	1	5.65
Франция	7	5.31	9	5.56	7	5.18	11	5.20
Канада	8	5.28	27	5.27	8	5.17	5	5.39
Швеция	9	5.24	12	5.54	23	4.89	8	5.30
Сингапур	10	5.23	6	5.74	4	5.31	25	4.64
Австралия	11	5.17	23	5.32	25	4.81	4	5.39
Новая Зеландия	12	5.17	4	5.75	12	5.06	22	4.69
Нидерланды	13	5.14	16	5.45	15	5.01	16	4.97
Япония	14	5.13	24	5.31	24	4.86	10	5.22

Гонконг	15	5.11	19	5.43	3	5.32	29	4.59
Исландия	16	5.10	3	5.77	13	5.06	36	4.47
Финляндия	17	5.10	5	5.74	22	4.89	24	4.65
Бельгия	18	5.04	18	5.43	26	4.78	18	4.90
Ирландия	19	5.01	7	5.68	19	4.96	40	4.41
Португалия	20	5.01	20	5.42	27	4.78	19	4.84
Дания	21	4.98	25	5.31	16	4.98	26	4.64
Индия	65	4.11	110	3.92	67	3.69	21	4.72
Страны СНГ:								
Россия	63	4.16	92	4.24	46	4.22	58	4.02
Грузия	66	4.10	30	5.18	80	3.46	91	3.67
Украина	76	3.98	60	4.73	71	3.62	99	3.59
Азербайджан	78	3.97	46	4.94	87	3.34	96	3.63
Армения	79	3.96	51	4.88	88	3.34	94	3.65
Казахстан	88	3.82	62	4.66	79	3.48	119	3.30
Молдова	102	3.60	65	4.61	97	3.16	133	3.04
Кыргызстан	111	3.45	93	4.23	131	2.61	103	3.51
Таджикистан	114	3.41	90	4.28	123	2.69	122	3.26
Примечание – Составлено автором по «The Travel & Tourism Competitiveness Report 2013». С. 18, 20, 22, 24[6].								

этому индексу занимает 6 место, Эстония (10), Барбадос (13), Уругвай (31), Маврикий (32), Латвия (35), Израиль (36), Иордания (37). Вызывает сомнение тот факт, что на Маврикии или Израиле такие параметры как экологическое регулирование, безопасность и охрана имеют высокие рейтинги.

По компоненту регулятивной структуры путешествий и туризма Индия заняла 110 позицию со значением 3,92, Казахстан – 62 место (4,66).

Компонент инфраструктуры и деловой среды путешествий и туризма также имеет свои позитивные и отрицательные стороны. Так, согласно поиндексу «инфраструктура туризма» Казахстан занимает 87-е место со значением 3,12; Индия находится на 67 позиции (3,69). Из стран Центральной Азии Кыргызстан находится на 138 месте, Таджикистан – на 139. Казахстан находится в одном ряду с такими странами, как Сальвадор (83), Суринам (85), Бруней (86), Никарагуа (88), Ботствана (89), что является не самым хорошим примером для нашего динамично развивающегося государства. В этом компоненте согласно подиндексу «инфраструктура интернета и телекоммуникаций» Япония занимает 7 место со значением 5,50, Люксембург (5 место), Республика Корея (1), Гонконг (2), Швейцария (6), Дания (4). Казахстан в этом параметре находится на 48 месте (в 2008 г. 77 место), что указывает на совершенствование и улучшение работы в данном направлении.

Компонент человеческих, культурных и природных ресурсов, как и другие индексы, рассчитывался с учетом количественных и качественных характеристик. По этому компоненту первое место занимает США со значением 5,65, второе Швейцария (5,63), третье Великобритания (5,57), Казахстан занимает 119 место со значением 3,30. Индия по данному компоненту находится на 21 позиции со значением (4,72). Этот показатель не совсем точно отражает действительную характеристику природных ресурсов.

Среди стран СНГ Республика Казахстан в 2013 г. находилась на 6 месте. Впереди нас находятся государства с менее развитым экономическим потенциалом, такие как Грузия, Армения, Азербайджан. Такое положение отчетливо показывает низкие позиции туризма Казахстана по конкурентоспособности. Казахстан посещают представители многих государств мира. Вместе с тем сложилась определенная группа стран, преобладающих в туристическом потоке (таблица 2).

Ранжирование нерезидентов по количеству посетивших Казахстан в 2012 г. показало, что наибольшее количество нерезидентов приходится на Российскую Федерацию, они составляют 27,3% от всех нерезидентов 2012 г. Это подтверждает мысль о традиционных связях с Россией.

Если рассматривать отдельно по странам, то самый большой рост посетителей-нерезидентов наблюдается из Испании в 7 раз по сравнению с 2004 г., из Финляндии в 6 раз, Индии в более чем 4 раз, по абсолютному количеству нерезидентов она занимает 8 место среди других стран. Если десять лет назад посетители из Индии не входили в число 10 основных стран-поставщиков туристов, то в настоящее время их количество значительно возросло. В 3,8 раза выросло число нерезидентов из Великобритании, очень большой рост по сравнению с 2004 г. наблюдается из Франции (3,2), Австрии (3,16 раза), Китая (3,12), Азербайджана (2,8 раза), Канады (2,4 раза), Италия (2,3 раза).

Рост абсолютных показателей свидетельствует об укреплении партнерских отношений и бизнес-контактов этих стран с Казахстаном. По таким странам как Турция, США, Германия рост составил 1,8, 1,7, 1,7 раза, соответственно, что характеризует снижение потока туристов в сравнении с 2008 г. Надо отметить, что такая тенденция наблюдается по некоторым странам. Это еще раз подтверждает нашу мысль о том, мировой финансовый кризис 2008-2009 гг. в целом не сильно повлиял на развитие деловых поездок. Выраженный рост количества нерезидентов характеризуется по всем странам в 2012 г. по сравнению с 2008 г. и рост в более чем 3 раза по сравнению с 2004 г. Официальная статистика свидетельствует об интересе к нашей стране и позволяет говорить о росте контактов с такими странами как Индия.

На наш взгляд, значительный потенциал развития различных направлений сотрудничества может быть реализован посредством участия Индии в такой сфере Казахстана как туризм. Если рассматривать перспективные направления сотрудничества в этой области, то можно выделить следующее:

Таблица 2 – Динамика въезжающих в Казахстан посетителей-нерезидентов по странам

	2004 г.	2006 г.	2008 г.	2010 г.	2011 г.	2012 г.	2012 г. в % к 2004 г.
Всего по Казахстану, чел.	219634	330817	543022	594 161	584 303	519 222	236,4
в том числе:							
Российская Федерация	61720	87584	120236	115 341	173 568	141 765	229,7
Великобритания	14077	16075	80173	101 371	68 124	53 944	383,2
США	22147	33040	51886	33 427	44 899	39 386	177,8
Турция	16956	38365	45798	37 070	39 551	32 044	189,0
Италия	13299	16502	37819	76 455	38 291	31 762	238,8
Германия	13805	19288	23741	21 378	25 075	24 677	178,7
Китай	7413	21130	21032	25 034	26 175	23 192	312,8
Индия	3860	5477	9882	11 007	12 802	16 198	419,6
Украина	5776	6464	8164	7 828	10 647	13 772	238,4
Франция	3592	4869	10615	11 269	13 774	11 601	322,9
Нидерланды	5748	7757	25050	31 752	21 719	9 679	168,4
Узбекистан	3638	6313	5347	4 744	6 610	8 265	227,2
Япония	4286	6670	3998	4 752	5 730	6 553	152,9
Кыргызстан	5097	3675	4546	4 406	5 563	5 611	110,1
Польша	2067	2753	3 739	3 564	7 093	5 004	242,1
Канада	2006	2439	5 601	7 630	6 299	4 925	245,5
Азербайджан	1471	2733	4901	5 446	5 218	4 072	276,8
Австрия	1271	907	4 588	2 776	3 908	4 017	316,0
Испания	533	992	1 562	1 996	2 787	3 762	705,8
Финляндия	600	1354	1 154	1 012	5 127	3 674	612,3

Примечание – Составлено и рассчитано автором по источникам[7,8]

- создание благоприятных условий для привлечения иностранных и отечественных инвестиций в туризм;
- создание благоприятной правовой среды для пребывания туристов в странах, предусматривающей упрощение процедуры получения виз, уменьшение ее стоимости, сокращение времени на прохождение пограничного и таможенного контроля, обеспечение безопасности туристов, находящихся на территории страны;
- осуществление широкомасштабной рекламной кампании для формирования и укрепления туристского имиджа Казахстана как страны с благоприятными политическими и экономическими условиями; усиление работы по распространению информации о Казахстане через дипломатические каналы, средства массовой информации Индии в целях увеличения потока туристов-нерезидентов и соответственно притока валюты в республику;
- государственная поддержка ежегодного участия туристских компаний Казахстана в международных туристских ярмарках, форумах, проводимых в Индии.

Для дальнейшего проактивного развития туризма как в Казахстане, так и в Индии необходима ориентация на расширение услуг в традиционных сферах (рекреационный и культурный туризм) и развитие альтернативного туризма, предоставление услуг новых видов (экологический, элитарный, этнический, религиозный, экстремальный, горно-приключенческий, деловой, конгресс-туризм и др.). Это станет визитной карточкой любой из рассматриваемых нами стран.

ЛИТЕРАТУРА

1. http://www.ereport.ru/stat.php?razdel=country &count=india&table
2. Дуйсен Г.М. Перспективы вовлечения объектов природного наследия Казахстана в туристско-рекреационную сферу // Общественно-научный журнал «Проблемы региональной экологии», Москва, 2006, № 3.
3. Сараев А.Р. О показателях статистики туризма // Вопросы статистики, 2007, № 9. С. 39-43.

4. The Travel & Tourism Competitiveness Report 2013. World Economic Forum // [Электронный ресурс]. – Режим доступа: www.weforum.org pp. 15-16.
5. Дуйсен Г.М. Рекреационное освоение регионов Казахстана в условиях вхождения в мировой туризм: теория, стратегия и практика. Монография. – Алматы, ТОО «Signet Print», 2010. – 256 с.
6. The Travel & Tourism Competitiveness Report 2013. World Economic Forum // [Электронный ресурс]. – Режим доступа: www.weforum.org pp. 18-24.
7. Туризм Казахстана 2004-2008. Статистический сборник. Агентство Республики Казахстан по статистике. Под ред. Ж.И. Омарова. – Астана, 2009. С.51-52.
8. Туризм Казахстана 2008-2012. Статистический сборник. Агентство Республики Казахстан по статистике. Гл. ред. Смаилов А.А. – Астана, 2012. С. 70-72.

34
Технологическое развитие Казахстана в контексте опыта Индии

Фархад Днишев

В современном мире парадигма развития во многом складывается под воздействием глобальных технологических сдвигов. Технологические прорывы, особенно в таких сферах, как информационно-коммуникационные технологии, биотехнологии и нанотехнологии, значительно расширили возможности решения задач экономического развития, повышения благосостояния и качества жизни, охраны окружающей среды. Глобализация открывает новые пути преодоления мирового технологического неравенства, все больше стран получают широкие каналы доступа к новым технологиям и их применению. Расширяется география технологического развития, в группу технологических лидеров, включавшую еще недавно только индустриально-развитые страны, начинает входить ряд развивающихся стран. Это, прежде всего, Китай и Индия. По всему миру появляются новые центры и сети развития технологий, одним из самых известных стал Бангалор.

Взаимодействие глобализации и технологий привело к формированию глобального технологического пространства. Производство и продвижение новых продуктов на мировые рынки теперь требует построения глобальных сетей, включающих специализированных поставщиков, основных производителей и потребителей, связанных технологической цепочкой. Усиливается интернационализация исследований и разработок, к их осуществлению все более активно привлекаются зарубежные партнеры, а нередко они выносятся за границы страны базирования компании-инноватора.

Построение глобальных технологических цепочек, глобальная миграция центров промышленного производства и последующее за этим перемещение центров НИОКР определяет развитие мирового инновационно-технологического сектора. Основной движущей силой этих сдвигов выступают транснациональные корпорации.

Сначала перемещение производства затронуло низкотехнологичные отрасли – добычу и первичную обработку природных ресурсов. Затем в страны-поставщики ресурсов переместились крупные металлургические компании, в районы заготовок леса переместилась лесопереработка. Все это обуславливается стремлением корпораций быть ближе к ресурсной базе, а также к крупным портам, упрощением логистики, то есть доступа товара к своим потребителям. Наиболее привлекательными странами для переноса ресурсоемких производств на сегодняшний день считаются страны БРИК (Бразилия, Россия, Индия, Китай). Нефтегазохимические производства размещаются в районах, богатых сырьем: тех же странах БРИК, на арабском Востоке, в Пакистане, Вьетнаме, а теперь все больше и в Африке.

В последние годы сдвиги в размещении мировой промышленности затрагивают и более технологичные отрасли. Развивающиеся страны все чаще выступают в качестве зон аутсорсинга и оффшоринга в автомобилестроении, судо- и самолетостроении, точном машиностроении, электронике и IT-индустрии. К примеру, в 2006 г. для производства iPod компания Apple создала 41 тысячу рабочих мест и только 14 тысяч из них в США.[1] Ожидается, что эти процессы будут набирать силу и дальше. Например, автомобилестроение будет все больше сосредотачиваться в странах БРИК, а центры гражданского крупнотоннажного судостроения – смещаться из Европы и Японии в Корею и Китай. В этих странах за последние 20-30 лет появились крупные промышленно-технологические кластеры судостроения, автомобилестроения, энергомашиностроения и т.д.

Сдвиги в размещении промышленности сопровождаются и перемещением инновационно-технологических центров. Глобальные инновационные стратегии крупных ТНК теперь включают перенос в развивающиеся страны программ исследований и разработок. Конечно, у ТНК есть свои экономические интересы. Побудительными причинами этих процессов для них выступает необходимость адаптации продукции и технологий ТНК к особенностям национальных рынков, приближение исследовательской базы к емким и быстро растущим рынкам сбыта, расширение возможностей по привлечению квалифицированного и сравнительно дешевого исследовательского персонала, получение доступа к активно формируемой в развивающихся странах инновационной инфраструктуре.[2]

Искусство политики догоняющих стран состоит в том, чтобы включиться в эти процессы с пользой для себя. Большой и поучительный для Казахстана опыт в этом отношении накоплен в Индии.[3] Индия умело использовала стремление крупнейших ТНК мира к перемещению инновационно-технологических центров на развивающиеся рынки. Многие ТНК открыли в этой стране оффшорные инновационные центры. Более 300 ТНК имеют в Индии подразделения оффшорного программирования. Компании из списка Fortune 500 (крупнейших компаний США) открыли 63 исследовательских центра в Индии. В Индии одна из крупнейших ТНК мира – General Electric – наняла более 2400 человек для разработок в сфере авиационных двигателей, потребительских товаров длительного пользования и медицинского оборудования.[4] Фармацевтические компании Astra-Zeneca, Eli Lilly, GlaxoSmithKline, Novartis, Pfizer и Sanofi-Aventis проводят в Индии клинические исследования.

Все это способствует не только активному развитию процесса трансфера технологий в эти страны, но и созданию там собственных технологических платформ, что позволяет им достигать конкурентных позиций на мировом рынке технологий: формирующиеся там центры производства технологий начинают ориентироваться уже не столько на внутреннее потребление, сколько на глобальный рынок. В результате конкурентные позиции Индии на мировых рынках технологий значительно усилились. Так, Индия является лидером на мировом рынке оффшорного программирования, занимает 3 место в мире на рынке фармацевтики.

Трансферт зарубежных технологий – широко распространенная мировая практика. Он охватывает и самые развитые, и среднеразвитые, и тем более развивающиеся страны. Главное – какого подхода при этом придерживаться. Было бы нежелательным ограничиваться простым «следованием за иностранной технологией». Для того, чтобы иметь благоприятные долгосрочные последствия, импорт технологий должен сопровождаться их обязательным улучшением, позволяющим вернуться на внешний рынок в качестве экспортера соответствующей продукции. Успешным в этом случае может быть движение от простого к сложному. Постепенное накопление знаний, опыта и капитала позволяет со временем проникнуть на рынки технологически сложной продукции.

Пример Индии показывает, что такой подход к распространению заимствованной современной технологии наряду с модернизацией технической базы приводит к широкому развитию собственно инновационной деятельности, дает толчок самостоятельному развертыванию современных направлений науки и технологий. Результатом становится обретение самостоятельности в научно-техническом развитии, что отражается на характере экономического развития, структуре национального хозяйства, структуре экспорта.

Мобилизации и укреплению имеющегося научно-технологического потенциала в интересах индустриальной модернизации Казахстана в последние годы уделяется много внимания. В то же время внешние факторы технологического развития пока задействованы недостаточно. Казахстан с учетом опыта Индии мог бы активно использовать внешние факторы технологического развития. В связи с этим можно выделить ряд приоритетов технологической политики использования внешних источников технологий. Это - трансферт зарубежных технологий, приход в страну несырьевых ТНК, использование схемы «сырье в обмен на технологии», НИОКР-аутсорсинг.

В Казахстане эти направления находятся в стадии становления. Так, в трансферте технологий пока преобладают поставки машин и оборудования, в то же время такие более сложные его формы, как приобретение ноу-хау и лицензий, не получили развития. В 2011 году предприятиями страны было приобретено за рубежом всего 38 прав на патенты, лицензий на изобретения и 6 ноу-хау и соглашений на передачу технологий. В балансе платежей за услуги на приобретение лицензий приходится только 1,2%.[5]

В стране практически отсутствуют производственные подразделения несырьевых ТНК. Они если и присутствуют в национальной экономике, то не более чем сбытовыми звеньями. В основном интересы ТНК сосредоточены вокруг сырьевого сектора. Необходима специальная политика по «принуждению» ТНК, приходящих в Казахстан, к осуществлению инновационных проектов в нашей стране. Следует стимулировать их к передаче своих новейших технологий в обмен на ресурсы и возможность работать в нашей стране. В Стратегии Казахстан 2050 подчеркивается, что необходимо «разрешать инвесторам добывать и пользоваться нашим сырьем только в обмен на создание новейших производств на территории нашей страны».[6] Иначе говоря, нужно запустить механизм «сырье в обмен на технологии». Элементы такого механизма были заложены в Программу 30 корпоративных лидеров, но так и не заработали. Тот же Китай постоянно вводит все новые «правила игры», вынуждая зарубежные корпорации, работающие в стране, делиться своими технологиями с китайскими государственными предприятиями, особенно в таких отраслях, как воздушный транспорт, энергетика, высокоскоростные железные дороги, IT и др.

Нужно учитывать, что возможности перемещения технологической деятельности связаны не только с экономическими, но и культурными факторами. В частности, привлекательности для аутсорсинга Китая и Индии способствует широкомасштабное распространение английского в качестве языка образования, исследований и технической документации, что существенным образом снижает коммуникационные барьеры.

Однако это не означает, что Казахстан не может использовать описанный выше путь интеграции в глобальное технологическое пространство. Начать можно с прихода на отечественные рынки мировых лидеров - поставщиков оборудования и сервисных компаний, которые обычно стремятся разместить свои сервисные центры ближе к рынкам сбыта. Например, это могут быть крупные поставщики нефтяного и горно-шахтного оборудования. В бурении на Западе Казахстана уже работает ряд иностранных компаний.

На следующем этапе, с ростом рынка потребления технологически сложной продукции, следует ожидать размещение в Казахстане высокотехнологичных производств в качестве аутсорсинга. Речь идет о производствах, использующих отечественную рабочую силу и зарубежные технологические платформы. Далее на этих рынках могут возникать научные центры, разрабатывающие высокотехнологичный продукт. В Казахстане уже имеется ряд таких центров: Казахстанско-французский центр трансферта технологий, Казахстанско-Корейский центр трансферта технологий.

Нужны также специальные меры, направленные на повышение привлекательности Казахстана как международной площадки для реализации исследовательских программ зарубежных компаний. Например, большую роль может сыграть введение режима СЭЗ в Назарбаев университете, что наряду с формирующейся здесь инфраструктурой и квалифицированным персоналом может стать серьезным мотивом для создания лабораторий ряда крупных ТНК в области информационно-коммуникационных, биотехнологий и др.

Когда говорят об усилении экономического сотрудничества между Казахстаном и Индией, то в качестве сдерживающего фактора зачастую называют логистику. В области науки и технологий логистические препятствия отходят на задний план. Поэтому наука и технологии должны быть объектом особого внимания для сотрудничества между Казахстаном и Индией. Это особенно относится к таким направлениям, как ядерные технологии, космические исследования, информационно-коммуникационные технологии, зеленая экономика, ирригационные технологии и т.д.

Литература

1. Portnoff André-Yves “Le retuar a l’industrie” *Futuribles.* P., №364, 2010, pp. 5-23.
2. Ерошкин А., Петров М. Новые тенденции взаимодействия развитых и развивающихся стран в инновационной сфере (Мировая экономика и международные отношения, 2012, №12) -pp. 3-20.
3. The Global Innovation Index 2012. Stonger Innovation Linkages for Global Growth. http://www.globalinnovationindex.org
4. Доклад о мировых инвестициях 2005: Транснациональные корпорации и интернационализация НИОКР. - Организация

Объединенных Наций, Нью-Йорк и Женева, 2005. http://unctad.org/en/docs/wir**2005**_en.pdf

5. Платежный баланс Республики Казахстансе. http://www.nationalbank.kz/?docid=343www.stat.kz
6. Стратегия «Казахстан - 2050»: новый политический курс состоявшегося государства. Послание Президента Республики Казахстан-Лидера нации Н.А. Назарбаева народу Казахстана, Астана, 2012. http://www.akorda.kz/en/page/page_poslanie-prezidenta-respubliki-kazakhstan-lidera-natsii-nursultana-nazarbaeva-narodu-kazakhstana-

35
Вопросы транспортных коммуникаций между Казахстаном и Индией

Дудар Жакенов

По утверждению Всемирной Торговой Организации, на сегодняшний день наблюдается замедление темпов экономики и рецессия в странах Европейского Союза, на которые приходится треть мировой торговли. Этот фактор негативно влияет на динамику мирового экспортно-импортных оборота, особенно, существенно сказывается на экспортные поставки в Европу из стран Азии и Америки.

Согласно статистики, объем мировой торговли в 2012 году составил US$ 18,328 триллионов, что на 2% больше чем в 2011 г. В этом контексте, развитие индийской внешней торговли в значительной степени определяется общим состоянием мировой торговли и конъюнктурой мирового рынка. Сегодня правительство Индии решает задачу диверсификации региональной структуры индийского экспорта путем расширения рынков сбыта в странах Азии и Африки. В число ведущих торговых партнеров Индии входят Китай, ОАЭ, США, Саудовская Аравия, Германия, Швейцария, Индонезия, Сингапур, Гонконг.

По данным Министерства торговли и промышленности Индии, объема внешнеторгового оборота за 2012 год составил US$ 809.4 миллиардов, из которых на экспорт приходится US$ 309.1 млрд. Несмотря на дефицит торгового баланса, индийская экономика по-прежнему одна из самых динамично развивающихся в мире. За последние 10 лет Индия добилась 50-процентного роста объема промышленного производства и 65-процентного увеличения экспорта высокотехнологичной продукции. В стратегии развития страны большая роль отведена программе «Индия: Видение – 2020», в которой определены стратегические направления развития индийской экономики на средне- и долгосрочную перспективу: энергетика (включая атомную), кластер информационных технологий, стратегические отрасли (оборонно-промышленный комплекс, аэрокосмический сектор, авиастроение, телекоммуникации и т.д.). При всем этом, развитие первого направления является высшим приоритетом Индии, т.к. 3 процента энергетических потребностей Индии покрываются атомной энергетикой, в перспективе планируется увеличть эту долю до 20 процентов.

Было время, когда страна не имела возможности получать обогащенный уран, в силу политических и экономических причин. Однако, сегодня Индия может заниматься как производством в сфере урановой промышленности и ядерных технологий, так и торговлей энергией получаемых АЭС. На территории страны действуют 20 атомных энергоблоков.

Сегодня Индии является одной из наиболее динамично развивающихся стран. Наряду с Китаем Индия позиционирует себя как будущая великая держава, и ее внешняя политика характеризуется глобальным охватом основных экономических и политических проблем.

Вместе с тем, будучи одной их ведущих региональных держав, Индия проводит политику под лозунгом «лицом к Востоку» и Центральная Азия рассматривается в качестве одного из приоритетных направлений. Внимание к региону обусловлено, как стремлением обеспечить национальные интересы, так и желанием повысить свой международный статус и не отстать от своего основного соперника в Азии – Китая.

Являясь одной из основных региональных держав, эта страна особое внимание уделяет дальнейшему повышению своей роли на международной арене. В начале 1990-х годов во внешнеполитической стратегии Индии появилось новое направление – Центральная Азия.

В рамках инициативы «Нового Шелкового пути индийской внешней политики", Индия придаёт большое значение развитию отношений с Центральной Азией, через территоирю которой издревле проходили политические, экономические, торговые, культурные потоки. Фактором сближения стала также общность интересов и угроз, которые присущи Индии и республикам Центральной Азией - борьба против исламского экстремизма, терроризма, наркобизнеса, урегулирование ситуации в Афганистане и обеспечение региональной безопасности.

В силу своего индустриального развития, Индия как и Китай, является большим импортером и крупнейшим мировой потребитель природных ресурсов. Индийская сторона открыто признается, что страны Центральной Азии являются огромным потенциальным рынком для промышленной продукции из Индии, а также перспективным источником приобретения топливо–энергетических ресурсов и полезных ископаемых, а это значит, что Индия может стать постоянным и надежным импортером нефти, газа и урана.

Интересы в области энергетики, наряду с обеспечением политической стабильности, являются, пожалуй, основным стимулом, подталкивающим Индию к укреплению своего влияния в регионе. Потребление энергии в Индии, как предполагается, будет расти в районе между 3.6 и 4.3 % ежегодно и более чем удвоиться к 2030 году. Это сделает Индию третьим крупнейшим импортером нефти к 2025 году. От обеспеченности страны поставками углеводородов, зависит ее стабильное экономическое развитие, а следовательно и национальная безопасность. На данный момент примерно 70 % нефти и газа Индия импортирует из стран Персидского залива. Конфликт в Ираке, повлиявший на рост цен на нефть, подтолкнул индийское правительство к поиску альтернативных источников сырья. Центральная Азия рассматривается как перспективный в этом отношении регион.

Это означает, что сегодня Индия всерьез связывает перспективы обеспечения собственной энергетической безопасности со странами Центральной Азии, а тема глобальной энергетической безопасности в долгосрочной перспективе будет представлять для Индии повышенную актуальность.

Кроме того, центральноазиатский регион является весьма удобным «коридором» для транспортировки индийских товаров в Россию, страны СНГ и далее в страны Европы. Товарооборот Индии в европейском направлении сегодня достиг US$ 57 миллиардов, а к 2015 году планируется довести данный показатель до рекордного уровня - US$ 237 миллиардов.

В настоящее время уровень торгово-экономического сотрудничества со странами Центральной Азии крайне неудовлетворителен, доля Индии в этой торговле составляет менее 1 % совокупного товарооборота. Одной из причин диспропорции дефицита торгового баланса Индии, можно объяснить слабостью транспортно-логистической составляющей. Для этого Индии необходимы поиски рынков и приемлемых транспортных маршрутов. Выгодным в этом кластере могут быть существующие транспортные коридоры.

Слабое присутствие индийских компаний на центральноазиатском рынке являются естественные транспортные и коммуникационные трудности, поскольку Индия не граничит ни с одной из республик региона, а сами республики не имеют выхода к океану. Вследствие чего, индийскому правительству приходится прилагать большие усилия по созданию условий для выхода индийских компаний на рынок Центральной Азии. Прежде всего, это касается налаживание транспортной инфраструктуры, поскольку эта отрасль отвечает общим интересам экономического развития всех стран азиатского региона и несомненно, будет способствовать расширению товарооборота между ними.

Для практической реализации торгово-экономических планов большую роль играют международные транспортные коридоры (МТК). К примеру, в направлении «Запад-Восток» и «Север-Юг» ресурсные объемы контейнерных перевозок в евроазиатском направлении в периоды 2000 – 2010 годы и на перспективу в 2015 году, имеют тенденцию в сторону увеличения.

Основными действующими коридорами соединяющих Европу с Азией, на сегодняшний день, являются ТАЖД, ТРАСЕКА и МТК «Север-Юг». Международные организации, в лице Евросоюза и ООН, а точнее ЕЭК и ЭСКАТО, выработали свою стратегию в развитии коридоров из Европы в Азию в рамках пилотных проектов ТРАСЕКА и СПЕКА. В начале 2013 года в Женеве, Европейским отделением ООН было подписано Совместное заявление о будущем развитии евро-азиатских транспортных связей.

Кроме того, этот вопрос был главным в повестке дня 16-й

международной конференции «TransBaltica - 2013", которая прошла в Риге 6-7 июня 2013 года с участием 20 европейских стран и СНГ. Материалы этих форумов можно найти в Интернете.

На сегодняшний день основные грузопотоки из Европы в Азию и обратно идут морским путем. Их объемы оцениваются в несколько миллиардов долларов. При этом грузопоток постоянно растет, а проходимость Суэцкого канала в Египте, является небезграничной. Если через Суэцкий канал груз из Южной Азии в Европу доставляется за 35 суток, то по коридору «Север – Юг» - за 20-25 суток. Сегодня компании из Европы и стран азиатского региона вынуждены искать альтернативные маршруты доставки своих грузов. В этом положительную роль мог бы сыграть МТК «Север-Юг».

Соглашение о создании данного коридора, было подписано в Санкт-Петербурге 12 сентября 2000 года, странами-участницами которого на первом этапе стали Россия, Иран и Индия. В мае 2002 года в Санкт-Петербурге министрами транспорта стран-участниц был подписан протокол об официальном открытии коридора. Позднее к договору присоединились Азербайджан, Армения, Беларусь, Казахстан, Оман, Сирия. Подали заявки на присоединение Турция и Украина. МТК «Север - Юг» призван обеспечить транспортную связь между странами страны Восточной, Центральной и Северной Европы, включая СНГ, со странами Персидского залива и Южной Азии (Индия, Пакистан через Иран), а также другими странами, которые изъявили желание участвовать в этом проекте. Основными преимущества МТК «Север - Юг» перед другими маршрутами (в первую очередь через Суэцкий канал): сокращение в два и более разы расстояния перевозок, а также снижение стоимости перевозки контейнеров по сравнению со стоимостью транспортировки по морскому пути.

Идея развития транзитного потенциала «Север - Юг» через Центральной Азии продиктовано самим географическим положением региона и даже историей. Сделать из Центральной Азии своеобразный мост между Европой и Азией для транзита грузов, безусловно, было бы выгодным как для самого региона, так и для транспортных компаний с разных частей континента.

В свою очередь Казахстан готов всяческому содействию

прохождению грузов по наземным транспортным коммуникациям, а также через морской порт Актау, имеющий самые современные терминалы и развитую инфраструктуру. Согласно проведенным пробным прогонам, транспортировка грузов по новому коридору обходится на 20% дешевле, чем через Суэцкий канал, Индия сможет ежегодно экономить на этом до US$ 16 миллионов. По оценкам экспертов, перевозка грузов по маршруту «Север – Юг» в перспективе может составить до 20-25 млн. тонн в год без учета транспортировки нефти и нефтепродуктов. Транспортный коридор "Север-Юг" принесет ощутимую финансовую выгоду Индии, он будет способствовать повышению конкурентоспособности индийских товаров на мировом рынке, а также дешевому и быстрому импорту. "Индиа тудей" считает, что транспортный коридор "Север-Юг" позволит не только расширить взаимовыгодную торговлю Индии со странами Центральной Азии, Закавказья, Скандинавии и Прибалтики, Дели рассматривает "ось доброй воли", как альтернативный канал стабильности внутреннего рынка.

В случае подключения индийских компаний к МТК «Север–Юг», выгода гарантирована всем участвующим сторонам, обеспечивающим законность, безопасность и доходность.

В заключении, необходимо учесть важную составляющую. Объединившись усилиями на выгодном транспортном направлении, Индия и страны центральноазиатского региона смогут лучше противостоять глобальным вызовам современности, при том понимании, что объединены одной географией и одним большим регионом по имени Азия.

Index